Bloom's Literary Themes

Alienation
The American Dream
Civil Disobedience
Dark Humor
Death and Dying
Enslavement and Emancipation
Exploration and Colonization
The Grotesque
The Hero's Journey
Human Sexuality
The Labyrinth
Rebirth and Renewal
Sin and Redemption
The Sublime
The Taboo
The Trickster

SIN AND REDEMPTION

Bloom's Literary Themes

SIN AND REDEMPTION

Edited and with an introduction by
Harold Bloom
Sterling Professor of the Humanities
Yale University

Volume Editor
Blake Hobby

BLOOM'S
LITERARY CRITICISM
An imprint of Infobase Publishing

Bloom's Literary Themes: Sin and Redemption

Copyright ©2010 by Infobase Publishing
Introduction ©2010 by Harold Bloom

Bloom's Literary Criticism
An imprint of Infobase Publishing
132 West 31st Street
New York NY 10001

Library of Congress Cataloging-in-Publication Data
Sin and redemption / edited and with an introduction by Harold Bloom.
   p. cm.—(Bloom's literary themes)
Includes bibliographical references and index.
ISBN 978-1-60413-446-9 (hc : alk. paper)
   1. Sin in literature.   2. Redemption in literature.   I. Bloom, Harold.   II. Hobby,
Blake.   III. Title.   IV. Series.
   PN56.S56S56 2010
   809'.93382022—dc22
                                        2009053496

Bloom's Literary Criticism books are available at special discounts when purchased
in bulk quantities for businesses, associations, institutions, or sales promotions.
Please call our Special Sales Department in New York at (212) 967-8800 or (800)
322-8755.

You can find Bloom's Literary Criticism on the World Wide Web at
http://www.chelseahouse.com

Text design by Kerry Casey
Cover design by Takeshi Takahashi
Composition by IBT Global, Inc.
Cover printed by IBT Global, Inc., Troy NY
Book printed and bound by IBT Global, Inc., Troy NY
Date printed: April 2010
Printed in the United States of America

10 9 8 7 6 5 4 3 2 1

This book is printed on acid-free paper.

Contents

Series Introduction by Harold Bloom: Themes and Metaphors

1. TOPOS AND TROPE

What we now call a theme or topic or subject initially was named a *topos*, ancient Greek for "place." Literary *topoi* are commonplaces, but also arguments or assertions. A topos can be regarded as literal when opposed to a trope or turning which is figurative and which can be a metaphor or some related departure from the literal: ironies, synecdoches (part for whole), metonymies (representations by contiguity) or hyperboles (overstatements). Themes and metaphors engender one another in all significant literary compositions.

As a theoretician of the relation between the matter and the rhetoric of high literature, I tend to define metaphor as a figure of desire rather than a figure of knowledge. We welcome literary metaphor because it enables fictions to persuade us of beautiful untrue things, as Oscar Wilde phrased it. Literary *topoi* can be regarded as places where we store information, in order to amplify the themes that interest us.

This series of volumes, *Bloom's Literary Themes*, offers students and general readers helpful essays on such perpetually crucial topics as the Hero's Journey, the Labyrinth, the Sublime, Death and Dying, the Taboo, the Trickster, and many more. These subjects are chosen for their prevalence yet also for their centrality. They express the whole concern of human existence now in the twenty-first century of the Common Era. Some of the topics would have seemed odd at another time, another land: the American Dream, Enslavement and Emancipation, Civil Disobedience.

I suspect though that our current preoccupations would have existed always and everywhere, under other names. Tropes change across the centuries: The irony of one age is rarely the irony of another. But the themes of great literature, though immensely varied, undergo transmemberment and show up barely disguised in different contexts. The power of imaginative literature relies upon three constants: aesthetic splendor, cognitive power, wisdom. These are not bound by societal constraints or resentments, and ultimately are universals, and so not culture-bound. Shakespeare, except for the world's scriptures, is the one universal author, whether he is read and played in Bulgaria or Indonesia or wherever. His supremacy at creating human beings breaks through even the barrier of language and puts everyone on his stage. This means that the matter of his work has migrated everywhere, reinforcing the common places we all inhabit in his themes.

2. CONTEST AS BOTH THEME AND TROPE

Great writing or the Sublime rarely emanates directly from themes since all authors are mediated by forerunners and by contemporary rivals. Nietzsche enhanced our awareness of the agonistic foundations of ancient Greek literature and culture, from Hesiod's contest with Homer on to the Hellenistic critic Longinus in his treatise *On the Sublime*. Even Shakespeare had to begin by overcoming Christopher Marlowe, only a few months his senior. William Faulkner stemmed from the Polish-English novelist Joseph Conrad, and our best living author of prose fiction, Philip Roth, is inconceivable without his descent from the major Jewish literary phenomenon of the twentieth century, Franz Kafka of Prague, who wrote the most lucid German since Goethe.

The contest with past achievement is the hidden theme of all major canonical literature in Western tradition. Literary influence is both an overwhelming metaphor for literature itself, and a common topic for all criticism, whether or not the critic knows her immersion in the incessant flood.

Every theme in this series touches upon a contest with anteriority, whether with the presence of death, the hero's quest, the overcoming of taboos, or all of the other concerns, volume by volume. From Monteverdi through Bach to Stravinsky, or from the Italian Renaissance through the agon of Matisse and Picasso, the history of all the arts demonstrates the same patterns as literature's thematic struggle with itself. Our country's great original art, jazz, is illuminated by what the great creators called "cutting contests," from Louis Armstrong and Duke Ellington on to the emergence of Charlie Parker's Bop or revisionist jazz.

A literary theme, however authentic, would come to nothing without rhetorical eloquence or mastery of metaphor. But to experience the study of the common places of invention is an apt training in the apprehension of aesthetic value in poetry and in prose.

Sin and redemption are *theological* categories, not *literary* themes. I disagree with many, perhaps most contributors to this volume, because nothing in Shakespeare can be illuminated by the application of theological touchstones. King Lear is neither sinful nor redeemed. I would make the same denial in regard to all the greater Shakespearean protagonists: Falstaff, Hamlet, Othello, Shylock, Macbeth, Cleopatra. As for the magnificent villains – Iago and Edmund – it is redundant to ascribe sin to them.

Yet what of Dostoevsky, who believed in the theology of sin and redemption? Raskolnikov in *Crime and Punishment* is an ideological murderer with little sense of sin, and he is not redeemed. His dark double, the nihilist Svidrigailov, is as cheerful as Iago and Edmund, and like them desires no redemption.

Devotional literature is always an oxymoron. Dr. Samuel Johnson, my critical hero, was a believing Christian but he denied the possibility of a spiritual literature:

> The good and evil of eternity are too ponderous for the wings of wit. The mind sinks under them, content with calm belief and humble adoration.

Calm belief and humble adoration doubtless alike are admirable, but they are not states of consciousness that animate artistic creation.

I suggest that *error*, not sin, is an authentic literary concept, and that *recognition*, rather than redemption, is the inevitable literary theme that emanates from error. Error starts the imagination into motion for Honor and the Athenian dramatists on to Proust and

Faulkner. Recognition is the consequent and answering theme. It is not just error that is recognized but rather the power that abides despite the wandering ways of having blundered.

By "recognition" I do not mean primarily Aristotle's tragic category of belated awareness, but a far more general literary principle. Delayed recognition is essential to the highest imaginative literature, from the Book of Job on to Faulkner's *As I Lay Dying* and Cormac McCarthy's *Blood Meridian*. When recognition is completed, the play, novel or poem ends.

Total self-recognition is anything but redemption, just as inaugural error is absolutely unlike original sin. The morality of literature evades good and evil. Shakespeare is not interested in saving you or in solving your problems.

ALL THE KING'S MEN
(ROBERT PENN WARREN)

"Sin and Redemption in *All the King's Men*,"
by John J. Han, Missouri Baptist University

On one level, Robert Penn Warren's *All the King's Men* (1946) is a political novel chronicling the life and death of Willie Stark, who resembles the real-life Huey Long (1893–1935), a charismatic Louisiana governor and U.S. senator nicknamed "The Kingfish." A self-made politician of a humble background in the deep South, Willie launches his career as an idealistic, winsome politician called "Cousin Willie from the country" (18). As he ascends the political ladder, he becomes a Machiavellian figure (4). He defeats the state legislature's attempt to impeach him, he dreams of becoming president of the United States, but his heavy-handed leadership style earns him many enemies. Then, at the peak of his career, he is assassinated.

On another level, however, *All the King's Men* is a novel about sin and redemption. Willie Stark commits the sin of adultery, and his political blackmail is directly responsible for Judge Irwin's suicide. Jack Burden misuses his research skills to uncover the secrets of Willie's political enemies, thereby becoming his boss's accomplice. Judge Irwin, known for his moral uprightness, turns out to have taken a bribe in office and to have had an adulterous relationship with Jack's mother. Finally, Jack's ancestor Cass Mastern is found to have committed adultery with a married woman in the 1850s, an action that led to the suicide of the woman's husband.

One of the ways *All the King's Men* comments upon sin and redemption is through its depiction of original sin. For example, when

1

Willie Stark directs Jack Burden to investigate Judge Irwin, a retired state attorney general, Jack is doubtful of finding corruption in the upright judge's political career. Scoffing at Jack's naiveté, Willie states, "Man is conceived in sin and born in corruption, and he passeth from the stink of the didie to the stench of the shroud. There's always something" (49). This somewhat crude remark does not come from a believer. Rather, Willie uses religious language he recalls from his Presbyterian Sunday school days to convince Jack that no person is without reproach. A believer in political expediency, Willie finds the church's teaching useful for understanding human nature—no human being is without sin. As Willie predicted, Jack's investigation reveals the judge's guilt. Tiny Duffy, Willie Stark's double, further embodies the sinfulness of human nature. Little human warmth can be found in his personality, and all of his decisions are based on political calculations. An ambitious man, he is a political animal willing to endure humiliation and abuse from Willie. When Duffy's act of betrayal causes Willie's death, he gladly replaces Willie as governor and shows little remorse. The pervasiveness of sin is also conveyed in Cass Mastern's journal. An entry contains the following words: "For all men come naked into the world, and in prosperity 'man is prone to evil as the sparks fly upward.' I write this down with what truthfulness a sinner may attain unto . . ." (161). Meanwhile, Ellis Burden, nicknamed the Scholarly Attorney in the novel, confirms the inherent sinfulness of human nature as follows:

> The creation of man whom God in His foreknowledge knew doomed to sin was the awful index of God's omnipotence. . . . Separateness is identity and the only way for God to create, truly create, man was to make him separate from God Himself, and to be separate from God is to be sinful. The creation of evil is therefore the index of God's glory and His power. (437)

The Scholarly Attorney's remark indicates a Christian-based dark view of original sin: Human beings are inferior to God in their moral capacity; it is their innate evil natures that separate humans from God.

Willie Stark is not simply a caricature of a Machiavellian, demagogic politician. He is a tragic hero who instills pity and fear in the reader. His physical features and public posture render him larger-than-life. His eyes "bulge" and "glitter" (9), he is very strong, and his speeches are spellbinding. In his early years, he exhibits remarkable energy. Working the fields during the day and studying law by himself at night, Willie becomes a lawyer and eventually county treasurer. Initially, Willie evinces a genuine desire to improve the lives of poor people. As a radical reformer, he views himself, and is viewed by his supporters, as a Christ-like figure. In the words of the managing editor of the *Chronicle*, Willie "thinks he is Jesus Christ scouring the money-changers out of that shinplaster courthouse" (51).

Willie, however, is a sinner in his misguided sense of mission. Though not an especially devout man, Willie is nonetheless convinced that God is calling him to the political appointments he covets; he thinks he is "on the Lord's side and the Lord [has] given him a sign" (71). When Willie encounters obstacles to his limitless ambition, he physically exhibits the same exalted sense of purpose: "His face [has] a high and pure and transparent look like a martyr's face just before he steps into the flame" (87–88).

Willie's motto is "My study is the heart of the people" (6). This seemingly harmless catchphrase conceals his double-mindedness. He studies the heart of the people for the sake of political manipulation. In Chapter One, Willie visits Mason City, his hometown. Urged by the adoring crowd, he delivers a speech that he claims is not politically motivated. Always conscious of his public image, he leaves the outside of his father's house intentionally unpainted to give the impression that he is one of them, not above them. He assumes humility before his dazzled crowd, but he is sometimes oblivious to its presence; after the speech, he walks "straight into the crowd as though the crowd [isn't] there" (12).

More important than Willie's political machinations, Willie believes that good ends justify the foulest of means. Willie rationalizes political blackmail by using the analogy of dirt:

> It's dirt that makes the grass grow. A diamond ain't a thing in the world but a piece of dirt that got awful hot. And God-a-Mighty picked up a handful of dirt and blew on it and made you and me and George Washington and mankind blessed in faculty and apprehension. It all depends on what you do with the dirt. That right?" (45)

In his conversation with Adam Stanton, Willie argues that politics is not always clean and that the best possible thing to do is to make good use of evil. When Adam asks him where good comes from, Willie replies, "Goodness.... Well you can't inherit that from anybody. You got to make it, Doc. If you want it. And you got to make it out of badness ..." (257). As Adam wonders how one can recognize the good if it comes only from the bad, Willie responds, "You just name it up as you go along" (257). Thus, Willie divides people into two groups: those who are useful to him and those who are not, and he uses ruthless tactics to crush his opponents.

Willie's political power makes him arrogant. In Chapter One, when he shakes hands with Tiny Duffy, then an underling he passionately despises, Willie grudgingly extends his hand "with the reserved air of the Pope offering his toe to the kiss of a Campbellite" (16). He also identifies himself with the hospital he envisions to build for the poor: "For it's mine, you hear—that's my hospital—it's mine!" (362).

Despite his lack of humility and professed amorality, Willie is at least partially redeemed when his life is struck by tragedy. The death of Willie's son forces Willie to reexamine himself and his conduct. He discontinues his extramarital affairs and goes back to his estranged wife. Before dying, Willie expresses remorse over the many sins he has committed throughout the novel, telling Jack Burden: "It might have been all different, Jack.... And it might even been different yet. If it hadn't happened, it might—have been different—even yet" (400). These words have a redeeming quality in them; if he survived the shooting, Willie might have lived his life differently.

Cass Mastern is the topic of Jack Burden's unfinished Ph.D. dissertation in American history. Mastern, the brother of Jack's grandmother, died during the Civil War after committing adultery. Cass was a native Mississippian who attended Kentucky's Transylvannia College in the 1850s, where he fell into the temptation of "the illicit sweetness of the flesh" (164): a tryst with Annabelle Trice, the wife of his best friend, Duncan Trice. In his journal, Cass recalls the first moment he saw her: "She came into the room and was the true goddess as revealed in her movement, and was, but for Divine Grace (if such be granted to a parcel of corruption such as I), my true damnation" (165). Their feelings were mutual, and they eventually committed adultery.

However, these pleasures of the flesh did not last long. After discovering his wife's unfaithfulness, Duncan shot himself in his library. Phebe, Annabelle's personal slave, then found Duncan's wedding ring, left under Annabelle's pillow before his suicide. Afraid that Phebe would spread the rumor about her affair with Cass, Annabelle sold her in the slave market. Stricken by guilt, Cass searched in vain for Phebe. Cass and Annabelle became estranged, he fell into despair, but he could not kill himself for fear that it might damn his soul. He came back to his plantation in Mississippi, where he freed his slaves. When the Civil War broke out, he sought death by joining the Confederate Army as a foot soldier. On battlefields, he did not shoot anyone; as his journal records, "How can I who have taken the life of my friend, take the life of an enemy, for I have used up my right to blood" (186). After patiently waiting for the enemy's bullet, he finally was shot, and with Duncan's wedding ring attached to a string around his neck, Cass slowly died in an Atlanta hospital.

Although Cass occupies only one chapter of the novel, it dramatically embodies the theme of sin and redemption. Cass's story illustrates the attractiveness of sexual sin, the grave consequences of adultery, and the sinner's atonement for his sin in the form of the sacrifice of his life. On his deathbed, Cass reflects on his sinfulness, his moral responsibility, and God's mercy:

> I have lived to do no man good, and have seen others suffer for my sin. I do not question the Justice of God, that others have suffered for my sin, for it may be that only by the suffering of the innocent does God affirm that men are brothers, and brothers in His Holy Name. And in this room with me now, men suffer for sins not theirs, as for their own. It is a comfort to know that I suffer only for my own.... Men shall come together yet and die in the common guilt of man and in the guilt that sent them hither from far places and distant firesides. But God in His Mercy has spared me the end. Blessed by His Name. (187–188)

Thus, Cass expiates his adultery and his violation of a friend's trust, comes to terms with God, and dies a peaceful death.

Harboring a guilt similar to Cass Mastern's, Judge Irwin—Jack Burden's father figure—kills himself at the revelation that he once accepted a bribe from the American Electric Power Company. Jack makes the discovery after an extensive investigation conducted at Willie's order. Jack learns that the judge's political corruption was directly responsible for the suicide of Mortimer L. Littlepaugh, then counsel for the company. Judge Irwin asserts his dignity by shooting himself rather than bowing to Willie's political pressure. It is unclear whether his suicide was motivated by a sense of humiliation or as an act of contrition. Jack learns from his mother that his biological father was not the Scholarly Attorney but Judge Irwin. Upon discovering his wife's infidelity with his friend, the Scholarly Attorney left his wife when Jack was about six, dedicating the rest of his life to the care of the unfortunate in the capital. Unlike Cass Mastern, who repents of his adultery and redeems himself for his act, Judge Irwin keeps his sexual sin secret. If Irwin had not committed suicide, Jack might not have known about his real father.

In his essay "Knowledge and the Image of Man," Robert Penn Warren identifies "the individual's right to exist as himself, the right to the hazards and glories of trying to develop most fully as himself," as "a heritage of Christianity" (237). According to Warren, "Every soul is valuable in God's sight, and the story of every soul is the story of its self-definition for good or evil, salvation or damnation. Every soul is valuable in God's sight. Or, with the secularization of things, we may say: every soul is valuable in man's sight" (237–38). In this regard, Jack Burden's story in *All the King's Men* is that of a journey toward self-definition and for knowledge that is essential for self-fulfillment. By the end of the novel, Jack achieves self-definition and self-knowledge, but at a price: the deaths of Judge Irwin, Adam Stanton, and Willie Stark, who all perish partly because of his amorality and irresponsibility.

For most of the novel, Jack remains a drifter. Unlike Willie, who is goal-oriented, he has no concrete plans for himself, either in his relationships or in his professional career. He loves Anne Stanton and thinks he will marry her someday, but his aimlessness makes her wonder whether he will be able to make a living. Jack marries Lois Seager for sex and then walks out of the marriage. His dissertation remains unfinished, and he briefly attends law school only to please Anne. Jack is surprised to discover that Anne has become Willie's mistress, but he fails to understand why such a shocking move could have happened. His lack of direction for life is partly responsible for Anne's affair with Willie, which leads to Adam's murder of Willie, which in turn leads to the murder of Adam himself. While Jack is an intelligent, reflective person, when he acts on behalf of Willie, Jack does so without considering the moral ramifications of his actions.

Despite his often cynical, contemptuous view of Willie, Jack carries out orders from him anyway, sometimes using threats and innuendos against Willie's opponents. Jack's greatest sin is to betray the trust of Judge Irwin, who has treated him with fatherly affection. Jack undergoes three periods of what he calls the Great Sleep (*All the Kings Men*, 100)—after he gave up on his doctoral dissertation, while his marriage to Lois was disintegrating, and after he resigned as a newspaper reporter. Rather than confronting problems, he avoids them by sleeping. In his lethargic non-action, he is akin to the title character of Ivan Goncharov's novel *Oblomov* (1859). A young nobleman in nineteenth-century Russia, Oblomov lacks vitality, practicality, and decisiveness, conducting his business from his bed or sofa. Like Jack Burden, he loses his sweetheart to a man with a more dynamic, vigorous personality. Jack's irresponsibility is also evidenced by his naturalistic philosophy of the Great Twitch. According to this theory, humans have no control over their environments, and, consequently, they are not responsible for their actions. On the return trip from California, he gives a ride to an old Arkansan. Jack observes a "twitch" in the man's left cheek—a part of his face, which, nevertheless, "was simply an independent phenomenon, unrelated to the face or to what was behind the face or to anything in the whole tissue of phenomena which is the world we are lost in" (313). *All the King's Men* concerns Jack's renunciation of the Great Twitch theory as he realizes his role in the deaths of Judge Irwin, Willie Stark, and Adam Stanton. In the final chapter of *All the King's Men*, Jack reflects on the process involved in his transformation. According to him, the novel is both about Willie Stark and about himself—"It is the story of a man who lived in the world and to him the world looked one way for a long time and then it looked another and very different way. . . . [H]e woke up one morning to discover that he did not believe in the Great Twitch any more. He did not believe in it because he had seen too many people live and die" (435–436). Jack does not die at the end of the novel. Instead, witnessing the deaths of other people makes him realize the importance of assuming responsibility for one's actions. Jack experiences redemption, but it comes largely from witnessing the tragedies that occur to others.

In Warren's novel, sin appears in the forms of pride, unbridled ambition, infidelity, amorality, and irresponsibility. Despite his initial good intentions for the people, Willie Stark falls from grace because of his lack of humility. His redemption is implied at the end of the novel. Cass Mastern has an affair with his best friend's wife, the incident leads to his friend's suicide, and Mastern redeems himself by seeking death in the Civil War. Jack, the narrator and observer of Willie's rise and fall, does not realize the danger of his own moral ambiguity until he loses his biological father, his boss, and his best friend. Jack comes to understand the importance of taking responsibility for one's actions, of maintaining honor and integrity, and of gaining self-knowledge and self-identity. Willie's deathbed conversation with Jack shows he has changed as a person, but his words, like all the words he has uttered in the political fray, do not clearly indicate he is redeemed. Repenting of his sexual sin and betrayal of trust, Cass Mastern seeks self-destruction in a war, thereby making expiation for his wrongdoing. Likewise, Judge Irwin kills himself rather than bending his sense of honor. Learning from both of their examples, Jack regains a sense of direction for life, better understands his past, and becomes ready to live as a responsible member of society.

Works Cited or Consulted

Warren, Robert Penn. *All the King's Men.* 1946. New York: Bantam, 1977.

———. "Knowledge and the Image of Man." *Robert Penn Warren: A Collection of Critical Essays.* Ed. John Lewis Longley, Jr. New York: New York UP, 1965. 237–246.

THE BIBLE

"Enchiridion to Laurentius on Faith, Hope, and Charity"
by Saint Augustine of Hippo, in
Seventeen Short Treatises of S. Augustine,
Bishop of Hippo (Circa 420 C.E.)

INTRODUCTION

Among the most influential philosophers and theologians of
the Western literary tradition, Saint Augustine of Hippo had a
profound effect on how we write and speak about the nature
of sin and redemption. In his *Enchiridion* ("handbook") written
for a friend named Laurentius, Augustine clearly articulates his
interpretation of biblical teachings and their philosophical implications for sin, redemption, free will, and the nature of faith.

8. [. . . (The cause)] of things evil is the will of a being mutably good
falling away from immutable good, first that of an angel, then of man.
This is the first evil of a rational creature, that is, the first withdrawing
of good: then after this there found way, now even against their will,
ignorance of things necessary to be done, and desire of things hurtful;
in company with which are brought in error and pain: which two

---

Augustine. "Enchiridion to Laurentius on Faith, Hope, and Charity." *Seventeen Short Treatises of S. Augustine, Bishop of Hippo*. Oxford: J.H. Parker, 1847. 85–159.

evils when they are perceived to be hanging over us, the emotion of the mind endeavouring to flee from them is called fear. Further, the mind when it obtains things desired, although hurtful or empty, in that through error it perceives it not, is either overpowered by morbid delight, or fanned it may be with vain joy. From these as it were the fountains of diseases, fountains not of plenty, but of want, all the misery of a rational nature issues. Which nature, however, in the midst of its evils could not lose the desire of blessedness. But these are the common evils, both of men, and of angels condemned by the justice of the Lord for their wickedness. But man has beside his own punishment, whereby he was punished by the death also of the body. Forasmuch as God had threatened him with the punishment of death if he sinned; thus gifting him with free will, as yet to rule him by His control, and affright him with destruction; and placed him in the happiness of Paradise as in the shadow of a life, from whence by observing righteousness he might ascend to better things. Hence after his sin being made an exile, his own race also, which by sinning he had corrupted in himself as in its root, he bound by the punishment of death and condemnation: so that whatever progeny should be born of him and of his wife, through whom he had sinned, condemned together with him, through carnal lust, wherein was repaid a punishment similar to the disobedience, should draw along with it original sin, whereby it should be drawn through various errors and pains, to that last never-ending punishment with the apostate angels, its corrupters, masters, and partners. Thus, *By one man sin entered into the world, and by sin death: and so death passed upon all men, in that all sinned.* By the world in that place the Apostle meaning the whole human race. This therefore was the case; the mass of the whole human race under condemnation was lying in evils, or even was rolling on and going headlong from evils into evils; and joined to the side of those angels who had sinned, was paying the deserved penalty of impious apostacy. Forasmuch as it pertaineth to the just anger of God, whatsoever the wicked willingly commit through blind and unsubdued lust, and whatsoever they unwillingly suffer by manifest and secret[1] punishments: the goodness of the Creator ceasing not to minister even to evil angels life and vital power, which ministration being withdrawn, they would straightway perish; and as for men, although they be born from a corrupted and condemned stock, ceasing not to give form and life to their seeds, to dispose their members, through periods of time and distances of place to quicken their senses, to bestow on them nutriment. For He judged it better to work good out of things evil, than to allow no things evil to exist. And truly had He willed that there should be no renewing at all of man for the better, even as there is none of impious angels, would it not be deservedly done, that the nature which deserted God, which, using evilly its own power, trampled upon and transgressed the command of its Creator, which it might most easily have kept, which corrupted in itself the image of its Creator, forwardly turning away from His light, which evilly broke off, by its free-will, its salutary subjection to His laws, should be all of it eternally deserted by Him, and suffer everlasting punishment according to its desert? Certainly He would thus act, were He only just, and not merciful also, and shewed not much more clearly His own free mercy rather in setting free the unworthy.

9. Certain angels therefore through impious pride deserting God, and being cast down from their high heavenly habitation into the lowest darkness of this air, that number of angels which was left continued in eternal blessedness with God, and in holiness. For the rest of the angels were not descended from one who fell and was condemned, that so original evil should bind them, as in the case of man, with the chains of succession subject to it, and draw down all to deserved punishments; but when he, who became the devil, had become lifted up together with the partners in his impiety, and, by being thus, lifted up, with them overthrown, the rest with pious obedience clave to the Lord, receiving also, what the others had not, a certain knowledge, to assure them of their eternal and unfailing steadfastness. It therefore pleased God, the Creator and Governor of the universe, that, seeing that not the whole multitude of angels had perished by deserting God, the part which had perished should remain in eternal perdition; whilst the part which had continued firm with God, when the other forsook Him, should rejoice in the full and certain knowledge of the eternity of its future happiness: but that, in that the other rational creature which was in man, had perished entire through sins and punishments both original and actual, out of the renewal of a part of it should be supplied whatever loss that fall of the devil had brought on the fellowship of the Angels. For this has been promised to the Saints at their resurrection, that 'they shall be equal to the Angels of God.' Thus Jerusalem which is above, our mother, the city of God, shall suffer no robbery of the multitude of her sons, or, it may be, shall reign with a yet fuller abundance.[2] For we know

not the number either of holy men, or of unclean devils, into whose place the sons of our holy Mother succeeding, of her who appeared barren upon earth, shall abide without any limit of time in that peace from which they fell. But the number of those citizens, whether it be that which is now, or that which shall be, is contemplated by that Artificer Who calls *the things which are not as the things which are*, and *orders all things in measure and number and weight*. But this portion of the human race, to whom God hath promised deliverance and an eternal kingdom, whether can it at all be restored by the merits of its own works? Far be it. For what good does one who is lost work, except so far as he hath been delivered[3] from destruction? Can it by the free choice of its will? Far be this also: for man using evilly his free will hath lost both himself and it. For in like manner as he who kills himself, assuredly by living kills himself, but lives not by killing himself, nor will be able to raise himself up again after he has killed himself: so when through free-will sin was committed, sin being conqueror, free-will was lost. *For of whom a man is overcome, to him is he made over as a slave also.* This is at any rate the judgment of Peter the Apostle: seeing then that this is true, what kind of liberty can that be of the slave who has been made over, except when it pleases him to sin? For he serves freely, who willingly does the will of his master. And thus he is free to commit sin, who is the slave of sin. Whence he will not be free to work righteousness, unless being set free from sin he shall begin to be the slave of righteousness. This is true liberty by reason of the joy in doing right, and at the same time godly slavery by reason of the obedience to the command. But this liberty to do well, when shall it be to man, made over and sold, unless He redeem him Whose is that saying, *If the Son hath set you free, then shall ye be truly free.* But before this begin to have place in man, how doth any one of free-will glory in any good work, who is not yet free to work what is good, unless he exalt himself, being puffed up with vain pride? Whom the Apostle restrains, saying, *By grace are ye saved through faith.* And lest they should so take to themselves at any rate the faith itself, as not to understand that it was given of God; (like as in another place the same Apostle says, that 'he had obtained mercy to be faithful;') here also he hath added, and says, *And this not of yourselves, but it is the gift of God; not of works, lest haply any one be exalted.* And lest it should be thought that good works will be wanting to believers, again he adds; *For we are His workmanship, created in Christ Jesus in good works, which*

God hath before prepared, that in them we may walk. Therefore then are we made truly free, when God fashions us, that is, forms and creates us, not that we may be men, which thing He hath already done; but that we may be good men, which thing His grace now does; that we may be *in Christ Jesus a new creature*, according to that which is said, *A clean heart create in me, O God.* For his heart, as far as respects the nature of the human heart, God hath not failed already to create. Also, that no one, although not of works, yet should glory of the very free choice of his will, as if the desert began of himself, which received the very liberty of working what is right, as a reward due; let him hear the same herald of grace saying, *For it is God who worketh in you both to will and to do, according to His good pleasure.* And in another place: *Therefore is it, not of him who willeth, nor of him who runneth, but of God who sheweth mercy.* Seeing that without doubt, if man be of such age, as already to exercise his reason, he cannot believe, hope, love, unless he be willing, or arrive at the prize of the high calling of God, unless he have run with his will. How then is it *not of him that willeth, nor of him that runneth, but of God who sheweth mercy*, except in that the will itself, as it is written, is *prepared before of the Lord.* Otherwise, if it was therefore said, *it is not of him who willeth, nor of him who runneth, but of God who sheweth mercy*, because it is brought to pass of both, both the will of man, and the mercy of God; and we understand it to be so said, *it is not of him who willeth, nor of him who runneth, but of God who sheweth mercy*, as if it were said, the will alone of man is not sufficient, unless there be also the mercy of God: therefore also the mercy alone of God is not sufficient, unless there be also the will of man; and thus if it be rightly said, *it is not of man who willeth, but of God who sheweth mercy*, because the will alone of man does not fulfil it; why is it not also on the other side rightly said, 'it is not of God who sheweth mercy, but of man who willeth, because the mercy alone of God does not fulfil it?' So then if no Christian will dare to say, 'it is not of God who sheweth mercy, but of man who willeth,' that he contradict not most openly the Apostle; it remains that it be understood therefore rightly to have been said, *it is not of him who willeth, nor of him who runneth, but of God who sheweth mercy*, that the whole may be given to God, who both prepares the good will of man hereafter to be assisted, and assists it when prepared. For the good will of man goes before many gifts of God, but not all[4]: but those which it goes not before, among them is itself. For both are Ps. 59, read in the sacred writings, both, *His mercy shall prevent* and, *His mercy shall follow me.* It prevents him who has not the will, that he may have the will; it follows after him who hath, that he may not have the will in vain. For why are we charged to pray for our enemies, who assuredly have no will to live godly, except that God may work in them the will also? And, again, why are we charged to ask that we may receive, except that He, by Whom it was brought to pass that we have the will, may bring to pass that which we will? We pray, therefore, for our enemies, that the grace of God may prevent them, as it has prevented us also: but we pray for ourselves that His mercy may follow after us.

10. Therefore the human race was holden under just condemnation, and all were children of wrath. Concerning which wrath it is written, *Since all our days have failed*, and *in Thy wrath have we failed; our years shall be thought on as a spider.* Concerning which anger Job also says, *For man born of a woman, is short of life and full of wrath.* Concerning which wrath the Lord Jesus Christ also says, *He who believeth on the Son, hath eternal life; but he who believeth not on the Son, hath not life, but the wrath of God remaineth upon him.* He says not, shall come; but remaineth. Forasmuch as with this every man is born. Wherefore the Apostle says, *For we too were by nature sons of wrath, as the rest also.* In this wrath when men were through original sin, and in so much the more grievous and deadly wise, as they had added greater or more sins besides, a Mediator was required, that is, a reconciler, to appease this wrath by the offering of a singular Sacrifice, whereof all the sacrifices of the Law and the Prophets were shadows. Whence the Apostle says, *For if, when we were enemies, we were reconciled to God by the death of His Son, much more, being reconciled now in His blood, shall we be saved from wrath through Him.* But when God is said to be angry, there is not implied of Him emotion, such as is in the mind of man when angry; but by a word transferred from human feelings, His vengeance, which is none other than just, hath received the name of Wrath. Therefore that through a Mediator we are reconciled to God, and receive the Holy Spirit, that of enemies we may be made sons; *For as many as are led by the Spirit of God, these are sons of God*; this is the grace of God through Jesus Christ our Lord. Concerning which Mediator it were long to speak so great things as are worthy to be spoken, although by man they cannot worthily be spoken. For who can set forth this alone in suitable words, that *The Word was made flesh, and dwelt among us,* that we should believe in the only Son of God the Father Almighty,

born of the Holy Ghost and the Virgin Mary? Thus, that is, the Word
was made flesh, the flesh being assumed by the Godhead, not the
Godhead changed into flesh. Further in this place we ought to understand by 'flesh' man, the expression from a part signifying the whole;
as it is said, *Since by the works of the Law no flesh shall be justified*; that
is, no man. For it is unlawful to say that any thing of human nature
was wanting in that assumption; but of nature every way free from
every tie of sin: not such nature as is born of both sexes through the
lust of the flesh with the bond of sin, the guilt whereof is washed away
by regeneration; but such as it was fitting that He should be born of
a virgin, whom the faith of His mother, not her lust, had conceived;
by whose very birth even were her virginity impaired, now no longer
would He be born of a virgin; and falsely, which God forbid, would
the whole Church confess Him born of the Virgin Mary; she who
following His Mother daily brings forth His members, and is a virgin
still. Read, if you will, on the virginity of holy Mary my letters to an
illustrious man whose name mention with honour and affection, Volu-
sianus. Wherefore Christ Jesus the Son of God is both God and Man.
God before all worlds,[5] Man in our world. God, because the Word of
God; for the *Word was God*: but Man, because unto unity of Person
there was added to the Word a reasonable soul and flesh." Wherefore
inasmuch as He is God, 'He and the Father are one;' inasmuch as He is
Man, 'The Father is greater than He.' For being the only Son of God,
not by grace, but by nature, that He might be full of grace also, He was
made the Son of Man likewise; and Himself the Same Both, of Both
One Christ. For *being in the form of God, He thought it not robbery*, what
He by nature, *to be equal with God*. Yet *He emptied Himself, receiving
the form of a servant*, not losing or diminishing the form of God. And
so He was both made less, and remained equal, Both in One, as has
been said: but one thing by reason of the Word, the other by reason
of His Manhood; by reason of the Word, equal with the Father, by
reason of His Manhood, less. One the Son of God, and the same the
Son of Man; One the Son of Man, and the same the Son of God: not
two sons of God, God and Man, but One Son of God; God without
beginning, Man from a certain beginning, one Lord Jesus Christ.

11. Here altogether greatly and evidently is God's grace commended.
For what merit had human nature in the Man Christ, that it should be
singularly assumed into the unity of Person of the only Son of God?
What good will, what good and zealous purpose, what good works

went before, such as that by them That Man should deserve to be made
one Person with God? Whether at all was He Man before, and was
this singular benefit afforded Him, in that He deserved singularly of
God? Truly from the time that He began to be Man, He began not to
be any thing other than the Son of God; and this the only Son, and
by reason of God the Word, Who by assuming Him was made flesh,
assuredly God: so that, in like manner as any man whatever is one
Person, that is, a reasonable soul and flesh, so Christ also may be one
Person, the Word and Man. Whence to human nature so great glory,
freely given undoubtedly with no merits going before, unless because
in this the great and alone grace of God is evidently shewn to them
who contemplate it faithfully and soberly, that men may understand
that they are themselves justified from their sins through the same
grace, through which it was brought to pass that the Man Christ
might have no sin? Thus also the Angel saluted His mother, when
he announced to her her future bringing-forth; *Hail*, said he, *full of
grace!* And a little after, *Thou hast found*, says he, *grace with God*. And
she indeed is said to *be full of grace*, and to have *found grace with God*,
that she might be the mother of her Lord, yea, of the Lord of all. But
of Christ Himself the Evangelist John, after having said, *And the Word
was made flesh, and dwelt among us*, says, *And we saw His glory, as of the
Only-begotten of the Father, full of grace and truth*. That which he says,
The Word was made flesh; the same is, *full of grace*: that which he says,
The glory of the Only-begotten of the Father, the same is, *full of truth*. For
the Truth Itself, the Only-begotten Son of God, not by grace, but by
nature, by grace took unto Him Man with so great unity of Person,
that Himself the Same was also the Son of Man. For the same Jesus
Christ the Only-begotten, that is, the only, Son of God, our Lord, was
born of the Holy Ghost and the Virgin Mary. And certainly the Holy
Ghost is the gift of God, which indeed Itself also is equal to the Giver:
and therefore the Holy Ghost also is God, not inferior to the Father
and the Son. From this therefore, that of the Holy Ghost is the birth of
Christ according to His Manhood, what else than very grace is shewn?
For when the Virgin had enquired of the Angel, how that should be
brought to pass which he announced to her, seeing that she knew not
a man; the Angel answered, *The Holy Ghost shall come upon thee, and the
power of the Highest shall overshadow thee; and therefore that Holy Thing
which shall be born of thee shall be called the Son of God*. And Joseph when
he wished to put her away, suspecting her to be an adulteress, whom he

knew to be with child not of himself, received such an answer from the Angel, *Fear not to take Mary thy wife; for that which in her is conceived, is of the Holy Ghost*: that is, What you suspect to be of another man, is of the Holy Ghost.

12. Yet do we therefore at all intend to say, that the Holy Ghost is the Father of the Man Christ, so that God the Father begot the Word, the Holy Ghost the Man, of both which Substances should be one Christ, both the Son of God the Father as touching the Word, and the Son of the Holy Ghost as touching the Man; in that the Holy Ghost as His Father had begotten Him of His virgin Mother? Who will dare to say this? Nor is there need to shew by discussion what other great absurdities follow; when now this very thing is of itself so absurd, that no faithful ears are able to bear it. Wherefore, as we confess, our Lord Jesus Christ, Who is God of God, but as Man was born of the Holy Ghost and the Virgin Mary, in both Substances, the divine, that is, the human, is the only Son of God the Father Almighty, from Whom proceedeth the Holy Ghost. In what manner then do we say, that Christ was born of the Holy Ghost, if the Holy Ghost begat Him not? Was it because He made Him? Seeing that our Lord Jesus Christ, so far as He is God, *all things were made by Him*: so far however as He is Man, Himself also was made, as the Apostle says: *He was made of the seed of David according to the flesh*. But whereas that Creature which the Virgin conceived and brought forth, although It belong to the Person of the Son alone, yet the whole Trinity made; for neither do the works of the Trinity admit of being separated; why in the making of It was the Holy Spirit alone named? Whether is it that even as often as one of the Three is named in any work, the whole Trinity is understood to work? It is so indeed, and may be shewn to be so by examples. But we must not delay any longer on this. For that moves us, how it is said, Born of the Holy Ghost, when He is in no way the Son of the Holy Ghost. For neither, because God created this world, may it lawfully be said to be the Son of God, or born of God; but made, or created, or built, or founded by Him, or whatever other such expression we may rightly use. He, therefore, when we confess Him born of the Holy Ghost and the Virgin Mary, how He be not the Son of the Holy Ghost, and yet be the Son of the Virgin Mary, is difficult to explain. Without any doubt, forasmuch as He was not so born of Him as of a father, and was so born of her as of a mother. It must not therefore be granted, that whatsoever is born of any thing, is straightway to be

called the son of that same thing. For not to notice that a son is born of a man in one sense, and in another sense a hair, a louse, a stomach-worm, no one of which is a son: not to notice then these, seeing that they are with ill grace compared to so great a thing; surely they who are born of water and of the Holy Ghost, no one would properly say that they are sons of the water; but they are expressly called sons of God their Father, and of their mother the Church. Thus, therefore, One born of the Holy Ghost is the Son of God the Father, not of the Holy Ghost. For what we said of hair and the rest, is only of use so far, that we be put in mind, that not every thing which is born of any one, can also be called the son of that of which it is born; in like manner, as it follows not, that all, who are called sons of any one, be said to be also born of him: as there are who are adopted. There are also named sons of hell, not as born of it, but prepared for it, as sons of the Kingdom, who are being prepared for the Kingdom. Therefore seeing that one thing may be born of another thing, and yet not in such a manner as to be a son, and again, that not every one, who is called a son, is born of him whose son he is said to be; doubtless the manner in which Christ was born of the Holy Ghost not as a Son, and of the Virgin Mary as a Son, suggests to us the grace of God, whereby Man, without any merits going before, in the very beginning of his nature in which he began to exist, was joined to God the Word unto so great unity of Person, that Himself the Same should be the Son of God, Who was the Son of Man, and the Son of Man, Who was the Son of God: and that thus in the taking upon Him human nature, in a certain way the very grace should be made natural to that Man, which should not be capable of admitting any sin. Which grace it was therefore necessary should be indicated by the Holy Ghost, because He properly is thus God, as to be called also the Gift of God. Whereof to speak sufficiently, even if it may be done, is matter for a very lengthened discussion.

13. Thus begotten or conceived through no pleasure of carnal lust, and therefore deriving no sin by way of descent; also by the grace of God in a wonderful and unspeakable manner joined, and grown together, in unity of Person, with the Word the Only-begotten of the Father, the Son, not by grace, but by nature, and so Himself also committing no sin; yet, by reason of the 'likeness of the flesh of sin' in which He had come, was He Himself also called sin, being to be sacrificed to wash away sins. Forasmuch as in the old Law sacrifices for sins were called 'sins;' which He truly was made, whereof they were

shadows. Hence the Apostle, after he had said, *We beseech you for Christ to be reconciled to God*; straightway adds and says, *Him who knew no sin, He made sin for us, that we may be the righteousness of God in Him*. He says not, as in certain faulty copies is read, "He Who knew no sin, for us wrought sin;" as if Christ Himself had sinned for us: but he says, '*Him* who had not known sin,' that is, Christ, 'God, to Whom we are to be reconciled, *made sin for us*,' that is, a Sacrifice for sins, through Which we might be able to be reconciled. He therefore sin, as we righteousness; nor that our own, but of God; nor in us, but in Him: as He sin, not His own, but ours; which that it had place not in Him, but in us, He shewed by the likeness of the flesh of sin, in which He was crucified: that, whereas sin was not in Him, so in a certain way He might die to sin, in dying to the flesh, wherein was the likeness of sin; and whereas He had never Himself lived according to the oldness of sin, He might by His own resurrection signify our new life springing to life again, from the old death, whereby we had been dead in sin. This is that very thing which is solemnized among us, the great Sacrament[6] of Baptism, that whosoever pertain to that grace, may die unto sin, as He is said to have died unto sin, who died unto the flesh, that is, the likeness of sin: and may live, by being born again from the laver, as He also by rising again from the grave, of whatever age their bodies be. For from the little child but lately born even to the decrepit old man, as no one is to be prohibited from Baptism, so is there no one who in Baptism dies not unto sin: but little children only unto original sin, elder persons however die unto all those sins also whatsoever by ill living they had added to that which they derived by birth. But therefore are they also generally said to die unto sin, when without any doubt they die not to one, but to many and all sins, whatsoever now of their own they have committed, either by thought, or word, or deed; since also by the singular number the plural is wont to be signified: as the poet says,[7] "And fill his belly with the warrior armed;" although they did this with many warriors. And in our own writings we read, *Pray therefore to the Lord that He may take away from us the serpent*; says not, the serpents, from which the people were suffering, so as thus to speak: and numberless other such. Whereas, however, also that original (sin, which is) one, is signified by the plural number, when we say that little children are baptized for the remission of *sins*, and say not for the remission of *sin*; that is an opposite form of speech, whereby by the plural the singular number is signified. As in the Gospel, Herod

being dead, it is said, *For they are dead who sought the child's life*: it is not
said, he is dead: and in Exodus, *They have made*, says he, *unto themselves
gods of gold*; whereas they had made one calf, of which they said, *These
are thy Gods, O Israel, who led thee forth out of the land of Egypt*: here also
putting the plural for the singular. Although in that one sin also, which
by one man entered into the world, and passed upon all men, by reason
of which young children also are baptized, more sins than one may be
understood, if that one be divided, as it were, into its separate parts.
For therein is both pride, in that man chose rather to be in his own
power, than in that of God; and sacrilege, in that he believed not God;
and murder, in that he cast himself headlong into death; and spiritual
fornication, in that the purity of the human mind was corrupted by the
persuasion of the serpent; and theft, in that forbidden food was taken;
and covetousness, in that he desired more than what ought to have
satisfied him; and whatever else in the commission of this one sin may
by careful thought be discovered. Also that little children are bound
by the sins of their parents, not merely of the first human beings, but
of their own parents, from whom they are themselves born, is said
not without show of reason. Forasmuch as that divine saying, *I will
repay the sins of the fathers upon the sons*; certainly is of force in them,
before that by spiritual regeneration they begin to belong to the New
Testament. Which Testament was prophesied of, when it was said by
Ezekiel, that the sons should not receive the sins of their fathers; and
that that parable should be no longer in Israel, *The fathers have eaten a
sour grape, and the teeth of the children have become numbed*[8]. For therefore is each one born again, that in him may be loosened whatever of
sin there be, with which he is born. For the sins which are afterwards
committed by evil conduct, may also by repentance be healed, as also
we see takes place after Baptism. And therefore regeneration was not
appointed, except only because our generation is corrupted; so much
so that even one begotten of lawful wedlock says, *In iniquities I was
conceived, and in sins my mother nourished me in the womb*. Neither
said he here, in iniquity, or, in sin, although this also might rightly
be said; but he chose rather to say iniquities and sins. Because in that
one sin also, which passed upon all men, and is so great, that by it
human nature was changed and turned unto necessity of death, there
are found, as I have shewn above, more sins than one; and other sins
of our parents, which, although they cannot so change our nature, yet
bind sons by a state of condemnation, unless the free grace and mercy

of God come to their help. But not without good reason may it be questioned, concerning the sins of our other parents, whom each of us succeed to as ancestors from Adam down to his own parent; whether he who is born be involved in the evil actions of all, and multiplied original transgressions, so that each one is born in so much the worse estate, the later it is; or whether it be for this reason that God threatens the posterity unto the third and fourth generation, concerning the sins of their parents, because He extends not His anger, as far as relates to the offences of their ancestors, further, through the tempering of His merciful kindness; lest they, on whom the grace of regeneration is not bestowed, might be weighed down with too heavy a burthen in their very eternal damnation, if they were obliged from the beginning of the human race to draw together by way of descent the sins of all their parents who went before them, and to suffer the punishments due to them: or whether any thing else in so great a matter, by more careful examination and handling of holy Scripture, may or may not be discovered, I do not venture to affirm unadvisedly.

14. That one sin, however, which was so great, and committed in a place and state of so great happiness, that in one man, by way of origin, and so to say, by way of root, the whole human race was condemned, is not loosed and washed away, but only through one Mediator between God and men, the Man Christ Jesus, Who alone could so be born, as that to Him there were no need to be born again. For they were not born again, who were baptized by the baptism of John, by whom He also was baptized: but by a certain ministry of him, as of a forerunner, who said, *Prepare a way for the Lord*, were prepared for that One in Whom alone they could be born again. For His baptism is, not in water only, as was that of John, but also in the Holy Ghost; according as of That Spirit, whosoever believeth in Christ, is regenerate, of Which Christ being generated, needed not to be regenerate. Whence that voice of the Father which came over Him when baptized, *I to-day have begotten Thee*; pointed not out that one day of time in which He was baptized, but that of unchangeable eternity, to shew that That Man pertained to the Person of the Only-begotten. For wherein the day is neither begun by yesterday's ending, nor ended by to-morrow's beginning, it is ever to-day. Therefore He willed to be baptized by John in water, not that any iniquity in Him might be washed away, but that His great humility might be commended. For in like manner in Him Baptism found nothing to wash away, even as

death found nothing to punish; that the devil, being overcome and vanquished by truth of justice, not by violence of power, in that he had most unjustly slain Him without any desert of sin, might through Him most justly lose them whom through desert of sin he had gotten in hold. Therefore He took upon Him both, both baptism and death, by reason of a determinate dispensation, not of pitiable necessity, but rather of pitying will; that One might take away the sin of the world, as one sent sin into the world, that is, upon the whole human race. Except only that that one sent one sin into the world, this One however took away not only that one sin, but at the same time all, which He found added to it. Whence the Apostle says, *Not as by one man sinning, so is the gift also: for the judgment indeed was of one unto condemnation, but the grace, of many offences unto justification.* Because assuredly that one sin which is derived by way of descent, even if it be alone, makes men liable to condemnation: but the grace justifies from many offences the man, who, beside that one which in common with all he hath derived by way of descent, hath added many of his own likewise. However, that which he says a little after, *As by the offence of one upon all men unto condemnation, also by the righteousness of one upon all men unto justification of life*; sufficiently shews, that no one born of Adam is otherwise than held under condemnation, and that no one is freed from condemnation otherwise than by being born again in Christ. Of which punishment through one man, and grace through one Man, having spoken as much as he judged sufficient for that place of his Epistle, next he commended the great mystery of holy Baptism in the Cross of Christ, in such manner as that we understand that Baptism in Christ is none other than the likeness of the death of Christ; and that the death of Christ crucified is none other than the likeness of the remission of sin: that, as in Him true death had place, so in us true remission of sin; and as in Him true resurrection, so in us true justification. For he says, *What shall we say then? shall we continue in sin, that grace may abound?* For he had said above, *For where sin abounded, grace abounded more.* And therefore he proposed to himself the question, whether one be to continue in sin, in order to obtain abundance of grace. But he answered, *Far be it*: and added, *If we are dead to sin, how shall we live therein?* Then, in order to shew that we are dead to sin: *What, know ye not*, says he, *how that we whosoever have been baptized in Jesus Christ, have been baptized in His death?* If therefore we are hence shewn to be dead to sin, in that we have been baptized in the death of Christ; assuredly little children also who are baptized in Christ, die unto sin, because they are baptized in His death. For without any exception it is said, *We whosoever have been baptized in Christ Jesus, have been baptized in His death.* And therefore is it said, that it may be shewn that we are dead to sin. But to what sin do little children die by being born again, except to that, which, by being born, they have derived? And thus to them also pertains what follows, wherein he says, *Therefore we have been buried together with Him through baptism unto death, that, in like manner as Christ rose from the dead through the glory of the Father, so we also may walk in newness of life. For if we have became planted together with the likeness of His death, so shall we be also of His resurrection: knowing this, that our old man hath been crucified together, that the body of sin may be made empty, that we serve not sin any longer. For he that hath died, hath been justified from sin. But if we have died with Christ, we believe that we shall also together live with Him: knowing that Christ rising from the dead, now dieth not, death shall no more have dominion over Him. For in that He hath died unto sin, He hath died once; but in that He liveth, He liveth unto God. Thus do ye also judge yourselves to have died indeed unto sin, but to live unto God in Christ Jesus.* For hence he had begun to prove that we must not continue in sin, that grace may abound; and had said, *If we have died to sin, how shall we live in it?* and, to shew that we had died to sin, had added, *What, know ye not that we whosoever have been baptized in Christ Jesus, have been baptized in His death?* Thus then he closed that whole passage as he began. Seeing that he so introduced the death of Christ, as to say that even He died to sin. To what sin, except to the flesh, in which was, not sin, but the likeness of sin; and therefore it is called by the name of sin? Therefore to them who have been baptized in the death of Christ, in which not only older persons, but little children also are baptized, he says, *So do ye also,* that is, in like manner as Christ, *So do ye also judge yourselves to have died unto sin, but to live unto God in Christ Jesus.* Whatever therefore was done in the Cross of Christ, in His Burial, in His Resurrection on the third day, in His Ascension into Heaven, in His Sitting at the right hand of the Father; was done in such sort, as that to these things, not only as spoken after a mystical manner, but also as done, the Christian life which is here lived might be conformed. For by reason of His Cross it is said; *But they that are Jesus Christ's, have crucified their flesh with its passions and lusts.* By reason of His Burial: *We have been buried together with Christ through*

Baptism unto death. By reason of His Resurrection: *That like as Christ rose again from the dead through the glory of the Father, so we also may walk in newness of life.* By reason of His Ascension into Heaven, and Sitting at the right hand of the Father: *But if ye have risen again with Christ, seek the things which are above, where Christ is sitting at the right hand of God, mind the things which are above, not the things which are upon earth: for ye have died, and your life is hid with Christ in God.* However, that which we confess concerning Christ as future; how that He is to come from Heaven, to judge the quick and dead, relates not to that life of ours which is lived here; in that neither is it among the things which He hath done, but among those which He is to do, at the end of the world. To this belongs what the Apostle goes on to add: *When Christ our life shall have appeared, then shall ye also appear with Him in glory,* But that He will judge the quick and the dead may be understood in two ways: either to understand by the quick them whom His coming shall find not yet dead, but still living in this flesh; but by the dead, them who, before His coming, have departed, or are to depart, from the body: or whether by the living the just, by the dead the unjust: since the just also shall be judged. For at times the judgment of God is used in an evil sense; whence is that saying, *But they who have done evil, unto the resurrection of judgment*: at times also in a good sense, according to that which is said, *O God, in Thy Name save me, and in Thy might judge me.* Forasmuch as by the judgment of God takes place that very separation of the good and bad, that the good, being to be freed from evil, not to be destroyed with the evil persons, may be set apart at the right hand. By reason of which he cried out, *Judge me, O God*: and as if setting forth what he had said, *And separate,* says he, *my cause from a nation not holy.*

NOTES

1. 'opertis.' Bened. 'apertis,' 'open,' most Mss.
2. Cf. de Civ. Dei, 1. xxii. c. 1.
3. al. 'quando'—'reparatus,' 'when he hath been restored.'
4. See S. Greg. Mor. xvi. 30. and xviii. 62. Tr. p. 363. and note c. where, in the passage cited, 'promeruit' is of course to be taken according to the Christian notion of the relation of works to reward, and as 'mereri' is repeatedly used in the present volume.

5. In this, and some other expressions, we have the very language of the Athanasian Creed, which was evidently rather collected than invented by its author.
6. 'Sacramentum,' perhaps here 'mystery.'
7. Of the Trojan Horse. Virg. Aen. ii. 20.
8. obstupuerunt, al. obstipuerunt.

THE POEMS OF SAMUEL TAYLOR COLERIDGE

"Coleridge's Divine Comedy"
by G. Wilson Knight, in *The Starlit Dome: Studies in the Poetry of Vision* (1941)

INTRODUCTION

In this chapter from his study of visionary poetry, noted scholar G. Wilson Knight analyzes the allusive symbolism of three poems by Coleridge which, taken together, "may be grouped as a little *Divina Commedia* exploring in turn Hell, Purgatory, and Paradise." Knight first examines the imagery of *Christabel*, which, like Dante's *Inferno*, "expresses fear of some nameless obscenity." Second, Knight finds "Rime of the Ancient Mariner" to be a "story of sin, loneliness, and purgatorial redemption." Finally, Knight meditates on the sublime symbols Coleridge records in "Kubla Khan," where readers reach the "marriage-point in life's progress half-way between birth and death: and even birth and death are themselves here mingled or married."

Knight, G. Wilson. "Coleridge's Divine Comedy." *The Starlit Dome: Studies in the Poetry of Vision*. London: Oxford UP, 1941; Barnes and Noble reprint, 1960. 83–178.

I

I shall concentrate first on *Christabel*, *The Ancient Mariner*, and *Kubla Khan*. Within a narrow range these show an intensity comparable with that of Dante and Shakespeare. As with those, strong human feeling mixes with stern awareness of evil; without artistic confusions. Coleridge's main negation tends to a subjective sin-fear: his use of *fear* is, indeed, the secret of his uncanny power, this being the most forceful medium for riveting poetic attention.

Christabel is one nightmare; so, pretty nearly, is *The Ancient Mariner*, and *Kubla Khan* at one point strikes terror. Coleridge is expert in nightmarish, yet fascinating, experience. The human imagination can curl to rest, as in a warm bed, among horrors that would strike pallor in actual life, perhaps recognizing some unknown release, or kinship: as in Wordsworth, who, however, never shows the nervous *tension* of Coleridge. These three poems, moreover, may be grouped as a little *Divina Commedia* exploring in turn Hell, Purgatory, and Paradise.

Christabel is akin to *Macbeth*. There is darkness (though moon-lit), the owl, the restless mastiff. There is sleep and silence broken by fearsome sounds. The mastiff's howl is touched with deathly horror: 'some say she sees my lady's shroud.' Opposed to the nightmarish are images of religious grace. This first part is strangely feminine: the mastiff is a 'bitch,' the heroine set between Geraldine and the spirit of her own mother as forces of evil and grace respectively. 'Mary Mother' and 'Jesu Maria' find a natural home in the phraseology. Some sort of sexual desecration, some expressly physical horror, is revealed by Geraldine's undressing. She insinuates herself into Christabel's religious, mother-watched, world; she is mortally afraid of the mother-spirit and addresses her invisible presence with extreme dramatic intensity. As so often a seemingly sexual evil is contrasted with a parental good, yet Geraldine gets her opportunity through Christabel's charity, and when she lies with her is imaged as a mother with a child. Some hideous replacing of a supreme good is being shadowed, with an expression of utter surprise, especially in the conclusion to Part I, that so pure a girl can have contact with so obscene an horror. It is something Christabel cannot confess: she is powerless to tell her father. She is under a spell. The evil is nerve-freezing yet fascinating. There is vivid use of light in the tongue of flame shooting from the dying brands, and before that Geraldine's first appearance in the moonlight is glitteringly pictured.

Stealth, silence, and sleep are broken by sudden, fearful, sound. In Part II we get perhaps the most intense and nightmarish use of the recurring serpent-image in our literature: both in Bracy's dream of Christabel as a 'sweet bird' (the usual opposite) with a 'bright green snake' coiled round it and Christabel's tranced hissing, later mesmerized by 'shrunken' serpent eyes. The poem expresses fear of some nameless obscenity. Christabel, we gather, has a lover, but he is of slight importance in the poem as we have it, though there is reason to suppose the conflict between him and Geraldine was to have been made dramatically explicit.

Christabel helps our understanding of *The Ancient Mariner*, which describes the irruption into the natural human festivity of a wedding party of the Mariner's story of sin, loneliness, and purgatorial redemption. These somewhat Wordsworthian elements are set against the 'merry din,' the 'loud bassoon.' The wedding guest is agonizedly torn from human, and especially sexual, normality and conviviality.

The story starts with a voyage into 'the land of ice and of fearful sounds.' There is snow and fog. From this the Albatross saves them: it is as 'a Christian soul.' Its snowy whiteness would naturally grip Coleridge: he is fascinated by whiteness. The bird seems to suggest some redeeming Christ-like force in creation that guides humanity from primitive and fearful origins. Anyway, the central crime is the slaying of it and by their wavering thoughts the crew 'make themselves accomplices'; and the dead bird is finally hung round the Mariner's neck 'instead of the cross' as a sign of guilt. Indeed, the slaying of the Albatross in the Mariner's story may correspond to the death of Christ in racial history. It is, moreover, an act of unmotivated and wanton, semi-sadistic, destruction, explicitly called 'hellish.' As a result the ship is calmed in a tropic sea. Parching heat replaces icy cold. The 'land of ice and snow' may be allowed to suggest primeval racial sufferings or primitive layers in the psychology of man; and yet also, perhaps, something more distant still, realms of ultimate and mysterious being beyond nature as we know it, and of a supreme, if inhuman, purity and beauty. The central crime corresponds to the fall, a thwarting of some guiding purpose by murderous self-will, or to loss of innocence in the maturing personality, and the consequent suffering under heat to man's present mental state. In poetic language you may say that whereas water parallels 'instinct' (with here a further reach in 'ice and snow' suggesting original mysteries of the distant and primeval), flames, fire, and light hold a more intellectual suggestion:

they are instinct becoming self-conscious, leading to many agonies and high aspirations. The bird was a nature-force, eating human food, we are told, for the first time: it is that in nature which helps man beyond nature, an aspect of the divine purpose. Having slain it, man is plunged in burning agony. The thirst-impressions recall Eliot's *Waste Land*, which describes a very similar experience. The new mode is knowledge of evil, symbolized in the 'rotting' ocean, the 'slimy things' that crawl on it, the 'death-fires' and 'witches oils' burning by night. It is a lurid, colourful, yet ghastly death-impregnated scene, drawn to express aversion from physical life in dissolution or any reptilian manifestation; and, by suggestion, the sexual as seen from the mentalized consciousness as an alien, salty, and reptilian force. It is a deathly paralysis corresponding, it may be, to a sense of sexually starved existence in the modern world: certainly 'water, water everywhere, nor any drop to drink' fits such a reading.

Next comes the death-ship. 'Nightmare Life-in-Death' wins the Mariner's soul. This conception relates to deathly tonings in literature generally, the *Hamlet* experience, and the metaphorical 'death' of Wordsworth's *Immortality Ode*. It is, significantly, a feminine harlot-like figure, and is neatly put beside Death itself. She 'begins her work' on the Mariner. The other sailors all die: observe how he is to endure *knowledge* of death, with guilt. He is 'alone on a wide wide sea' in the dark night of the soul; so lonely—compare Wordsworth's solitaries—that God Himself seemed absent. The universe is one of 'beautiful' men dead and 'slimy things' alive, as in Shelley's *Alastor*. The 'rotting sea' is now directly associated with the 'rotting dead,' while he remains eternally cursed by the dead men's 'eyes.' At the extremity of despair and therefore self-less feeling, his eyes are suddenly aware of the beauty of the 'water-snakes' as he watches their rich colours and fiery tracks: 'O happy living things.' The exquisite prose accompaniment runs: 'By the light of the moon he beholdeth God's creatures of the great calm.' A fertilizing 'spring of love' gushes from his 'heart' and he blesses them *'unaware'*—the crucial word is repeated—with unpremeditated recognition and instinctive charity. Immediately the Albatross slips from him and sinks like lead into the sea. An utterly organic and unforced forgiveness of God conditions God's forgiveness of man.

The exact psychological or other conceptual equivalents of poetic symbolism cannot be settled. If they could, there would be no occasion for such symbols, and my use of the term 'sexual' might seem rash to anyone unaware of the general relation of snakes and water to sexual instincts in poetry, as in *Antony and Cleopatra* and Eliot's use of water and sea-life. Christabel's enforced and unhappy silence whilst under Geraldine's serpent spell may be directly related to the water-snakes of *The Ancient Mariner*. She, like the becalmed ship, is helpless; perhaps, in her story too, until a certain frontier, involving spontaneous, but not willed recognition, is reached. Just as she cannot speak, that is, confess, so the Mariner, when, as it were, saved, spends the rest of his life confessing.

The immediate results of conversion are (i) gentle sleep after feverish and delirious horror, and (ii) refreshing rain after parching heat. These are imaginative equivalents and may be said to touch the concept of *agapé* as opposed to *eros*, and are here logically related to Christian symbols. A sense of purity and freedom replaces horror and sin. Energy is at once released: the wind blows and the dead rise and work, their bodies being used by a 'troop of spirits blest,' who next make music, clustering into a circle, with suggestion of Dante's paradisal lives. Now the ship starts to move like Eliot's similar ships in *The Waste Land* and *Ash Wednesday*; yet no wind, but rather the 'lonesome spirit from the South-pole,' is causing the motion, and demanding vengeance still. Why? and who is he? Coleridge's prose definition scarcely helps. He works 'nine fathom' deep—in man or creation, at once instinct and accuser, and not quite stilled by conversion. At last he is placated by the Mariner's penance. Next '*angelic* power' drives on the ship. There is more trouble from the dead men's eyes and another release. As the ship draws near home, each body has a burning seraph upright above it. These seraphic forms that twice seem conditioned by dead bodies, yet not, as individuals, precisely the 'souls' of the men concerned, must, I think, be vaguely identified with the concept of human immortality, the extra dimension of their upright stature over the bodies being pictorially cogent.

At home there is the 'kirk,' the woodland 'hermit,' and safety. After such fiery experience the normality of the hermit's life, its homely and earthy quality, is emphasized. We meet his 'cushion' of 'moss' and 'oak-stump' and his daily prayers. He is a figure of unstriving peace such as Wordsworth sought, associated with earth and solid fact after nightmare and transcendent vision. Extreme sensual and spiritual adventure has brought only agony. Therefore:

> O sweeter than the marriage-feast,
> 'Tis sweeter far to me,

> To walk together to the kirk
> With a goodly company.

It is an embracing of *agapé* with a definitely lower place, if not a rejection, accorded to *eros*; a welcoming of earth and refreshing rain ('the gentle rain from heaven' is an *agapé*-phrase in Shakespeare) with a rejection of the sun in its drawing, tormenting heat. I doubt if there is any relieving synthesis implicit in the 'youths and maidens' that go to church at the end of the poem with the Wordsworthian 'old men and babes': the balance is scarcely in favour of youthful assertion. The final lesson is a total acceptance of God and his universe through humility, with general love to man and beast. But the specifically sexual is left unplaced: the wedding-guest is sadder and wiser henceforth, and presumably avoids all festive gatherings from now on; though forgiveness of *reptilian* manifestation remains basic.

This is Coleridge's *Purgatorio*, as *Christabel* is a fragmentary attempt at a little *Inferno*. Whether we can call the central criminal act 'sexual' is arguable: it certainly resembles that in Wordsworth's *Hart-leap Well*, but the Mariner's compulsion to tell his tale suggests rather Eliot's Sweeney and his grim account. One might notice that the imaginative tonings in *Lucrece* and *Macbeth* are identical, and that 'sadism' may be only a conscious recognition of a deeper relation than has yet been plumbed: motiveless cruelty is, moreover, a general and most valuable poetic theme, as in Heathcliff's ill-treatment of a dog. Such thoughts help to integrate into the whole the mystery of an unmotivated action which, with the South-pole spirit itself, is left rationally undefined, as Shakespeare leaves the motives of Macbeth and Iago and the pain of Hamlet rationally undefined. The new life comes from acceptance of the watery and the reptilian, at which the sea no longer appears to be 'rotting,' that is, dead, though all these drop out of the picture afterwards. The crime, together with rejection of the unrefreshing 'rotting sea' and its creatures, brings parched agony, but acceptance of those brings the other, heavenly and refreshing, water of rain. Also acceptance precedes repentance, not vice versa. A spontaneous, unsought, upspring of love alone conditions the down-flow of grace.

The poem is lively and colourful, as A. C. Bradley has well emphasized. The movement and appearance of sun and moon are described in stanza after stanza; and stars too. The sun peeps in and out as though uncertain whether or not to give its blessing on the strange scene. The poem glitters: the Mariner holds the Wedding Guest with a 'glittering eye,' which, if remembered with his 'skinny hand,' preserves a neat balance. The light is somewhat ghastly: as in the strange sheen of it on ice or tropic calm, and the witches' oils burning 'green and blue and white.' Green light is a favourite in Coleridge (cp. in *Dejection* 'that green light that lingers in the west'). The snakes move in 'tracks of shining white,' making 'elfish' illumination. Their colours are 'blue, glossy-green and velvet black' and by night their every motion pencils 'a flash of golden fire.' The ghost-ship comes barred across the blood-red sun. The 'charmed water' is said to burn 'a still and awful red.' There is a very subtle interplay of light and colour. The Life-in-Death figure is a garish whore with red lips, yellow hair, white leprosy skin; the evil creatures are colourful; the supernatural seraphs brilliant. The whole is dominated by a fearful intensity summed in the image, rather dark for this poem, of a night-walker aware of a demon following his steps. But the play of light and colour helps to give the somewhat stringy stanza succession and thinly narrative, undramatic sequence of events a certain intangible poetic mass. I doubt if the rhyme-links, the metrical rhythms, even the phrase-life, so to speak, would be considered fine poetry without this and, what is equally important, the substance of idea and meaning we have been analysing.

The strangeness and ghastly yet fascinating lights of the experience must guide our judgement of the solution. The experience is of fearful fascination; a feverish horror that is half a positive delight, mental pre-eminently; and the return is a return to earth, the hermits' cell and mossy stone, a return to reality and sanity. Whatever our views of the implied doctrine there is no artistic confusion or lack of honesty. The balancing of symbols, as in the contrast of bird-life and the reptilian, is subtle as Dante's (the *Purgatorio* has a very similarly reiterated observation of the sun in varied position and mood) and Shakespeare's, though without the massive scheme of the one or the sympathetic range of the other. It is a little poem greatly conceived. The supernatural figures dicing for the Mariner's soul suggest, inexactly, the balancing of the Eumenides against Apollo in respect of Orestes in Aeschylus; while the 'lonesome spirit' from the South Pole in its office of accuser performs exactly the function of those Eumenides, furies of guilt and accusation. It is replaced eventually by swift angelic power, as in Eliot's *Family Reunion* the furies of *Sweeney Agonistes* turn into angels.

Poetry of any worth is a rounded solidity which drops shadows only on the flat surfaces of philosophical statement. Concretely it bodies forth symbols of which our ghostly concepts of 'life,' 'death,' 'time,' 'eternity,' 'immortality' are only very pallid analogies. They are none the less necessary, if we are to enchain our normal thinking to the creations of great literature, and I next translate the domed symbolism of *Kubla Khan* into such shadow-terms corresponding to the original in somewhat the same way as the science of Christian theology corresponds, or should correspond, to the New Testament.

The pleasure-dome dominates. But its setting is carefully described and very important. There is a 'sacred' river that runs into 'caverns measureless to man' and a 'sunless sea.' That is, the river runs into an infinity of death. The marked-out area through which it flows is, however, one of teeming nature: gardens, rills, 'incense-bearing' trees, ancient forests. This is not unlike Dante's earthly paradise. The river is 'sacred.' Clearly a sacred river which runs through nature towards death will in some sense correspond to life. I take the river to be, as so often in Wordsworth (whose *Immortality Ode* is also throughout suggested), a symbol of life.

Born on a *height*, it descends from a 'deep romantic chasm,' a place 'savage,' 'holy,' and 'enchanted,' associated with both a 'waning moon' and a 'woman wailing for her demon lover.' The river's origin blends romantic, sacred, and satanic suggestions. Whatever our views on sex it would be idle to suppose them anything but a tangle of inconsistencies. Moreover, the idea of original sin, the 'old serpent,' and its relation to sex is not only Biblical but occurs in myth and poetry ancient and modern. We have not yet compassed the straightforward sanity on this vital issue which D. H. Lawrence said would, if attained, make both nasty sex stories and romantic idealisms alike unnecessary: a certain obscene and savage sex-desecration seems to have fixed itself as a disease in the human mind. That is why we find the virgin-symbol, in both paganism and Christianity, sublimated; especially the virgin mother. Sex is overlaid with both high romantic and low satanic conceptions, complexities, fears, taboos, and worship of all sorts, but the necessity and goodness of pure creativeness no one questions. Our lines here hint a mystery, not altogether unlike Wordsworth's dark grandeurs, blending satanism with sanctity and romance with savagery. They express that mystic glamour of sex that conditions human creation and something of its pagan evil magic; and touch the enigma of the creator-god beyond good and evil, responsible for eagle and boa-constrictor alike.

Whatever our minds make of them, sex-forces have their way. Nature goes on cheerily blasting families and uniting true lovers in matrimonial bonds of 'perdurable toughness,' with an equal efficiency working through rake and curate alike, and not caring for details so long as her work be done. Goethe's poetry well presents this seething, torrential, over-mastering creative energy. Look now at our next lines: at the 'ceaseless turmoil,' the earth-mother breathing in 'fast thick pants,' the fountain 'forced' out with 'half intermitted burst,' the fragments rebounding like hail, the 'chaffy grain beneath the flail,' the 'dancing rocks.' What riotous impression of agony, tumult, and power: the dynamic enginery of birth and creation.

Then off the river goes 'meandering in a mazy motion': observe the rhythm of this line. The maze is, of course, a well-known figure suggesting uncertain and blind progress and is sometimes expressly used for the spiritual complexities of human life; and the general symbolism of mazes and caves throughout my present study might be compared with my brother's inspection of such symbolisms in the ancient world (*Cumaean Gates*, by W. F. Jackson Knight). After five miles of mazy progress the river reaches the 'caverns measureless to man,' that is, infinity, nothingness; and sinks, with first more tumult (i.e. death-agony), to a 'lifeless ocean,' that is to eternal nothingness, death, the sea into which Timon's story closes. This tumult is aptly associated with war: the principle of those conflicting and destructive forces that drive man to his end. The 'ancestral voices' suggest that dark compulsion that binds the race to its habitual conflicts and is related by some psychologists to unconscious ancestor-worship, to parental and pre-parental authority: We find an interesting analogy in Byron's *Sardanapalus*.

So in picture-language we have a symbolical pattern not unlike Addison's *Vision of Mirza*, though less stiffly allegorical. As for Kubla Khan himself, if we bring him within our scheme, he becomes God: or at least one of those 'huge and mighty forms,' or other similar intuitions of gigantic mountainous power, in Wordsworth. Or we can, provisionally—not finally, as I shall show—leave him out, saying that the poet's genius, starting to describe an oriental monarch's architectural exploits, finds itself automatically creating a symbolic and universal panorama of existence. This is a usual process, since the poet continually starts with an ordinary tale but universalizes as he proceeds: compare the two levels of meaning in *The Tempest*, where Prospero performs a somewhat similarly superhuman role to Kubla Khan here; or Yeats's emperor in *Byzantium*.

In *The Christian Renaissance* I wrote at length on the concept of immortality as it emerges from interpretation of poetry. I concluded that, though we must normally think in temporal terms and imagine immortality as a state after death, yet poetry, in moments of high optimistic vision, reveals something more closely entwined than that with the natural order. It expresses rather a new and more concrete perception of life here and now, unveiling a new *dimension* of existence. Thus immortality becomes not a prolongation of the time-sequence, but rather that whole sequence from birth to death lifted up vertically to generate a super-temporal area, or solidity. I used such a scheme to explain parts of the New Testament, Shakespeare, Goethe, and other poets: especially here I would point to my interpretation of Wordsworth's *Immortality Ode*. But I did not use *Kubla Khan*, my scheme being evolved from inspection of other poets.

I come now to the latter movement of our poem, whose form is not unlike an expansion of the Petrarchan Sonnet. This is the sestet. Observe that the metre changes: a lilting happy motion, a shimmering dance motion, replaces heavy resonance and reverberation. Our minds are tuned to a new apprehension, something at once assured, happy, and musical. A higher state of consciousness is suggested: and see what it shows us.

The dome's *shadow* falls half-way along the river, which is, we remember, the birth-death time-stream. This shadow—a Wordsworthian impression—is cast by a higher, more dimensional reality such as I have deduced from other poets to be the pictured quality of immortality. It is directly associated with the 'mingled measure' of the sounds coming from the two extremes. In Wordsworth, and elsewhere, immortality may be associated closely with birth, though that is by way of a provisional and preliminary approach to the greater truth; while in our own thinking it is found most often to function in terms of a life after death. But both are finally unsatisfying; birth and death are both mysteries that time-thinking distorts, and personal life beyond their limits a somewhat tenuous concept. The true immortality is extra-dimensional to all this: it is the *pleasure-dome itself*, arching solid and firm above creation's mazy progress and the 'mingled' sounds of its conflicts, just as in Wordsworth the child's immortality is said to 'brood' over it 'like the day': that is, arching, expansive, immovable.

The 'mingled-measure' suggests the blend and marriage of fundamental oppositions: life and death, or creation and destruction. These 'mingle' under the shadow of the greater harmony, the crowning dome-circle. Observe that it is a paradoxical thing, a 'miracle of rare device'; 'sunny,' but with 'caves of ice,' which points the resolution of antinomies in the new dimension, especially those of light and heat, for Eros-fires of the mind; and ice, for the coldness of inorganic nature, ultimate being, and death, the ice-caves being perhaps related to our earlier caverns, only more optimistically toned; light instead of gloomy, just as 'sunny' suggests no torturing heat. The 'caves of ice' may also hint cool cavernous depths in the unconscious mind (a usual Wordsworthian cave-association) blending with a *lighted* intelligence: whereby at last coldness becomes kind. These, ice and sun-fire, are the two elemental antitheses of *The Ancient Mariner*, and their mingling may lead us farther. We are at what might be called a marriage-point in life's progress half-way between birth and death: and even birth and death are themselves here mingled or married. We may imagine a sexual union between life, the masculine, and death, the feminine. Then our 'romantic chasm' and 'cedarn cover,' the savage and enchanted yet holy place with its 'half intermitted burst' may be, in spite of our former reading, vaguely related to the functioning of a man's creative organs and their physical setting and, too, to all principles of manly and adventurous action; while the caverns that engulf the sacred river will be correspondingly feminine with a dark passivity and infinite peace. The pleasure-dome we may fancy as the pleasure of a sexual union in which birth and death are the great contesting partners, with human existence as the life-stream, the blood-stream, of a mighty coition. The poet glimpses that for which no direct words exist: the sparkling dome of some vast intelligence enjoying that union of opposites which to man appears conflict unceasing and mazed wandering pain between mystery and mystery.

I would leave a space after 'caves of ice.' I am not now so sure about the sonnet form: those six lines are central. So next we have our third and final movement, starting with the Abyssinian damsel seen in a vision playing music. The aptness of a girl-image here is

obvious. In Shakespeare and Milton music suggests that consciousness which blends rational antinomies, and so our poet equates the
once-experienced mystic and girl-born music with his dome. Could
he revive in himself that music he would build the spiritual dome 'in
air'; that is, I think, in words, in poetry. Or, maybe, he would become
himself the domed consciousness of a cold, happy, brilliance, an
ice-flashing, surf-smitten, wisdom. The analogy between music and
some form of architecture is not solitary: it receives a fine expression in Browning's *Abt Vogler*, a valuable commentary on *Kubla Khan*.
The analogy is natural enough for either music or poetry: we talk of
architectonics in criticizing poetry or a novel, for the very reason that
literary or musical art bears to rational thought the relation of a solid,
or at least an area, to a line. Tennyson's *Palace of Art* is a direct analogy,
and Wordsworth compares his life's work to a 'Gothic Church.'

The poem's movement now grows ecstatic and swift. There is a hint
of a new speed in the drawn-out rhythm of 'To such a deep delight
'twould win me. . . .' Now the three rhymed lines gather up the poet's
message together with his consciousness of its supreme meaning with
a breathless expectancy toward crescendo. Next follows a fall to a ritualistic solemnity, a Nunc Dimittis, phrased in long vowels and stately
measured motion, imaged in the 'circle' and the eyes dropped in 'holy
dread' before the prophet who has seen and re-created 'Paradise': not
the earthly, but the heavenly paradise; the 'stately' permanence above
motion, the pleasure-dome enclosing and transcending human agony
and frustration. To tune our understanding we might go to such a
passage as Wordsworth's:

> incumbencies more awful, visitings
> Of the Upholder of the tranquil soul,
> That tolerates the indignities of Time,
> And, from the centre of Eternity
> All finite motions overruling, lives
> In glory immutable. (*The Prelude*, iii. 116)

Which transmits a similar recognition.

Kubla Khan is a comprehensive creation, including and transcending not only the dualisms of *The Ancient Mariner* ('sun,' 'ice,'
and sexual suggestions recurring with changed significance) but also
the more naturalistic, Wordsworthian, grandeurs. Though outwardly

concentrating on an architectural synthesis, it has too another, mountainous, elevation suggested in Mount Abora; and indeed the dome itself is a kind of mountain with 'caves,' the transcendent and the natural being blended, as so often in Wordsworth. It must be related to other similar statements of an ultimate intuition where the circular or architectural supervenes on the natural: in particular to the mystic dome of Yeats's *Byzantium*. The blend here of a circular symbolism with a human figure (the Abyssinian maid) and images of human conflict may be compared both to Dante's final vision and an important passage in Shelley's *Prometheus*. *Kubla Khan* is classed usually with *Christabel* and *The Ancient Mariner*, both profound poems with universal implications. The one presents a nightmare vision related to some obscene but nameless sex-horror; the other symbolizes a clear pilgrim's progress (we may remember Coleridge's admiration of Bunyan's work) through sin to redemption. It would be strange if *Kubla Khan*, incorporating together the dark satanism and the water-purgatory of those, did not, like its sister poems, hold a comparable, or greater, profundity, its images clearly belonging to the same order of poetic reasoning. Its very names are so lettered as to suggest first and last things: Xanadu, Kubla Khan, Alph, Abyssinian, Abora. 'A' is emphatic; Xanadu, which starts the poem, is enclosed in letters that might well be called eschatological; while Kubla Khan himself sits alphabetically central with his alliterating 'k's. Wordsworth's line 'of first, and last, and midst, and without end,' occurring in a mountain-passage (*The Prelude*, vi. 640) of somewhat similar scope, may be compared. The poem's supposed method of composition is well known. How it comes to form so compact and satisfying a unit raises questions outside the scheme of my study. The poem, anyway, needs no defence. It has a barbaric and oriental magnificence that asserts itself with a happy power and authenticity too often absent from visionary poems set within the Christian tradition.

DIVINE COMEDY
(DANTE ALIGHIERI)

༄ ༄

"Dante"
by George Santayana, in *Three Philosophical Poets:*
Lucretius, Dante, and Goethe (1910)

INTRODUCTION

In this excerpt from a lengthy chapter on the *Divine Comedy*, Spanish-American philosopher, critic, and poet George Santayana examines the metaphysical, ethical, and religious framework guiding Dante's poetic vision. Drawing upon Platonic and Aristotelian notions of morality and cosmic order, as well as Catholic doctrines regarding sin and redemption, Santayana asserts that Dante's creation has a special significance in our shared literary tradition: "Probably for the first and last time in the history of the world a classification worked out by a systematic moralist guided the vision of a great poet."

༄

The subject-matter of the *Divine Comedy* is accordingly the moral universe in all its levels,—romantic, political, religious. To present these moral facts in a graphic way, the poet performed a double work of imagination. First he chose some historical personage that might plausibly illustrate each condition of the soul. Then he pictured this

---

Santayana, George. "Dante." *Three Philosophical Poets: Lucretius, Dante, and Goethe.* Cambridge, MA: Harvard UP, 1910. 73–135.

person in some characteristic and symbolic attitude of mind and of
body, and in an appropriate, symbolic environment. To give material
embodiment to moral ideas by such a method would nowadays be very
artificial, and perhaps impossible; but in Dante's time everything was
favourable to the attempt. We are accustomed to think of goods and
evils as functions of a natural life, sparks struck out in the chance shock
of men with things or with one another. For Dante, it was a matter of
course that moral distinctions might be discerned, not merely as they
arise incidentally in human experience, but also, and more genuinely,
as they are displayed in the order of creation. The Creator himself was
a poet producing allegories. The material world was a parable which
he had built out in space, and ordered to be enacted. History was a
great charade. The symbols of earthly poets are words or images; the
symbols of the divine poet were natural things and the fortunes of
men. They had been devised for a purpose; and this purpose, as the
Koran, too, declares, had been precisely to show forth the great difference there is in God's sight between good and evil.

In Platonic cosmology, the concentric spheres were bodies formed
and animated by intelligences of various orders. The nobler an intelligence, the more swift and outward, or higher, was the sphere it moved;
whence the identification of "higher" with better, which survives,
absurdly, to this day. And while Dante could not attribute literal truth
to his fancies about hell, purgatory, and heaven, he believed that an
actual heaven, purgatory, and hell had been fashioned by God on
purpose to receive souls of varying deserts and complexion; so that
while the poet's imagination, unless it reechoed divine revelation, was
only human and not prophetic, yet it was a genuine and plausible
imagination, moving on the lines of nature, and anticipating such
things as experience might very well realize. Dante's objectification of
morality, his art of giving visible forms and local habitations to ideal
virtues and vices, was for him a thoroughly serious and philosophical
exercise. God had created nature and life on that very principle. The
poet's method repeated the magic of Genesis. His symbolical imagination mirrored this symbolical world; it was a sincere anticipation of
fact, no mere laboured and wilful allegory.

This situation has a curious consequence. Probably for the first
and last time in the history of the world a classification worked out
by a systematic moralist guided the vision of a great poet. Aristotle
had distinguished, named, and classified the various virtues, with their

opposites. But observe: if the other world was made on purpose—as
it was—to express and render palpable those moral distinctions which
were eternal, and to express and render them palpable in great detail,
with all their possible tints and varieties; and if Aristotle had correctly
classified moral qualities, as he had—then it follows that Aristotle
(without knowing it) must have supplied the ground-plan, as it were,
of hell and of heaven. Such was Dante's thought. With Aristotle's
Ethics open before him, with a supplementary hint, here and there,
drawn from the catechism, and with an ingrained preference (pious
and almost philosophic) for the number three and its multiples, he
needed not to voyage without a chart. The most visionary of subjects,
life after death, could be treated with scientific soberness and deep
sincerity. This vision was to be no wanton dream. It was to be a sober
meditation, a philosophical prophecy, a probable drama,—the most
poignant, terrible, and consoling of all possible truths.

The good—this was the fundamental thought of Aristotle and
of all Greek ethics,—the good is the end at which nature aims. The
demands of life cannot be radically perverse, since they are the judges
of every excellence. No man, as Dante says, could hate his own soul;
he could not at once be, and contradict, the voice of his instincts and
emotions. Nor could a man hate God; for if that man knew himself, he
would see that God was, by definition, his natural good, the ultimate
goal of his actual aspirations.[1] Since it was impossible, according to
this insight, that our faculties should be intrinsically evil, all evil had
to arise from the disorder into which these faculties fall, their too great
weakness or strength in relation to one another. If the animal part of
man was too strong for his reason, he fell into incontinence,—that is,
into lust, gluttony, avarice, wrath, or pride. Incontinence came from
an excessive or ill-timed pursuit of something good, of a part of what
nature aims at; for food, children, property, and character are natural
goods. These sins are accordingly the most excusable and the least
odious. Dante puts those who have sinned through love in the first
circle of hell, nearest to the sunlight, or in the topmost round of purgatory, nearest to the earthly paradise. Below the lovers, in each case, are
the gluttons,—where a northern poet would have been obliged to place
his drunkards. Beneath these again are the misers,—worse because
less open to the excuse of a merely childish lack of self-control.

The disorder of the faculties may arise, however, in another way.
The combative or spirited element, rather than the senses, may get

out of hand, and lead to crimes of violence. Violence, like incontinence, is spontaneous enough in its personal origin, and would not be odious if it did not inflict, and intend to inflict, harm on others; so that besides incontinence, there is malice in it. Ill-will to others may arise from pride, because one loves to be superior to them, or from envy, because one abhors that they should seem superior to oneself; or through desire for vengeance, because one smarts under some injury. Sins of these kinds are more serious than those of foolish incontinence; they complicate the moral world more; they introduce endless opposition of interests, and perpetual, self-propagating crimes. They are hateful. Dante feels less pity for those who suffer by them: he remembers the sufferings these malefactors have themselves caused, and he feels a sort of joy in joining the divine justice, and would gladly lash them himself.

Worse still than violence, however, is guile: the sin of those who in the service of their intemperance or their malice have abused the gift of reason. *Corruptio optimi pessima*; and to turn reason, the faculty that establishes order, into a means of organizing disorder, is a perversity truly satanic: it turns evil into an art. But even this perversity has stages; and Dante distinguishes ten sorts of dishonesty or simple fraud, as well as three sorts of treachery.

Besides these positive transgressions there is a possibility of general moral sluggishness and indifference. This Dante, with his fervid nature, particularly hates. He puts the Laodiceans in the fringe of his hell; within the gate, that they may be without hope, but outside of limbo, that they may have torments to endure, and be stung by wasps and hornets into a belated activity.[2]

To these vices, known to Aristotle, the Catholic moralist was obliged to add two others: original sin, of which spontaneous disbelief is one consequence, and heresy, or misbelief, after a revelation has been given and accepted. Original sin, and the paganism that goes with it, if they lead to nothing worse, are a mere privation of excellence and involve in eternity merely a privation of joy: they are punished in limbo. There sighs are heard, but no lamentation, and the only sorrow is to live in desire without hope. This fate is most appropriately imputed to the noble and clear-sighted in the hereafter, since it is so often their experience here. Dante was never juster than in this stroke.[3] Heresy, on the other hand, is a kind of passion when honest, or a kind of fraud when politic; and it is punished as pride in fiery tombs,[4] or as faction by perpetual gaping wounds and horrible mutilations.[5]

So far, with these slight additions, Dante is following Aristotle; but here a great divergence sets in. If a pagan poet had conceived the idea of illustrating the catalogue of vices and virtues in poetic scenes, he would have chosen suitable episodes in human life, and painted the typical characters that figured in them in their earthly environment; for pagan morality is a plant of earth. Not so with Dante. His poem describes this world merely in retrospect; the foreground is occupied by the eternal consequences of what time had brought forth. These consequences are new facts, not merely, as for the rationalist, the old facts conceived in their truth; they often reverse, in their emotional quality, the events they represent. Such a reversal is made possible by the theory that justice is partly retributive; that virtue is not its own sufficient reward, nor vice its own sufficient punishment. According to this theory, this life contains a part of our experience only, yet determines the rest. The other life is a second experience, yet it does not contain any novel adventures. It is determined altogether by what we have done on earth; as the tree falleth so it lieth, and souls after death have no further initiative.

The theory Dante adopts mediates between two earlier views; in so far as it is Greek, it conceives immortality ideally, as something timeless; but in so far as it is Hebraic, it conceives of a new existence and a second, different taste of life. Dante thinks of a second experience, but of one that is wholly retrospective and changeless. It is an epilogue which sums up the play, and is the last episode in it. The purpose of this epilogue is not to carry on the play indefinitely: such a romantic notion of immortality never entered Dante's mind. The purpose of the epilogue is merely to vindicate (in a more unmistakable fashion than the play, being ill acted, itself could do) the excellence of goodness and the misery of vice. Were this life all, he thinks the wicked might laugh. If not wholly happy, at least they might boast that their lot was no worse than that of many good men. Nothing would make an overwhelming difference. Moral distinctions would be largely impertinent and remarkably jumbled. If I am a simple lover of goodness, I may perhaps put up with this situation. I may say of the excellences I prize what Wordsworth says of his Lucy: there may be none to praise and few to love them, but they make all the difference to me.

Dante, however, was not merely a simple lover of excellence: he was also a keen hater of wickedness, one that took the moral world tragically and wished to heighten the distinctions he felt into something absolute and infinite. Now any man who is *enragé* in his preferences will probably say, with Mohammed, Tertullian, and Calvin, that good is dishonoured if those who contemn it can go scot-free, and never repent of their negligence; that the more horrible the consequences of evil-doing, the more tolerable the presence of evil-doing is in the world; and that the everlasting shrieks and contortions of the damned alone will make it possible for the saints to sit quiet, and be convinced that there is perfect harmony in the universe. On this principle, in the famous inscription which Dante places over the gate of hell, we read that primal love, as well as justice and power, established that torture-house; primal love, that is, of that good which, by the extreme punishment of those who scorn it, is honoured, vindicated, and made to shine like the sun. The damned are damned for the glory of God. This doctrine, I cannot help thinking, is a great disgrace to human nature. It shows how desperate, at heart, is the folly of an egotistic or anthropocentric philosophy. This philosophy begins by assuring us that everything is obviously created to serve our needs; it then maintains that everything serves our ideals; and in the end, it reveals that everything serves our blind hatreds and superstitious qualms. Because my instinct taboos something, the whole universe, with insane intensity, shall taboo it for ever. This infatuation was inherited by Dante, and it was not uncongenial to his bitter and intemperate spleen. Nevertheless, he saw beyond it at times. Like many other Christian seers, he betrays here and there an esoteric view of rewards and punishments, which makes them simply symbols for the intrinsic quality of good and evil ways. The punishment, he then seems to say, is nothing added; it is what the passion itself pursues; it is a fulfilment, horrifying the soul that desired it.

For instance, spirits newly arrived in hell require no devil with his prong to drive them to their punishment. They flit towards it eagerly, of their own accord.[6] Similarly, the souls in purgatory are kept by their own will at the penance they are doing. No external force retains them, but until they are quite purged they are not able, because they are not willing, to absolve themselves.[7] The whole mountain, we are told, trembles and bursts into psalmody when any one frees himself and reaches heaven. Is it too much of a gloss to say that these souls

change their prison when they change their ideal, and that an inferior
state of soul is its own purgatory, and determines its own duration? In
one place, at any rate, Dante proclaims the intrinsic nature of punishment in express terms. Among the blasphemers is a certain king of
Thebes, who defied the thunderbolts of Jupiter. He shows himself
indifferent to his punishment and says: "Such as I was alive, such I
am dead." Whereupon Virgil exclaims, with a force Dante had never
found in his voice before: "In that thy pride is not mortified, thou
art punished the more. No torture, other than thy own rage, would
be woe enough to match thy fury."[8] And indeed, Dante's imagination cannot outdo, it cannot even equal, the horrors which men have
brought upon themselves in this world. If we were to choose the most
fearful of the scenes in the *Inferno*, we should have to choose the story
of Ugolino, but this is only a pale recital of what Pisa had actually
witnessed. A more subtle and interesting instance, if a less obvious one,
may be found in the punishment of Paolo and Francesca di Rimini.
What makes these lovers so wretched in the Inferno? They are still
together. Can an eternity of floating on the wind, in each other's arms,
be a punishment for lovers? That is just what their passion, if left to
speak for itself, would have chosen. It is what passion stops at, and
would gladly prolong for ever. Divine judgement has only taken it at
its word. This fate is precisely what Aucassin, in the well-known tale,
wishes for himself and his sweetheart Nicolette,—not a heaven to be
won by renunciation, but the possession, even if it be in hell, of what
he loves and fancies. And a great romantic poet, Alfred de Musset,
actually upbraids Dante for not seeing that such an eternal destiny as
he has assigned to Paolo and Francesca would be not the ruin of their
love,[9] but the perfect fulfilment of it. This last seems to be very true;
but did Dante overlook the truth of it? If so, what instinct guided him
to choose just the fate for these lovers that they would have chosen
for themselves?

There is a great difference between the apprentices in life, and the
masters,—Aucassin and Alfred de Musset were among the apprentices; Dante was one of the masters. He could feel the fresh promptings of life as keenly as any youngster, or any romanticist; but he had
lived these things through, he knew the possible and the impossible
issue of them; he saw their relation to the rest of human nature, and
to the ideal of an ultimate happiness and peace. He had discovered
the necessity of saying continually to oneself: Thou shalt renounce.

And for this reason he needed no other furniture for hell than the literal ideals and fulfilments of our absolute little passions. The soul that is possessed by any one of these passions nevertheless has other hopes in abeyance. Love itself dreams of more than mere possession; to conceive happiness, it must conceive a life to be shared in a varied world, full of events and activities, which shall be new and ideal bonds between the lovers. But unlawful love cannot pass out into this public fulfilment. It is condemned to be mere possession—possession in the dark, without an environment, without a future. It is love among the ruins. And it is precisely this that is the torment of Paolo and Francesca—love among the ruins of themselves and of all else they might have had to give to one another. Abandon yourself, Dante would say to us,—abandon yourself altogether to a love that is nothing but love, and you are in hell already. Only an inspired poet could be so subtle a moralist. Only a sound moralist could be so tragic a poet.

The same tact and fine feeling that appear in these little moral dramas appear also in the sympathetic landscape in which each episode is set. The poet actually accomplishes the feat which he attributes to the Creator; he evokes a material world to be the fit theatre for moral attitudes. Popular imagination and the precedents of Homer and Virgil had indeed carried him halfway in this symbolic labour, as tradition almost always carries a poet who is successful. Mankind, from remotest antiquity, had conceived a dark subterranean hell, inhabited by unhappy ghosts. In Christian times, these shades had become lost souls, tormented by hideous demons. But Dante, with the Aristotelian chart of the vices before him, turned those vague windy caverns into a symmetrical labyrinth. Seven concentric terraces descended, step by step, towards the waters of the Styx, which in turn encircled the brazen walls of the City of Dis, or Pluto. Within these walls, two more terraces led down to the edge of a prodigious precipice—perhaps a thousand miles deep—which formed the pit of hell. At the bottom of this, still sinking gently towards the centre, were ten concentric furrows or ditches, to hold ten sorts of rogues; and finally a last sheer precipice fell to the frozen lake of Cocytus, at the very centre of the earth, in the midst of which Lucifer was congealed amongst lesser traitors.

Precision and horror, graphic and moral truth, were never so wonderfully combined as in the description of this hell. Yet the conception of purgatory is more original, and perhaps more poetical.

The very approach to the place is enchanting. We hear of it first in the fatal adventure ascribed to Ulysses by Dante. Restless at Ithaca after his return from Troy, the hero had summoned his surviving companions for a last voyage of discovery. He had sailed with them past the Pillars of Hercules, skirting the African shore; until after three months of open sea, he saw a colossal mountain, a great truncated cone, looming before him. This was the island and hill of purgatory, at the very antipodes of Jerusalem. Yet before Ulysses could land there, a squall overtook him; and his galley sank, prow foremost, in that untraversed sea, within sight of a new world. So must the heathen fail of salvation, though some oracular impulse bring them near the goal.

How easy is success, on the other hand, to the ministers of grace! From the mouth of the Tiber, where the souls of Christians congregate after death, a light skiff, piloted by an angel, and propelled only by his white wings, skims the sea swiftly towards the mountain of purgatory, there deposits the spirits it carries, and is back at the mouth of the Tiber again on the same day. So much for the approach to purgatory. When a spirit lands it finds the skirts of the mountain broad and spreading, but the slope soon becomes hard and precipitous. When he has passed the narrow gate of repentance, he must stay upon each of the ledges that encircle the mountain at various heights, until one of his sins is purged, and then upon the next ledge above, if he has been guilty also of the sin that is atoned for there. The mountain is so high as to lift its head into the sphere of the moon, above the reach of terrestrial tempests. The top, which is a broad circular plain, contains the Garden of Eden, watered by the rivers Lethe and Eunoe, one to heal all painful memories, and the other to bring all good thoughts to clearness. From this place, which literally touches the lowest heaven, the upward flight is easy from sphere to sphere.

The astronomy of Dante's day fell in beautifully with his poetic task. It described and measured a firmament that would still be identified with the posthumous heaven of the saints. The whirling invisible spheres of that astronomy had the earth for their centre. The sublime complexities of this Ptolemaic system were day and night before Dante's mind. He loves to tell us in what constellation the sun is rising or setting, and what portion of the sky is then over the antipodes; he carries in his mind an orrery that shows him, at any given moment, the position of every star.

Such a constant dragging in of astronomical lore may seem to us puerile or pedantic; but for Dante the astronomical situation had the charm of a landscape, literally full of the most wonderful lights and shadows; and it also had the charm of a hard-won discovery that unveiled the secrets of nature. To think straight, to see things as they are, or as they might naturally be, interested him more than to fancy things impossible; and in this he shows, not want of imagination, but true imaginative power and imaginative maturity. It is those of us who are too feeble to conceive and master the real world, or too cowardly to face it, that run away from it to those cheap fictions that alone seem to us fine enough for poetry or for religion. In Dante the fancy is not empty or arbitrary; it is serious, fed on the study of real things. It adopts their tendency and divines their true destiny. His art is, in the original Greek sense, an imitation or rehearsal of nature, an anticipation of fate. For this reason curious details of science or theology enter as a matter of course into his verse. With the straightforward faith and simplicity of his age he devours these interesting images, which help him to clarify the mysteries of this world.

There is a kind of sensualism or aestheticism that has decreed in our day that theory is not poetical; as if all the images and emotions that enter a cultivated mind were not saturated with theory. The prevalence of such a sensualism or aestheticism would alone suffice to explain the impotence of the arts. The life of theory is not less human or less emotional than the life of sense; it is more typically human and more keenly emotional. Philosophy is a more intense sort of experience than common life is, just as pure and subtle music, heard in retirement, is something keener and more intense than the howling of storms or the rumble of cities. For this reason philosophy, when a poet is not mind-less, enters inevitably into his poetry, since it has entered into his life; or rather, the detail of things and the detail of ideas pass equally into his verse, when both alike lie in the path that has led him to his ideal. To object to theory in poetry would be like objecting to words there; for words, too, are symbols without the sensuous character of the things they stand for; and yet it is only by the net of new connections which words throw over things, in recalling them, that poetry arises at all. Poetry is an attenuation, a rehandling, an echo of crude experience; it is itself a theoretic vision of things at arm's length.

Never before or since has a poet lived in so large a landscape as Dante; for our infinite times and distances are of little poetic value while we have no graphic image of what may fill them. Dante's spaces were filled; they enlarged, to the limits of human imagination, the habitations and destinies of mankind. Although the saints did not literally inhabit the spheres, but the empyrean beyond, yet each spirit could be manifested in that sphere the genius of which was most akin to his own. In Dante's vision spirits appear as points of light, from which voices also flow sometimes, as well as radiance. Further than reporting their words (which are usually about the things of earth) Dante tells us little about them. He has indeed, at the end, a vision of a celestial rose; tier upon tier of saints are seated as in an amphitheatre, and the Deity overarches them in the form of a triple rainbow, with a semblance of man in the midst. But this is avowedly a mere symbol, a somewhat conventional picture to which Dante has recourse unwillingly, for want of a better image to render his mystical intention. What may perhaps help us to divine this intention is the fact, just mentioned, that according to him the celestial spheres are not the real seat of any human soul; that the pure rise through them with increasing ease and velocity, the nearer they come to God; and that the eyes of Beatrice—the revelation of God to man—are only mirrors, shedding merely reflected beauty and light.

These hints suggest the doctrine that the goal of life is the very bosom of God; not any finite form of existence, however excellent, but a complete absorption and disappearance in the Godhead. So the Neoplatonists had thought, from whom all this heavenly landscape is borrowed; and the reservations that Christian orthodoxy requires have not always remained present to the minds of Christian mystics and poets. Dante broaches this very point in the memorable interview he has with the spirit of Piccarda, in the third canto of the *Paradiso*. She is in the lowest sphere of heaven, that of the inconstant moon, because after she had been stolen from her convent and forcibly married, she felt no prompting to renew her earlier vows. Dante asks her if she never longs for a higher station in paradise, one nearer to God, the natural goal of all aspiration. She answers that to share the will of God, who has established many different mansions in his house, is to be truly one with him. The wish to be nearer God would actually carry the soul farther away, since it would oppose the order he has established.[10]

Even in heaven, therefore, the Christian saint was to keep his essential fidelity, separation, and lowliness. He was to feel still helpless and lost in himself, like Tobias, and happy only in that the angel of the Lord was holding him by the hand. For Piccarda to say that she accepts the will of God means not that she shares it, but that she submits to it. She would fain go higher, for her moral nature demands it, as Dante—incorrigible Platonist—perfectly perceived; but she dare not mention it, for she knows that God, whose thoughts are not her thoughts, has forbidden it. The inconstant sphere of the moon does not afford her a perfect happiness; but, chastened as she is, she says it brings her happiness enough; all that a broken and a contrite heart has the courage to hope for.

Such are the conflicting inspirations beneath the lovely harmonies of the *Paradiso*. It was not the poet's soul that was in conflict here; it was only his traditions. The conflicts of his own spirit had been left behind in other regions; on that threshing-floor of earth which, from the height of heaven, he looked back upon with wonder,[11] surprised that men should take so passionately this trouble of ants, which he judges best, says Dante, who thinks least of it.

In this saying the poet is perhaps conscious of a personal fault; for Dante was far from perfect, even as a poet. He was too much a man of his own time, and often wrote with a passion not clarified into judgement. So much does the purely personal and dramatic interest dominate us as we read of a Boniface or an Ugolino that we forget that these historical figures are supposed to have been transmuted into the eternal, and to have become bits in the mosaic of Platonic essences. Dante himself almost forgets it. The modern reader, accustomed to insignificant, wayward fictions, and expecting to be entertained by images without thoughts, may not notice this lack of perspective, or may rejoice in it. But, if he is judicious, he will not rejoice in it long. The Bonifaces and the Ugolinos are not the truly deep, the truly lovely figures of the *Divine Comedy*. They are, in a relative sense, the vulgarities in it. We feel too much, in these cases, the heat of the poet's prejudice or indignation. He is not just, as he usually is; he does not stop to think, as he almost always does. He forgets that he is in the eternal world, and dips for the moment into a brawl in some Italian market-place, or into the council-chamber of some factious *condottiere*. The passages—such as those about Boniface and Ugolino—which Dante writes in this mood are powerful and vehement, but they are not beautiful. They brand the object of their invective more than they reveal it; they shock more than they move the reader.

This lower kind of success—for it is still a success in rhetoric—falls to the poet because he has abandoned the Platonic half of his inspiration and has become for the moment wholly historical, wholly Hebraic or Roman. He would have been a far inferior mind if he had always moved on this level. With the Platonic spheres and the Aristotelian ethics taken out, his *Comedy* would not have been divine. Persons and incidents, to be truly memorable, have to be rendered significant; they have to be seen in their place in the moral world; they have to be judged, and judged rightly, in their dignity and value. A casual personal sentiment towards them, however passionate, cannot take the place of the sympathetic insight that comprehends and the wide experience that judges.

Again (what is fundamental with Dante) love, as he feels and renders it, is not normal or healthy love. It was doubtless real enough, but too much restrained and expressed too much in fancy; so that when it is extended Platonically and identified so easily with the grace of God and with revealed wisdom, we feel the suspicion that if the love in question had been natural and manly, it would have offered more resistance to so mystical a transformation. The poet who wishes to pass convincingly from love to philosophy (and that seems a natural progress for a poet) should accordingly be a hearty and complete lover—a lover like Goethe and his Faust—rather than like Plato and Dante. Faust, too, passes from Gretchen to Helen, and partly back again; and Goethe made even more passages. Had any of them led to something which not only was loved, but deserved to be loved, which not only could inspire a whole life, but which ought to inspire it—then we should have had a genuine progress.

In the next place, Dante talks too much about himself. There is a sense in which this egotism is a merit, or at least a ground of interest for us moderns; for egotism is the distinctive attitude of modern philosophy and of romantic sentiment. In being egotistical Dante was ahead of his time. His philosophy would have lost an element of depth, and his poetry an element of pathos, had he not placed himself in the centre of the stage, and described everything as his experience, or as a revelation made to himself and made for the sake of his personal salvation. But Dante's egotism goes rather further than was requisite, so that the transcendental insight might not fail in his philosophy. It extended so far that he cast the shadow of his person not only over the terraces of purgatory (as he is careful to tell us repeatedly), but over the whole of Italy and of Europe, which he saw and judged under the evident influence of private passions and resentments.

Moreover, the personality thrust forward so obtrusively is not in every respect worthy of contemplation. Dante is very proud and very bitter; at the same time, he is curiously timid; and one may tire sometimes of his perpetual tremblings and tears, of his fainting fits and his intricate doubts. A man who knows he is under the special protection of God, and of three celestial ladies, and who has such a sage and magician as Virgil for a guide, might have looked even upon hell with a little more confidence. How far is this shivering and swooning philosopher from the laughing courage of Faust, who sees his poodle swell into a monster, then into a cloud, and finally change into Mephistopheles, and says at once: *Das also war des Pudels Kern!* Doubtless Dante was mediaeval, and contrition, humility, and fear of the devil were great virtues in those days; but the conclusion we must come to is precisely that the virtues of those days were not the best virtues, and that a poet who represents that time cannot be a fair nor an ultimate spokesman for humanity.

Perhaps we have now reviewed the chief objects that peopled Dante's imagination, the chief objects into the midst of which his poetry transports us; and if a poet's genius avails to transport us into his enchanted world, the character of that world will determine the quality and dignity of his poetry. Dante transports us, with unmistakable power, first into the atmosphere of a visionary love; then into the history of his conversion, affected by this love, or by the divine grace identified with it. The supreme ideal to which his conversion brought him back is expressed for him by universal nature, and is embodied among men in the double institution of a revealed religion and a providential empire. To trace the fortunes of these institutions, we are transported next into the panorama of history, in its great crises and its great men; and particularly into the panorama of Italy in the poet's time, where we survey the crimes, the virtues, and the sorrows of those prominent in furthering or thwarting the ideal of Christendom. These numerous persons are set before us with the sympathy and brevity of a dramatist; yet it is no mere carnival, no *danse macabre*: for throughout, above the confused strife of parties and passions, we hear the steady voice, the implacable sentence, of the prophet that judges them.

Thus Dante, gifted with the tenderest sense of colour, and the firmest art of design, has put his whole world into his canvas. Seen there, that world becomes complete, clear, beautiful, and tragic. It is vivid and truthful in its detail, sublime in its march and in its harmony. This is not poetry where the parts are better than the whole. Here, as in some great symphony, everything is cumulative: the movements conspire, the tension grows, the volume redoubles, the keen melody soars higher and higher; and it all ends, not with a bang, not with some casual incident, but in sustained reflection, in the sense that it has not ended, but remains by us in its totality, a revelation and a resource for ever. It has taught us to love and to renounce, to judge and to worship. What more could a poet do? Dante poetized all life and nature as he found them. His imagination dominated and focused the whole world. He thereby touched the ultimate goal to which a poet can aspire; he set the standard for all possible performance, and became the type of a supreme poet. This is not to say that he is the "greatest" of poets. The relative merit of poets is a barren thing to wrangle about. The question can always be opened anew, when a critic appears with a fresh temperament or a new criterion. Even less need we say that no greater poet can ever arise; we may be confident of the opposite. But Dante gives a successful example of the *highest species* of poetry. His poetry covers the whole field from which poetry may be fetched, and to which poetry may be applied, from the inmost recesses of the heart to the uttermost bounds of nature and of destiny. If to give imaginative value to something is the minimum task of a poet, to give imaginative value to all things, and to the system which things compose, is evidently his greatest task.

Dante fulfilled this task, of course under special conditions and limitations, personal and social; but he fulfilled it, and he thereby fulfilled the conditions of supreme poetry. Even Homer, as we are beginning to perceive nowadays, suffered from a certain conventionality and one-sidedness. There was much in the life and religion of his time that his art ignored. It was a flattering, a euphemistic art; it had a sort of pervasive blandness, like that which we now associate with a fashionable sermon. It was poetry addressed to the ruling caste in the state, to the conquerors; and it spread an intentional glamour over their past brutalities and present self-deceptions. No such partiality in Dante; he paints what he hates as frankly as what he loves, and in all things he is complete and sincere. If any similar adequacy is attained again by any poet, it will not be, presumably, by a poet of the supernatural. Henceforth, for any wide and honest imagination, the supernatural must figure as an idea in the human mind,—a part of the natural. To conceive it otherwise would be to fall short of the insight of this age, not to express or to complete it. Dante, however, for this very reason, may be expected to remain the supreme poet of the supernatural, the unrivalled exponent, after Plato, of that phase of thought and feeling in which the supernatural seems to be the key to nature and to happiness. This is the hypothesis on which, as yet, moral unity has been best attained in this world. Here, then, we have the most complete idealization and comprehension of things achieved by mankind hitherto. Dante is the type of a consummate poet.

NOTES

1. *Purgatorio*, xvii. 106–11:

> Or perchè mai non può dalla salute
>   Amor del suo suggetto volger viso,
>   Dall' odio proprio son le cose tute:
> E perchè intender non si può diviso,
>   E per sè stante, alcuno esser dal primo,
>   Da quello odiare ogni affetto è deciso.

2. *Inferno*, iii. 64–66:

> Questi sciaurati, che mai non fur vivi,
>   Erano ignudi e stimolati molto
>   Da mosconi e da vespe ch' erano ivi.

3. *Ibid.*, iv. 41, 42:

> Semo perduti, e sol di tanto offesi
>   Che senza speme vivemo in disio.

Cf. *Purgatorio*, iii. 37–45, where Virgil says:

> "State contenti, umana gente, al *quia*;
>   Chè se potuto aveste veder tutto,
>   Mestier non era partorir Maria;
> E disiar vedeste senza frutto
>   Tai, che sarebbe lor disio quetato,
>   Ch' eternalmente è dato lor per lutto.
> Io dico d' Aristotele e di Plato,
>   E di molti altri." E qui chinò la fronte;
>   E più non disse, e rimase turbato.

4. *Inferno*, ix. 106–33, and x.

5. *Ibid.*, xxviii.

6. *Inferno*, iii. 124–26:

> E pronti sono a trapassar lo rio,
>> Chè la divina giustizia gli sprona
>> Si che la tema si volge in disio.

7. *Purgatorio*, xxi. 61–69:

> Delia mondizia sol voler fa prova,
>> Che, tutta libera a mutar convento,
>> L'alma sorprende, e di voler le giova. . . .
> Ed io che son giaciuto a questa doglia
>> Cinquecento anni e più, pur mo sentii
>> Libera volontà di miglior soglia.

8. *Inferno*, xiv. 63–66:

> "O Capaneo, in ciò che non s'ammorza
>> La tua superbia, se' tu più punito:
>> Nullo martirio, fuor che la tua rabbia,
>> Sarebbe al tuo furor dolor compito."

9. Alfred de Musset, *Poésies Nouvelles, Souvenir*:

> Dante, pourquoi dis-tu qu'il n'est pire misère
>> Qu'un souvenir heureux dans les jours de douleur?
> Quel chagrin t'a dicté cette parole amère,
>>> Cette offense au malheur?
>> . . . Ce blasphème vanté ne vient pas de ton coeur.
> Un souvenir heureux est peut-être sur terre
>>> Plus vrai que le bonheur. . . .
> Et c'est à ta Françoise, à ton ange de gloire,
>> Que tu pouvais donner ces mots à prononcer,
> Elle qui s'interrompt, pour conter son histoire,
>>> D'un eternel baiser!

10. *Paradiso*, iii. 73–90:

> "Se disiassimo esser più superne,
>> Foran discordi li nostri disiri
>> Dal voler di colui che qui ne cerne, . . .
> E la sua volontate è nostra pace;
>> Ella è quel mare al qual tutto si move
>> Ciò ch' ella crea, e che natura face."
> Chiaro mi fu allor com' ogni dove
>> In cielo è Paradiso, e sì la grazia
>> Del sommo ben d' un modo non vi piove.

11. *Paradiso*, xxii. 133–39:

> Col viso ritornai per tutte e quante
> Le sette spere, e vidi questo globo
> Tal, ch' io sorrisi del suo vil sembiante;
> E quel consiglio per migliore approbo
> Che l' ha per meno; e chi ad altro pensa
> Chiamar si puote veramente probo.

FAUST
(JOHANN WOLFGANG VON GOETHE)

❧

"Goethe's *Faust*"
by B.W. Wells, in *Sewanee Review* (1894)

INTRODUCTION

In his study of Goethe's play and its antecedents, B. W. Wells explores the way the Faust legend has portrayed sin and the way Goethe's *Faust* inverts the myth of the fall, with a chorus of angels saving Faust from eternal damnation.

❧

Goethe's "Faust" is by the unanimous consent of German critics the greatest work of their literature, the most characteristic product of the German mind. And because of this very national quality it is perhaps more difficult of just appreciation than many less excellent works of less individualized art.

In any study of this drama it is necessary to bear in mind *how* and *from what* it came to be. In the early part of the sixteenth century we hear of a certain charlatan named Faust who went about Germany swindling the credulous by fortune-telling, necromancy, and wonders of healing. He must have made a deep popular impression, for after a violent death, in 1540, he became almost immediately the nucleus around which gathered a great number of diabolical tales, which

---

Wells, B.W. "Goethe's *Faust*." *Sewanee Review* Vol. 2 (August 1894): 385–412.

seemed to spring naturally from the gloomy fancy of this first century
of German Protestantism, and in 1587, these legends were collected
into a "Historia von D. Johann Faustus," written by an anonymous but
zealous and mortally serious Lutheran.

This legend, consciously or unconsciously, makes Faust the coun-
terpart, as he was the contemporary, of Luther.[1] Son of a peasant, he
achieves great distinction at the University of Wittenberg, but falling
into what the legend calls "a foolish and arrogant mind," he seeks by
magic to deepen his knowledge of nature. A devil, Mephostophiles,
becomes his servant for twenty-four years, after which Faust is to
belong to the evil one, and the treaty is signed with his blood. At first
the devil amuses Faust and his professorial famulus, Wagner, with high
living, then with sexual pleasures, then he whets his curiosity in regard
to the unseen world. This tending to rouse remorse, Faust takes to
mathematics for consolation, and after a time visits hell and the stars.
Then he makes wide travels on earth, playing various magical pranks,
in the course of which he shares in wild student revelry and conjures
up the Grecian Helen, whom he takes as concubine, and has by her a
soothsaying child. When the twenty-four years are passed, the devil
carries away Faust, who ruefully points out the moral of his folly.

The point of this moral in the original Faust legend is directed
against those humanists who were no more content with the obscu-
rantism of Luther than they had been with that of Rome. In the
reformed as in the unreformed Church a man must not seek to know
beyond what is written, and above all he must eschew Helena and
Greek ideals of life. Both the Luther of history and the Faust of the
legend lecture on ancient culture, but Faust yields to it and Helena,
while Luther marries after the christian ordinance; Luther clings
to the Bible, Faust wishes to search beyond and behind it; Luther
fights with the devil, Faust compacts with him. Both visit Rome
where Luther is shocked, but Faust is amused and cynical. In short,
this "Historia" is orthodoxy brandishing its theological birch at the
freedom of human inquiry.

This remains essentially the characteristic of all prose versions of
the Faust legend, for of these there were several in the next century.
Some, to be sure, endeavor to connect him with the idolatry they
attributed to Rome, and some introduce the episode of Helena by an
abortive attempt of Faust to seduce a servant girl, a *motif* afterward
used by Goethe. Meantime, however, the "Historia" had been translated

into English and dramatized by Christopher Marlowe (1589), with no essential change in plot or theology. After Marlowe's death (1603) a good deal of *diablerie* was added to his serious tragedy in order to tickle the ears of the groundlings. In this shape English actors brought the story back to Germany where it attained much popularity as a spectacular drama, in which the clown, representing the shrewd philistine common-sense of the middle class, plays the chief part, counterfeiting and parodying Faust and almost masking the original serious purport of the piece. But a still lower fall, and greater vulgarization, awaited the legend. It became a puppet play, a sort of "Punch and Judy Show," to amuse children, and as such it was seen by the boy Goethe.

Meanwhile, however, Lessing with critical insight had perceived the great possibilities of a subject that involved the deepest problems of man's moral existence. Dr. Faust, he wrote in 1759, "has a number of scenes in it that only a genius akin to Shakspere could have conceived." He even began, himself, a drama on the subject, though of this Goethe was probably ignorant. But what appealed to Lessing appealed equally, and perhaps more forcibly, to Goethe, for there were many things in the young man's career that might make him feel allied to the Faust whom he discerned behind the tinsel of the puppet-play. If Faust had explored all the branches of knowledge and found satisfaction in none, Goethe in his Leipzig years had been disappointed in his legal and metaphysical studies, of which latter "he thought he knew about as much as the teacher himself." Nor was he better satisfied with his critical instructors. "What I wanted," he writes, "was a standard of judgment, and that no one seemed to possess." Then in Frankfort he had had a touch of speculative theology through Frau von Klettenberg, and with it had been mixed a certain amount of pietistic alchemy and spirit-lore, which might fascinate but could not satisfy; and to all these we must add the powerful solvent of Rousseau's social philosophy. That he found in his personal student experience suggestions of Faust was not remarkable. He had a cynical friend, Behrisch, who, to judge from a letter, seems to have counselled him to play Faust's part toward a Leipzig Gretchen; but the subject was more probably brought home to him by a sympathetic study of Paracelsus, the sixteenth century physician, in whom Goethe found the connecting link between Faust and himself.

Now the moment Goethe saw Faust in himself, the necessity of giving this subject literary expression became imperative to him.

"Faust," as he would treat the subject, would contain his views of man, of destiny, of ethics, and of the spiritual world. It would be his testament to mankind. But there was a vast scope of intellectual and moral development that separated the young man who went to Strassburg in 1770, hiding his cherished scheme from the critical and captious Herder, from the venerable octogenarian who at eighty-two sealed the manuscript of the concluding part of what had been truly the work of his life, and wrote of it to Reinhard: "Await no finality. The last-solved problem of the history of the world and of mankind discloses immediately a new one to be solved." Incompleteness lay in the nature of the task, nor could we expect to find either in matter or form a unity of composition or plan. Much is unexplained, more is left without a clearly obvious purpose, and the sequence of some scenes offers insuperable chronological difficulties. As Scherer has said: "The whole plan is not carried out. Important scenes, which Goethe had proposed are wanting. Inequalities were not avoided. It is only when looked at in general and from a distance that the poem has unity, somewhat as the Homeric epics, or the 'Nibelungenlied,' or the 'Gudrun.' Just as the work of various hands in the broad popular epics produced only a partly unified whole, or hid and swelled the original whole, so here, this work of sixty years, long continued, interrupted, and subject to the most various moods, could not attain a true inner uniformity and completeness. While in the great mass of the First Part we admire the sure, bold hand of the young or mature artist, the Second offers, beside astonishingly successful portions, weaker parts also, in which the hand of the aged master seems to tremble."

Goethe was entirely conscious of this. He calls it, in writing to Schiller, his "tragelaph," or goat-stag, a fantastic creature, and again he speaks of it as a "rhapsodical drama." In 1797 he found some of the early prose scenes "quite intolerable in their naturalness," and proposed to put them into rhyme, which he did in every case but one.

[...]

The poem opens with a prelude in which a Poet, a Manager, and a Merry-Andrew, exchange their views on the conditions of the German stage and of theatrical success. We have then a Prologue in Heaven, where God and the devil are introduced with the naïveté of Hans Sachs. In this Prologue we are told, on the very highest authority, that Faust is God's servant. His service is indeed momentarily "confused," but God will bring him in due time to "clearness." Still, since man is prone to err as long as he strives, God is willing that Mephistopheles should tempt him if he will. Thus the reader or auditor is assured at the very outset that Faust will be saved. Indeed Goethe's Mephistopheles tells the attentive reader that he cares less to win Faust's soul than to prove that he is right in his materialistic and pessimistic view of life. The point of interest is therefore no longer: What will become of Faust?, but how this "clearness" is to come to him; and the action is thus raised wholly out of the sphere of Marlowe's tragedy of sin and damnation to a serener ethical plane. But the reader should not forget that this Prologue was written after Goethe himself had come to greater clearness about his intentions than when most of the First Part was composed.

The play opens with Faust in his study. He is apparently an old man though he has been professor but ten years. He has studied every profession and is profoundly discouraged at the narrow scope of the human mind. He even contemplates suicide; for magic, though it had enabled him to conjure the spirit world, had not given him power to comprehend or control it. The carols of Easter morning bring him back to a healthier frame of mind, and we next find him with his famulus, the narrowly contented scholar Wagner, who, like Hanswurst in the earlier drama, is the philistine antitype of Faust, mingling with the people on a spring holiday, but escaping at length from what he knows to be their unmerited gratitude for his medical aid in the pestilence.

As they walk together and Faust speaks of his longings, they are met by a black dog whom Faust takes to his study, where after some hocus-pocus the dog reveals himself as the diabolical spirit Mephistopheles, for the moment dressed as a wandering scholar, who announces himself as "a part of that force which always wills the ill and always works the good," or again as "the spirit that denies," whose "element is what you call sin, destruction, evil," and that, because "all that exists is worthy of perishing." In so far, then, Mephistopheles is a sort of Nihilist. His attendant spirits lull Faust to sleep in exquisite dimeters and on his awaking he has become disposed to sign a compact by which, if the spirit can satisfy him, he may have him. "When on an idler's bed I stretch myself in quiet, There let at once my record end. Canst thou with lying flattery rule me, Until self-pleased myself I see,—Canst thou with rich enjoyment fool me, Let that day be the last for me."[2] But this, as appears from the Prologue, means nothing more than that he will then be driven to admit that Mephistopheles' pessimism is justified. Faust signs the compact with his blood, and after Mephistopheles has given cynical advice to a young scholar on his choice of a profession, he begins his task by introducing his master to an orgy of student debauchery in Auerbach's wine cellar in Leipzig.

The scene that follows is vivid and, alas, not untrue to student nature, though the reader will sympathize with Faust in the disgust it aroused in him. He was not to be satisfied with such chaff. It lay in the natural sequence of things that the obsequious devil should now shift from gluttony to lust. But at this point Goethe found a personal experience to embody, and thus there was developed a drama within a drama that so outgrew its subordinate place as to seem to many the central point of the entire work, as it is of the First Part. It is the Gretchen episode that for a time absorbs the poet's entire interest.

It was essential for the drama that Faust should not wholly reject these untried attractions of sensual love. But in yielding he must carry our sympathy with him, since the Prologue has told us, what indeed must from the first have been clear, in the very nature of the case and from the character of the author, that Faust is to be brought by his trials to "clearness" and not to moral ruin. This Goethe sought to accomplish by the "Witches' Kitchen," where a rejuvenating potion is given to Faust, which, as Mephistopheles tells the spectators aside, is a love potion also. Helena, the ideal of womanly beauty, is shown him in a glass and "with this drink in his veins, he shall soon see Helena in every woman." But, after all, this attempt to enlist our sympathy for Faust the seducer, with his rather childish "I must," was not, perhaps could hardly be, successful, and it was probably the consciousness of this that made Goethe speak so slightingly of the work at this stage in letters to Schiller. As for the Apes' mysterious talk in this scene of the "Witches' Kitchen," Goethe afterward spoke of it as "dramatic-humoristic nonsense," and barring the "humorous," we may take his word for it. It is wholly impertinent to the main action of the play.

With scene vii. and Gretchen we pass into a quite different atmosphere. Mephistopheles does little more than a cynical friend might do. The action is now no longer guided by the old play or puppet-show but by Goethe's recollections of Leipzig and Sesenheim. It is the theme treated already in "Götz," in "Clavigo," in "Egmont," the love of a girl of lower culture and station for a man socially and intellectually her superior, though morally, if not inferior, at least more complex.

The whole episode, in its delineation of character, and in its tragic development, is a masterpiece hardly equalled, save by Shakspere, in the range of literature. It is thoroughly popular, universally comprehensible, and thus it fixed itself immediately in the public mind as *the* Faust drama, while the higher unity of the whole was perceived only by the thoughtful few.

The episode, for such it is essentially, though artistically complete in itself, opens with the meeting of Faust and Gretchen as she leaves the church. With the boldness of a gallant adventurer he offers her his escort, which she refuses as a girl of the middle class might do, resolutely, but without indignation, and in a language that marks at the very outset her lack of culture. Here and throughout she is a girl of the people. She has the faults common to her class in Germany and elsewhere; she is inclined to sentimentality, fond of dress and ornament, but yet she is industrious, neat, and with the motherly instinct natural in a simple child of nature. Faust, thanks we must suppose rather to the witch's potion than to any peculiar elective affinity between his nature and hers, is fascinated by her and demands Mephistopheles' aid to win her. But his diabolical arts would fail here. "I have no power over souls so green," he says contemptuously, while the facile Faust thinks: "had he but seven hours he could win her by his own persuasion," and would have no need of the devil. Mephistopheles is pledged to help him but, save for certain buried treasures which he unearths, he resorts only to ordinary means of seduction. We have left for the moment mediaeval witchcraft for modern naturalism.

The next scene (viii.) takes us to Gretchen's "small but neatly kept chamber," where, as she braids her hair, she muses, a little flattered by the attentions of a gallant, who "would not have been so bold if he had not been of noble family." Presently she goes out, and Mephistopheles nurses Faust's passion by bringing him to this sanctuary of maidenhood where each feels and speaks according to his nature, Faust as a lover, Mephistopheles as a cynical sensualist. They leave a casket of jewelry in her clothes-press. Gretchen returns and with the instinct of innocence notes the sultry air, and feels a dim foreboding. She finds the casket and, without much questioning whence it came, she is carried away by the contents. She decks herself with the ornaments and talks the while with a childlike pathos of the disadvantages of a poor girl in this worldly world. "To gold still tends, On gold depends, All, all! Alas! we poor."

The ground being thus prepared, the willing go-between is found in the shape of neighbor Martha, whose prudent flirtation with the cautious Mephistopheles forms a powerful foil in the ardent passion of Faust and the budding love of Gretchen. Tender feelings that might purify Faust's love are for the moment shipwrecked on the cynical promptings of his ally (xi.). In Martha's garden they meet, and Faust wins the promise of her love in two exquisite scenes (xii., xiii.), skillfully set off by the recurring bits of dialogue between Martha and Mephistopheles, as each couple in turn is brought before the audience.

There follows a scene (xiv.) which in its present place involves a contradiction, when viewed in the light of the last scene of the Second Part. Originally it had been placed much later and after Gretchen had long given all she had to give. In his youth and up to the period of his union with Schiller, Goethe was willing to let Faust's relation to Gretchen continue until broken by an unwelcome interruption. In old age, he found symbolical use for Gretchen and wished to make her appear as one: "Who had forgot herself but once, Who dreamed not that she erred." It then became necessary to cancel this scene or change its place, which leaves it, as is usual in such revisions, out of place. This scene is entitled "Forest and Cavern," and shows Faust in a gloomy mood. He has torn himself away from Gretchen, as the boy Goethe is said to have done from his first unhappy passion, and sought refuge in the bosom of nature. Now such moods are not apt to intervene between the promise and the fulfillment of love, and Mephistopheles in painting the longing of the deserted Gretchen has an easy victory, hardly requiring the consummate skill with which he presents his temptation. In its original place and with the original assumption of a prolonged relation, the scene would have had a far deeper note of moral tragedy.

After an exquisite song in which Gretchen expresses her love-longing (xv.) there follows a second scene in Martha's garden where Gretchen naïvely questions Faust of his religious faith and gets an answer which is the poetry of pantheism, and wholly outside the sphere of her intellect. It is interesting to see how clearly in a few speeches Goethe has placed the religious instinct in contrast to speculative theology, neither comprehending the other, the lower yielding to the higher, but not without moral loss. Gretchen instinctively shrinks from Mephistopheles, but for Faust she will give her mother a sleeping potion, a poison with which Mephistopheles has provided him, that they may love undisturbed; for in him whom she loves the simple Gretchen can conceive no harm.

No long interval can intervene between the first and second "Garden" scenes (xii., xvi.), for the "Forest and Cavern" (xiv.) was apparently intended to represent no more than such an excursion as the boy Goethe was wont to make with his tutor in Frankfort, as he has told us in "Wahrheit und Dichtung." The first interview (xii.) had been in the time of the flowering daisies, perhaps in April, for it must have been after Easter and before May 1st, the Walpurgis-Night that is to follow.[3] But in the scene that follows the second meeting, "At the Fountain," (xvii.), Gretchen has already fallen. Her prayer in the "Donjon" scene (xviii.) shows that she is conscious of approaching motherhood and is already abandoned, and when her brother Valentin is introduced and killed by Faust in scene xix. her condition has become common talk; yet this, as we learn from that very scene, was on the 29th of April.

Then, too, it will be noted that in no one of these scenes is the death of Gretchen's mother from the potion mentioned or assumed, or indeed reconcilable with what is said, though if, as is stated in the Second Part, Gretchen erred but once, this death must have already taken place and it is, in fact, mentioned in the "Cathedral Scene" (xx.) that follows. All this has come, like the previous trouble with "Forest and Cavern" (xiv.) from the changed conception of Faust's connection with Gretchen, at first conceived as a lasting liaison in which the mother's death is to be caused by the growing recklessness of Gretchen's absorbing passion, but afterward as a momentary aberration, as of a magnetic needle that turned immediately back to its celestial pole.

The scenes "At the Fountain" and "Donjon" (xvii., xviii.) show first how sin in Gretchen's gentle nature fills the heart with tender and pathetic sympathy for fellow-sinners, then the penitent turns in impassioned prayer to the sorrow-laden Virgin-Mother, her soul recovering its purity and gaining infinite depth by its acquaintance with sorrow and pain. This scene, even though originally intended to allude to Gretchen's repentance for her mother's death and afterward changed in its intention, might surely imply that Gretchen was abandoned. She speaks in the preceding scene (xvii.) of Faust in the past tense, and indeed it is difficult to conceive that such feelings as she utters there could coexist with their former relation. But yet in "Night" (xix.), the scene that follows these, Faust is disturbed at the thought of going to see his mistress (*Buhle*) without a gift, and Gretchen must surely be meant.

It was important to Mephistopheles' purpose, however, that Faust should not be present at the crisis that was now approaching in Gretchen's fate. Hence Valentin, her brother, was introduced, first that by publicly proclaiming her fault he might plunge her deeper into purifying shame; second that by killing him and so depriving her of the only relative to whom she could look for help, Faust might intensify his guilt and the final catastrophe be justified; and, lastly, that in order to escape from the consequences of this murder, Faust might be compelled to leave the city and therefore to abandon Gretchen. "Night," then, belongs to an earlier plan than the two preceding scenes. And the conceptions were never satisfactorily reconciled. If Faust had already abandoned Gretchen, as those scenes presuppose, the Valentin episode would be unnecessary, and the "Cathedral Scene" which succeeds might appropriately follow Gretchen's prayer (xviii.). But the character of Valentin has a vigor and clearness of conception that gives enduring life.

The "Cathedral Scene" (xx.) with its funeral sequence, *Dies Irae*, was originally headed "Obsequies of Gretchen's Mother." As the verses of the Judgment Hymn resound in the penitent's ear, an evil spirit whispers to Gretchen thoughts of despair, and she falls fainting in the passion of her purgation, at the thought that "the glorified turn their faces from her." This scene in its present position must fall in the Autumn, though, if Gretchen "erred but once" and this single error was the occasion of her mother's death, it must have taken place in April, and such is the assumption of the scene that immediately follows.

For the tension of the tragedy, which has here become intense, is now broken by the witches' carnival on Walpurgis Night (May 1st). One may justify the introduction of such a scene on ironical grounds, as Heine does in the case of Shakspere's clowns, but the scene is too long for this purpose, and wholly foreign matter dealing with the personal and literary controversies of the time has been wantonly intruded in "Oberon's Wedding." Nothing connects the traditional Faust with the Walpurgis Carnival, though he was brought by the legend to the Brocken, the peak of the Harz on which it took place. But this is purely indifferent. We are here transferred from the modern realism of the Gretchen episode to the mediaeval atmosphere of the early scenes, and the Faust who meets us here, singing with will-o'-the-wisps, dancing with witches, enjoying the wild rout and Rabelaisian wit, is not the Faust who loved Gretchen nor he who killed Valentin. This, too, like the "Witches' Kitchen" was "dramatic-humorous nonsense," we have Goethe's word for it, and here the humor is not lacking, if one does not insist too anxiously on sense. Goethe wrote it in 1800, and as late as 1830 he still rejoiced in it. "Really," he said to Falk, "one ought to play the joke oftener in one's youth and give 'em such bits (*Brocken*) as the Brocken."

An interruption in the course of the drama was justified, for fate was hurrying it to a close. We are brought back to the tragic mood by the scene named "Dreary Day." Some interval has elapsed, Faust has not seen Gretchen again, and is now far away when startled by the news, which comes to him we know not whence,[4] that Gretchen has been a wretched outcast and is now an accused prisoner, or rather, as appears later, convicted of infanticide and destined to execution. This is one of those prose scenes that Goethe in 1798 had found "intolerable in comparison with the rest" and had not succeeded in versifying. It is strong, but the extravagance of the language smacks of "Storm and Stress." Faust insists on being taken to her cell that they may attempt her rescue, and on magic horses they urge their nightly flight, while beneath a gallows, witches soar and sweep, bow and bend, scatter, devote and doom.

And so we are brought to the climax of Gretchen's prison cell. Her mind is shaken by grief and the misery of her lot. Her tragic madness suggests Ophelia's and perhaps surpasses its model. Faust finds her lying on the straw, singing words of an old song, which she turns to apply to her dead child. She takes her lover for her jailer and pleads pathetically with him. Now she asks for her child, now imagines hell beneath her prison. At last she recognizes Faust and half-incoherently recalls the course of their love. She clings to him with tenderest passion, but she will not fly, "it is so wretched to beg, and with a bad conscience beside." Suddenly she remembers that the child is drowned and cries to Faust to haste to save it for it still quivers, or she tells him how she will be buried with her mother and brother, a little aside, the baby on her right breast, alone, for she can no longer feel a perfect sympathy even with her lover.

"It seems as though you repelled me," she cries, "and yet 't is you, and you look so kind and good." This is noteworthy. She cannot unite herself with Faust again because she has gone through a stage of spiritual development that separates her from him. When at the close of the Second Part, Gretchen is bidden to rise to higher regions that if Faust dimly comprehend her, he may follow, the clue is given to the reason why she has this feeling here. And thus every tragic element is combined to deepen Faust's agony. At last Mephistopheles warns him that day is dawning. Gretchen shrinks in terror from that unspiritual spirit, and when Faust, a last time, urges her to fly, she commits herself rather to the judgment of God, her last breath a prayer, and the last quiver of life a shudder for her lover. "She is judged," says Mephistopheles. But Faust is not to be left in this error. A voice from above proclaims: "Is saved," and, as her appealing voice, calling him, dies away, Mephistopheles, snatching Faust to his side, vanishes.

So closes the First Part and with it the microcosmic portion of Faust's experience, which has come to take a larger place than its function in the general plan would make artistically justifiable. But rules of proportion, and indeed of formal criticism in general, cannot be applied to Faust as a whole. What has given the First Part its preeminent place in German literature, at least in the popular consciousness, is in part the gnomic wisdom of Mephistopheles, which takes up and embodies a view of the world and of life which all recognize and too many share; but, more even than that, it is the unique portrayal of guilty innocence and betrayed simplicity in the drama of Gretchen's fall and purgation through suffering.

The Second Part of "Faust," in bringing us to the greater world and its wider activities, follows more closely in its outline the old legend. Magic resumes its sway and the whole becomes more spectacular and operatic. A thread of esoteric meaning, or rather, perhaps, many threads, can be traced through all, now plainly in sight, now masked almost completely from view; sometimes because they deal with a state of feeling and political conditions that are no longer present to our minds, sometimes because various allegorical interpretations run for a time side by side and at last become inextricably involved, sometimes too because, as occasionally in the First Part, the poet with wanton irony mystifies his readers.

[...]

No analysis of the Second Part of "Faust" can bring out its manifold beauties, but it is necessary to recall the sequence or rather succession of scenes to justify any judgment of the drama as a work of art, in which all the parts, to be fitly joined together, must be in due proportion to each other and to the whole.

The close of the tragedy of Gretchen should have left Faust crushed with guilty despair. The Second Part finds him "bedded on flowery turf, tired, restless, seeking sleep," while graceful little spirits, accompanied by Aeolian harps, sing soothing strains. The purpose of their song is "to calm the fierce struggle of the heart, to remove the bitter glowing arrows of reproach and purify his breast from the horror it has experienced." They will "bathe him in dew from Lethe's flood and give him back to holy light." Thus Faust is prepared to enter on the new experiences of the Second Part, and at the same time it is made very clear that, to Goethe, action, not penitential brooding, is to be the means by which Faust is to overgrow the wounds of his soul's fault and be brought to "clearness." And so we are already prepared to find that in submitting Gretchen to Faust, Mephistopheles has realized his own saying, he has "willed the ill and wrought the good." Faust is stronger, wiser, deeper, for having known Gretchen, but she is to him as the *roses d'antan*, and he looks forward, not back, until at the very close, the circle of his life is joined and the beginning meets the end. Such seems to be the ethical import of the introductory scene, darkened a little toward the close by interwoven allusions to Goethe's theory of colors. A considerable part of this prelude, as indeed of the whole Second Part, is operatic in character.

The spectator is now transported to the palace of an Emperor, who is here represented as a frivolous and incompetent ruler, perhaps that he may the more require the aid of Faust's magic arts, and the more freely grant him scope for future activity. But it is hard to win much interest for services that cost only the wave of a magician's wand and serve only to atone for the results of incompetence. Hence the scenes at the imperial court, here and in the Fourth Act, are aesthetically the least pleasing.

We learn first that extravagance has brought want in all quarters of the empire. Then Mephistopheles, who has introduced himself as court-fool, offers to relieve the embarrassment by means of countless buried treasures, the property of the crown. But from the question how he is to recover them the emperor turns gladly to a carnival which in the main is also of Mephistopheles' preparation. Commentators say that the buried treasure is undiscovered knowledge, but it is difficult to carry the allegory through in this sense.

[...]

Pleased with his imaginary riches, the emperor wishes to be amused. He demands that Helena and Paris, types of ideal man and womanhood, be conjured up before him. That is, wealth, material and intellectual, arouses the desire for culture, of which Greek culture is the universal type and model. But over this classic realm of the beautiful Mephistopheles, the demon of an ascetic and supernatural religion, has no power. He turns to Faust and bids him descend to the Mothers who dwell in the nether world, the incomprehensible creators of the ideal. Yet Mephistopheles, though he cannot seek the ideal himself, can give Faust a key to guide him; and this key grows in his hand, burns bright, and gives new strength and courage, though when Faust vanishes with it Mephistopheles utters a sneering doubt whether he will ever return from his quest. The Key seems to be enthusiasm, by which alone the ideal is revealed, but which may become destructive unless he who holds it in his hand stand firm on reality.

A scene of strong satire on the petty German courts now intervenes to give space for Faust's search, but he returns at length with power to summon the Trojan Paris, on whom the courtiers comment each after his kind. Helena then appears. She does not attract Mephistopheles, for Greek beauty is not, like this demon of Northern fancy, the sensuous negation of mediaeval asceticism, but is outside of it and incomprehensible to it. Nor can the courtiers comprehend her charm. But Faust's past life has attuned his mind to thrill responsive to this new vision of beauty. With overwhelmed longing he endeavors to grasp it, crying: "Whoe'er has seen her, cannot bear her loss." But the Greek spirit is still too foreign for his Teutonic mind. She vanishes, and he lies fainting, to be borne away by Mephistopheles. The close of this first act, the "Key," the "Mothers," and "Helena," is all that is essential to the ethical thesis of "Faust."

The Second Act opens in Faust's study, where he still lies in a swoon while the conversation of Mephistopheles with a famulus, with Wagner, now a famous professor and physicist, and with a skeptical bachelor, once the student whom Mephistopheles had counselled, brings before us the conceptions of metaphysics, aesthetics, and ideal culture that might be contending in Faust's mind; all not without pointed satire at the conceited self-assurance of Young Germany and the metaphysicians of 1820.

Wagner has made chemically an Homunculus, but since he cannot give his little man a body, he must stay sealed in the flask where he was created. This Homunculus is clearly the artificial conception of the ideal that comes not from the experience of life but from study. It, too, as well as Faust, has Greek aspirations and therefore it seeks to draw its parent to classic ground. Suddenly it escapes from Wagner's hand, hovers over the head of Faust and reveals the course of the sleeper's mind as his soul gradually accustoms itself to the Greek view of life and happiness, the view, it may be added, of Goethe's "Roman Elegies." But the Homunculus is a student's creation, and the classical life that he seeks is found in the shadowy visions of Pharsalia's Walpurgis-Night, whither he counsels that Faust be taken. Of this classic carnival Mephistopheles has heard nothing. "How should you?" says Homunculus. "You know romantic ghosts alone. A genuine ghost, that must be classic, too." Though Mephistopheles dreads the Greeks who "entice man's breast to bright sins, so that ours seem gloomy beside them," yet the temptation of Thessalian witches overcomes his repulsion, and they all follow the Homunculus, dependent, as Mephistopheles pregnantly observes, "on creatures we ourselves have made."

The Classical Walpurgis-Night has little direct connection with the course of Faust's development. Seeking everywhere Helena, he is borne, as one insane, to Mantho for his cure, but she "loves the man who seeks the unattainable," and directs him to Persephoneia's realm. Of this journey, however, we hear no more, nor is it made clear by what means Helena is brought to the upper world. But, aside from this, the scene serves a useful purpose in bringing the reader or spectator to a classical frame of mind by the introduction of the various ideals of antiquity that are here brought before him. Mephistopheles, counselled by the Sphinx and teased by the Lamiae, feels first at home with the personified ugliness of the Phorkyades, while Homunculus, in his zeal to obtain incorporation, loses himself among the philosophers, to be dashed to pieces at last against Galatea's throne, who is herself that realized ideal of which he was the scholar's reflection. To follow out these allegorical threads in all their twisted windings would perhaps go beyond the poet's intention, for he has clearly laid them aside himself to weave into this scene an allegorized debate between Anaxagoras and Thales, the former representing those who held the volcanic origin of the earth and opposed the investigations of the "Neptunists," among whom Goethe, who speaks here under Thales' mask, reckoned himself a leader. And so important does this second allegory become in the mind of the poet that he allows the Classical Walpurgis-Night to close with an operatic scene on the Aegean Sea, where sirens, nereids, and tritons, with Nereus, Proteus, and Thales, sing the praises of the sea and the triumph of the sea-born Galatea, while we are left uncertain how or why Helena is brought to the upper world.

For the opening of the Third Act finds her with a chorus of captured Trojan women before Menelaus' palace in Sparta, anxiously veiling from her own eyes the memory of all that has intervened since Paris carried her away, as though, perhaps, this were a condition of her return from the under world. She thinks herself just landed, sent before by Menelaus to prepare a sacrifice. With her is Mephistopheles, disguised as Phorkyas, type of ugliness, a servile contrast to Helena's queenly beauty and bearing. Through Phorkyas she learns that she is the destined victim of Menelaus' jealous rage. This signifies that the political jealousy of Greece destroyed its culture and its art. Though willing to die calmly, Helena does not disdain the proferred protection of a settlement of Northmen in the hills just north of Sparta, "made some twenty years ago," a hint that tells us exactly what is meant, for if we count back twenty years from 1808, when this scene was completed, we have the date of Goethe's return to Germany from Rome (1788) with all the wonderful results of that journey for him and for the culture of his country. Faust, the leader of this bold and venturous band, is praised by Phorkyas as of a gentler nature than the Greeks, which seems an allusion to the christian element in modern civilization, and his fortress-palace is made to typify Gothic art. To bring Helena to Faust's palace is to bring Greek ideals to Germany, while, of course, here as before, in the details there is much that may be explained in this way, or in that, or more wisely, sometimes, in no way at all.

For such a man as Goethe, to know Greek art was to make it a part, an inseparable part, of his artistic being; and Greek art found in him a protector who yet preserved his German nature. And so in the drama Faust and Helena need for their union no long wooing though in the brief play of its delicate fancies, Faust teaches her the unwonted German rhyme, into which the chorus falls a little later, after Faust has taken his bride to the peaceful retreat of Arcadia. Here a child is born to them, Euphorion, whom Goethe told Eckermann (December

20, 1829) was the personification of Poetry, who had appeared, also, as has been said, in another form in the First Act. But there is something in the manner of Goethe's announcement that suggests mystification, and it is very clear that at the close of his brief career, Euphorion is but a thin mask for Lord Byron.

All of what is said by and of Euphorion seems consistent with no interpretation that has yet been suggested by the commentators, but still the essential elements of the episode embody a profound aesthetic truth. Euphorion is introduced as a naked genius without wings, faun-like but not animal, springing higher and higher from the ground, while his mother cautions him that he may leap but not fly, and, like Antaeus, will gain strength by touching earth. The German Faust at first is less disturbed, than his Grecian spouse at these soaring leaps, but Euphorion's flight is ever wilder, more unrestrained, until at last he falls like Icarus, dead at his parents' feet, and disappears in light, leaving behind his mantle and lyre and calling on his mother to follow. The fire and throbbing energy of this scene are indescribable, and the threnody to Lord Byron with which the chorus bewails Euphorion's death is a sympathetic and discriminating tribute of exquisite beauty. Helena follows the summons of her son, and having embraced Faust, she vanishes, leaving her garment and veil in his arms. They dissolve into clouds, lift Faust, and bear him away.

Here the essential allegory seems to be that a perfect and fruitful union between modern and classic life is impossible. It produces an idealism that destroys itself because it is not in touch with the actualities of our life. Therefore Euphorion perishes and therefore Helena must return to the shades. But she leaves behind her all that we can take up into our modern life of the classic ideals, the Garment, that is "love of beauty," especially in artistic form. Hence Phorkyas, falling a moment from Mephistopheles' role, bids Faust:

Hold fast to what remains to thee of all.
The garment! Leave it not; for demons pluck
Already at its skirts, and to the underworld
Would drag it gladly. Cling the faster to it.
. . . .
Above all commonplace it lifts thee up
Upon the air, long as thou canst endure.

It is, then, through the Greek view of life that Faust is to gain the foundation for his future experience, and this foundation is to be a practical idealism. The influence of Helena on Faust is that he no longer gazes in the stars while his feet are in the mire. He will from this time look more about him than above him. He will still strive, but his activity will be in this world and for his fellow men.[5] It is not, then, merely aesthetic teaching that Helena has for Faust, but a profoundly ethical one, and one of sufficient importance to the drama to make the subordinate and introductory position of the First and Second Acts artistically justifiable. The Fourth Act, so far as it concerns the main theme, exists only to make the Fifth possible, and this in turn is only putting into action the ethics of the "Helena," which is thus the cardinal point of the whole. How this fact accounts for the long comparative neglect and present growing appreciation for the Second Part will appear presently.

The Fourth Act shows us Faust on a mountain, full of life and energy which draw their inspiration from classical memories. His ambition is now useful labor. He wishes to redeem broad tracts of land for settlement from the destroying ocean. That he may gain imperial aid and sanction in this project, Mephistopheles proposes that he should assist the emperor, now engaged in hopeless war with rebellious vassals. All this has no other dramaturgical purpose than to introduce the activities of the Fifth Act. It serves, however, as the vehicle of much political satire, of which the general tendency is that government should be left to those who make it their business to govern.[6] This act was the last written and shows clear traces of old age. It is incomplete also. The scene in which Faust receives the reward of his magical aid, in a cause for which, again, it is hard to feel much sympathy, was not written when Goethe sealed the manuscript in August, 1831.

The Fifth Act shows Faust's ambition in good part realized. He is now a century old.[7] He has compelled the evil spirits to his service, and trade and agriculture flourish in spite of their perversity. He is impatient of opposition, however, and has still to learn moderation in prosecuting a good cause. This lesson is taught him by Mephistopheles' officious murder of Baucis and Philemon, whose small possession was a thorn to his unsatiated desire. Once more that cynical spirit has "willed the ill and wrought the good." And now the end draws on. Want, Guilt, Need, and Care, approach his palace. Care alone can enter, and under her breath Faust grows blind, but she cannot touch him, although he refuses from henceforth magic aid. The four depart, but Death appears. Faust sees him not, but in his blindness he urges on his unselfish task, to provide dwellings which will prove for men a doubly precious possession, because they must be maintained by constant effort against the encroaching sea. He thinks he hears the busy spades of his laborers, but they are the Lemures who dig his grave. With the vision of his accomplished purpose before his sinking eyes, he enjoys even now, in anticipation, that highest moment in which he could say to the present: "Ah! linger still, thou art fair." And so he dies and is laid in the grave.

There follows a fantastic scene in which Mephistopheles and his attendant spirits endeavor to prevent the escape of the soul from Faust's body. This cynical degradation of the ideal is interrupted by a heavenly choir and a glory shining from above. For a time these strains of mystic beauty alternate with Mephistopheles' sensuous animalism. But the roses of penitence that the angels strew, burn and scatter the demons, and, in a moment when Mephistopheles is distracted by the sensuous charms of certain angel boys, Faust's soul escapes him. This scene is essentially operatic, and that which concludes the drama can hardly be conceived without a musical accompaniment. A chorus of blessed children and various typical figures of the mediaeval church, the Ecstatic, the Profound, the Seraphic Father, here conceived as anchorites, sing celestial hymns. Then the "younger," and the "more perfect" angels take up the strain; and from the highest, purest, of the hermit cells, the "Marian Doctor" hails the advent of Mary, the Merciful, surrounded by Her penitents.

By turns and together, the Woman who washed the Lord's feet with ointment, the Woman of Samaria and the Egyptian Mary beg the Blessed Virgin's pardon for "this good soul, that forgot itself but once, and thought not that it erred." And now first since the close of her tragic life, Gretchen appears and, in a stanza that suggests her impassioned prayer to the Blessed Virgin in the First Part (xviii.), she begs that Mary will bend her countenance graciously on her joy since "the early love brought to 'clearness' at last, returns again." "Grant me to teach him. The new day blinds him still." But Mary answers: "Rise to higher spheres. If he dimly apprehend you, he will follow." And the mystic chorus concludes with those well known words: "The eternal-womanly draws us upward and on."

In this gnomic saying we ought to find, if Goethe is serious with us, the key to all. What, then, is "eternally womanly," and who are meant by "us," human beings, or men as distinct from women? Was it this "eternally womanly" that drew Gretchen upward, or was it not rather the eternal manly? This, at least, will afford us a clear interpretation to that last word of the mystical drama. If by "us" we understand "men," then the "eternal" essential element in women that draws "us" is "love," but this love is, in its essence, unselfish, altruistic, fruitful, and hence the teaching of the drama is here proclaimed to be that we rise, or are raised, by altruistic effort.[8]

As Scherer has observed,[9] Faust "chooses not wealth but work," and in that work finds his "salvation." To this choice he is brought, mediately by Gretchen, immediately by Helena, for beauty is positive, creative, and so here, as in life contrasted with the ugly, the evil, the negative, as it appears in Mephistopheles-Phorkyas. It is Helena that reveals to Faust the worth of life, of this life, and so frees him from the spirit that denies. Both pass from a sensitive, groping, contemplative, searching, aesthetic existence, under the spur of negative spirits and ideal models, to active, useful labor. In both Goethe puts unselfish activity above the claims of aesthetics or learning. He does not let his poet and actor, nor yet his groping student, find satisfaction. He calls to them: "You must act, work." The greatest representative of German poetry, a many-sided and successful investigator, bows before practical life. He does not look longingly over into strange regions, conscious of his own weakness. No! He knows the practical world, has been of it, has worked successfully in it, and yet has left it. He recommends in his poem what he neglected in his life. Thus "Faust" expressed in a time that was poor in noble deeds the longing for heroic action. It echoed the protest of the statesman vom Stein against the excess of metaphysical speculation that had thinned the life-blood of Germany.

But already the tide had turned. The change that Goethe demanded, he lived to see in a fair way to be accomplished, and we have lived to see the real exalted above the ideal, action above thought, perhaps in undue measure. Hence the general popular comprehension of "Faust" as a whole in this period more than ever before, because more than ever before it reflects the popular mind to which as to Faust the "logos" is neither "word," nor "thought," nor "power" but "action."[10] The dangers of such a philosophy of life are obvious, some of them are already realized in the luxury of our hedonists and the socialism and nihilism of our proletariat, but "Faust," if rightly apprehended, offers two poisons, each an antidote of the other, which joined together help and strengthen. Neither Euphorion's idealism that will not touch earth, nor Mephistopheles' realism that will not rise above it, but that just mean, that idealizes the real and realizes the ideal, that is the world-wisdom of "Faust."

NOTES

1. Ch. Scherer, Faust-Buch, xxi.
2. The metrical citations of the First Part are from Taylor's translation.
3. This cannot be the Walpurgis-Night of the next year because Valentin is killed two days before the Walpurgis and also before Gretchen's child is born, but, as will appear, a satisfactory chronology has become hopeless. How this came about is clearly stated by Thomas, I. c. 324.
4. It had been proposed to reveal it to him on the Brocken, but the intention was not realized.
5. Let him to whom this seems strange read what Goethe says to Eckermann on thoughts of immortality, Feb. 25, 1824.
6. Compare Eckermann, March, 1832, toward the end of the second volume, where among much else in the same spirit, Goethe says: "I hate bungling like sin, especially bungling in politics, from which nothing but evil for thousands and millions can come."
7. See Eckermann, June 6, 1831.
8. If love is selfish, the result, as Bleihtreu cynically says, is:
    "Das Ewig-weibliche zieht uns herab
    Und wird des mannlichen Stolzes Grab."
9. This paragraph is based throughout on, and in part translated from Scherer, *Litteraturgeschichte*, 719, seq., for I have not found it possible to state what I wished without seeming to borrow from him.
10. Part I, Sc. 3. Not *Wort*, nor *Sinn*, nor *Kraft*, but *That*.

THE NOVELS OF F. SCOTT FITZGERALD

✦

"Gods and Fathers in F. Scott Fitzgerald's Novels"
by James Gindin, in
Modern Language Quarterly (1969)

INTRODUCTION

In his study of F. Scott Fitzgerald's novels, James Gindin focuses on Fitzgerald's doomed romantic heroes and his conception of original sin. Arguing that Fitzgerald became more sympathetic in his late novels and less moralizing, Gindin shows how "his concern for his characters increased, as did his sympathy for their human struggles and relationships, for all the questions they could never answer. Correspondingly, the element of morality or judgment diminished, and God or truth disappeared; the romantic hero, although still doomed, seemed doomed less by a moral order or original sin than by accident."

✦

Fitzgerald's fiction always, in one form or another, reveals a strong element of moral judgment against which the heroes can be seen. The Fitzgerald hero is charming, intelligent, impressed by the glitter of a sparkling new world, and sensitive, a special person in the sense that the romantic hero is always someone particularly sensitive, intelligent,

Gindin, James. "Gods and Fathers in F. Scott Fitzgerald's Novels." *Modern Language Quarterly* (March 1969): 64–85.

and vulnerable. But against the romantic hero Fitzgerald places a moral judgment, a stern rebuke, functioning either within the character or from the outside, which inevitably limits the freedom and possibility of the romantic hero. The romantic hero would be God, would dominate through his own individual capacity, but the moral judgment demonstrates that no man, no matter how special in secular terms, can play God. The hero is also, simultaneously, the archetypal contemporary American, the confident and eager representative of his country trying his talents against an older and more universal moral order.

In Fitzgerald's earliest novel, *This Side of Paradise* (1920), the moral framework is not fully developed, and the romantic hero's sin never reaches proportions sufficient to earn inevitable damnation. The next novel, *The Beautiful and Damned* (1922), however, articulates the doom of the special creature, and in *The Great Gatsby* (1925), Fitzgerald echoes the paradox implicit in the doctrine of original sin, the concept of man inevitably trapped by the difference between what he would desperately like to be and what he is. In subsequent novels, *Tender Is the Night* (1934) and the unfinished *The Last Tycoon* (1941), the romantic hero is also doomed, but the moral framework, the judgment that makes the usurping hero's damnation inevitable, is more equivocal, more questionable, less confidently a statement about man's destiny. God weakens in Fitzgerald's last two novels, and although the hero, the man who would be God, never achieves his vision of experience, the forces that prevent him are more accidental and capricious, less articulately a moral order. The hero sometimes seems doomed by the lingering residue of firm moral commitment.

Most of *This Side of Paradise* depicts the trivial glitter of Amory Blaine's social conquests and the student-like notebook of his philosophical and literary observations. Yet Amory Blaine is one of Fitzgerald's special creatures, established less by anything he does than by the quality of his introspection and by the assurances the author gives of Amory's special talents and sensitivity. Like many romantic heroes, Fitzgerald's heroes are distinguished within themselves and, until the later novels, need not do anything to prove their special capacity. Although Amory spends most of his time at parties and in random intellectual speculation, he is conscious of the morality of his thought and actions. At times, he is fiercely puritanical, disdaining the juvenile country-club vamps at the very moment he is attracted to them. As he goes through Princeton and the army in World War I, he continues to lament the moral vacuum of his wild weekends and to question the unapologetic materialism of the society he sees around him. Amory is also a patriot, looking for an American literature, an American destiny, a unique and valuable national synthesis of experience.

Apart from the moralism and nationalism, however, Amory is explained most frequently as the Keatsian romantic hero strung between inevitably abstract polarities. Not as profound as the polarity involved in the doctrine of original sin, Amory's polarity is that of the "cynical idealist" (p. 84),[1] a paradox that both the author and Amory himself use frequently to explain the man always aware of two different sides of his own nature. Amory's ideal of nobility and magnanimity is undercut by shallow social snobbery; his interest in rising materially in the world batters his honest sympathy and concern for others; his pride in his exterior charm fights his intellectual self-examination. His language often expresses his doubleness: his charm at parties is "a spiritual tax levied" (p. 77); he fears his need for money may cause him to "commit moral suicide" (p. 257); he tells one of his girl friends that "selfish people are in a way terribly capable of great loves" (p. 184). Fitzgerald's point of view parallels Amory's two-sidedness, for the author often switches scenes and interjects comments to inflate, then explode, the romantic bubble. One chapter ends with Amory and a young girl moving together toward a cinematic kiss; the next chapter begins with her "Ouch!" and her continued petulance because his shirt stud had touched her neck. The paradoxes from the nineties, including the epigraph from Oscar Wilde's work, are Fitzgerald's as well as Amory's, the language and structure that give the novel its dated smartness.

Although the doubleness of the "cynical idealist," the paradoxical characterization of the romantic hero, provides the novel with whatever unity it possesses, other elements important for Fitzgerald's later fiction appear. The novel contains many sharp observations on how social barriers operate between people, as well as a careful development of the complexities of combined close friendship and competition in the relationship between Amory and Alec. In addition, Amory acknowledges his sense of morality and connects it to established religion. Although he sometimes doubts and blasphemes, he sharply rebukes an unconventional girl friend who is completely atheistic, invariably centers his self-examination on religious principles, and makes his intellectual confessions to Monsignor Darcy.

Wise and sophisticated, Monsignor Darcy serves as Amory's surrogate father, guiding Amory's reading, debating his ideas, maintaining frequent connection with him through letters and visits. He regards Amory as part of his "family," his spiritual descendant. Since Amory's real father is shadowy and irrelevant (having abrogated all except financial responsibilities toward him) and Amory has been brought up by his eccentric, cosmopolitan, hypochondriacal mother (who keeps losing and regaining her faith in the Roman Catholic church because she enjoys being converted), the turn toward the surrogate is necessary for the transmission of any moral and spiritual ideas. Amory never loses his respect and affection for the older man; when he learns of Monsignor Darcy's death, he recognizes that he must become a man, must perpetuate, in his own terms, the humanity, spirituality, and wisdom of the Monsignor. The transmitted value has some effect. At the end of the novel, when Amory feels that he has finally found himself, Fitzgerald explains:

> His mind turned a corner suddenly and he found himself thinking of the Catholic Church. The idea was strong in him that there was a certain intrinsic lack in those to whom orthodox religion was necessary, and religion to Amory meant the Church of Rome. Quite conceivably it was an empty ritual but it was seemingly the only assimilative, traditionary bulwark against the decay of morals. Until the great mobs could be educated into a moral sense some one must cry: "Thou shalt not!" Yet any acceptance was, for the present, impossible. . . . He wanted to keep the tree without ornaments, realize fully the direction and momentum of this new start. (p. 281)

Like Amory, Fitzgerald is keeping his moralism in reserve, just barely below the surface.

As a central force in Fitzgerald's fiction, the moralism emerged soon thereafter. One of the most brilliant early stories, "May Day" (published in *Tales of the Jazz Age* in 1922), chronicles the waste and emptiness of selfish party-going and dissipation, contrasting this with the humane concern for all the inequities and injustices in American society. *The Beautiful and Damned* is also, in many ways, a moral parable. At the beginning of the novel, the author inserts a Faustian dialogue between "Beauty" and "The Voice," in which "The Voice" promises "Beauty" fifteen years of triumph as "a ragtime kid, a flapper, a jazz-baby, and a baby vamp" (p. 29) in the new and opulent America, in return for which "Beauty" will inevitably be spoiled and tarnished by vulgarity. The dialogue serves as the model for the novel: Anthony and Gloria Patch, the special people, the beautiful couple of the new and exciting America, spoil and squander themselves, are damned as finally as if they had sold their souls to the devil. In part, they tarnish their own beauty. Gloria is selfish and extravagant, afraid to spoil her figure by having a child, reckless, imperious, and narcissistic. Anthony, externally gracious and intelligent, superficially the perfect product of upper-class America, is centrally weak. He drifts, never works despite his many resolutions, and can exert his will only when he is drunk, making petulant scenes in public.

Fitzgerald's judgment of Anthony and Gloria springs from a puritanical perspective: indolence breeds decay, and hard work would save a man; behaving badly in public, the loss of public composure no matter what the circumstances, is the surest sign of hollowness and dissolution. In addition, Fitzgerald views his characters as originally "clean," spiritually antiseptic, not the "clean like polished pans," but the "blowy clean" connected with "streams and wind." As the novel progresses, as indolence, parties, and selfishness take their inevitable toll, the characters, particularly Gloria, become sullied and unclean, the beauty is tarnished. This is not caused by any particular act—Gloria is never unfaithful to Anthony—but there remains an aura, a judgment that indicates both the decay of Gloria's freshness and beauty and the puritanical severity of Fitzgerald's perspective. The antiseptic sense of virtue seems to require a spiritual virginity. Once the woman is no longer the idol, remote and virginal, she introduces sin into the world. Had Anthony remained single, he might have been able to save himself, to redeem his transgressions by hard work and abstinence. But married—he first met Gloria at a time when he was feeling despondent about himself and then substituted living through sexual attraction for working through despondency—Anthony has no chance for salvation; he is tied to the devil's agent.

Anthony's moral hollowness is also caused by the fact that he has no father, no law-giver, no agent to transmit a usable moral framework. His father, an ineffectual dandy of the nineties, had died when Anthony was very young, and the boy had been raised by his grandfather. In *The Beautiful and Damned*, the father-surrogate is too distant and too unconcerned to provide an acceptable substitute for a real father. Adam Patch, Anthony's grandfather, is a rigorous and strong old puritan who amasses a fortune and then decides to "consecrate the remainder of his life to the moral regeneration of the world" (p. 4). He educates Anthony carefully and expensively, but then expects him to engage in useful, ennobling work and to support puritanical causes like prohibition. In the climactic scene of the novel, the staged drama that marks the inevitability of Anthony's doom, his grandfather visits him unannounced to discover a particularly wild and dissolute party in progress. The judgment against Anthony, like his grandfather's withdrawal of financial support, is final and unyielding. Although severe and bitter from Anthony's point of view, his grandfather is highly respected by others, especially by those who see him only from a remote and public distance, like Bloeckman, the alien within the society, who calls old Adam Patch "a fine example of an American" (p. 94). The example, removed and hardened by an extra generation, cannot help Anthony.

Other surrogates in the novel are no more successful. Like Amory Blaine, Anthony is both cynic and idealist. But in this novel the possibilities are extrapolated into polar characters, Anthony's friends, the idealist Dick Caramel and the cynic Maury Noble (the names themselves are ironic tags), who function as surrogates, constantly providing instructions and propounding their solutions to the dilemmas that face Anthony. The surrogates provide no help, for the cynic and the idealist cannot be reconciled. Each polar extreme goes in its own direction: Dick Caramel becomes foolish, soft-headed, unconsciously corrupt; Maury Noble becomes embittered and completely materialistic. When Anthony tries to combine the two, he does nothing; finally, cut off from any father figure, any morality, he lapses into madness.

As they live out their doom, without morality, Anthony and Gloria are forced to feed more completely on each other, to exist only in terms of the relationship that is an inadequate substitute for a sense of human purpose. Their concentration on their relationship is the initial symptom of their decline; but Fitzgerald also probes the relationship itself with insight: the strong sexual attraction, the disastrous mixture of her nervous recklessness and his cowardice, the complete lack of self-knowledge at the beginning, the spoiled childishness of both, yet the moments of fierce loyalty to the marriage. The relationship develops with an ironic reversal of the initial balance. At the beginning of the marriage, Gloria is willing to abandon people or relationships the moment she no longer feels attracted to them, just as she has no interest in antiques or traditions, whereas Anthony says he is more committed to his choice and marriage, just as he is more sentimental about history and period furniture. Yet, finally, it is Anthony who is unfaithful and petulant, while Gloria tries to keep the marriage together just because it is a marriage. Gloria, the spoiled beauty who had married for "safety," needs to assume the dominant role and is capable of staking everything on their staying together. Anthony, having always evaded the hollowness at his center, increasingly lacks the capacity to deal with any relationship and is driven to literal madness when his wartime mistress later demands that her love be returned. A woman, if not governed by the dictates of a moral framework, is invariably the agent of destruction.

Fitzgerald's interest in character itself, however, keeps obtruding into the structure of using character to illustrate the parable of doom. Another example is Bloeckman, the Jew, the character who represents what in America is alien to the central moral tradition. Originally uncouth, naïve, commercial, and too desperate in his attempt to get every social custom right, Bloeckman develops dignity as the novel progresses; he is also the only person willing to help Anthony when all his supposed friends have turned against him. In view of Anthony's anti-Semitism, the use of Bloeckman demonstrates the hollowness of Anthony, who would hold rigidly to superficial social standards while at the same time ignoring moral standards completely; but for Fitzgerald the rise of Bloeckman is also, in part, a story of character, of humanity, apart from any moral framework. Yet Bloeckman is not at the center of the novel, nor, despite all its fascination, is the alternating humanity in the relationship between Anthony and Gloria; rather, the center is the moral parable, the dissolution of the potentially special couple.

The fact that Gloria and Anthony spend so much time within their relationship, within themselves, reflects their hollowness and eventual doom. But the complexity with which the relationship is presented, besides enriching the texture of the novel, adds another dimension to the parable. In contrast to all the other simple illustrations in the parable, Anthony is complex. Unable or unwilling to adopt a single pose, to live by a single attitude like that of the "idealist" or the "cynic," he is damned. His choice of Gloria, of marriage, is sinful, but it is also more complex, more fully human, than the choices of his simplified celibate friends. Anthony and Gloria are the only fully human characters in the novel, the only people who do not hypocritically limit themselves to the singularity that survives. Contemporary America, as Fitzgerald depicts it, rewards hypocrisy, simplification, the person who restricts his humanity to the salvageable single pose and rules out any humanely contradictory impulses. Anthony and Gloria are "beautiful" because they do not simplify, and they are spoiled because they represent something exceptional to the people around them; but their inability or unwillingness to simplify, to restrict themselves, insures their damnation in contemporary America.

The novel's flaw lies in Fitzgerald's failure to work out convincingly the balance between the couple's inability and unwillingness, or to develop any coherent relationship between their responsibility for their doom and an indictment of the American society that dooms its "beautiful." Responsive, directionless, impulsive, capable at times of love for each other, as no other characters in the novel are capable of love, Anthony and Gloria try to sustain their status as special people. Even toward the end, Anthony defends his own feelings of aristocracy: "Aristocracy's only an admission that certain traits which we call fine—courage and honor and beauty and all that sort of thing—can best be developed in a favorable environment, where you don't have the warpings of ignorance and necessity" (p. 407). In the novel, however, contemporary America, despite all its opulence, is a land of "ignorance and necessity," a land that requires hard simplification, callous dishonesty, or rigorous moral restriction from those who are determined to survive. The "beautiful," the flexible and evanescent, are "damned." Because of the depiction of America, the relentless environment that promises so much and punishes so fiercely, Anthony and Gloria gain sympathy well beyond that usually accorded to illustrations in a moral parable. Hollow as they finally are, and harshly as Fitzgerald judges them, Anthony and Gloria are still preferable to all the self-seeking simplifications around them. Although Fitzgerald never makes the relevance of the moral judgment clear, never allows the judgment to stand as a final statement about the principal characters, he never modifies the stringency of the judgment itself.

The moral structure of *The Great Gatsby* is far more coherent. The narrator of the novel, Nick Carraway, more honest than anyone else, serves as "a guide, a pathfinder, an original settler" (p. 4). Frequently obtruding with judgments on characters and general observations on society, Nick provides the perspective through which the issues of the novel are apparent. He speaks for the author when he cries across the lawn to the defeated, deluded, hopelessly naïve Gatsby, "You're worth the whole damn bunch put together" (p. 154). Appropriately, Nick is close to his real father, whom he quotes at the very beginning of the novel and returns to at the end. A solid, sane, highly moral Midwesterner, Nick's father provides the secure basis from which his son can see and judge the chaotic modern world morally and effectively.

Jay Gatsby, the subject of the novel, is the embodiment of the American Dream: the mystery of its origins, its impossible romanticism, its belief in its capacity to recapture a past that may never have existed (as Gatsby believes he can re-create his past with Daisy), its faith in an unknown future, its ultimate futility. He attempts to create a new Eden, derived from the past, through money, silk shirts, and an Oxford accent. Gatsby is also the Horatio Alger hero in his dedication to "dumbbell exercise," the study of "needed inventions," and the pure vision of the future that involves making a lot of money. Like the Horatio Alger hero, Gatsby abandons his own ineffectual and undistinguished father (a man only too willing to relinquish his son to the demands of commercial manifest destiny) and attaches himself to a surrogate, the millionaire miner, Dan Cody. The romantic American myth, predicated on the democratic unpredictability of the origins of the specially virtuous and sensitive man, requires a surrogate father, a willful and deliberate attachment. But, in Fitzgerald's terms, the failure of Gatsby is further demonstration that the myth is false, for the moral guide can only be transmitted by a real father, a true God. The vertical line of virtue must be direct and close, from father to son, and only the vertical line can preserve the sensitive son from the chaos of the modern world.

Gatsby's vision might have been a more plausible version of experience in an earlier, simpler America which had not yet become increasingly materialistic and increasingly distant from the morality of true fathers. His aspirations, then, might not have necessarily involved him, as they do now, with the criminal, the callous, and the corrupt.

> And as I sat there brooding on the old, unknown world, I
> thought of Gatsby's wonder when he first picked out the green
> light at the end of Daisy's dock. He had come a long way to

this blue lawn, and his dream must have seemed so close that he could hardly fail to grasp it. He did not know that it was already behind him, somewhere back in that vast obscurity beyond the city, where the dark fields of the republic rolled on under the night. (p. 182)

Yet in another sense, as Nick clearly sees at the end of the novel, the dream Gatsby represents was always flawed, always impossible to achieve, the promise of the glittering new land which could never be fulfilled no matter how dedicated the aspirant:

And as the moon rose higher the inessential houses began to melt away until gradually I became aware of the old island here that flowered once for Dutch sailors' eyes—a fresh, green breast of the new world. Its vanished trees, the trees that had made way for Gatsby's house, had once pandered in whispers to the last and greatest of all human dreams; for a transitory enchanted moment man must have held his breath in the presence of this continent, compelled into an aesthetic contemplation he neither understood nor desired, face to face for the last time in history with something commensurate to his capacity for wonder. (p. 182)

The difference between promise and achievement, between vision and reality, is the story of America, but it also suggests, in Fitzgerald's terms, the story of man, the aspiring creature limited by himself and the world around him, the worthwhile human creature who invariably wants to have more than he has, to be more than he is. Man's two-sidedness, the difference between his vision and his inevitable destiny, has developed in range and meaning, far from Amory Blaine's superficial "cynical idealism." In *The Great Gatsby*, Fitzgerald's tightest novel both artistically and theologically, both sides of man are locked, the romantic hero's aspiration and defeat are equally necessary. Man's destiny, the sin of the attractive romantic hero, is immutable in Fitzgerald's moral and religious perspective.

The continuity of the human paradox is also applied specifically to America, for all the characters are products of history, are intrinsically related to the past. Tom Buchanan, the stupid and corrupt aspect of the American past, triumphs over Gatsby, the idealized and romanticized version of the past, to win Daisy, the prize in the present which has been spoiled, corrupted, and victimized by the past. What Gatsby's vision represents has, in America, both past and present, never been articulated or imagined in concrete terms, has always been attenuated by Tom's kind of callous, brutal, stupid materialism. Another paradox implicit in Fitzgerald's version of American history is apparent in the incompatibility of two American myths: the democratic myth of the importance of the common man and the myth of the opportunity for the special creature, the exceptionally visionary, resolute, and dedicated. The common man, Wilson, in revenge for the death of his common wife, kills the specially visionary and idealistic Gatsby rather than the specially corrupt and culpable Tom and Daisy. The common man cannot tell one special man from another and finally destroys the American Dream that theoretically provides the symbol for his own aspiration. All these paradoxes, all these, for Fitzgerald, necessary destructions of the ideal or of the transcendence of human possibility, make the novel a moral fable. But Fitzgerald's morality in *The Great Gatsby* is not the simple morality of single-minded judgment, of excoriating the unrighteous. Rather, as articulated through the wise and temperate Nick, the morality is the inflexible necessity of the harsh dilemma of human experience, the invariable human defeat involved in the difference between vision and reality. Because he understands and accepts this, Nick is able to survive and look back on the events of the novel through distance and time.

Dick Diver, the hero of *Tender Is the Night*, is characterized as an American moral agent in the amoral world of Europe after World War I. Initially puritanical in respect to women and to his work, Dick is depicted as a superior representative of America, powerful, intelligent, charming and not aware of his charm, full of fresh ideas and naïve illusions: "the illusions of eternal strength and health, and of the essential goodness of people: illusions of a nation, the lies of generations of frontier mothers who had to croon falsely, that there were no wolves outside the cabin door" (p. 117). Dick recognizes that the American is not perfect, that he needs to be less strident, to cultivate a "repose" that traditional culture brings easily to the European. At the same time, he attempts to exert an American moral force within European society, a force expressed in terms of personal relationships, of consideration for others, of humanity. And he does, at least early in his career, build the small, humane moral society around the small

Riviera beach he discovers, then molds and carefully rakes. Fitzgerald consistently points out the moral center of Dick's charm, the exquisite consideration, the recognition of the value of everything around him, the capacity to extract the full humanity from his associates in the way that the priest, ideally, both guides and understands his parishioners. Dick's psychiatry, too, is moral, attempting to "cure" homosexuality and to "save" his patients from themselves. Even Abe North, the most self-destructive of the American characters, acknowledges that everyone must have a moral code; ironically and bitterly, he claims that his is an opposition to burning witches. For Fitzgerald, such a flippantly limited moral implies certain destruction.

Dick fails, like Jay Gatsby, partly because his innocent and moral ideals no longer apply to contemporary experience. Increasingly throughout the novel, Dick's public moralism is inappropriate in a new, more private world that he cannot understand. Although he is much less the smugly dense American than McKisco is, he never appreciates Tommy Barban's private justifications for wandering service as a mercenary soldier. Dick never understands the world of Mary North's Levantine second husband, or the cosmopolitan skepticism of the newer rebels like Lady Caroline Sibly-Biers, or, finally, the female nature of his wife, the new and revitalized Nicole, who successfully poses her "unscrupulousness against his moralities" (p. 802). Despite all his external charm, Dick is too committed to the past, to an old American morality, ever to recognize fully the private, separate particles of contemporary European life. At one point, Dick sees a party of middle-aged American women who impress him as forming a cohesive unit, and he discovers that they are a group of goldstar mothers who have come to Europe to visit their sons' graves:

> Over his wine Dick looked at them again; in their happy faces, the dignity that surrounded and pervaded the party, he perceived all the maturity of an older America. For a while the sobered women who had come to mourn for their dead, for something they could not repair, made the room beautiful. Momentarily, he sat again on his father's knee, riding with Moseby while the old loyalties and devotions fought on around him. Almost with an effort he turned back to his two women at the table and faced the whole new world in which he believed. (pp. 100–101)

Dick may believe in two worlds, the moral one of the old America and the new one of his women, but he cannot live in both. And as he fails, his own morality, his own center, begins to dissolve. He works less and less, becomes more dependent on Nicole's money, and is increasingly drunken, careless, and inconsiderate. When Rosemary Hoyt, who had once idolized him, tells him that he still seems the man he was, he replies, "The manner remains intact for some time after the morale cracks" (p. 285)—almost as if he is Dorian Gray with a deeply imbedded sense of sin just under the easy façade. Dick's "manner" eventually cracks, too, for he becomes violent and petulant, picks fights, indulges in self-pity, and is pointlessly vulgar in talking with Nicole. All these are symptoms of an advanced stage of dissolution: for Fitzgerald, not behaving well, not observing superficial amenities and conventions, always indicates the hero's irreversible defeat.

The doom is not as elemental and universal as that of *The Great Gatsby*, for *Tender Is the Night* is a more complicated novel. For example, the father figures proliferate, suggesting a more equivocal morality than that of *The Great Gatsby*. Dick's real father is an American clergyman who had taught Dick all he knew of "manners" and "matters of behavior," a man halfway between Nick Carraway's wise and sophisticated father and Gatsby's humble simpleton. Though honest and direct, he lacks the intellect, the range, and the insight to be transportable to the new and more complicated world of postwar Europe. Despite the distance in space and time between Dick and his father, Dick often "referred judgments to what his father would probably have thought or done" (p. 203). Yet he recognizes that, in choosing Europe, he has abandoned his father. He temporarily returns to America to attend his father's funeral: "These dead, he knew them all, their weather-beaten faces with blue flashing eyes, the spare violent bodies, the souls made of new earth in the forest-heavy darkness of the seventeenth century. 'Good-by, my father—good-by, all my fathers'" (p. 205). Dick attaches himself to a surrogate father, Dr. Dohmler, the psychiatrist in charge of the clinic where Dick initially works. Dr. Dohmler is fiercely moral, an instructor, a guide, and Dick is strongly influenced by his precepts and judgments. Yet in marrying Nicole, in confusing the separate relationships between husband and wife and between doctor and patient, Dick disobeys one of Dr. Dohmler's strongest injunctions. The real father is not necessarily preferable to the surrogate, for either might have served to transmit his morality to Dick. But Dick abandons one and disobeys the other; left alone, he cannot sustain himself. The father also has responsibilities toward his child: Nicole's father, in forcing incest upon her, actually converts his daughter into his mistress and so violates the relationship between father and child in the most disastrous way possible.

In this complicated novel, Dick Diver is a multiple father as well as a multiply errant son. Having rejected the gods offered him, Dick establishes himself as a series of gods, playing a different kind of father in each of his varying relationships. Although certain moral judgments still obtain in *Tender Is the Night* (*e.g.*, the prescription against incest), the plurality of gods makes the moral issues more equivocal and perplexing than those of *The Great Gatsby*. As a real father to his two children, Dick finds his only lasting success. To Lanier and Topsy, he is warm and firm, able to mean something even after he has ceased to mean anything to anyone else. Dick is less successful as a surrogate father to Rosemary, the starlet who gains recognition in *Daddy's Girl*. For her, Dick is the cosmopolitan father, introducing her to Europe, to history, to the world of sensitivity. When first attracted to her, he regards her as too much the child to make love to her, but Rosemary, who has always sensed the ambivalence between the father and the lover, eventually grows beyond the need of a surrogate and recognizes the hollowness within Dick. Even so, in the scene in which they recognize that their whole relationship has been superficial, that they have only been playing parts like the actors they are, that neither is really capable of loving the other, Rosemary says, "I feel as if I'd quarrelled with Mother" (p. 219).

More importantly, Dick is a surrogate father for Nicole, replacing the father who had violated her. First as psychiatrist and then as husband, Dick still plays the father, sheltering Nicole from the world, guiding her, and giving her the time and understanding necessary for her restoration to psychic health. But the roles of father and of husband are incompatible: Nicole, once restored, must reject Dick because, as a grown-up woman, she no longer needs a father; Dick, in marrying the woman he needed to guide, had really committed a kind of symbolic incest. In the multiplicity of his fatherhood, Dick tries to be a universal father, the controller and guide for all the relationships around him, the lord and creator of the beach. Images like the "deposed ruler," or the "spoiled priest," applied to Dick after his decline is evident, underline the universal nature of his fatherhood.

In general terms, Dick's doom is unambiguous, the folly and presumption of playing God, of attempting, while still a human being, to guide and control all the lives around him. Yet the specific moral framework of the novel is far more ambiguous. The reader wonders which God, if any, might have been the true one: Dr. Dohmler? Dick's father? Dick as psychiatrist? Dick as the charming and responsive master of the civilized world? The novel charts Dick's doom, but part of his doom is the confusion and ambiguity of whatever moral order specifically destroys him. When, in his final defeat, Dick makes the sign of the cross over the populous beach he had once created from the debris between shore and sea, his action is neither an ironically unrecognized truth nor a presumptuous falsehood, but, rather, a pathetic and irrelevant gesture of his failure.

In the moral ambiguity of *Tender Is the Night*, much of Fitzgerald's attention shifts from the vertical relationship, the transmission of truth or moral values from parent to child, to the lateral relationship, the equivalent relationship between man and woman, the mutual recognition of humanity. The focus often changes from fathers to women, to the representatives of an amoral principle of accepting what is and holding "things together." For Fitzgerald, the father is more characteristically, although not entirely, connected with America, a continent that is a "nursery." In contrast, the new world of postwar Europe neglects the transmission of moral values, the father, and concentrates on the woman. Early in the novel, after Dick has been presented at the apex of his talent and control, there is a shooting at the railway station, an unforeseen and unexpected event. Both Rosemary and Nicole wait in vain for "Dick to make a moral comment on the matter and not leave it to them" (p. 85). From that moment on, as a kind of counterpoint to the theme of Dick's dissolution, Fitzgerald develops an interest in the two women's attempt to discover themselves. Both Rosemary and Nicole begin to understand the world around them without Dick's guiding judgment.

Because she has had more to overcome and has been more completely involved with Dick, Nicole's is the more interesting consciousness, and, appropriately, Fitzgerald devotes more time to her gradual breaking away from dependence on Dick and developing an independent self-awareness. Like Gloria in *The Beautiful and Damned*, Nicole has a kind of reckless courage. Originally dependent, she is able to become wiser, more competent, more self-assured as the man she regarded as her master dissolves. To some extent both novels show the roles of the partners reversing within the marriage. But Fitzgerald's attitude changed. In *The Beautiful and Damned*, as the wife became more human and competent, less the porcelain trophy, she was inevitably soiled, unclean; in *Tender Is the Night*, the loss of spiritual virginity indicates the capacity for human relationship, and no moral judgment, no antisepsis, is involved. When Nicole realizes that Dick, the father, cannot also be a husband, she turns, in her new self-confidence, toward Tommy Barban:

> Her ego began blooming like a great rich rose as she scrambled back along the labyrinths in which she had wandered for years. She hated the beach, resented the places where she had played planet to Dick's sun.
>
> "Why, I'm almost complete," she thought. "I'm practically standing alone, without him." And like a happy child, wanting the completion as soon as possible, and knowing vaguely that Dick had planned for her to have it, she lay on her bed as soon as she got home and wrote Tommy Barban in Nice a short provocative letter. (p. 289)

After she and Tommy Barban make love, Nicole almost expects an explanation or interpretation of the experience, such as Dick would have given. But Tommy provides none, and Nicole is content and a "child" no longer. Fitzgerald indicates his final approval of Nicole, or at least his refusal to pass judgment against her, by portraying her as neither bitter nor petulant when she decides to leave Dick; indeed, she can recognize that in her need she had contributed to his indolence and unwittingly encouraged his decline. She can be gracious, always the sign of a kind of virtue in Fitzgerald's terms. Most of the events in the last third of the novel are seen from Nicole's point of view. And, using her point of view, Fitzgerald shows that he is as interested in dissecting an incompatible relationship—the strain between a woman who needed a surrogate father before she was ready for a husband and a man who was too much of a father to change himself into a husband—as he is in chronicling the destruction of the romantic ego.

Despite the use of Nicole's point of view, the structure of the novel does not justify reading the emphasis on Nicole as equal to the emphasis on Dick's decline. A consideration of the structure, of the movement from one episode to another, focuses attention on Dick and his failure. Yet Fitzgerald himself was uneasy and dissatisfied with the shape of the novel. As originally published and as usually read today, the novel begins with Rosemary's point of view toward Dick on the beach, Rosemary naïvely worshiping the Dick who is then at the height of his power and charm. Then, following Dick, with flashbacks into the past and the meeting between Dick and Nicole, the novel traces Dick's decline. In some editions the first ten chapters of Book II have been placed before Book I, a change that Fitzgerald later advocated and one that would make the novel read chronologically. Like the original version, however, the chronological version emphasizes the rise and fall of the hero, the only real difference being that the chronological version places greater emphasis on psychological causes, on Nicole's illness, Dick's work, and Dick's disobedience of Dr. Dohmler's injunction. Since Fitzgerald's explicit treatment of psychological issues (in contrast with his implicit treatment of character in a way that could be explained in psychological terms) is so heavily moralistic and simplistically unconvincing to contemporary readers, the chronological organization seems even less satisfactory than does the original. The counterpoint to the theme of Dick's dissolution—the growth of Nicole's capacity to understand experience and the partial shift to the amoral female perspective—is not represented in either structure or given coherently meaningful shape. A conversation about Abe North between Nicole and Dick illustrates something of the problem:

> Nicole shook her head right and left, disclaiming responsibility for the matter: "So many smart men go to pieces nowadays."
>
> "And when haven't they?" Dick asked. "Smart men play close to the line because they have to—some of them can't stand it, so they quit."
>
> "It must lie deeper than that." Nicole clung to her conversation; also she was irritated that Dick should contradict her before Rosemary. "Artists like—well, like Fernand don't seem to have to wallow in alcohol. Why is it just Americans who dissipate?"
>
> There were so many answers to this question that Dick decided to leave it in the air, to buzz victoriously in Nicole's ears. (pp. 99–100)

Nicole is right, for the novel shows that it does "lie deeper than that." But whatever is "deeper," like whatever version of God dooms Dick, is never made fully coherent, never brought finally into focus. The structural reliance on only the theme of Dick's decline almost seems a substitute for the failure to control fully the ultimate skepticism about God and the issues of lateral relationship in the novel. Yet, despite this failure and the lack of a universal order as tight as that of *The Great Gatsby*, a sense of richness, density, and disordered humanity emerges from *Tender Is the Night*.

No fathers exist in *The Last Tycoon*. The protagonist, Monroe Stahr, is the man of enormous talent who has achieved his dominance over others, his special stature, by his own brilliance, energy, and hard work. No moral code or dedication to manners or principle infuses his background. In a scene with Kathleen, he explains:

> "When I was young I wanted to be a chief clerk—the one who knew where everything was. . . . I'm still a chief clerk. . . . That's my gift, if I have one. Only when I got to be it, I found out that no one knew where anything was. And I found out that you had to know why it was where it was, and whether it should be left there." (p. 96)

Stahr has sympathy as well as talent, the capacity to understand people around him, the willingness to soothe the narcissistic actor and to help the cameraman ruined by rumor. Yet all his talents and humanity are solely individual, not part of any country or code or truth. A humane employer, he is still not willing to side with labor in a struggle against capital in the principal issue of his time (this aspect was never fully worked out in the portion of the novel finished; Fitzgerald's notes indicate that he planned to develop the labor agitation further, but arguing further from notes and guesses would not be very rewarding); a capitalistic moviemaker, he is far from a defender or a representative of the system. When in power, Stahr relies only on himself, even if he is not always sure just what that self is. While flying in a plane, Stahr goes up to the cockpit to talk with the pilot:

> He was looking down at the mountains.
> "Suppose you were a railroad man," he said. "You have to send a train through there somewhere. Well, you get your

surveyors' reports, and you find there's three or four or half a
dozen gaps, and not one is better than the other. You've got to
decide—on what basis? You can't test the best way—except by
doing it. So you just do it."

    The pilot thought he had missed something.

    "How do you mean?"

    "You choose some one way for no reason at all—because
that mountain's pink or the blueprint is a better blue. You see?"
(p. 28)

In addition, Stahr is a Jew, an alien in America, a force without locus
and a talent without background. The novel revolves around a man
and his relationships rather than around an inherited principle and its
application to the modern world.

    In *The Last Tycoon*, the American past is false or irrelevant in
the Hollywood that manufactures dreams for contemporary society.
Abraham Lincoln eats the forty-cent dinner, including dessert, in the
studio cafeteria, and the Danish visitor who notices him feels that
Lincoln now makes more sense than he ever had before; a telephone
call to Stahr, supposedly from the President, turns out to be a joke
to get Stahr to talk with an ape; a trip to the Hermitage, Andrew
Jackson's home, taken because the plane is delayed by bad weather,
holds no message for the characters and provides only the setting
for a suicide. Comically, absurdly, the men of Hollywood make their
myths, legends just as true and just as false as the ones enshrined by
history. Stahr's dream woman, Kathleen, attractive to him because she
resembles his dead wife, is also not American. An English girl who has
been to "all the places that Stahr made movies of" (p. 132), Kathleen
is first seen riding on the head of a Hindu goddess, a stage prop for a
movie, through a flood in the studio.

    Throughout the novel, fortunes change rapidly, people appear and
disappear unexpectedly, and those concerned with the movies are apt
to be powerful and arrogant one minute and jobless and desolate the
next. No one is secure and no one is sure of himself. Kathleen tells
Stahr that he is three or four people, a comment echoed by Cecilia
Brady, the narrator of part of the novel, who claims that all writers
are several people; a genuine Russian prince refuses to play the part
of a Russian prince because he has turned Communist; in looking for
Kathleen, after he has seen her once, Stahr gets the wrong woman

first. In fact, the wrong woman is named Smith, a name Stahr also uses for anonymity when he flies across the country. And the man Kathleen marries, as a result of both mistiming and misunderstanding between herself and Stahr, is also named Smith. As the multiple Smiths, some true and some false, indicate, the principal concern of the novel is identity, discovering who or what one is, rather than any form of moral judgment or evaluation.

At the same time, Stahr is another of Fitzgerald's doomed romantic heroes whose attempt to play God must inevitably be defeated. His role as the "last" tycoon amidst the changes of social history, the verdict from the doctor that gives him only a few months to live, and prophetically introduced observations from other characters demonstrate, even in the completed portion of the novel, that Stahr's dissolution and defeat were to be inescapable. Yet, as in *Tender Is the Night*, the cause of the doom, the triumphant morality or the true God, is never manifest. Playing God, for Fitzgerald, is a sin no matter how attractive, and it is a sin even in a chaotic universe with no moral framework or principle that can define or label what sin is. The guilt, the sense of sin, lingers even after the intellect and understanding can no longer accept the system that assigned the sin.

Like all Fitzgerald's romantic heroes, Stahr tries to relieve the barren dedication of his quest with an interest in women. But, unlike the earlier heroes, Stahr changes, learns from his relationship with a woman. Kathleen, Stahr's mistress, is formless, can play mother, "trollop," temporary wife, anything Stahr might momentarily need. Kathleen's previous relationship, too, had been defined by the man, and, in the course of the novel, she marries Smith because he happens, decisively, to arrive unexpectedly at the moment when she and Stahr are between definitions. The other woman who loves Stahr, Cecilia Brady, also makes the point that women exist to understand men, to be defined by them and attach themselves to them. Significantly, Cecilia is "in" but not "of" the movies, and Kathleen refuses to let Stahr show her around the studio: both women are less interested in the thing itself, the life outside the man, than in the definition the man creates of his own "thing." This, to Fitzgerald, makes them genuine women in contrast to the starlets who gain their only identity through being "of" the movies, created by the glittering and fabricated dreams.

That Kathleen can marry Smith because of her uncertainty about Stahr indicates that Stahr himself, despite his success as a talented producer, is far from certain about his own identity or about the definitions he wants to impose upon experience. Until too late, he does not know what he feels about Kathleen, what his personal identity is. At one point, Kathleen gives him a note, then later asks that it be returned, but neither can find it in the car. After he has taken her home, Stahr finds the note and brings it back to his house:

> He was proud of resisting his first impulse to open the letter. It seemed to prove that he was not "losing his head." He had never lost his head about Minna [his dead wife], even in the beginning—it had been the most appropriate and regal match imaginable. She had loved him always and just before she died, all unwilling and surprised, his tenderness had burst and surged forward and he had been in love with her. In love with Minna and death together—with the world in which she looked so alone that he wanted to go with her there.
>
> But "falling for dames" had never been an obsession—his brother had gone to pieces over a dame, or rather over dame after dame after dame. But Stahr, in his younger days, had them once and never more than once—like one drink. He had quite another sort of adventure reserved for his mind—something better than a series of emotional sprees. Like many brilliant men, he had grown up dead cold.... And so he had learned tolerance, kindness, forbearance, and even affection like lessons. (pp. 115–16)

Stahr's belated growth refers to public issues as well as personal ones. Only during the course of the novel does he, the capitalistic entrepreneur of dreams, begin to realize how unfairly he has always used labor. Although he is still fascinated by the power one man can hold, by playing God, he begins to question himself and his aims more closely. He becomes more concerned with others, with politics, with art, as well as with women. Yet, for all his richer sense of humanity, Stahr is still doomed, and, if Fitzgerald's notes for the rest of the novel can be credited, he might have been finished off melodramatically because the sense of doom has no logical corollary in terms of the novel.

The point of view of *The Last Tycoon* is never developed sufficiently to order all the elements. The novel's action is ostensibly seen through Cecilia Brady, the daughter of Stahr's partner. Cecilia is a Bennington girl, a "new" woman, honest, flippant, and direct. She is not even disillusioned when she accidentally surprises her father making love to his secretary in his office, for she has seen that before and has already shifted from a childish reliance on fathers and moralities to an interest in the humane development of the self. In this sense, she is a satisfactory narrator for the novel. But the subject of the novel is Stahr, and Cecilia tells more than she could possibly know. Fitzgerald has her collecting information from others, piecing together stories of Stahr's life in the studio from several sources, and acting like a zoomar-lens consciousness when she enters Stahr's mind as he approaches Kathleen, Cecilia standing a hundred yards away. The device of Cecilia's narration breaks down entirely in its irrelevance to the central and private love scenes between Stahr and Kathleen. The gossip and the quick cutting from one scene to another, which disrupt Cecilia's narrative, are justified, even effective, as a mirror of Hollywood. Cecilia can also see the ironic pathos in Stahr's decline. But as a device to record Stahr himself and what defeats him, to present his growing humanity, and to suggest the order in terms of which he sins, Fitzgerald's use of Cecilia as narrator is inadequate. She is even further from the God who may not exist than is Stahr himself. And, in secular as well as religious terms, no structurally coherent device, at least none apparent in the unfinished novel, manages to articulate all that is there.

In his last two novels, Fitzgerald's compassion grew. His concern for his characters increased, as did his sympathy for their human struggles and relationships, for all the questions they could never answer. Correspondingly, the element of morality or judgment diminished, and God or truth disappeared; the romantic hero, although still doomed, seemed doomed less by a moral order or original sin than by accident. Still unable to control his own destiny as he so powerfully wanted to, the romantic hero turned his attention to the very human relationships that contributed to his doom, sometimes even, as in the instance of Monroe Stahr, ironically learning from them. Yet despite the interest in the strictly secular relationship and the lack of an implicit moral order, Fitzgerald's form was always that of the parable, no less in *Tender Is the Night* than in *The Beautiful and Damned*. In the last two novels, the parable form was less appropriate, less able to summarize and direct the issues of the novel, and Fitzgerald never found a form to express coherently the greater human dimensions and complexity of his later fiction. The form broke, particularly in *Tender*

Is the Night, in which the energy and perception of the novel leap out from the inadequate structure and the ultimately superficial point of view. Yet in the very breaking of the form, the very collapse of the parable as an explanation that can support the weight of contemporary experience, the sense of Fitzgerald's achieved compassion inheres. Compassion seldom is tidy or neatly measurable in a formal equation, and Fitzgerald's last two novels explode from the tidiness of judgment and evaluation of the "American experience" into deeper questions, as well as richer and less systematic understandings about the perplexities of man.

NOTE

1. Page references in the text are to the Scribner Library editions of Fitzgerald's novels, except in the case of *The Last Tycoon*, for which I have used the edition published in London in 1949.

THE NOVELS OF WILLIAM GOLDING

"William Golding: Island"
by Jean E. Kennard, in *Number and Nightmare:*
Forms of Fantasy in Contemporary Fiction

INTRODUCTION

For Jean E. Kennard, William Golding is concerned with
sin, and "the great sin is to see everything in terms of self."
Kennard concludes that, "Like Anthony Burgess and Iris
Murdoch, Golding refutes the Sartrean view of man as an
alienated being in absurd relation to the universe with what
amounts to a leap of faith. He believes that there is meaning,
unity, but recognizes this is unprovable. Redemption from
the Post-existential dilemma, nevertheless, lies in each man's
recognition of his place in the universal scheme."

Critics vary almost as much about William Golding's philosophy
as they do about Iris Murdoch's. They are agreed that each of his
six novels[1]*—with the possible exception of *The Pyramid*—has basic
metaphysical concerns, that Golding is concerned with the human
condition rather than with the condition of contemporary man, but
they differ considerably over what his metaphysics are. Many believe

Kennard, Jean E. "William Golding: Island." *Number and Nightmare: Forms of*
Fantasy in Contemporary Fiction. Hamden, CT: Archon Books, 1975. 176–202.

him to be an orthodox Christian, some taking him as Catholic, others as Calvinist; and one cannot deny that he writes primarily in terms of Christian mythology. James Baker, however, thinks that this is the great error of Golding criticism, that because critics have concentrated on Golding's debts to Christian sources "he is now popularly regarded as a rigid Christian moralist."[2]

Bernard Dick is one of several critics who discuss Golding in relation to Existentialism. He claims that in *Free Fall* "Golding has abandoned myth for Existentialist soul-bearing"[3] and that "Sartre did it much better in *Nausea*."[4] Baker, too, suggests that Golding sees reality as a purely subjective pattern "which we compose according to the limitations of our own nature"[5]—an Existentialist premise—but recognizes that he considers man's creation of God in his own image as presumptuous, not heroic. In *Pincher Martin*, as Baker points out, Golding inverts "the existential formula certain of the critics wished to impose upon it."[6]

Golding denies that there is any direct Existentialist influence upon him, just as he denies any Freudian influence, but he has admitted that we are all living in an Existentialist climate: "People have done a sort of Freudian exegesis on me. Well, I don't know my Freud, but both Freud and I have been looking at ourselves and human society. There must be points at which we agree. Well, now, my generation is the existentialist generation."[7] Given his interest in metaphysical matters, Golding is, as he wisely points out, bound to be concerned in this society at this time with many of the same questions as the Existentialists. Such questions as what is human identity? does man have "a center"? how far is man free? is there a reality transcending man's subjectivity? dominate his novels.

In every instance, though, he opposes the Post-existential view and comes up with answers very similar to those of Anthony Burgess and Iris Murdoch. It is untrue that Golding's novels leave us without answers, as Mark Kinkead-Weekes and Ian Gregor suggest.[8] Golding admits that he cannot subscribe to any particular religion, but insists that he is a fundamentally religious man: "The whole thing surely *has* to *be* a unity. If there is one faith I have, it is that there *is* a unity. And it seems to me—that man hasn't seen this."[9] This faith in a pattern that transcends man is not the only difference between Golding's position and that defined in the early work of Sartre and Camus, but it is the basic one. As with Anthony Burgess and Iris Murdoch it is this belief which underlies all other aspects of his philosophy and determines the techniques of his novels.

It is because "man hasn't seen this" that he is in trouble, according to Golding. Golding sees man as trapped in himself, "islanded," a condition he appears to believe comes inevitably with consciousness of self, with the loss of innocence. In his discussion of *Free Fall* Bernard Dick explains that to Golding "loss of freedom comes ... with the creation of a macrocosm inhabited and orbited by the self."[10] All Golding's major characters—Sammy Mountjoy, Pincher Martin, Dean Jocelyn—are men who have created the world in their own image, who turn everything into themselves.

As one might expect, metaphors of entrapment, cellars or prisons, and of absorption by self, eating, dominate the novels. The "eating" image is, of course, associated with greed, as Bernard Oldsey and Stanley Weintraub point out, and greed is a form of pride. The passage they quote from W. Burnet Easton, Jr.'s *Basic Christian Beliefs*, is worth quoting again since it makes clear Golding's associations with greed: "The fundamental sin according to the Bible is pride, egocentricity, self-deification, and the insistence that each of us is the final arbiter of what is good for him."[11] For Golding, then, the great sin is to see everything in terms of self, a sin Iris Murdoch, opposing Sartre on the same grounds, calls neurosis.

To what extent, though, can man be held responsible for this islanding of the self which, after all, happens to him inevitably with maturity? And what, if anything, can he do to save himself? Golding suggests, most clearly in *The Inheritors*, that man in a state of innocence is an integral part of his universe. The separation of man from the rest of his world through consciousness is apparently Golding's way of defining original sin. At this point man is islanded. As Baker suggests: "The island is an important symbol in all of Golding's works. It suggests the isolation of man in a frightening and mysterious cosmos."[12] This is perhaps true, though it puts too little emphasis on man's responsibility for his own condition to be a completely accurate account of Golding's views. Baker concludes by saying the island also represents "The futility of his attempt to create an ordered preserve for himself in an otherwise patternless world."[13] This is simply not true. There are bridges to the mainland, if not for Sammy Mountjoy, at least for William Golding.[14] In one conversation Jack Biles reminds Golding of a comment in his essay on Copernicus: there is an "overriding human necessity of finding a link between separate phenomena."[15]

Golding is an antirationalist, as are Murdoch and Burgess. He does not, however, believe that salvation lies in a reacknowledgement of the primitive with its concomitant violence, as does Iris Murdoch; nor does he, like Burgess, demand our acceptance of the violence he admits is a basic part of man's nature. Golding believes man's salvation lies in a recognition of the macrocosm in which he is a microcosm; man must find a bridge off the island of himself into an outer reality. As Golding himself explains it, "I see, I think I can see, that the only kind of real progress is the progress of the individual towards some kind of—I would describe it as *ethical*—integration."[16]

Howard Babb's account of Sammy's experience in *Free Fall* introduces another element necessary for salvation: the willingness to express one's awareness of an external reality, through a cry for help; in other—Christian—words, man needs the grace of God. Babb's comments are interesting also in that they could apply equally well to so many Iris Murdoch characters: "Sammy Mountjoy—at the moment of being sunk most completely in his self—can cry out for help, thereby acknowledging the otherness of the universe and indeed experiencing its divinity. . . . he both feels enclosed within a guilty self yet is periodically visited, when the demands of the self are in abeyance, by perceptions of the world about him as miraculous."[17]

Each of Golding's novels is a fantasy fable in the sense in which I have defined the term, except *The Pyramid*, an attempt at comic realism which has no place in this discussion. Samuel Hynes's general comments on the form of the other five novels are interesting primarily because they exactly describe the basic elements of fantasy fable: "Golding so patterns his narrative actions as to make them the images of ideas, the imaginative forms of generalizations; the form itself, that is to say, carries meaning apart from the meanings implied by the character or those stated more or less didactically by the author. Consequently we must look for human relevance to the patterned action itself; if we identify, it must be with the moral—with conception of man and the shape of the universe—and not with this character or that one."[18] Even in Golding's most realistic novel,[19] *Free Fall*, set in present time and in a familiar England, the scenes are separated from one another, only flashes in Sammy Mountjoy's mind, so that we are forced to search for the pattern, the relationship between them. Kinkead-Weekes and Gregor write of *Free Fall*, "Page by page the scenes convince, but they are always felt to be in the service of some governing purpose which frames them, islands them ... out of the complexities of living."[20] In their more general discussion of the novels in their concluding chapter, they point out that the reader, continually trying to piece together a pattern, is involved in a process of reading with a continuous need for translation: "Our awareness of meaning depends on our awareness of correspondence. Nothing is offered for its own sake. Situations, relationships, protagonists, figures are selected; controlled for a purpose beyond themselves, serving an analytic design or debate."[21]

In spite of this accurate observation of the effect of Golding's novels, Kinkead-Weekes and Gregor seem to have missed Golding's intention. They see this method as a dramatization—presumably ironic—of "the limitations of the pattern-maker and the tragic consequences of his vision."[22] Surely this is a distortion designed to make their account of technique fit their view of Golding's thesis. What they describe dramatizes much more obviously the necessity for microcosm to recognize macrocosm. The reader moves steadily outward, from the islands of Golding's beginning situation to the mainland of his whole pattern, until he begins to suspect, as Golding himself says to Biles, that "everything is symbolic."[23]

Each novel is a microcosm of a greater whole: in *Lord of the Flies* the innate violence of the children alone on the island is a version in miniature of the adult world represented by the officer with his cruiser; the prehistoric world of *The Inheritors* is one episode in a history repeating itself in every man, as each loses his innocence; Pincher Martin, actually centered on his own nagging tooth, is living out in miniature the story of his whole life; *Free Fall* is closely related to *The Inheritors* and again deals with each man's loss of innocence in terms of one man, Sammy Mountjoy; Dean Jocelyn's obsession with building a spire is revealed as every man's drive to find meaning. Each islanded situation is gradually seen to incorporate more significance until one has the feeling that Golding has incorporated everything. "Everything is there at once." This, of course, is the great art of myth Golding himself has described to Frank Kermode as "something which comes out from the roots of things in the ancient sense of being the key to existence, the whole meaning of life, and experience as a whole."[24]

The experience of expansion the reader goes through in Golding's novels happens with every aspect of his technique: his characters, first recognizable as individuals, are seen to function also as allegorical figures; the patterning of the plot gradually adds increasing significance to each episode as its place in the overall scheme becomes clearer; each novel is related to earlier books by other writers, as Oldsey and Weintraub demonstrate, and thus is seen to be part of a larger culture; and, perhaps most importantly, Golding's language is so densely metaphoric that the reader is constantly given the sense of one thing's relation to another. These techniques are, of course, Joycean, and in many ways serve the same ends. They are, in fact, the defining characteristics of the novel of nightmare.

As every student knows, *Lord of the Flies* concerns a group of children who are plane-wrecked on a friendly South Seas island during World War II. After reverting to savagery, they are finally "rescued" by a naval officer with a cruiser who presumably returns them to a world as violent as that which they created for themselves on the island. This comparison is Golding's final word to the reader. As James Baker points out in his introduction to the Casebook edition of *Lord of the Flies*, the appearance of the naval officer generalizes the experience of the novel.[25] The island society is a microcosm of a larger whole.

The failure of the island society comes about because of an innate tendency towards violence in the boys. Golding is, then, in opposition to the romantic notion of noble primitives. Human beings are not innately innocent, so human progress is unlikely. Like Burgess, Golding is Augustinian rather than Pelagian. Like Burgess, too, his belief in certain predetermined tendencies in human nature and his belief in a patterned universe set him in opposition to the Post-existential world view. The violence of the boys marooned on the island is, Golding makes clear to us, only part of what is to be found in nature as a whole. The novel opens after a violent storm "that wasn't half dangerous with all them tree trunks falling" (p. 6); the forest is swept by a raging fire Golding describes in terms of wild animals; even the clouds, Simon feels, "were sitting on the land; they squeezed, produced moment by moment this close, tormenting heat" (p. 127). In this final quotation the use of the word *squeezed* in connection with heat and clouds suggests the relationship between the boys and the natural world. During the ritual dance Ralph feels the desire to "squeeze and hurt" Robert; this scene is a foreshadowing of the one where Simon is killed by the fire and his death is followed by a cloudburst.

What happens to the children is in large measure seen to be inevitable, though they are at first innocent because ignorant of their own natures. In an interview with James Keating, Golding has explained:

> They don't understand their own natures and therefore, when they get to this island, they can look forward to a bright future, because they don't understand the things that threaten it. This seems to me to be innocence; I suppose you could almost equate it with ignorance of men's basic attributes, and this is inevitable with anything which is born and begins to grow up. Obviously it doesn't understand its own nature.[26]

The decline of the children's society on the island and the gradual revelation of evil is paralleled to the boys', particularly Ralph's, increasing self-consciousness. He begins to have a recurring "strange mood of speculation that was so foreign to him" (p. 70). Self-consciousness is, of course, the separation of self from the not-self, the outside world; and it is in terms of a breaking up of an initial harmony that Golding defines evil in the novel. At first the "littl'uns" separate themselves from the older children and then from each other; then Jack's group separates from Ralph's. "Things are breaking up. I don't understand why" (p. 75), Ralph says to the meeting and then later to Piggy, "what makes things break up like they do?" (p. 129) Finally each boy is alone, an island, afraid of everyone else.

Mistakenly the children feel that the evil is outside, a beast they can hunt and kill. Only Piggy and Simon realize that they themselves contain the seed of the trouble: Piggy tentatively suggests, "What I mean is . . . maybe it's only us" (p. 82); Simon is told in a vision by the pig's head on a stick, "You knew, didn't you? I'm part of you? Close, close, close. I'm the reason why it's no go? Why things are what they are" (p. 133). The decline of their society is also marked in the novel by their gradual forgetting that rescue must come from outside. At first talking of almost nothing else but parents, home, and rescue, they make fewer and fewer references to the world, of which they are a part. Percival Wemys Madison, trained by his parents to memorize his address and telephone number, his place in the world, gradually forgets them and when the officer comes at the end, finds he can remember nothing about his life outside the island. Similarly, the fire Ralph recognizes they need in order to send smoke signals to possible rescuers is neglected by the others and goes out. The scene in which Ralph discovers this is significantly followed by the first pig hunt. Jack later takes the fire to cook his pig, and it becomes associated not with rescue and the outside world, but with eating, Golding's image for self-absorption. Piggy's increasing blindness is also a parallel loss of vision in a wider sense; he, too, becomes trapped in his own body, unable to see the outer reality.

If human nature is innately violent and selfish, then what hope does Golding offer us? Not much in *Lord of the Flies*. In various interviews and essays he has suggested a possibility of curbs voluntarily imposed by individuals upon themselves, though he does not talk very optimistically about the likelihood of this. In the interview with Keating, Golding says of the children in *Lord of the Flies*:

> They're too young to look ahead and really put the curbs on their own nature and implement them, because giving way to these beasts is always a pleasure, in some ways, and so their society breaks down. Of course, on the other hand, in an adult society it is possible society will not break down. It may be that we can put sufficient curbs on our own natures to prevent it from breaking down.[27]

There is some suggestion in the novel that others act as a curb on violence, that social organization has its values in spite of the history of Western civilization. Initially Roger, the most savage of the boys, does not throw stones at the littl'uns because his "arm was conditioned by a civilization that knew nothing of him and was in ruins" (p. 57). Golding obviously believes that the parliament organized by Ralph is a force for good, in spite of the fact that the boys are incapable of making the necessary allowances for others that would help it work. When Jack and Ralph work together early in their stay on the island, they find two can lift logs too heavy for one.

Although Golding suggests the harmony of an ideal society, he does not indicate any faith in its creation. If man is to be helped, he appears to need help from God, represented in this novel, not altogether successfully, by Simon, the boy Golding himself has called a saint. More sensitive, more farseeing than the others, Simon has visions and attempts to communicate them to the others, only to be murdered by mistake as the beast. Golding in a conversation with Jack Biles says that Ralph should have been weeping for Simon at the end of the novel, not Piggy.[28] James Baker agrees that "In his martyrdom Simon meets the fate of all saints," and adds, "the truth he brings would set us free from the repetitious nightmare of history, but we are, by nature, incapable of perceiving that truth."[29] There is no way of refuting this from the evidence available in the novel. It may or may not be true. It is not clear. What is clear, however, is that Simon represents for Golding a supernatural world which does exist. As long as it exists, then, there must be hope that we can recognize it, unless to Golding's God we really are as flies to wanton boys. The later novels at least reject this concept of God.

The techniques of *Lord of the Flies* are all designed to move the reader outward to a recognition of the macrocosm of which the situation in the novel is a microcosm. On the simplest level the violence on the island is echoed by constant references to the adult world beyond, to atom bombs, naval cruisers, parents in the various services. This world is represented by the dead parachutist, whom Golding has explained to Frank Kermode, he intended to represent history, the past.[30] The reader is constantly being drawn to compare his disappointment, his horror at the boys' savagery, with the institutionalized savagery of his own world.

The action of the novel is a gradual expansion. Each event foreshadows another or, to put it another way, eventually becomes the event of which it had earlier been an imitation or representation. Everything is, then, seen to be an integral part of everything else, as in all novels of nightmare. The first page of the novel describes the plump boy, Piggy, being caught and scratched by the unfamiliar twigs and thorns on the island. This scene with its suggestion of a trapped, plump animal is echoed by the later scene in which an actual pig is trapped by the boy hunters in the undergrowth. The real significance of such hunting is revealed only in the final scene in which Ralph is hunted by the boys through the thickets. The description of Ralph at this point has overtones of all the earlier hunting scenes: "There was a shout from beyond the thicket and then Ralph was running with the swiftness of fear through the undergrowth. He came to a pig-run, followed it perhaps for a hundred yards, and then swerved off.... Ralph thought of the boar that had broken through them with such ease" (p. 180). Similarly, the episode in which the boys push the rock over the cliff in play gains its full significance when the rock is later dropped on Piggy and kills him; the ritual dance in which all the boys pretend Robert is the pig they have killed and Ralph feels the first desire in him to destroy living flesh culminates in the killing of Simon in a later ritual.

Samuel Hynes comments accurately that Golding's characters, "while they are usually convincing three-dimensional human beings, may also function as exemplars of facets of man's nature—of common sense or greed or will."[31] Golding's ability to create characters which function both realistically and allegorically is illustrated particularly well in *Lord of the Flies*. It is necessary for Golding to establish the boys as "real" children early in the novel—something he achieves through such small touches as Piggy's attitude to his asthma and the boys' joy in discovering Piggy's nickname—because his major thesis is, after all, about human psychology and the whole force of the fable would be lost if the characters were not first credible to us as human beings.

Increasingly, though, Golding shows the children responding differently to the same object or event and the highly patterned nature of these episodes makes it clear that the reader is intended to read them as allegory. Typical are the reactions of Jack, Ralph, and Simon to some evergreen bushes: Simon sees them as candles, associating them and himself with religious services; Ralph, the practical one, points out that they cannot be lit; Jack, concerned as always with eating, first slashes at the buds and then decides they can't be eaten. Golding associates each boy with a certain set of images. Jack is animalistic, "bent double," "dog-like," "naked," "with flared nostrils, assessing the current of warm air for information" (p. 43). Simon becomes increasingly Christlike and is seen helping to feed the "littl'uns." The strength of Golding's characterization lies in the fact that while the reader is led out from the reality of individuals to a wider significance, his initial sense of real people is not lost. When, for example, at the death of Piggy the reader recognizes this is the death of reason or logic, he nevertheless retains the sense of horror at a child's being murdered by other children.

The allegorical aspects of the characterization and the action lead the reader imaginatively into other worlds of the cultural macrocosm. There are, as so many critics have pointed out, innumerable Biblical associations with the Eden myth and many political implications in the democracy/fascism opposition represented in Ralph and Jack. Oldsey and Weintraub, among others, have shown how Golding is in fact answering Ballantyne's boys' adventure story *Coral Island* in *Lord of the Flies*;[32] James Baker relates the novel to classical Greek literature, particularly to Euripides's *The Bacchae*. These critics are, of course, illustrating the same point about Golding's work, that one of its important aspects is its relation to a cultural whole he wishes the reader to perceive.

The final and perhaps most important way in which Golding's techniques dramatize his theme is the metaphorical density of the language itself. Golding describes everything in terms of something else. This is particularly true of his descriptions of natural phenomena. Here Ralph watches the lagoon and imagines its rise and fall as the breathing of a sea creature. The passage is thus related in the reader's mind to the beast the children think is causing their problems on the island and which Ralph is at this moment hunting. It also points up the fact that the violence of nature—albeit their own—is in fact the cause of the breaking-up:

> Ralph shuddered ... Now he saw the landsman's view of the swell and it seemed like the breathing of some stupendous creature. Slowly the waters sank among the rocks, revealing pink tables of granite, strange growths of coral, polyp, and weed. Down, down, the waters went, whispering like the wind among the heads of the forest. There was one flat rock there, spread like a table, and the waters sucking down on the four weedy sides made them seem like cliffs. Then the sleeping leviathan breathed out, the water rose, the weed streamed, and the water boiled over the table rock with a roar. (pp. 97–98)

Golding frequently uses the images of worlds or globes to illustrate his theme of the necessity for relating microcosm to macrocosm. Jack and Ralph walk along like "two continents of experience and feeling, unable to communicate" (p. 49); Ralph examines his bitten nail and watches "the little globe of blood that gathered where the quick was gnawed away" (p. 122). The ability to use metaphor and simile, to perceive relations, is an essential characteristic of the loss of innocence, as Golding makes clear in his second novel, *The Inheritors*. But even though one must perceive things as separate before one can compare them, the act of comparison, of course, is a putting together and thus a sign of hope, of possible salvation from the prison of oneself.

The Inheritors, like *Lord of the Flies*, is concerned with the fall of man and with the loss of innocence. Set in prehistoric times, it tells of the destruction of a Neanderthal tribe and particularly of one member of it, Lok, by a group of "new" men, homo sapiens, led by Tuami. But the new men are not superior to the Neanderthals in much that Golding feels matters; Golding has reversed the notion of history as progress to suggest the notion of history as spiritual decline. The notion he rejects is that represented by H. G. Wells in his *Outline of History*, that Neanderthal man was bestial, hairy, gorilla-like, with possible cannibalistic tendencies. Golding uses a quotation from Wells as an epigraph to the novel and explains it in a conversation with Frank Kermode: "Wells' *Outline* played a great part in my life because my father was a rationalist, and the *Outline* was something he took neat. It is the rationalist gospel in excelsis. . . . By and by it seemed to me not to be large enough . . . too neat and too slick. And when I reread it as an adult I came across his picture of Neanderthal man, our immediate predecessors, as being these gross brutal creatures who were possibly the basis of mythological bad men. . . . I thought to myself that this is just absurd. . . ."[33]

Like the boys in *Lord of the Flies*, at the opening of the novel Lok's people are innocent. They live in a harmonious world, in which, what-ever its physical dangers and difficulties, they are one with each other. Lok takes for granted that "People understand each other" (p. 59), that "it is bad to be alone. It is very bad to be alone" (p. 178). Going away, separation, is an evil for them. On returning to familiar places they are pleased to discover that a stone "has not gone away. It has stayed by the fire until Mal came back to it" and that "the river had not gone away either or the mountains" (p. 20).

They do not need language to communicate but use a form of telepathy or shared pictures. Language apparently carries implica-tions of the separation of name and object, of distortion, that Golding does not wish to assign to the state of innocence. The pictures they share may be less exact, in some ways less useful than language, but they undoubtedly indicate a closer communication. The early scenes of the novel are full of such remarks as: "[Fa] did not need to speak" (p. 2); "as so often happened with the people, there were feelings between them" (p. 4); "without warning, all the people shared a

picture inside their heads" (p. 27). The pictures not only transcend
the barriers among people, but also those between present and future.
After they have found food by following Lok's directions, he says,
"And Lok saw a true picture, Honey for Liku and little Oa" (p. 47).
Lok's people are totally responsible for one another and provide that
sort of warmth and acceptance of each other contemporary sensitivity groups attempt to imitate. After searching for the "new" man,
Lok is welcomed back to the group and restored spiritually through
physical means: "But the strings that bound him to the people were
still there ... they drove in until they were being joined to him, body
to body. They shared a body as they shared a picture. Lok was safe"
(pp. 79–80).

The loss of a log and the disappearance of one of them, Ha, leads
Lok's people to suspect the existence of others in their area. Lok's
ability to relate to another, ironically, makes him "become" a "new"
man through hunting him: "as the smell of cat would evoke in him a
cat-stealth of avoidance and a cat-snarl ... so now the scent turned
Lok into the thing that had gone before him" (p. 64). He learns from
this that the "other" is frightened and greedy, not at one with his
world as are Lok's people. Unlike Lok's tribe, "new" people kill and eat
meat; their sexuality is a form of rape. Lok observes that the mating
of Tuami and the fat woman is a "fierce and wolflike battle" (p. 159).
Tuami's people have already lost their innocence. They are afraid of
the darkness. Golding has written in a letter to John Peter that "God
is the thing we turn away from into life, and therefore we hate and
fear him and make a darkness of him."[34] Tuami's people, then, in their
inability to see beyond themselves, in their sense of being surrounded
by a frightening darkness, have in Golding's terms lost touch with the
macrocosm which is the unity of God.

Lok gradually takes on the characteristics of the "new" people.
Their existence forces him into self-consciousness. He discovers
metaphor. There are now two parts of Lok, inside-Lok and outside-
Lok. After drinking the new people's alcohol, he becomes violent,
snatching at the pot, hitting Fa with a stick. "He found that when
he looked at the trees they slid apart and could only be induced to
come together with a great effort that he was not disposed to make"
(p. 185). He has indeed become, as he says, one of the "new" people.
This connection between Tuami and Lok has already been suggested
by the fact that they both have chestnut hair. The "new people with

their intelligence, violence, and strength supersede the Neanderthals by literally destroying them, but it is also clear that their characteristics are dominant anyway; "Neanderthalness" is dead in Lok before Tuami destroys Lok's people.

The Inheritors is a pessimistic book in the sense that Golding does not show the way to salvation for fallen man. Does he mean hope to lie in the implications of metaphor: "Likeness could grasp the white-faced hunters with a hand, could put them into the world where they were thinkable and not a random and unrelated irruption" (p. 176)? Does he mean it to lie in the brief picture of the two children Tanakil and Liku together? In the hope of unity offered by the baby Neanderthal Tuami's people take with them? It is hard to say. Salvation must lie through the darkness, on its other side, but, like Tuami at the end of the novel, we cannot "see if the line of darkness had an ending" (p. 213).

The Inheritors is a microcosm of the whole of human history. What happens here is repeated in every child as he grows to maturity. Read this way, Golding's view is Wordsworthean in its stress on the loss of childhood vision through self-consciousness, although *The Inheritors*, less than *Lord of the Flies*, emphasizes the paradisiacal elements of innocence. Lok's integration with his world is, however, no different in kind from the boy Wordsworth's in *The Prelude*.

The action of the novel functions in two ways. On the simplest level it traces the separation and death of Lok's people brought about by Tuami's. Mal dies first of a fever brought about by falling in the river; he falls in the river because the "new" people have removed their log bridge. Ha disappears on a hunt for the "new" people. Liku, the little girl, and her baby brother are stolen by Tuami's tribe and Liku is eaten. Fa goes over the waterfall. Finally Lok is alone, separated from his people, and separated from the reader by a sudden shift in point of view at the end of the novel. For the reader the plot is an opening out; his view is, for much of the novel, as limited as Lok's. Golding forces the reader to leap ahead guessing at what Lok cannot see, placing him in the macrocosm of human history. At the end, when the reader suddenly sees Lok from the point of view of Tuami, "a red creature," and "it," he has passed beyond Lok and Tuami both, since he is able to compare them with each other. The novel allows the reader, then, to make the relationship necessary in Golding's view, to transcend the Fall, even if it is not possible for Lok or Tuami.

Golding's descriptions of nature follow the pattern of separation in the plot. At first nature is seen as a harmonious whole; there are numerous images of inclusiveness and expansion:

> Over the sea in a bed of cloud there was a dull orange light that expanded. The arms of the clouds turned to gold and the rim of the moon nearly at the full pushed up among them.... The light crawled down the island and made the pillars of spray full of brightness.... it discovered grey forms that slid and twisted from light to shadow or ran swiftly across the open spaces on the sides of the mountain. It fell on the trees of the forest so that a scatter of faint ivory patches moved over the rotting leaves and earth. (pp. 31–32)

Everything is personified. Lok's people make no distinction between animate and inanimate—flames, stones, logs are as alive as Fa and Liku—and, as the previously quoted passage indicates, neither initially does Golding. As Lok loses his innocence his world becomes one of separate objects, of contrast not similarity: "Ivy and roots, scars of earth and knobs of jagged rock—the cliff leaned over so that the top with its plume of birch was looking straight down on to the island. The rocks that had fallen were still jumbled against the cliff at the bottom and their dark shapes, always wet, contrasted with the grey gleam of the leaves and the cliff" (p. 111).

The avalanche at the end causes this world to crumble and separate even more violently but, if indeed it marks the end of the ice age, as some critics have suggested, then it is also a sign of hope, of a new world. The description of the avalanche contains the two elements; images of separation and disintegration are followed by those of expansion and inclusiveness: "The hyenas lifted their hindquarters off the earth, separated and approached the interior of the hollow from either hand. The ice crowns of the mountains were a-glitter. They welcomed the sun. There was a sudden tremendous noise that set the hyenas shivering back to the cliff. It was a noise that engulfed the water noises, rolled along the mountains, boomed from cliff to cliff and spread in a tangle of vibrations over the sunny forests and out towards the sea" (p. 202).

Golding seems to have talked more about *Pincher Martin* than about any of his other novels. This is probably because of the critical controversy that has arisen about two aspects of the novel: the so-called trick ending, a final chapter in which the reader learns that Christopher Martin, who he had thought was struggling for his life on a rock, has been dead since the first page;[35] and the response to the central character, about whom critics hold diametrically opposed views. Is *Pincher Martin* an Existentialist novel with Pincher an heroic, Promethean figure standing out against death, forging his own identity with his intelligence? Are we to take as good in a Sartrean sense Pincher's awareness that he can have no "complete identity without a mirror" (p. 116), that he has created God in his own image, or not? Certainly it is hard to believe Golding is not consciously concerned with Existentialism here. The passage in which Pincher analyzes his feeling of lost identity, his comments on the way he used mirrors to watch himself as if he were watching a stranger, his use of others to assure himself of his own existence would not be out of place in *The Myth of Sisyphus* or in *Being and Nothingness*. It is difficult, too, for the reader not to feel some respect for the tenacity and courage Pincher displays. Nevertheless, Golding does not think Pincher heroic but presumptuous; critics who judge the experience by Existentialist criteria have, as James Baker points out, "made a hero out of Golding's villain."[36]

Golding makes the significance of *Pincher Martin* clear in some comments in the British BBC publication *Radio Times*:

> Christopher Hadley Martin had no belief in anything but the importance of his own life; no love, no God. Because he was created in the image of God he had a freedom of choice which he used to centre the world on himself. . . . The greed for life which had been the mainspring of his nature, forced him to refuse the selfless act of dying. He continued to exist in a world composed of his own murderous nature. His drowned body lies rolling in the Atlantic but the ravenous ego invents a rock for him to endure on. It is the memory of an aching tooth. . . . He is not fighting for bodily survival but for his continuing identity in the face of what will smash it and sweep it away—the black lightning, the compassion of God.[37]

"To achieve salvation, individuality—the persona—must be destroyed,"[38] Golding has written elsewhere; and it is his individuality that Pincher refuses to surrender. He is physically and spiritually islanded, clinging to his own identity as to his rock. Relieved to find his identity disc around his neck, he shouts, "Christopher Hadley Martin. Martin. Chris. I am what I always was! (p. 68); he survives by shouting, "I am! I am! I am!" (p. 129), knowing only that he "must hang on" (p. 144).

He is nothing but greed, as the flashbacks to his past life reveal; his role of Greed in the morality play is type casting. Everything and everyone is food to feed Pincher Martin and, as he realizes himself, "eating with the mouth was only the gross expression of what was a universal process. You could eat with your cock or with your fists, or with your voice" (p. 79). He is guilty of Golding's greatest sin, self-obsession; he turns everything into himself, just as he has created his own purgatory on the rock. A recurring image in the novel, that of the Chinese box, in which a fish is buried and gradually eaten by maggots who subsequently eat each other, is obviously intended to reflect Pincher's experience: "The big ones eat each other. Then there are two and then one and where there was a fish there is now one huge and successful maggot. Rare dish" (p. 120). Throughout the novel Pincher hears a sound like the knocking of a spade against a tin box.

As in *The Inheritors*, man's intelligence is not seen as a good. Frank Kermode points out that "Golding is fascinated by the evidence—in the nature of the case ubiquitous—that human consciousness is a biological asset purchased at a price."[39] It is possible to go further than this, I think and suggest that for Golding the price is too high and the extent to which it is an asset debatable. It is precisely Pincher's intelligence, as he himself recognizes, that makes the purgatorial experience possible and prevents his surrender to God. Pincher knows that man makes patterns and superimposes them on nature, that he labels objects to control his world, and he uses this talent, apparently, to survive on the rock. But if the struggle for survival is here an evil, then the means used to achieve it are a liability not an asset. Pincher's intelligence has isolated him, kept him in that dream of a dark cellar that haunted his childhood. The last few pages of the novel are dominated by Pincher's recognition of his aloneness: "I'm so alone! Christ! I'm so alone! ... Because of what I did I am an outsider and alone.... Now there is no hope" (pp. 160–161). Hope, however, has already been implied for Pincher in that in his aloneness he has called out, "Christ," even if blasphemously, and in that his next comment is the name of the Christ figure in the novel, his friend Nathaniel.

The scene in Pincher's memory immediately following is one in which he recognizes that the only genuine love he ever felt was for Nat. Once again in a Golding novel salvation lies through love, a reaching out to someone else. It is, of course, too late for Pincher to reach out for Nat now, but he has come to terms with a reality other than himself through a recognition of his place in the pattern. It is important to note that there is an essential difference between recognizing the pattern and imposing it; Golding's distinction is the one made by Burgess in *MF* between creating riddles and solving them. If we can take Nat's words as Golding's, Golding really believes in Vonnegut's ironic Bokononist term "karass": "One is conscious when meeting people that they are woven in with one's secret history. Don't you think?" (p. 138). Pincher has learned how people fit into his secret history.

What is more important he knows that he is not the last maggot, but "the last maggot but one" (p. 163). He recognizes something beyond himself, that there is a God, even if up to the end he is shouting, "I shit on your heaven!" (p. 178). It is not necessary to read the ending of *Pincher Martin* pessimistically. The mouth may be blaspheming but "the centre knew what to do. It was wiser than the mouth" (p. 177). The centre, Pincher's inner core, always described as black, finally merges with the black lightning which is God "in a compassion that was timeless and without mercy" (p. 179). The gap between the island, which is Pincher, and the mainland, which is not, is finally bridged; of course in spite of, rather than with, Pincher's conscious will.

In one sense the apparent experience Pincher Martin undergoes is the macrocosm of which he is actually experiencing the microcosm. The reader is asked to believe that he is in his own head; the rock he imagines he is on is his own tooth. This is a dramatization of Pincher's whole life; he is smaller, less significant than he thinks. Although there are various clues to the fact that Pincher is inside his own head, it is really only on a second reading that this becomes clear. The discovery in the last chapter that Pincher was dead all along comes as a shock, not as a confirmation of suspicions. The clues are frequently in the form of metaphors: Pincher compares his experience to lying "on a rim of teeth in the middle of the sea" (p. 82); he feels as if "the pressure of the sky and air was right inside his head" (p. 141). Much of the metaphoric density of the novel lies in this set of images. But in order for the reader to see these comments as ironic, he already has to know the truth of Pincher's situation. Other clues come in the form of

Pincher's dawning awareness of the familiarity of the rock. He resists recognizing the truth, refuses to connect himself with a reality beyond his illusory world, but the awareness comes to him anyway. At the end of the novel his realization of the nature of his own character, his place in the pattern of his experiences, is paralleled to his realization of the truth about the rock: he "understood what was so hauntingly familiar and painful about an isolated and decaying rock in the middle of the sea" (p. 154).

The pattern the reader, with Pincher, pieces together is the pattern formed by the flashback sequences in Pincher's mind. Memories of his past life: his cuckolding of his friend Alfred, his rape of Mary, his responsibility for Peter's injury, and Nat's death, are each a microcosm of his whole life. He watches them as if they are a film being projected on to the pebbles in front of him. The first picture is of a jam jar on a table which "was interesting because one could see into a little world there which was quite separate" (p. 8). In piecing the separate worlds together, the reader and Pincher come to realize that he is indeed what he always was, and that "an hour on this rock is a lifetime" (p. 40), all the experiences of the book have happened in a moment, but a moment which is the microcosm of a whole life.

The techniques of characterization Golding uses in this novel are very similar to those he uses in *Lord of the Flies*; the characters function midway between realism and allegory. Mary is the girl Pincher rapes and Nat marries, but she is also the Virgin Mary; Pincher's rape of her is presumptuous in terms of the allegory, too, then. He acts as God. Nathaniel is the Christ figure, and his name is always juxtaposed with Christ's in Pincher's exclamations: "Nat! Nathaniel! For Christ's sake! Nathaniel! Help!" (p. 12). Martin, who was baptized Christopher, has destroyed Christ—in the form of Nat—rather than carried him as his name implies and has literally become his nickname, Pincher. But in brief snatches of description or dialogue Golding keeps every character functioning on the human level also, even as the reader is beginning to see the allegorical pattern. Mary remains the rather uninteresting girl with "the remote and unconquered face" (p. 130); Nat, the gentle, concerned friend.

Through allegorical characterization Golding makes the reader relate his microcosmic world of Pincher on the rock to Christian mythology, and through references to Prometheus to Greek mythology also. Oldsey and Weintraub point out the extent to which the reader is invited to relate the novel to a cultural macrocosm, claiming that the book has echoes of Bierce, of Hemingway, of *King Lear*, of *Paradise Lost*, of Eliot, of Conrad, and of a minor adventure story called *Pincher Martin*.[40] As Nat says to Pincher, "our lives must reach right back to the roots of time, be a trail through history" (p. 138). And in a good fable they must be seen to.

Many critics have commented that the title of Golding's fourth novel, *Free Fall*, has both a theological and a scientific significance, but Golding himself has, as usual, expressed it best: "Everybody has translated this in terms of theology; well, okay, you can do it that way, which is why it's not a bad title, but it is in fact a scientific term. It is where your gravity *has gone*; it is a man in a space ship who has no gravity; things don't fall or lift, they float about; he is completely divorced from the other idea of a thing up *there* and centered on *there* in which he lives."[41] Sammy Mountjoy, narrator of *Free Fall*, has more insight and perhaps more conscience than Pincher Martin, but basically his is Pincher's problem. He is islanded, trapped in himself, "completely divorced from the other idea of a thing up there."

There are images of cells everywhere. The whole novel can be read as taking place in a prison cell where Sammy is held by the Germans in World War II. Dr. Halde, his interrogator, tells him, "You do not believe in anything enough to suffer for it or be glad. There is no point at which something has knocked on your door and taken possession of you. You possess yourself" (p. 144). Since he recognizes no reality beyond himself, for Sammy, as for Pincher, other people are merely objects for his use. He knows the way out is to make contact with something beyond himself, to build a bridge; he wants to know what it is like to be Beatrice, for example, but finds himself doomed to isolation: "Our loneliness ... is the loneliness of that dark thing that sees as at the atom furnace by reflection, feels by remote control and hears only words phoned to it in a foreign tongue. To communicate is our passion and our despair" (p. 8).

The novel is Sammy's attempt to build the bridge, to find his place in a reality beyond himself. One way in which he attempts this is to search for the pattern of his own life, particularly for the moment when he lost his freedom. As in *The Inheritors*, loss of freedom is equated with loss of innocence, with self-consciousness; like Lok's people, Sammy begins in Paradise, here a slum area known as Paradise Hill. On looking back he sees himself and his friend Johnny as "two points of perception, wandering in Paradise. I can only guess our innocence, not experience it" (p. 45). As a child he was fully integrated with his world, spontaneous, free, a quality which the best of his later paintings capture. As Kinkead-Weekes and Gregor say, in this novel "Golding is questioning the nature of understanding itself."[42]

Golding establishes a relationship between an understanding of others and an ability to manipulate them. A series of characters in the novel—Philip Arnold, who "knew about people" (p. 49), Miss Pringle, "a past-master of crowd psychology and momentum" (p. 195), and Dr. Halde, Sammy's tormentor at the prison camp—suggests that for Golding, here as elsewhere, the price of understanding can be too high. Sammy's loss of freedom comes when he recognizes that he can make a choice, that he has the power to manipulate events. Told by his headmaster that one can have anything one is prepared to pay the price for, he makes a Faustian bargain for Beatrice Ifor:

> "What is important to you?"
> "Beatrice Ifor."
> "She thinks you depraved already. She dislikes you.
> "If I want something enough I can always get it provided I
> am willing to make the appropriate sacrifice."
> "What will you sacrifice?"
> "Everything." (p. 236)

Sammy attempts to build the bridge from his island also in the sense of trying to find unity in the outer reality. Golding represents the apparent chaos of the world in the two teachers of the young Sammy; Nick Shales, rationalist and scientist, and Rowena Pringle, teacher of religion. Baker believes that at the end of the novel Sammy has not made sense of the dichotomy represented by these two world views, that he has to remain "uncertain, unsatisfied."[43] It is important to remember, though, that as children Sammy and his friends "held both universes in our heads effortlessly" (p. 211), since this indicates that Golding, if not Sammy, believes in a unified reality. There is no need to resolve the paradox; in Paradise there is only harmony. The title of the novel, combining a scientific and a religious significance in one phrase, also suggests this harmony.

As at the end of *Pincher Martin* though, it is possible to accept Golding's belief in a patterned universe without believing Sammy ever finds salvation. Nevertheless, I agree with Oldsey and Weintraub here that an important indication of Sammy's salvation is his cry for help, his willingness to put self aside and recognize "the other idea of a thing up there." However ambiguous the final page of the novel may be, Sammy does leave the cell, his island, and does, like Pincher, receive compassion. The bridge is, after all, love, as Sammy recognizes. Commenting on his treatment in a hospital ward as a child, he writes, "I have searched like all men for a coherent picture of life and the world, but I cannot write the last word on that ward without giving it my adult testimony. The walls were held up by sheer, careful human compassion" (p. 77). The child Sammy, then, who had chosen Nick Shales's irrational world for nonrational reasons, because Nick gave love and Rowena Pringle was cruel, is seen to be right after all. Love is the only truth that matters: "People are the walls of our room, not philosophies" (p. 222).

Although *Free Fall* resembles *Pincher Martin* in that the physical situation of the central character, here a prison cell, is a microcosm of his spiritual life, it is only in terms of its time scheme a fantasy novel. It takes place in recognizably modern times in familiar English places. The novel has been criticized for its lack of a controlling myth; Babb says that in *Free Fall* Golding "would seem to be running a . . . risk; of including materials that do not eventuate in a realized paradigm of meaning."[44] It has been criticized also for the extent to which Sammy comments on his own experience.[45] This, surely, is perfectly defensible given Golding's thematic concerns in this novel. Sammy's desperate desire to communicate, to find a link with an outside reality, is dramatized very well in those passages of commentary directed to the reader. They are not in fact comments upon the action, but rather the essential action of the book itself. As the book progresses and the reader comes closer to Sammy in sharing his search for a pattern, they become fewer in number. Sammy no longer tells the reader at the end, "we share nothing but our sense of division" (p. 10). Sammy's communication with the reader is in itself a sign of health, a bridge built.

For there is a pattern in Sammy's experiences as related in the novel; Hynes is wrong in saying, "the scenes do not compose a myth or fable."[46] The experience of reading *Free Fall* is, like that of reading Golding's other novels, a piecing together of a puzzle, a working from the microcosm to the macrocosm. Each scene of the novel illustrates a paradox: the world of feeling is not parallel to the rational world. Sammy's mother lies to him when he asks who his father was, inventing different stories every time he asks. The little boy is told lies, but emotionally given the truth. His search for his place in the world, which the questions about his father represent, is answered every time his mother shows her love for him. The older girl, Evie, who takes him to school, lies to him too, but holds his hand. When his passion for Beatrice is fulfilled sexually, he feels farther from her than ever; in his head he loves her, but he feels no real emotion. The pattern is clearest, of course, in the conflict between Nick's world and Miss Pringle's: "The beauty of Miss Pringle's cosmos was vitiated because she was a bitch. Nick's stunted universe was irradiated by his love of people" (p. 226).

The existence of a pattern is underscored by parallel events and characters the reader is invited to compare. The boy Sammy laughs at the retarded girl, Minnie, who urinates on the classroom floor; the man Sammy mourns Beatrice who does the same thing on the floor of the hospital. As I mentioned above, Philip Arnold, Rowena Pringle, and Dr. Halde share a knowledge of people enabling them to exploit them. But it is only one side of people, their weaknesses, that they know; love and compassion are unknown to each of these three. The commandant's final comment, "The Herr Doctor does not know about peoples" (p. 253), is in that sense true.

Babb has demonstrated the extent certain paragraphs of the novel turn out to be microcosms of the whole story.[47] The language of *Free Fall* is as dense metaphorically as that of the earlier novels. Here too Golding gives one the sense in which this particular situation is all inclusive; the reader is taken to worlds beyond the novel and is left with the feeling that these worlds may well be infinite. As in other novels of nightmare the reader moves towards infinity. A passage in which Sammy discusses what the Germans wish him to endure in the dark cell literally refers to the possible discovery of a corpse in the center of the room, but has both sexual and religious overtones: "We want you to feel forward over the slope and spread your fingers till you have found the sole of a shoe. Will you go on then, pull gently and find that the sole resists? Will you, under the erected hair in the blindness, deduce without more effort the rigor, the body curled there like a frozen foetus? How long will you wait?" (p. 175). All man's, as well as all Sammy's, experience is here; the womb, sexual intercourse, the search for meaning, death. Golding's language confirms his belief in a unified cosmos.

Oldsey and Weintraub mention literary echoes of Poe's "The Pit and the Pendulum," of Orwell: *1984*, and of *Pincher Martin* but stress that *Free Fall* can be read most successfully as a comment on Camus' *The Fall*: "Golding reverses one of the basic existential tenets: man's position in the universe is not absurd; the universe itself is not; but man's proclivity toward self, toward sin without a concept of atonement, can make him absurd."[48]

The Spire is thematically and technically the culmination of Golding's four earlier novels. Here the central character is Jocelin, Dean of a medieval English cathedral, whose driving ambition is to build a spire taller than any built before. Unlike Sammy Mountjoy and Pincher Martin, he is a religious but not for that reason any less subject to their vices. Like them he sacrifices people—ultimately in Golding's scheme equivalent to selling his soul—to achieve his ambition, justifying it on the grounds that his ambition is a vision of God's will. He uses an adulterous passion between his master builder Roger and the wife of a church official, Pangall, to keep the builder on the job; he prevents Roger from getting work elsewhere; he is responsible for Goody Pangall's death which results from the affair; he allows workmen to die attempting to achieve the impossible; he neglects church services; he makes an unsuitable boy a canon in exchange for his father's gift of timber for the spire. As Jocelin himself puts it at the end, "I traded a stone hammer for four people" (p. 212). He succeeds in manipulating others because he, like Philip Arnold, Rowena Pringle, and Dr. Halde, know how to exploit people. Indeed he takes pride in this fact: "I know them all, know what they are doing and will do, know what they have done" (p. 2). The action of the novel is like the action of *Pincher Martin* and *Free Fall*, that of the central character's gradual discovery of the meaning of his life. Jocelin, too, is islanded, "locked in his head" (p. 83), and looking back says to Roger Mason, "I was driven too. I was in some net or other" (p. 200).

The metaphorical implications of Jocelin's spire are multiple, but the most important is the significance of the spire as a symbol for man's reaching towards another world, in religious terms Heaven, in an attempt to understand it. The building of the spire, then, is a metaphor for Camus' premise that man seeks meaning. When Jocelin climbs the spire, he shouts, "Up here we are free of all the confusion" (p. 96), and on a second climb asks numerous questions: "What's this called? And this?" (p. 139). The movements of the mind are frequently described in terms of climbing: he asks Roger, "What's a man's mind, Roger? Is it the whole building . . . ?" (p. 203); the questions of his confessor "Wormed over him, expanded, became a mountain. He saw to what a height a mind must climb, ladder after ladder, if it were to answer, so he prepared once more to climb" (p. 160).

It is not that the search for meaning is in itself wrong in Golding's terms, but the motive for the search is all important. It may be vision, a true search; it may be presumption, mere will. Jocelin believes he is fulfilling a mission that began when he was first chosen Dean by God. The action of the novel questions this assumption: Jocelin's position as Dean was in fact given him as a sort of joke by his aunt, then mistress of the king; the spire may have inadequate foundations. As T. S. Eliot demonstrates in *Murder in the Cathedral*, the final temptation of the visionary is pride in the vision, and Jocelin is undoubtedly proud. A deacon says, "He thinks he is a saint! A man like that!" (p. 7). The face of the Holy Spirit carved on the spire is to be Jocelin's; he believes his will and God's are synonymous: "You'll see how I shall thrust you upward by my will. It's God's will in this business" (p. 33). For Golding, to forget oneself in another reality is the chief good; it is indeed necessary for salvation. But Jocelin thrusts himself up, makes himself God.

Jocelin clearly comes to realize his folly. He recognizes that God is indeed love—"If I could go back, I would take God as lying between people and to be found there" (p. 210)—and at the end, dying, apparently calls upon God for help as do Sammy and perhaps, although not willingly, Pincher. In this novel Golding answers the problem critics raise about *Free Fall*, that Sammy himself does not fully recognize the unity he seeks. The answer he gives is that of Anthony Burgess and Iris Murdoch, the other novelists of nightmare: some mystery is both inevitable and necessary. "God knows where God may be" (p. 212), says Jocelin at the end. He may indeed mean, as the critics believe, that man cannot find where God is. But the words can also be read more optimistically to mean that even though man does not know where God is, God indeed does.

The confirmation of God's existence comes finally in the vision of the apple tree given to Jocelin before he dies: "His head swam with the angels, and suddenly he understood there was more to the apple tree than one branch. It was there beyond the wall, bursting up with cloud and scatter, laying hold of the earth and the air, a fountain, a marvel, an apple tree" (p. 195). As Babb points out, the tree includes the divine and the secular, the earth and the sky; it "manifests a miraculous totality."[49] But the tree is an apple tree and must carry overtones of the Garden of Eden. The transformed apple tree is a perfect image for Golding's concept of salvation. Man, a child, lives alongside the apple tree in innocence; adult, he eats of its fruit and falls into sin as he gains self-consciousness and knowledge. But knowledge is also the way forward to salvation; man must see that he is part of a macrocosm, that the tree touches earth and heaven. In this way the original sin may be transcended, the tree transformed.

The spire is the symbol around which multiple meanings cluster. It is, as Babb says, both a physical fact in the external world and a presence within Jocelin himself.[50] It is simultaneously church spire, male organ, and Jocelin's will as the metaphorical language of the novel indicates: "The model was like a man lying on his back. The nave was his legs placed together, the transepts on either side were his arms outspread. The choir was his body; and the Lady Chapel, where now the services would be held, was his head. And now also, springing, projecting, bursting, erupting from the heart of the building, there was its crown and majesty, the new spire" (p. 2). It is a microcosm gradually expanding for the reader towards an infinity of meanings, including a paradigm of the action of the novel itself.

The plot, too, is an expansion. Kinkead-Weekes and Gregor point out that "The first four chapters are intensive, the next four extensive, as the tower rises and permits wider and wider views.... But this is only for a time. The cellarage cannot be ignored by climbing into the tower. 'Up here,' 'out yonder,' 'down there,' turn out to be part one of the other."[51] All is seen to be one; "Everything is there at once."

Golding has said that he would prefer his books to be thought of as "myths of total explanation."[52] Like Anthony Burgess and Iris Murdoch, Golding refutes the Sartrean view of man as an alienated being in absurd relation to the universe with what amounts to a leap of faith. He believes that there is meaning, unity, but recognizes this is unprovable. Redemption from the Post-existential dilemma, nevertheless, lies in each man's recognition of his place in the universal scheme. Like Iris Murdoch, he frequently defines this recognition as love. What convinces his reader is not the logic of his argument, but his techniques, those of the novelists of nightmare. He forces the reader outward from the island of a particular situation over the bridges that lead in all directions. Only from the macrocosm can one see that the island is a microcosm of everything else. Golding, as Kermode says, "has found in experience and embodies in his own myths the truths that inform all others."[53]

NOTES

1. *Lord of the Flies* (1954; rpt. New York: Putnam's, Capricorn Books, 1959); *The Inheritors* (1955; rpt. New York: Pocket Books, Cardinal Edition, 1963); *Pincher Martin* (1956; rpt. New York: Putnam's, Capricorn Books, 1962); *Free Fall* (London: Faber and Faber, 1959); *The Spire* (1964; rpt. New York: Pocket Books, Cardinal Edition, 1964); *The Pyramid* (1966; rpt. New York: Harcourt, Brace and World, Harvest Books, 1967). All page references in the text are to the most recent editions listed here.
2. James R. Baker, *William Golding* (New York: St. Martin's Press, 1965), p. 15.
3. Bernard F. Dick, *William Golding* (New York: Twayne, 1967), p. 73.
4. *Ibid.*, p. 74.
5. Baker, p. 24.
6. *Ibid.*, p. 40.
7. Jack I. Biles, *Tal: Conversations with William Golding* (New York: Harcourt, Brace and Jovanovich, 1968), p. 240.
8. Mark Kinkead-Weekes and Ian Gregor, *William Golding: A Critical Study* (New York: Harcourt, Brace and Jovanovich, 1968), p. 240.
9. Biles, p. 102.
10. Dick, p. 99.
11. Quoted by Bernard S. Oldsey and Stanley Weintrub, *The Art of William Golding* (1965; rpt. Bloomington: Indiana Univ. Press, 1968), p. 80.
12. Baker, p. 26.
13. *Ibid.*
14. The confusion of Sammy's statements in *Free Fall* with Golding's own beliefs has been a major problem with critical accounts of the novel.
15. Biles, p. 105.
16. *Ibid.*, p. 41.

17. Howard S. Babb, *The Novels of William Golding* (Columbus: Ohio State Univ. Press, 1970), p. 97.

18. Samuel Hynes, *William Golding* (New York: Columbia Univ. Press, 1964), pp. 4–5.

19. I mean here, of course, the most realistic of the five novels I'm considering.

20. Kinkead-Weekes and Gregor, p. 194.

21. *Ibid.*, p. 241.

22. *Ibid.*, p. 240.

23. Biles, p. 19.

24. Frank Kermode and William Golding, "The Meaning of It All," *Books and Bookmen*, 5 (October, 1959), 9–10.

25. James R. Baker, *William Golding's Lord of the Flies: A Casebook*, ed. James R. Baker and Arthur P. Ziegler, Jr. (New York: Putnam's, 1964), XXIII.

26. *Ibid.*, p. 190.

27. *Ibid.*, pp. 190–191.

28. Biles, p. 12.

29. Baker, *William Golding*, p. 13.

30. *Casebook*, pp. 200–201.

31. Hynes, p. 5.

32. This material is so well known that there is little point in repeating it here. See Oldsey and Weintraub and Carl Niemeyer, "The Coral Island Revisted," *College English*, 22 (1961), 241–245. It is perhaps worth noting that *The Lord of the Flies* reverses a whole tradition of children's adventure stories of the nineteenth and twentieth centuries in which children, bereft of adult supervision, prove themselves morally mature.

33. Frank Kermode, "The Novels of William Golding," *International Literary Annual*, 3 (1961), 11–29.

34. Letter to John Peter, quoted in "Postscript [to 'The Fables of William Golding']," *William Golding's Lord of the Flies: A Sourcebook*, ed. William Nelson (New York: Odyssey Press, 1963), p. 34.

35. The title of the first American edition of the novel, *The Two Deaths of Christopher Martin*, revealed the truth right away.

36. Baker, *William Golding*, p. 38.

37. "Pincher Martin," *Radio Times*, 138 (March 21, 1958), p. 8.

38. Quoted in Archie Campbell, "William Golding: *Pincher Martin*," in *From the Fifties* (BBC, Sound Drama Radio Series), ed. Micheal Bakewell and Eric Evans (London, 1961), p. 34.

39. Frank Kermode, "William Golding," *On Contemporary Literature*, p. 374.

40. Oldsey and Weintraub, p. 76.

41. Biles, p. 81.

42. Kinkead-Weekes and Gregor, p. 165.

43. Baker, *William Golding*, p. 68.

44. Babb, p. 99.

45. Both Hynes and Kermode make this criticism.

46. Hynes, p. 39.

47. Babb, pp. 119 ff.

48. Oldsey and Weintraub, pp. 116 and 121.

49. Babb, p. 161.

50. *Ibid.*, p. 137.

51. Kinkead-Weekes and Gregor, p. 212.

52. *On Contemporary Literature*, p. 369.

53. *Ibid.*, p. 381.

KING LEAR
(WILLIAM SHAKESPEARE)

"The Human Bond, Loosened and Tightened: Ciceronian Sin and Redemption in *King Lear*"
by Scott F. Crider, University of Dallas

For Renaissance England, all ethics were Christian ethics. Shakespeare wrote plays for a culture defined by religious controversy, as the Reformation led Catholics and Protestants in England to quarrel over what their national Christianity should be, but everyone believed that answers to ultimate questions were Christian ones. Shakespeare's audience believed sin and redemption were governed by the Christian Lord and his son, who redeemed humankind from the first sin of Adam. In the world of Shakespeare studies, there was a time when all this went without saying; then, as Jeffrey Knapp has argued, there entered a "secularist bias." According to Knapp, secularist readings cannot fully explain a number of Shakespeare's recurring themes, including sin and redemption.

Yet there is a peculiar feature of most of the plays Shakespeare wrote after 1606, including *King Lear*: There is no mention of either the Lord or Jesus Christ. In fact, most of Shakespeare's imaginative worlds are, in some form or another, pagan. This apparent paganism was due in great part, no doubt, to censorship. In 1606, the Revel's Office, which governed the theaters, established an act to restrain the theater companies from what Andrew Gurr calls "profane oaths," and this act explains "why the pagan gods begin to be called on with more frequency in the drama after this date."[3] The first oath of our play is Lear's "by Apollo," for example (1.1.161), the remaining ones to the other deities of the pantheon. But this reticence to mention the Christian God is also due to the fact that, in Shakespeare's sources, Lear ruled before England was either Roman or Christian,[4] so the play's fictive world is, as one critic argues, governed by syncretist paganism.[5] Yet its gods are specifically Roman. In Medieval and Renaissance Europe, the ancient gods were often used as types for the Christian God, and Apollo was often imagined as a figure for Christ. Even so, the restraint of the law allowed Shakespeare liberty to fashion fictions whose precise mythology and metaphysics are difficult to identify. In *King Lear*, Shakespeare imagines this syncretist paganism through Roman ethical categories inherited from Cicero, even though (at moments) he has characters put Christian pressure on those categories by giving them distinctly Christian diction.

Shakespeare's *King Lear* suggests that the only significant "sin" is to loosen or untie the natural bond of association that joins human beings to each other, what Kent calls "the holy cords atwain / Which are too intrince t'unloose" (2.2.73). The play suggests, as well, that the only "redemption" is to tighten such a loosened bond.[6] Though Kent calls the cords "holy," the play may or may not agree. The gods appear to have nothing to do with the matter; they may even be hostile to human happiness. To be sure, Shakespeare questions how "natural" the bond can be, when characters routinely violate it. But, even if it is only a natural potential without necessary actualization (since human beings are free), the bond between us exists, according to Shakespeare, and it entails duties toward one another. The play's characters continually assume that the bond is natural and loosening or untying it unnatural, and they continually appeal to the duties following from such bonds.[7] Yet Shakespeare's play indicates that people are just as likely, if not more so, to scant such duties; after all, two of Lear's three daughters abuse him. In Shakespeare generally, whatever the foundation of duty—be it human nature or divine grace—human beings share a bond.

Cicero was probably the most important philosopher of the Renaissance, and Ciceronian humanism may very well be the defining characteristic of the period.[8] Cicero was also a philosopher of some achievement, especially in the area of ethics. One of the great ethical problems that he identified and explored is the apparent tension between the honorable and the advantageous—what he calls the honest and the useful. Cicero argues that there is no real tension, and that anything truly advantageous will also be honorable. And his foundation for this belief is a principle of human society, a principle which takes precedence over any advantages apparently adverse to that society, even philosophical speculation itself:

> Now it is not in order to make honeycombs that swarms of bees gather together, but it is because they are gregarious by nature that they make honeycombs. In the same way, but to a much greater extent, men, living naturally in groups, exercise their ingenuity in action and reflection. Therefore unless learning is accompanied by the virtue that consists in protecting men, that is to say in the fellowship of the human race, it would seem solitary and barren. In the same way, if greatness of spirit were detached from sociability, and from *the bonding between humans*, it would become a kind of brutal savagery.[9]

For Cicero, human beings in society share a bond or conjunction: It is strongest within the family, then the polity, yet it extends to all human beings as such. Human justice—the greatest of the shared goods—begins in our shared human nature. All ethical duties are, for Cicero, then, evaluated by their effect upon that social bond or conjunction, without which we become savage, no better than, and perhaps worse than, animals. An added point especially important for drama is this: That bond ought to guide one's speech. As Cicero argues, "[E]loquence embraces those to whom we are joined in social life" (1.156). After all, drama represents human action in the family and the city by giving its characters dialogue—speech within, between, and among those characters who are so very like human beings. Cicero argues in his works on rhetoric that it is speech that makes possible human sociality itself.[10]

Cicero's understanding of the social bond can illuminate a reading of sin and redemption in *King Lear*. The only sin of *King Lear* is the brutal savagery of loosening/untying the human bond between and among family members, other members of clan and polity, and even fellow humans whose only relation to one is shared species, and the only redemption is the tightened/retied bond. As we see, many in the play violate such bonds, but only those who respect or repair them qualify as characters. In Aristotle's *Poetics*, he explains that "[c]haracter is that which reveals moral choice," by which he means that a fictive character is essentially his or her habitual choices.[11] This is true in life, as well, as he explains in his *Nicomachean Ethics*. What is important for our purposes is that a character chooses between and among thoughts, speeches, and actions. However, a mere villain simply *is* unethical. One recognizes no choice since, like the psychopath, he or she has no conscience to determine choice. Self-serving will is all. Accordingly, the play's personages fall into interesting categories. Cordelia and Edgar do not violate the human bond at all, even if they are tempted to do so, but their siblings do, without any ethical deliberation. While Goneril and Regan do not mend their broken bonds, Edmund tries to do so at play's close. The play's central action is Lear's recognition of the tragic error of untying his bond with Cordelia and his attempt to retie it. The play's sub-plot action is Gloucester's untying with Edgar. Kent and the Fool never forsake their duty to Lear, but countless other servants do. While Cornwall is savage, Albany is a relatively just ruler. Those who respect or repair bonds are full characters; those who do not are not—they are mere villains. If characters are like human beings, then villains are like human beings who have given up their humanity and become like animals. Within the play, only redeemed sociality establishes humanity.

Sins against the human bond occur both in the family and in the polity. And, of course, in a monarchy, the two are intimately related. Lear's misguided attempt to have his children compete for his affection, a contest his two elder daughters engage in with zeal, brings a cool reply by his youngest daughter, Cordelia: "I love your majesty / According to my *bond*, no more nor less."[12] Given the political situation and her sisters' villainy, whatever the prudence of Cordelia's response to her father's emotional neediness, Lear's disowning of her loosens and unties their natural bond:

> By all the operation of the orbs
> From whom we do exist and cease to be,
> Here I disclaim all my paternal,
> Propinquity and property of blood,
> And as a stranger to my heart and me
> Hold thee from this for ever. The barbarous Scythian
> Or he that makes his generation messes
> To gorge his appetite, shall to my bosom
> Be as well neighboured, pitied and relieved,
> As thou my sometime daughter. (1.1.112–121)

Because Cordelia would not speak of her love for him as more or less than what is called for by her daughterly bond, Lear "disclaims" his fatherly one with a strange simile: Cordelia will be to him like a barbarian who commits infanticide and cannibalism; neither his daughter nor the barbarian shall receive his neighborliness, pity, and relief. One of the strange qualities of the simile is that Lear is accidently revealing his own sin: an appetite for love that leads him to gorge on his own daughters, since by play's end all three daughters are dead due to his sin of bond-breaking with Cordelia. Later, when his two volubly "affectionate" daughters play psychological ping-pong with him, he calls upon the very bond Cordelia claimed but was inadequate:

> No, Regan, thou shalt never have my curse.
> Thy tender-hafted nature shall not give
> Thee o'er to harshness. Her [Goneril's] eyes are fierce, but thine
> Do comfort and do not burn. 'Tis not in thee
> To grudge my pleasures, to cut off my train,
> To bandy hasty words, to scant my sizes
> And, in conclusion, to oppose the bolt
> Against my coming in. Thou better knowst
> The offices of nature, bond of childhood,
> Effects of courtesy, dues of gratitude. (2.2.359–368)

Lear believes that the familial bond necessitates "offices of nature": ethical duties that follow from the bond. His sin against his bond with Cordelia leads to their sin against theirs with him, and Regan's cold reply indicates that the offices the bond demands will not be executed affectionately, if at all: "Good sir, to the purpose" (370). When Gloucester tries to persuade Goneril and Regan to allow him to take Lear in and protect him from the coming storm, Regan's response is harsh: "O sir, to willful men / The injuries that they themselves procure / Must be their Schoolmasters. Shut up your doors" (492–494). Goneril and Regan treat their father like a child, then even like an animal. The violated bond in the family leads to psychological and political tyranny, which itself leads to self-consuming savagery. This savage violation will so offend Albany's ethical sense that he fears that, if the heavens do not punish their injustice, "Humanity must perforce prey on itself, / Like monsters of the deep" (4.2.51), and the horrors of the play enact just such tyrannical self-consumption.

The violated bond plays out in the subplot, as well. Like Lear, Gloucester abuses his children, first Edmund for his illegitimacy (1.1.1–32), then Edgar for Edmund's slander and plot against him (2.1.78–85). What is interesting for our purposes is that, to defend his own "unnatural" sin against the bond he shares with his father and his half-brother, Edmund invokes nature: "Thou, Nature, art my goddess; to thy law / My services are *bound*" (1.2.1–2, emphasis mine). Against "the plague of custom" that precludes him from inheritance because he is a bastard, Edmund defends the vigorous offspring that come from illicit sexuality as truly "legitimate" (3–21): "Now gods, stand up for bastards" (22). Against the ethical bond of nature that would preclude his unethical schemes, Edmund puts forward another, extraethical power of nature: He violates the bond because he can, contriving the exile of his half-brother (1.2) and cooperating in the blinding, exile, and death of his own father (3.3, 3.5, and 3.7). For Edmund, he *may* do whatever he *can* do. Interestingly, characters treat "nature" as univocally good or bad, but the play sees it as double, depending upon human choice and action. A Ciceronian confidence animates the play's ethical characters; not so its monsters of the deep. Yet the play itself stages both.

Once Lear's bond with his daughters is loose and untied, he real-izes that this bond of sociality is all that distinguishes human beings from the animal kingdom. For all his supposed "madness" in the storm scene (3.3–4), his reflections on poor Tom's nakedness lead him to see that, without the ethical offices necessitated by the human bond, human beings are no longer human: "Unaccommodated man is no more but such a poor, bare, forked animal as thou art" (3.4.105–106). The accommodation Lear discusses here is not simply shelter but indeed all of human culture, which is itself both the condition of possibility for the bond and its reinforcing result. Without the cultural bond of human care, we are animals. Lear questions the natural quality of the bond and its offices, a quasi-Christian recognition that sin may vitiate human nature so fully that only grace can achieve human community: "Is there any cause in nature that make these hard hearts?" (3.6.74–75). After all, if the bond is natural, why and how do people fail to act upon it? Yet *King Lear* represents a world without divine grace (even if characters speak of it [for example, 5.2.4]), so the bond's actualization will require human beings to be and act human. Lear and other characters often interrogate the Ciceronian model from a

Christian perspective, a perspective that the play itself does not fully share. Or, if it does, it is a Christian perspective that must accommodate the Book of Job's recognition that the divine appears sanguine in response to the suffering of the just.[13] If so, short of an apparently indifferent divine, the human bond is all that we have.

Redemptions of the sinned-against human bond also occur in the family. The rebinding of the bond between Lear and Cordelia requires forgiveness for the violated bond: As Lear says to her once she and her army have saved him from his other daughters, "Pray you now, forget and forgive; I am old and foolish" (4.7.83–84). And their moving embrace before her death—"Have I caught thee? / He that parts us shall bring a brand from heaven, / and fire us like foxes" (5.3.21–23)—is a figure for the bond which, though loosened, is tightened through forgiveness for the earlier error of loosening it. By means of the binding embrace, we catch and redeem one another. Forgiveness continues to inform Lear's understanding of his reunion and new life with Cordelia in prison, though that new life will be brief since Cordelia is shortly murdered:

> Come, let's away to prison;
> We two alone will sing like birds i'the cage.
> When thou dost ask me blessing I'll kneel down
> And ask thee forgiveness. So we'll live
> And pray, and sing, and tell old tales, and laugh
> At gilded butterflies, and hear poor rogues
> Talk of court news; and we'll talk with them too—
> Who loses and who wins, who's in, who's out—
> And take upon us the mystery of things
> As if we were God's spies. And we'll wear out
> In a walled prison packs and sects of great ones
> That ebb and flow by the moon. (5.3.8–20)

Lear imagines the mended bond as a new family life for him and his daughter, one sanctioned by the gods. Though "God" is capitalized in First Folio, there is no apostrophe, so we don't know if they are to be "God's spies" or "Gods' spies."[14] Be that as it may, Lear thinks of the mundane eloquence of the mended familial bond—blessing, forgiving, praying, singing, and talking—as the very activities of the bond. Though there is nothing alien to a Christian understanding here, and indeed the first two acts have distinctly Christian resonance, it is also a thoroughly Ciceronian understanding of speech as the human cord of conjunction.

Lear is never reunited with his other daughters, and they remain villains throughout the play until their bitter ends. Nor is Edmund reunited with his father. Like Cordelia, Edgar's bond with his father is mended; unlike Cordelia's with Goneril and Regan, so too is his bond with Edmund. In fact, Edgar's account of his reunion with his father (5.3.180–198) moves a dying Edmund to recognize the force of the bond: "This speech of yours hath moved me, / And shall perchance do good" (198–199). Fewer than fifty lines later, he tries to undo his earlier order to have Lear and Cordelia murdered: "Some good I mean to do, / Despite my own nature" (241–242). He fails and is responsible for one of the greatest horrors of Western literature: Cordelia's death. Yet Edmund is, at the end, moved to mean to do some good. The recognition of the sin of breaking the bond with his father and half-brother inspires him to attempt to act upon his recognition of the bond, not here with a family member, but with a fellow human being. While Goneril and Regan remain villains—like people who fail to discern and act upon the bond—Edmund, a villain almost until the end, becomes a full character—like a person who does discern and act upon human fellowship. It is too late, and Cordelia's death is Lear's final suffering, but Edmund does mean to do some good. Unlike the savage sisters in love with him, he redeems his bond with his species before dying, even if not soon enough to redeem Cordelia from hanging.

The power of the human bond can redeem sins against that bond, but human beings must choose to act upon it. Why and how do we do so? In part, by attending to stories about just such choice and action. Characters in Shakespeare seldom narrate actions the audience has already seen enacted, but Edgar's "brief tale" is a miniature *King Lear*. In response to Albany's questioning, Edgar tells of his disguised reunion with his father:

>   ... and in this habit
> Met I my father with his bleeding rings,
> Their precious stones new lost; became his guide,
> Led him, begged for him, saved him from despair,
> Never—O fault!—revealed myself unto him
> Until some half-hour past, when I was armed,

Not sure, though hoping of good success.
I asked his blessing and from first to last
Told our pilgrimage. But his flawed heart,
Alack, too weak the conflict to support,
'Twixt two extremes of passion, joy and grief,
Burst smilingly. (5.3.187–198)

Edgar's narration of their pilgrimage, of the broken and mended bond, moves even Edmund to goodness. Notice the diction: A "pilgrimage" is a Christian journey, but there is no Christian God here toward whom the characters journey. Be that as it may, if even so monstrous a fictive character as Edmund can be moved by Edgar's narration to late (and, alas, ineffectual) virtue, how shall we respond who have read or seen a dramatic enactment of the play itself? No doubt with imaginative identification and sympathy with the fictive characters. Fictions can assist us in our ethical lives by binding us to fictional characters but only if we look up from the page or leave the theater ready to take up the real bond shared with actual human beings. We must not be men and women of stone, unmoved by such speech to do some actual good. Christian, pagan, or even atheist; in tune with our human nature, or ajar: We must catch one another in a conjunctive embrace that makes us human. Cordelia's imperative to herself in the play's opening is clear: "Love and be silent." She is not silent, but she does love.[15] And so should we. Shakespeare is famously ambiguous about many things in the testament of his poems and plays, but upon our ethical duty to one another, bonded in humanity, tied to each other, our poet-playwright is quite clear: love.[16]

Notes

1. Trans. is from Lloyd B. Berry's *The Geneva Bible: A Facsimile of the 1560 Edition* (Madison: U of Wisconsin P, 1969), 1.7, emphasis mine.
2. *Shakespeare's Tribe: Church, Nation, and Theater in Renaissance England* (Chicago: U of Chicago P, 2002), 2.
3. *The Shakespearean Stage, 1574–1642* (Cambridge: Cambridge UP, 1992), 76.
4. Geoffrey Bullough, ed. *Narrative and Dramatic Sources of Shakespeare*, Vol. 7 (New York: Columbia, 1973), 269–420.

5. See William R. Elton's *"King Lear" and the Gods* (San Marino, California: The Huntington Library, 1966), where he concludes that the play, "despite its Christian allusions, is intentionally more directly a syncretically pagan tragedy" (338). Although I agree that the play is pagan, its characters' Christian diction puts some pressure on that characterization.

6. Kent's use of the word "cord" for the bond indicates that Cordelia's own name—whose etymological history usually isolates "heart" in Latin and French—might also come from "cord" in Greek, Latin, and French: string or rope, including the string of an instrument. See *The Oxford English Dictionary*, A.1. The character herself, then, figures and acts upon the heart's knowledge of the bond.

7. For an astute discussion of "nature" in the play, see Paul Cantor's "Nature and Convention in *King Lear*" in *Poets, Princes, and Private Citizens*, ed. Joseph M. Knippenberg and Peter Augustine Lawler (Lanham, Md.: Rowan and Littlefield, 1996), 213–233.

8. For the classic account, see Jerrold Seigel's *Rhetoric and Philosophy in Renaissance Humanism: The Union of Eloquence and Wisdom, Petrarch to Valla* (Princeton: Princeton UP, 1968).

9. Trans. is from Cicero, *On Duties*, ed. M.T. Griffin and E.M. Atkins (Cambridge: Cambridge UP, 1991), 1.157, emphasis mine.

10. See H.M. Hubbell's Loeb ed. of *De inventione* (Cambridge: Harvard UP, 1993), 1.2, and E.W. Sutton and H. Rackam's ed. of *De oratore* (Cambridge: Harvard UP, 1988), 1.5. In both works, Cicero provides a myth of the first orator whose language brings people together into community.

11. Trans. is from Aristotle, *Poetics*, ed. and trans. Stephen Halliwell (Cambridge: Harvard UP, 1995), 53.

12. All references to the play are to R.A. Foakes' Arden ed. (Victoria, Australia: Thomas Nelson and Sons, Ltd., 1997), 1.1.92–93. Hereafter, cited internally.

13. For an interesting discussion of the play from this perspective, see Steven Marx's *Shakespeare and the Bible* (Oxford: Oxford UP, 2000), 59–78, although Marx is not as acute on the terror of the Book of Job as Harold Bloom is in *Shakespeare and the Invention of the Human* New York: Penguin, 1998), 476–515, esp. 477.

14. I have left F's punctuation-less version in my quotation. For an investigation of the different texts of the play, see Gary Taylor and Michael Warren's *The Division of the Kingdoms: Shakespeare's Two Versions of "King Lear"* (Oxford: Oxford UP, 1983).

15. On the topic of love, see Stanley Cavell's "The Avoidance of Love: A Reading of *King Lear*" in *Disowning Knowledge in Six Plays of Shakespeare* (Cambridge: Cambridge UP), 39–123.

16. I would like to thank two colleagues and fellow Shakespeareans, Andrew Moran and Gerard Wegemer, who offered timely, helpful comments on a draft of this essay. It is dedicated to my sister, Paige Weed.

MOBY-DICK
(HERMAN MELVILLE)

"Sin and Redemption in Melville's *Moby-Dick*: The Humaneness of Father Mapple"
by Robert C. Evans,
Auburn University at Montgomery

No one interested in the topics of sin and redemption in Herman Melville's *Moby-Dick* should overlook the famous sermon by Father Mapple, which is the focus of chapters seven and eight of Melville's epic masterpiece. Nowhere else in the book are such words as "sin," "sinners," "sinful," and "redemption" used more frequently than in Mapple's sermon; indeed, such terms are employed extremely sparingly elsewhere in the novel. It makes sense, of course, that a Christian minister preaching a sermon should use this kind of language, but in a book that deals so strikingly and obsessively with moral and even religious issues, one might have expected such words to turn up far more often in later chapters than in fact they do. Mapple's sermon, then, is significant partly because it deals so openly and so insistently with ethical issues in general and with matters of sin and redemption in particular. After all, matters of ethics and morals, as well as questions concerning man's relationship with God, are key themes raised by the novel as a whole, and they are central to the sermon. The sermon is also important because it comes so early in the book, because its topics seem highly relevant to the later plot of the novel, and because the focus of the sermon—the experiences of the biblical Jonah—is so obviously relevant to the experiences of two of the novel's major figures: Ishmael (the narrator of the text) and Captain Ahab (who is arguably the book's tragic hero).

Few analysts dispute the thematic significance of Father Mapple's sermon. Howard P. Vincent long ago asserted that "Melville undoubtedly intended" that the sermon "should be the vehicle for the central theme of *Moby-Dick*," and Vincent further contended that *Moby-Dick* remains philosophically "closed to us until we understand Father Mapple's sermon on Jonah and the Whale. With this key Melville unlocked his novel" (70). Yet the meanings of the sermon, as well as the attitudes we should adopt toward Mapple, have long been disputed. For some readers, the sermon—which concerns Jonah's initial refusal to serve God as a prophet, his consequent effort to flee from God, the punishment he suffered as a result of his flight, and his eventual repentance and redemption—stands as an eloquent and trustworthy account of the dangers of sin and pride and the rewards of humility, obedience, repentance, and virtue. Tyrus Hillway, for instance, praises "the beautiful and moving discourse of Father Mapple" and sees it as an implied indictment of the sinful, ungodly behavior of Captain Ahab (26). Likewise, D.B. Lockerbie asserts that Melville expresses the "essence" of his novel "through the lips of Father Mapple" (qtd. in Paffenroth 113). John Paul Wenke suggests that "Ishmael not only speaks of Mapple with awe and reverence but affirms Christian orthodoxy" (126), while Joel Porte describes Mapple himself as a noble figure (209). In an important early biography, Newton Arvin also saw Mapple as a reliable moral guide. Arvin claimed that even if Melville did not necessarily endorse the precise Christian teachings of Father Mapple, his novel could be read as supporting Mapple's basic point that "one might arrive at a kind of peace by obeying" nature, if not exactly by obeying the Christian God himself. Clearly Arvin assumes that Melville respects Mapple, and Harold Bloom likewise calls Mapple "[a]dmirable," although Bloom is quick to note that "we need not conclude (as so many critics do) that Melville chooses Mapple's stance over Ahab's" (163).

Fewer and fewer recent critics, in fact, do now conclude that Melville endorses Mapple. Indeed, more and more analysts see Melville's attitude toward the sermon (and its preacher) as ironic and even sarcastic. According to increasing numbers of readers, Melville mocks Mapple and satirizes his teachings. This ironic reading of the sermon had been sketched out as long ago as 1952 in Lawrance

Thompson's famous book *Melville's Quarrel with God*, and it has been developed and elaborated many times since then. Thompson argued that Melville's own viewpoint in *Moby-Dick* "represents a sarcastic and sneering burlesque of Christian doctrine," and, specifically, that "Father Mapple's sermon on Jonah and the whale is also ridiculed and burlesqued" (163). Many later commentators have agreed. In 1953, for instance, Henry A. Murray asserted that Ahab's "self-assertive sadism" is matched by the "masochistic submission" preached by Father Mapple (10). Likewise, in 1971, Ray B. Browne condemned Mapple as himself a kind of "fanatical" and "religious Ahab" (50), while in 2003 Michael T. Gilmore also saw Mapple, like Ahab, as a dangerous "fanatic for truth" (88). Many critics now see Mapple as at least as destructive as Ahab, and in fact some see Ahab as the more admirable figure of the two. Robert Milder, for instance, has recently asserted that "*Moby-Dick* does more to vindicate Ahab than it does Mapple" (106).

A response to Mapple's sermon is important to any effort to understand sin and redemption in *Moby-Dick*. If we take Mapple and his words seriously, it is easy to see them as implying a negative evaluation of the pride, sin, and lack of redemption of Captain Ahab. If, on the other hand, we assume that Melville is mocking Mapple and his sermon, then Mapple can be seen as at least as bad as Ahab and perhaps even worse. Indeed, Ahab can even be seen as a far more noble and heroic figure than Mapple, who can be regarded either as a fool or a charlatan, either as self-deceived or as deliberately deceptive.

Recent attacks on Mapple may have gone too far, and the old preacher is a more admirable figure than many commentators have been willing to concede. Abundant evidence (which tends to be overlooked in recent interpretations) suggests that Mapple is not as bad as (or even worse than) Ahab and that, in fact, Mapple expresses values ratified by the novel as a whole. These values may not necessarily be the strictly Calvinist Christian values that Mapple sometimes articulates, but those are hardly the only values Mapple endorses. Even more striking than Mapple's Calvinism (which is mentioned only briefly) is his fundamental humanism—his concern for the good of other people, especially the poor and downtrodden. Mapple lingers in the mind as one of the most fundamentally decent, compassionate, and humane figures in *Moby-Dick*, and it is his humanity and humaneness that both Ishmael and Melville seem to find attractive. Mapple is indeed concerned with sin, but he is just as concerned with redemption. Mapple is undoubtedly concerned with serving God, but he is also concerned with treating one's fellow humans with dignity, compassion, mercy, and respect. The fundamental humaneness of Father Mapple and his teachings tends to be overlooked in recent criticism, but it is that humaneness (combined with his own humility) that makes him, finally, a far more admirable figure than Ahab.

One initial point worth emphasizing about Ishmael's decision to visit Father Mapple's chapel is that he goes voluntarily; he feels no pressure to attend the service. If Melville had wished to present Father Mapple ironically, he could easily have made Ishmael's attendance somehow enforced or compelled. Likewise, although William V. Spanos (one of Mapple's severest recent critics) continually insists that Mapple's sermon is "not addressed to a general public" but rather to a motley collection of disreputable cast-off sailors whom Mapple apparently tries to control and manipulate (99), Melville in fact goes out of his way to emphasize the large proportion of women in attendance, including many "sailors' wives and widows" (*MD* 39). Some of these women and widows who attend Father Mapple's church are apparently wealthy enough to have been able to afford to pay for the placement of commemorative stone "tablets" to memorialize their lost loved ones (39). Mapple's congregation, in short, seems more broadly representative of humanity as a whole than Spanos admits, and it is worth emphasizing again that all the people present to hear Mapple's sermon choose to attend his church.

In fact, when Mapple finally appears, Ishmael makes it obvious that the old preacher is a well-respected man who has earned the admiration in which he is widely held. If Melville had intended to make Mapple a tyrannical Calvinist manipulator, he could easily have done so much more clearly. Instead, Mapple is described as "a man of a certain venerable robustness"—a "fine old man" who is "a very great favorite" among the "whalemen" themselves (42). It is always possible, of course, that these sturdy whalemen have been deceived by a cunning old fraud, but, if that is the case, neither Melville nor Ishmael offers much evidence. Instead, Ishmael stresses that Mapple had himself "been a sailor and harpooneer in his youth" but that he now "for many years past had dedicated his life to the ministry" (42). The phrase "dedicated his life" may, of course, be sarcastic and satirical, and, if it were obvious that Mapple were making a handsome financial profit from his ministry, suspicions of sarcasm and satire might seem warranted. At no point, however, does Melville imply that Mapple is wealthy, and indeed the old man doesn't even bother to pass the collection plate before or after his sermon. In fact, when Mapple comes into the chapel from a raging storm outside, Ishamel is careful to note that "he carried no umbrella, and certainly had not come in his carriage" (42). His simple outer garments are dripping with rain, but Mapple himself is described in ways that link him with energy, vitality, and strength: "Father Mapple was in the hardy winter of a healthy old age; that sort of old age which seems merging into a second flowering youth, for among the fissures of his wrinkles, there shone certain mild gleams of a newly developing bloom—the spring verdure peeping forth beneath February's snow" (42). Critics who want to link Mapple with Ahab because both are old men (Gilmore 88) need to explain why Ishmael describes Mapple as such a vital and attractive old man. Mapple does resemble Ahab in age, but in most other respects the contrasts between the two men is very striking. Mapple seems to symbolize life, whereas Ahab is repeatedly linked with death long before his maniacal pursuit of the white whale leads to destruction for himself and most of his crew.

One charge commonly leveled against Mapple is that he separates himself from his congregation, not only by climbing up a ladder into his pulpit but then by pulling the ladder up after him. He is thus, allegedly, in a smugly superior position—a position that allows him, both literally and figuratively, to look down on his congregants. According to Spanos, Father Mapple can now "panoramically survey and speak the Word to his congregation of seamen, or errant sinners, with immunity" (93), while according to Bainard Cowan, "the sanctimoniousness of this staged allegory ... places the man performing it in a privileged, even inaccessible, position to the rest of mankind" (82). There are serious problems with such claims. But, before discussing those problems, it seems worth mentioning that some critics are also bothered when Ishmael reports that Mapple, before beginning his sermon, "ordered the scattered people [in the congregation] to condense" (*MD* 44), as if he is already behaving like a tyrant. But Ishmael is careful to note that Mapple issues his orders "in a mild voice of unassuming authority," and the actual words Mapple uses are clearly comic: "Starboard gangway, there! side away to larboard—larboard gangway to starboard! Midships! midships!"

(44). Melville and Ishmael obviously have a sense of humor, and so, perhaps, does Mapple himself, but this may be less true of some of Mapple's critics.

The charge that Mapple adopts a condescending tone toward his congregants is difficult to support. Repeatedly, Mapple speaks to them as "shipmates" (45), and in fact he uses that term eighteen different times in his sermon, also once addressing them as his "friends" (48). Nowhere else in *Moby-Dick* is the term "shipmate" used so often, especially by a single character, and not once, of course, does the truly tyrannical Ahab address his fellow-sailors with that sense of comradeship and familiarity. It is certainly possible to claim that Mapple's repeated use of the term "shipmates" (along with such other oft-repeated words as "we," "us," "our," "ourselves," etc.) may merely be a calculated, insincere rhetorical ploy, but, if it is, Melville (or Ishmael) obviously could have made that possibility clearer. Instead, Mapple truly seems to regard his congregation as his brothers and sisters—as people with whom he has much in common, including many of the same foibles, flaws, and sins. Mapple repeatedly demonstrates a kind of humility that is utterly lacking in Ahab (except in a few vulnerable moments, such as his interactions with Pip). Mapple proclaims that the story of Jonah is "a lesson to us all as sinful men, and a lesson to me as a pilot of the living God. As sinful men, it is a lesson to us all" (45). Later, near the conclusion of the sermon, Mapple again declares—after "bowing his head lowly, with an aspect of the deepest yet manliest humility" (49)—that "I am a greater sinner than ye" (50), and later still he proclaims, "woe to him who, as the great Pilot Paul has it, while preaching to others is himself a castaway" (50). Mapple, in other words—unlike Ahab—shows himself willing to judge himself, find himself wanting, confess his flaws, and, even more important, submit himself to the judgment of others (including not only his congregants but also God). He lacks the kind of horrific egotism that makes Ahab such an intriguing, but also such a tragic, destructive, and self-destructive figure. No one ever suffers or dies as a result of listening to Mapple's sermons, and thus it seems a strange kind of moral equivalence to claim that because "Ahab is as faithful to his conception of God as Mapple is to *his*," within "the fictively realized world of *Moby-Dick*, it is hard to condemn Ahab as morally or spiritually wrong" (Milder 105).

Mapple's sermon, in fact, suggests plenty of reasons to think that Ahab is indeed morally wrong, if not also spiritually. In other words, whether or not Melville and/or Ishmael endorses Mapple's view of the Christian God, they almost certainly agree with Mapple's assumptions about common human decency—a decency largely lacking in Ahab. Ahab tends to think of his crew merely as instruments to use and exploit in pursuing his own selfish designs; Mapple, on the other hand, repeatedly shows a genuine concern for his fellow human beings, especially for the poor and downtrodden. Thus, Mapple condemns the captain of the ship on which Jonah pays for refuge as a man "whose discernment detects crime in any, but whose cupidity exposes it only in the penniless. In this world, shipmates" (Mapple continues) "sin that pays its way can travel freely, and without a passport; whereas Virtue, if a pauper, is stopped at all frontiers" (47). Thus, if Spanos is correct in thinking that Mapple's congregation is made up mainly of poor and exploited sailors, it is no wonder that Mapple's congregants respect him. He not only speaks up on behalf of the poor and disadvantaged, but (as we shall see) he even regards such outspokenness as one of the prime obligations of a true Christian preacher. Mapple condemns Jonah's cupidinous captain, just as he later calls for condemnation of any captains of this earth who exploit and manipulate their fellow creatures.

Much of what Mapple says about Jonah and the other men aboard Jonah's ship reflects favorably on Mapple himself. When Mapple repeatedly emphasizes Jonah's troubled "conscience," he implies that he himself considers a clear conscience important. Likewise, when he praises Jonah for being "self-condemning" (46), Mapple suggests that he himself is capable of similar self-condemnation. In addition, when Mapple describes the subject of his sermon as "poor Jonah" (48), he shows that he is not only capable of condemning Jonah's sins but is also capable of treating a sinner with tenderness and compassion. Similarly, when Mapple praises the pity and mercy that the other sailors on the storm-tossed ship eventually show Jonah (49), he shows his own capacity for mercy and pity. Jonah (in Mapple's account) feels conscience-stricken because his presence on the ship has put the other men in danger of death, and so the "wretched Jonah cries out to them to take him and cast him forth into the sea, for he knew that for *his* sake this great tempest was upon them" (49). Yet the men do not immediately sacrifice Jonah (as might have been expected);

instead, "they mercifully turn from him, and seek by other means to save the ship" (49)—conduct that Mapple obviously admires. Only when it becomes clear that God will not be satisfied until Jonah is cast overboard do the men "not unreluctantly" lay hold of him (49). Both Jonah and his shipmates, in other words, show far more concern and compassion for their fellow men than Ahab ever does. Jonah is willing to risk his life to save his "shipmates," and his shipmates are willing to risk their own lives to try to save Jonah. Ahab, however, rarely deviates from his egocentric, monomaniacal, and destructive course.In the end, he destroys not only himself but the lives of almost his entire crew. Whether Ahab sins against God is unclear, because it is unclear whether God exists. However, that Ahab sins against his fellow human beings (including his own wife and child) is hard to deny. Mapple, devoted as he obviously is to the Christian God, seems just as clearly devoted to humane compassion for other persons.

It is this sense of compassion that motivates the most controversial portion of Mapple's sermon: its conclusion, in which he seems most obviously to speak as a fire-and-brimstone Calvinist preacher. In that conclusion, Mapple declares, "Delight is to him, who gives no quarter in the truth, and kills, burns, and destroys all sin though he pluck it out from under the robes of Senators and Judges" (51). Such language might indeed be disturbing if it were literal—if Mapple were calling for the actual killing, burning, and destruction of sinners. He is, however, speaking only metaphorically; he is calling for the destruction of sin (including, as he has made abundantly clear, his own), not sinners. He has already shown, in his discussion of Jonah, his willingness to condemn sin while forgiving the sinner, and the point of his final words is not to unleash literal destruction on sinful people but to urge his listeners—and himself—to remain true to their spiritual and moral principles. When Mapple proclaims "a far, far upward, and inward delight" to anyone "who against the proud gods and commodores of this earth, ever stands forth his own inexorable self" (51), he implicitly sanctions both a rejection of, and a rebellion against, proud and tyrannical persons like Ahab. He implicitly condemns any oppressors and exploiters of the poor and downtrodden. He vows his determination (as the cliché has it) to "speak truth to power." He speaks partly as a man of God, but he speaks also as a man of the people, and it is his basic humanity rather than his particular theology that both Ishmael and Melville seem to admire.

One needn't assume that Ishmael accepts every single detail of Mapple's religious beliefs in order to argue that Mapple does provide a basic moral touchstone by which the behavior of many other characters—especially Ahab—can be judged. Clearly Ishmael comes to admire Queequeg even more than he admires Mapple, and Ishmael even participates with Queequeg in worshipping the latter's little wooden God. Mapple, assuredly, would not approve, but this is no reason to assume that either Ishmael or Melville entirely rejects Mapple or all of his teachings. Ishmael learns, both from Mapple and from Ishmael, how to appreciate, value, love, and forgive his fellow man. It is mostly from Ahab that he unfortunately learns the brutal power of destructive hate and unremitting vengeance.

WORKS CITED OR CONSULTED

Arvin, Newton. *Herman Melville*. 1950. New York: Grove Press, 2002.

Bloom, Harold. *The Epic*. Philadelphia: Chelsea House, 2005.

Browne, Ray B. *Melville's Drive to Humanism*. Lafayette, IN: Purdue University Studies, 1971.

Cowan, Bainard. *Exiled Waters: Moby-Dick and the Crisis of Allegory*. Baton Rouge: Louisiana State University Press, 1982.

Gilmore, Michael T. *Surface and Depth: The Quest for Legibility in American Culture*. New York: Oxford University Press, 2003.

Hillway, Tyrus. "A Preface to *Moby-Dick*." *Moby-Dick Centennial Essays*. Ed. Tyrus Hillway and Luther S. Mansfield. Dallas: Southern Methodist University Press, 1953. 22–29.

Melville, Herman. *Moby-Dick: An Authoritative Text*. Ed. Harrison Hayford and Hershel Parker. New York: Norton, 1967.

Milder, Robert. *Exiled Royalties: Melville and the Life We Imagine*. New York: Oxford University Press, 2006.

Murray, Henry. A. "In Nomine Diaboli." *Moby-Dick Centennial Essays*. Ed. Tyrus Hillway and Luther S. Mansfield. Dallas: Southern Methodist University Press, 1953. 3–21.

Paffenroth, Kim. *In Praise of Wisdom: Literary and Theological Reflections on Faith and Reason*. New York: Continuum, 2004.

Porte, Joel. *In Respect to Egotism: Studies in American Romantic Writing*. Cambridge: Cambridge University Press, 1991.

Spanos, William V. *The Errant Art of Moby-Dick: The Canon, the Cold War, and the Struggle for American Studies*. Durham, NC: Duke University Press, 1995.

Thompson, Lawrance. *Melville's Quarrel with God*. Princeton, NJ: Princeton
    University Press, 1952.
Vincent, Howard P. *The Trying-out of* Moby-Dick. Boston: Houghton Mifflin,
    1949.
Wenke, John Paul. *Melville's Muse: Literary Creation and the Forms of
    Philosophical Fiction*. Kent, OH: Kent State University Press, 1995.

THE SHORT STORIES
OF FLANNERY O'CONNOR

"Light and Enlightenment in Flannery O'Connor's Fiction"
by Patricia D. Maida,
in *Studies in Short Fiction* (1976)

INTRODUCTION

In her reading of O'Connor's short stories, Patricia D. Maida declares, "The momentum of Flannery O'Connor's fiction is basically hopeful in assessing man's limitations amid the constant possibility of redemption. Although man is thwarted by his lack of vision, the light remains a hovering presence–ready to pursue, if necessary, the recalcitrant. The process of enlightenment, so basic to O'Connor's works, is reinforced by natural imagery–through the tree-line, the sun, and the color purple." Thus, Maida describes how natural imagery signifies the spiritual experience of O'Connor's characters as they sin and are redeemed.

Vision functions as the dynamic principle in Flannery O'Connor's fiction. From her first novel *Wise Blood*, through *The Violent Bear It Away*, and in both collections of short stories, O'Connor portrays

Maida, Patricia D. "Light and Enlightenment in Flannery O'Connor's Fiction." *Studies in Short Fiction* 13 (Winter 1976): 31–36.

characters who are morally blind.[1] Her people project their true selves through the physical qualities of their eyes—through color, shape, and intensity. And their perception of the world is controlled by their limited powers of sight. The reader enters this world through the eyes of the characters, experiencing an environment fraught with extraordinary signs in the form of natural imagery. Among the recurring images a triad dominates: the tree-line, the sun, and the color purple. Essentially, the tree-line suggests a delineation between the known and the unknown; the sun reflects light or enlightenment; and the color purple indicates bruising and pain. But on the metaphysical level, this triad represents an existential awareness and a spiritual process.

The prototype of the O'Connor hero, Haze Motes of "Wise Blood," embodies the very essence of the problem common to O'Connor's protagonists—moral blindness, self-deception. As Stanley Edgar Hyman points out in his study of the novel, "Haze" indicates lack of clarity and "Motes" is a term used to describe particles in the eye.[2] The focus on vision is reinforced by the impression of a stranger who meets Haze Motes: "[His eyes] were the color of pecan shells and set in deep sockets. . . . Their settings were so deep that they seemed . . . almost like passages leading somewhere . . ." (WB, pp. 10–11). As the imagery suggests alienation has prevented Motes from achieving his potential; the depth of his personality remains blocked within the shell he has maintained. Finally realizing his folly, Motes blinds himself in the belief that "if there's no bottom in your eyes, they hold more" (WB, p. 222). Although he believes in the possibility of attaining truth, Motes is stung by the irony of having eyes that really do not see—much like the classical Oedipus. Illumination comes to him ultimately because he is forced to look within himself.

The focus on the eyes of the characters not only provides greater insight for the reader, but it also increases the reader's awareness of the conflict between individual perception and truth. For example, in "A Good Man Is Hard to Find," an escaped convict wears silver-rimmed spectacles that make him look rather scholarly and calculating. But when he removes them, the facade is gone: his eyes are "red-rimmed and pale and defenseless looking" (GM, p. 143). At this point the reader's sympathy is redirected from the old woman the man is about to kill to this man himself—an escaped convict, a social outcast known only as the "Misfit." By assuming the objective point of view, O'Connor the narrator focuses closely on the telling details, especially the eyes of the characters and other elements that will inform the reader: "For the writer of fiction, [according to O'Connor] everything has its testing point in the eye, an organ which eventually involves the whole personality. . . ."[3] One gains a sense of the emotional disorder affecting the villain in "A Circle in Fire" by the distortion in his vision: " . . . his gaze seemed to be coming from two different directions at once as if it had [other people] surrounded" (GM, p. 218). And in "Good Country People," Hulga, a highly educated young woman has eyes that are "icy blue, with the look of someone who has achieved blindness by an act of the will and means to keep it" (GM, p. 244). This self-imposed blindness prevents her from seeing the truth and allows her to be duped by a salesman who has eyes "like two steel spikes" (GM, p. 260). One gains some insight into personality and character through the eye imagery, and also a judgmental perspective on motivation and behavior.

Vision controls not only the way a person views himself and others, but also the way he perceives nature. One of the recurring images O'Connor employs from the natural environment is the "tree-line," a demarcation of what is immediate to a character's experience and that which lies beyond. Sudden consciousness of the tree-line on the part of a character foreshadows an impending crisis. For example, in "The Violent Bear It Away" when the protagonist becomes obsessed with the desire to baptize the child who accompanies him on a boat ride, he becomes hypersensitive to the environment: "It [the lake] lay there, glass-like, still, reflecting a crown of trees and an infinite overarching sky" (V, p. 167). Later, when he goes through a traumatic experience, he notices the tree-line again: "Planes of purpling red above the tree-line stretched back like stairsteps to reach the dusk" (V, p. 238). The staircase image above the tree-line indicates a change in his outlook, allowing him to reach above and beyond his limitations. In "The Enduring Chill," a foreshadowing of movement beyond the hero's narrow experience occurs as he looks at the horizon: "The sky was a chill gray and a startling white gold sun, like some strange potentate from the east, was rising beyond the black woods that surrounded Timberboro" (ETR, p. 82). Here, the woods mark the limits of his experience, but the sun implies light and movement beyond the limits.

Sun images work along with the tree-line images to convey impending light or enlightenment. In an O'Connor story the intensity of the sun is most acute at the point where the hero is suddenly enlightened, having experienced a moment of truth—a process like James Joyce's epiphany. For example, in "Greenleaf" when the heroine has a prophetic dream, she begins to see her environment differently:

> She became aware after a time that the noise was the sun trying to burn through the tree-line and she stopped to watch, safe in the knowledge that it couldn't, that it had to sink the way it always did outside of her property. When she first stopped it was a swollen red ball, but as she stood watching it began to narrow and pale until it looked like a bullet. (ETR, p. 47)

Just before the crucial moment—the point where she is gored by the very bull she had hoped to destroy—the sun becomes so intense that she closes her eyes. In her last moments of life, the victim of an ironic sacrifice, she perceives a radical change: "the entire scene in front of her changed—but the tree-line was a dark wound in a world that was nothing but sky—and she had the look of a person whose sight has suddenly been restored but who finds the light unbearable" (ETR, p. 52). The strength of the sun is not only a reflection of the illumination occurring in the psyche of the character; it also highlights the source of power—truth and Divine intervention. This intervention is obvious in the coercive force given the sun in the following images. In "The Life You Save May Be Your Own," Mr. Shiftlett is literally pursued by the sun as it "began to set directly in front of the automobile" which he is driving (GM, p. 109). In "Parker's Back" at the moment when Parker has an accident that changes the course of his life "the sun, the size of a gold ball, began to switch regularly in front to behind him, but he appeared to see it both places as if he had eyes in the back of his head" (ETR, p. 242). In each instance the light is the dynamic force.

The red-golds of the sun contrast with the purple tones of the imagery surrounding the moment of enlightenment. Purple suggests bruising, pain, and self-abnegation—it is always part of the process of change depicted in an O'Connor story. Thus in "Greenleaf" when Mrs. May decides to destroy her nemesis, "The sky was creased with thin red and purple bars and behind them the sun was moving slowly as if it were descending a ladder" (ETR, p. 45). Mrs. May is about to experience physical and psychological pain as she is forced to come to terms with the truth. In some of O'Connor's fiction the purpling effect is seen in natural imagery; in others, it is visible in the physical person of the individual character. The heroine's face turns purple in "Good Country People" when she is tricked in a strange reversal that turns into a valuable experience. The heroine's eyes are affected in "Everything That Rises Must Converge": "The blue in them seemed to have turned a bruised purple" (ETR, p. 17). In this instance also the character suffers a painful shock that prepares her for the truth. The classical idea of suffering as a prelude to knowledge as well as the irony operative in classical tragedy permeates O'Connor's fiction. If illumination is to occur, the individual's defenses must be shattered in a kind of shock therapy. The outcome is a collision with truth—a metaphysical experience.

The totality of the natural imagery that reflects this metaphysical experience represents ultimately a spiritual process basic to O'Connor's orientation. The juxtaposition of earth and sky, the role of the sun, the use of the color purple portray the process of Redemption. Representing infinity and the omnipresent Divinity, the sky hovers over the earth separated by the horizon or tree-line. The barrier is penetrated by the rays of the sun—the influence of God called grace.[4] The sun causes a purpling effect or a form of self-abnegation on the part of the individual that prepares him for change. The color purple is traditionally used in Christian liturgy to symbolize penitential seasons. The fact that the occasion for the moment of illumination arrives unexpectedly, often ironically, indicates the unique power of Divine intervention. In discussing her perspective on life, O'Connor acknowledges a commitment to make her values apparent in her work:

> I see from the standpoint of Christian orthodoxy. This means that for me the meaning of life is centered in our Redemption by Christ and that what I see in the world I see in relation to that. I don't think that this is a position that can be taken half-way or one that is particularly easy in these times to make transparent in fiction.[5]

All of O'Connor's works are concerned with Christian values, even though some of her short stories do not touch upon religion directly. She manages to evoke a sense of the redemptive process throughout her works, however, by reinforcing the moment of truth with symbolic imagery.

One of her last stories, "Revelation," provides in itself a synthesis of the dynamics of vision operative in her work. A distorted self-image leads Mrs. Turpin, the heroine, to see the world in her own limited terms:

> On the bottom of the heap were most colored people, not the kind she would have been if she had been one, but most of them; then next to them—not above, just away from—were the white trash; then above them were the home-owners, and above them the home-and-land owners, to which she and Claud belonged. Above she and Claud were the people with a lot of money and much bigger houses and much more land. (ETR, p. 195)

An apparently routine visit to a doctor's office initiates a change in her point of view. Mrs. Turpin becomes the object of a disturbed girl's wrath: "in the girl's seared face her eyes … appeared alternately to smolder and to blaze … the ugly girl's eyes were fixed on her … as if she had some very special reason for disliking her" (ETR, pp. 196–197). Just at the point when Mrs. Turpin is thanking God for making her such a good woman with so many advantages, the girl throws a book and strikes her directly over the eyes. Her vision begins to change: "it suddenly reversed itself and she saw everything large instead of small" (ETR, p. 206). The eye imagery focuses precisely on Mrs. Turpin's defective vision, the crux of her problem. Confused and awaiting an explanation, she is shocked when the girl shouts, "Go back to hell where you came from you old wart hog" (ETR, p. 207). Believing she has received some kind of revelation, Mrs. Turpin returns home filled with self-doubt, suffering anxiety and a battered ego.

The moment of truth comes only after some soul searching and extraordinary enlightenment. The process is reflected in the natural imagery—in the tree-line, the sun, and color purple. We learn that "The sun was a deep yellow now like a harvest moon and was riding westward very fast over the far tree line …" (ETR, p. 214). As Mrs. Turpin dwells on her experience, "The pasture was growing a peculiar glassy green and the streak of highway had turned lavender" (ETR, p. 216). Even though she really has no intellectual awareness of what is taking place in her psyche, the light has begun to dawn:

> A visionary light settled in her eyes. She saw the streak of a vast swinging bridge extending upward from the earth through a field

of living fire. Upon it a vast horde of souls were rumbling toward heaven. There were whole companies of white-trash, clean for the first time in their lives, and bands of black niggers in white robes, and battalions of freaks and lunatics shouting and clapping and leaping like frogs. And bringing up the end of the procession was a tribe of people whom she recognized at once as those who, like herself and Claud, had always had a little of everything and the God-given wit to use it right. (ETR, pp. 217–218)

She has an apocalyptic vision that promises a total reversal of her values.

Considering how complacent Mrs. Turpin appears before this experience, she would seem to be most unlikely to have such a radical change of heart. The confrontation with the girl in the doctor's office appears to be an accident, yet it acts as a catalyst in the process of awakening. But it is no accident that the girl is named Mary *Grace*. In fact, as the imagery of the tree-line, the sun, and the color purple suggests, the incident reveals how grace operates in the natural order. As the provocative force of God, grace operates subtly, usually without the individual's being aware of it; it evokes an existential response forcing the individual to verify the terms of his existence. Although such a response may be painful, the outcome is positive. In Mrs. Turpin's case, she receives the vision, however painful it may be, which she has asked for and which may provide the way to salvation. And she does receive a "revelation"; the "visionary light" reveals a new perspective on human worth and responsibility.

The momentum of Flannery O'Connor's fiction is basically hopeful in assessing man's limitations amid the constant possibility of redemption. Although man is thwarted by his lack of vision, the light remains a hovering presence—ready to pursue, if necessary, the recalcitrant. The process of enlightenment, so basic to O'Connor's works, is reinforced by natural imagery—through the tree-line, the sun, and the color purple. The fusion of character, situation, and imagery culminates in a unique experience, a metaphysical awakening, a spiritual illumination.

Notes

1. *Wise Blood* (New York: Farrar, Straus & Cudahy, 1949), referred to as "WB" in text references; *The Violent Bear It Away*: (New

York: Farrar, Straus & Cudahy, 1955), referred to as "V" in text references; *A Good Man Is Hard to Find* in *Three by Flannery O'Connor* (New York: The New American Library, 1964), referred to as "GM" in text references; *Everything That Rises Must Converge* (New York: Farrar, Straus & Giroux, 1966), referred to as "ETR" in text references.

2. Stanley Edgar Hyman, *Flannery O'Connor* (Minneapolis: University of Minnesota Press, 1966), p. 9.
3. "The Church and the Fiction Writer," *America*, 30 March 1957, p. 733.
4. For a detailed study of the operation of grace in O'Connor's work see Carter W. Martin, *The True Country* (Kingsport, Tennessee: Vanderbilt University Press, 1969), Chapters 3 & 4.
5. "The Fiction Writer and His Country," *The Living Novel*, ed. Granville Hicks (New York: The Macmillan Company, 1962), p. 162.

PARADISE LOST
(JOHN MILTON)

"Ingratitude as Sin in Milton's *Paradise Lost*"
by Michael Gillum, University of
North Carolina at Asheville

Why was it wrong for Eve and Adam to taste the forbidden fruit in Paradise? Many biblical interpreters have invoked the sin of pride, or wanting to rise above humans' rightful place in the scale of being. The Genesis text does support that view, since the serpent promises Eve "that when you eat of it your eyes will be opened, and you will be like God, knowing good and evil" (Gen. 3:5, *RSV*). God later ratifies the serpent's claim by saying, "Behold, the man has become like one of us, knowing good and evil ..." (Gen. 3:22). However, John Milton interpreted Scripture in his own way. In *Paradise Lost*, he does not imagine Eve as motivated by foolish pride or a desire to rival God. True, during the temptation Milton's serpent virtually quotes the Biblical serpent on those points (*PL* 9.705–710),[1] but Milton's Eve, mulling her decision, does not speak of becoming godlike. Rather, in that speech (9.745–779), she focuses on the thought that, since knowledge is a good, it seems unjust that knowledge should be forbidden. In Milton's interpretation of the Fall, the primal sin was not pride but simply disobedience.

The notion that an act of disobedience could justly lead to the ruin of a world might be a stumbling-block for modern readers. Obviously, disobedience can be courageous and virtuous. In his prose tracts *The Tenure of Kings and Magistrates* (1650), *Defense of the English People* (1651), and the *Second Defense of the English People* (1654), Milton vigorously defended political rebellion and the execution of King

Charles I. But in *Paradise Lost*, the archrebel Satan is the villain, and Eve, who apparently thinks she is acting virtuously and courageously, receives a sentence of death for the petty crime of eating a piece of stolen fruit. How does Milton in *Paradise Lost* "justify" this particular way of God to men? (1.26).

Although Milton was a radical and a rebel in English politics, in his religious thought and in *Paradise Lost* he endorsed God's absolute monarchical power over creation. This apparent contradiction has troubled Milton criticism from Shelley's *Defence of Poetry* (1821) to Michael Bryson's recent *The Tyranny of Heaven* (2004). However, the tension is not hard to resolve, as Barbara K. Lewalski and others have shown. Milton rejected earthly kingship on the grounds stated by Aristotle in the *Politics* (Book 3, ch. 16–17). That is, if a king were clearly superior to all his subjects in virtue and intelligence, then he would justly rule over them permanently with unlimited power. But in reality, few, or more likely, no kings at all are so superior to their subjects. Since it is unjust that a person should rule absolutely over his or her equals and superiors, earthly monarchy is fundamentally unjust. In similar terms, Milton's Archangel Michael, previewing human history for Adam's instruction, criticizes the first kingship:

> . . . [O]ne shall rise
> Of proud ambitious heart, who not content
> With fair equality, fraternal state,
> Will arrogate dominion undeserved
> Over his brethren. . . . (12.24–28)

Adam gets the point and responds:

> O execrable son so to aspire
> Above his brethren, to himself assuming
> Authority usurped, from God not giv'n:
> . . . .
> man over man
> He made not lord; such title to himself
> Reserving, human left from human free. (12.64–71)

Both speakers refer to humans as "brethren," meaning they are fundamentally equal to each other. The first king, Nimrod, like all humans, was also a "son" to God, but a bad one, in that he claimed a lordship that properly belongs only to God. In usurping lordship, he was also a bad brother to his human siblings, his natural equals under God. According to these political ideas, humans owe absolute obedience to God but to no human person.

God, as Adam says, reserves lordship for himself and retains ultimate authority. So, although Milton rejects political hierarchy in human affairs, he asserts a hierarchy in the cosmos: God over angels and humans, humans (collectively and by God's delegation) over the animals and the Earth. God's right authority over humans and angels derives both from his having created them and from his absolute superiority. This unequal relationship between the Father and his creatures justifies God's requirement of obedience. In *Paradise Lost*, God does not demand obedience in order to demonstrate his power or gratify the divine ego. Rather, he wants this obedience because it is inherently good and right, in that God is the creator and benefactor superior in wisdom. And further, by following God's lead, the creatures would become progressively better and more like him. The angel Raphael instructs Adam about this spiritual evolution that God intends:

> Your bodies may at last all turn to spirit,
> Improved by tract of time, and winged ascend
> Ethereal, as we [angels], or may at choice
> Here or in heav'nly paradises dwell,
> If ye be found *obedient....* (5.497–501, emphasis mine)

Obedience or conformity to God is the mechanism for this evolution, which is a Miltonic addition to traditional theology. Similarly, the Father speaks of a future time when the creatures will have evolved through obedience to such perfection that the Son, as King of Heaven, will resign his power, because God will then be "all in all" (3.339–341).

According to Milton's interpretation of Genesis, the Tree of Knowledge, in its true signification, is really the Tree of Obedience. When God decrees the prohibition to Adam, he describes the tree as "The pledge of thy obedience, and thy faith ..." (8.325)—"faith" here meaning fealty or loyalty. Adam, explaining to Eve, calls the tree "the only sign of our obedience left / Among so many signs of power and rule / Conferred upon us ..." (4.428–430). Apparently the fruit of this tree has no special properties except that it is forbidden. God has arbitrarily chosen to prohibit this particular tree as a "sign" of obedience. Why the arbitrariness? It is because Adam and Eve were created so perfect that their unfallen human will and reason naturally led them to choose rightly—that is, to follow God's will without any particular effort. As Eve explains to the serpent:

> But of this tree we may not taste or touch,
> God so commanded, and left that command
> Sole daughter of his voice; the rest we live
> Law to ourselves, our reason is our law. (9.651–654)

Since the prohibition is arbitrary, or outside natural law and reason, Adam and Eve cannot follow it naturally, as they follow the laws of their nature in all other matters. Rather, they must make a conscious choice to avoid the fruit as a demonstration of their fealty to God. The prohibition is a test that in a paradoxical way enlarges the creatures' liberty and dignity. In order to be fully free, they must have the opportunity to fail, as the Father says at 3.98–111. Again, this understanding of the prohibition is one of Milton's unconventional interpretations and not commonplace theology.

But the arbitrariness of the prohibition raises the question whether it was truly wrong in an ethical sense to eat the fruit. Milton was a "moral realist"—that is, one who thought right and wrong are objectively real categories. Rightness and wrongness are not created/defined by God's will and decree, as John Calvin and many other Protestants believed, but rather God wills and decrees what is (already) inherently right. Milton was also a rationalistic humanist who believed that human reason can generally discern the objective moral law.[2] If we look at the Fall from these viewpoints, the wrongness of eating the fruit becomes an important question, because if the punishment results from a morally neutral action, then God becomes a cosmic bully throwing his weight around like the Calvinist God that Milton rejected. In constructing the scheme of *Paradise Lost*, Milton was careful to shield God from this charge insofar as he could.

Although some critics have felt Milton was not successful in this shielding, I think the poem makes a solid case for the ethical wrongness of Eve's and Adam's acts. The answer that unfolds is this: Though the fruit itself is morally neutral, the eating is not, because the eating is disobedient, and disobedience to God is objectively wrong in the world of *Paradise Lost*. As we have seen, obedience is right because God, unlike mortal kings or parents, is immeasurably wiser than those he commands. Obedience to God is good for those who obey—it makes them better people. But beyond that, Milton asserts that obedience is owed according to the principle of gratitude.

The idea of obedience in *Paradise Lost* is grounded in the knowledge of being created and in the knowledge of one's creator. Self-understanding creatures accept their subordinate position and feel grateful for their existence. We can see this pattern clearly in the newly-created Adam's first speech:

> Thou sun, said I, fair light,
> And thou enlightened earth, so fresh and gay,
> Ye hills and dales, ye rivers, woods, and plains,
> And ye that live and move, fair creatures, tell,
> Tell, if ye saw, how came I thus, how here?
> Not of my self; by some great Maker then,
> In goodness and in power preeminent;
> Tell me, how may I know him, how adore,
> From whom I have that thus I move and live,
> And feel that I am happier than I know. (8.273–282)

Through reason, and on the evidence of creation, Adam immediately concludes that he was created by a superior being who excels in goodness and power. Because he feels intense gratitude for his existence, Adam wants to know his Maker so he can "adore" or worship.

Gratitude such as Adam experiences plays a crucial role in the ethical scheme of *Paradise Lost*. Archangel Raphael says God created our species as one that might

> Govern the rest, self-knowing, and from thence
> Magnanimous to correspond with heav'n,
> But *grateful* to acknowledge whence his good
> Descends ... (7.510–513, emphasis mine)

Peter E. Medine, who has studied the background for Milton's treatment of gratitude, summarizes the traditional Judeo-Christian idea of gratitude in this way: "Gratitude is fundamentally the acknowledgement of God's originary power in creating the universe; in the nature

of things, gratitude is literally a universal debt, and the perfection
of the universe depends on its expression in hymns and thanks and
praise" (117). Of course, in *Paradise Lost*, "thanks and praise" make up
the content of Adam and Eve's morning and evening prayers and also
of the angels' ceremonies in heaven.

Certainly there are elements of rationality and ethical justice in
gratitude. As Medine explains, Thomas Aquinas connected gratitude
to Aristotle's idea of commutative (contractual) justice, in that, if we
receive a good, we owe a debt. However, since gratitude owed cannot
be extracted or compelled, it is a "debt of honor" (119–120), according
to Aquinas. In his moment of clarity on Mt. Niphates, Milton's Satan
judges his own disobedience in light of the traditional Judeo-Christian
idea of gratitude:

> Ah wherefore! he deserved no such return
> From me, whom he created what I was
> In that bright eminence, and with his good
> Upbraided none; nor was his service hard.
> What could be less than to afford him praise,
> The easiest recompense, and pay him thanks,
> How due! (4.42–48)

Even fallen Satan acknowledges that God is the good and generous
creator to whom Satan justly owed a debt and to whom service, praise,
and thanks were due. In rebelling, he sought to renege on his debt, to
"quit / The debt immense of endless gratitude, / So burdensome still
paying, still to owe" (4.51–53). Thus Satan clearly associates gratitude
with natural law and commutative justice. The loyal angel Abdiel
brands Satan as "ingrate" (5.811), while the Father hurls the same
charge at Adam and Eve as he foresees their disobedience (3.97).
Ingratitude is near the heart of the primal sins of Satan, Adam, and
Eve, because heartfelt gratitude would entail steadfast loyalty and
obedience to the creator and benefactor.

While gratitude is a rationally grounded ethical obligation, it is also
an emotion. Gratitude connects with natural law on the one hand and
with love on the other. Satan recognized his debt but felt resentment
instead of love, because the debt reminded him of his inferiority to
God. By contrast, in Adam's awakening scene, the emotional warmth
of his gratitude is obvious. Also, the good angels say repeatedly that

they obey God out of love. Raphael explains, "freely we serve / Because we freely love, as in our will / To love or not" (5.538–540). Since service entails obedience, the failure to obey is a failure of love as well as a failure to keep an ethical obligation or debt.

Moreover, Eve and Adam explicitly recognize the moral obligation to obey, its positive rightness as opposed to the negative threat of punishment. This is how Adam explains the prohibition to Eve:

> Needs must the Power
> That made us, and for us this ample world
> Be infinitely good, and of his good
> As liberal and free as infinite,
> That raised us from the dust and placed us here
> In all this happiness, who at his hand
> Have nothing merited, nor can perform
> Aught whereof he hath need, he who requires
> From us no other service than to keep
> This one, this easy charge, of all the trees
> In Paradise that bear delicious fruit
> So various, not to taste that only Tree
> Of Knowledge.... (4.412–424)

Adam acknowledges that proper gratitude requires the service of obedience to the special command. Eve then responds that what Adam has said is "just and right" (4.443). Later, Adam judges the special command itself to be just; he urges obedience to God, "whose command / Single, is yet so just" (5.551–552). How is the command just, since it seems outside the scope of reason or natural law? Why shouldn't free people eat what they want when they are hungry? Adam, who recognizes that obedience is due, must consider that God is reasonable in imposing an explicit test of obedience. God did explain to Adam that such testing was the intent behind the prohibition (8.325), so the command has a rational purpose that Adam and Eve understand.

Paradise Lost seeks to shield God against the charge of irrational bullying. The text presents grateful obedience as the primary moral obligation for the creatures who owe everything to their Father, and it makes clear that the creatures understand the positive obligation to obey beyond the threat of punishment for disobedience.

A look at Eve's speech immediately before her Fall (9.745–779) shows how the failure of love and gratitude enables her sin of disobedience. Forgetting that God has "placed [her] here in all this happiness," she responds to Satan's characterization of God as the "Threat'ner" (9.686) who unjustly seeks to keep her "low and ignorant" (9.704) by prohibiting valuable knowledge. She notes that the "worthy" fruit has been "kept from man" (9.746), while she repeats forms of the word "forbid" five times. If God "Forbids us good, forbids us to be wise," then "Such prohibitions bind not" (9.759–760): That is, God himself is unethical and unworthy to be obeyed.

After the Fall, Eve denies that God (now reduced to "the gods") even created the Tree (9.805–807). She embraces Satan's earlier suggestion that God (or "the gods") did not really create the world but falsely claimed authorship of a system that actually arose through spontaneous natural processes (9.718–723). This denial of creation is crucial, because in the system of the poem, knowledge of having been created is the ground of grateful obedience. The irony here is that Eve must know that she herself was directly created by God, since Adam witnessed her creation from his rib (8.461), and surely he has told her about it. During the temptation, Eve claims "ignorance ... of God" (9.774–775). But in her direct experience, Eve has heard God's voice (4.467–475) and been led by him to her perfect mate and heart's desire. She is not really ignorant of God, but rather she is forgetting or setting aside what she knows about God and her duty to him.

We should note that Milton imagined a test for Eve that was much harder than the one sketchily indicated by Genesis or assumed by the many biblical commentators who had put down the biblical Eve as merely prideful, greedy, and foolish. By making the temptation so strenuous, Milton paid a sort of compliment to Eve's dignity and intelligence. The cards are stacked against her in several ways. First, the name of the tree is misleading in that the fruit does not actually convey knowledge of good and evil. Not the fruit itself but the sin of disobedience is what brings knowledge in its wake, the unhappy knowledge of "good lost, and evil got" (9.1072). In naming the tree, God played the ironist, using language in a way that could not be understood by the humans until after the Fall. Then, unlike in the Bible story, the serpent in *Paradise Lost* has suddenly acquired the power of speech, a power that Satan claims was imparted by the fruit. Language itself becomes evidence supporting the claims that the serpent voices about the fruit's potency. And finally, Satan as tempter has extraordinary powers of persuasion guided by a superhuman, if perverted, angelic intelligence. In the biblical account, Eve does not face any of these extra difficulties.

Eve failed the test. Could she have passed it? Readers properly feel sorry for overmatched Eve as Satan entangles her in his web of false reasoning, but we may also recognize that she has a weapon ready at hand that is capable of cutting her free. As we have seen previously, Eve has rationally understood and emotionally felt her obligation to obey God. Therefore, to escape Satan's logical snares, she has only to say, "We love and obey our creator because we owe him everything." This response would not represent blind obedience or blind faith but rationally grounded fealty. Given Milton's account of moral psychology, this is likely how he would defend God's statement that Eve was created "sufficient to have stood" (3.99) on the basis of free will armed with reason. The rightness of obedience under these circumstances is a moral principle fully accessible to Eve's reason.

Having fallen through disobedience, Eve's psyche is immediately disordered so that she runs through a repertory of other sins, including aspiration to godhead, gluttony, idolatry of the Tree, selfishness, jealousy toward Adam, and a determination to feed her husband death (9.790–836). After Adam eats the fruit, both fall into lust, then anger, and finally despair. Why do these things happen? In his theological treatise *De doctrina christiana* or *Christian Doctrine* (1823), Milton vigorously reinterprets the biblical concept of death as the punishment for sin (Book 1, ch. 12). He says "death" is not only the dissolution of the body: It includes every sadness and evil introduced into the world by the disordering of the mind, the unfallen intellect, through sin. This disorder is not a punishment imposed by God like an angry parent beating a misbehaving child. Rather it is a natural, internal process of derangement and deterioration caused by Adam and Eve losing their moral balance and breaking fealty with God. *Paradise Lost* dramatizes this process through the sudden, violent changes in their speech and behavior as disordered passions rise:

> They sat them down to weep, nor only tears
> Rained at their eyes, but high winds worse within
> Began to rise, high passions, anger, hate,
> Mistrust, suspicion, discord, and shook sore

> Their inward state of mind, calm region once
> And full of peace, now tossed and turbulent:
> For understanding ruled not, and the will
> Heard not her lore, both in subjection now
> To sensual appetite.... (9.1121–1129)

Milton's idea is that sin is its own punishment and the cause of further sin.

The most radical reinterpretation Milton imposes on the Genesis account is to imagine that Adam and Eve were redeemed during their earthly lives. In Book 10, they undergo a Protestant-style conversion involving the usual stages—the agonized awareness of sin, confession, repentance, forgiveness from God, and strengthening by grace. After hearing Michael tell the story of the Son's future incarnation, sacrificial death, and atonement, Adam even acknowledges Christ as his redeemer (12.572–573).

Strikingly, Milton has Eve start this process of redemption. After the Fall and Judgment, Adam has spent an anguished, sleepless night alone wrestling with his new condition, alternately blaming Eve, God, and himself. When Eve finds him and tries to make up, he attacks her with a vicious, misogynistic tirade: "Out of my sight, thou serpent, that name best / Befits thee with him leagued, thyself as false / And hateful ..." (10.867–868). Instead of counterattacking in typical human fashion, Eve unexpectedly falls at Adam's feet, expressing her love and dependence, accepting the blame. She intends to return to the place of judgment and

> There with my cries importune Heaven, that all
> The sentence from thy head removed may light
> On me, sole cause to thee of all this woe.
> Me, me only just object of his ire. (10.933–936)

Here Eve not only accepts moral responsibility, as opposed to the "mutual accusation" (9.1187) that prevailed earlier, but she invents confession and repentance on the spot. Predictably, Adam softens immediately and forgives her. Inspired by this result, they confess to God and pray for forgiveness. In response, God sends regenerating grace to hold them up.

In their contrition, Adam and Eve have returned to the state of obedience that was broken by their sin. In Adam's last speech in the poem, he sums up Michael's instruction as "Henceforth I learn, that to obey is best . . ." (12.561), while Eve's last words are an expression of gratitude: "though all by me is lost, / I all unworthy am vouchsafed, / By me the Promised Seed shall all restore" (12.621–623).

NOTES

1. Quotations of *Paradise Lost* are from the Elledge edition, cited by book and line number.
2. For reason and natural law in Milton's thought, see Bennett, *Reviving Liberty*.

WORKS CITED OR CONSULTED

Bennett, Joan S. *Reviving Liberty: Radical Christian Humanism in Milton's Great Poems.* Cambridge, MA: Harvard U. Press, 1989.

Bryson, Michael. *The Tyranny of Heaven: Milton's Rejection of God as King.* Newark: U. of Delaware Press, 2004.

Empson, William. *Milton's God.* London: Chatto & Windus, 1965.

Lewalski, Barbara K. "*Paradise Lost* and Milton's Politics." *Milton Studies* 38 (2000): 141–168.

Medine, Peter E. "Gratitude and *Paradise Lost*: A Neglected Context." In *Milton and the Grounds of Contention.* Ed. Mark A. Kelley, Michael Lieb, and John T. Shawcross. Pittsburgh: Duquesne U. Press, 2003. 115–149.

Milton, John. *De doctrina christiana.* Trans. Charles Sumner as *The Christian Doctrine.* In *The Works of John Milton*, gen. ed. Frank Allen Patterson. 18 vols. New York: Columbia U. Press, 1933. Vol. 15.

———. *Paradise Lost.* Ed. Scott Elledge. 2nd ed. New York: W. W. Norton, 1993.

Shelley, Percy B. "A Defence of Poetry." In *Shelley's Prose.* Ed. David Lee Clark. Albuquerque: U. of New Mexico Press, 1954. 275–298.

"THE PARDONER'S TALE"
(GEOFFREY CHAUCER)

❧

"The Pardoner's Homosexuality and How It Matters"
by Monica E. McAlpine, in *PMLA* (1980)

INTRODUCTION

Chaucer's "The Pardoner's Tale" focuses on a trickster who plays to human guilt, in his own allegory of sin and the need for redemption. In this historically informed reading of the tale, Monice E. McAlpine suggests that Chaucer makes a daring move in portraying the Pardoner as not only a sinner and homosexual but also a fellow pilgrim, who, along with other members of the social strata, seeks redemption as he travels to Canterbury.

∞

The famous pronouncement of Chaucer's narrator on Chaucer's Pardoner—"I trowe he were a geldyng or a mare"[1] (1.691)—poses several questions for modern readers. What are the options that it offers for the interpretation of the Pardoner? Why is the narrator unable to decide between them? To what extent does Chaucer maintain this indeterminacy about the Pardoner and require the reader, like the narrator, to remain forever undecided? Does Chaucer in any way

---

McAlpine, Monica E. "The Pardoner's Homosexuality and How It Matters." *PMLA* 95.1 (January 1980): 8–22.

lead the reader to a greater certitude? If so, what is the sexual status of the Pardoner? Finally, what is the moral significance of that status? These questions arise partly from the complexity of Chaucer's poetry and partly from present-day ignorance of medieval sexual concepts and terminology.

The term "mare," in particular, has proved notoriously difficult for modern readers to interpret, and even when the term is glossed, the possibility that the Pardoner may be a "mare" is often ignored in favor of the belief that he is certainly a "geldyng," or eunuch. Psychological, moral, and spiritual interpretations of the Pardoner's eunuchry and of the sterility and, less accurately, the impotence with which it is associated permeate current critical treatments of this pilgrim. A faithful reading of Chaucer's line requires that the balance be restored. We need a gloss for "mare," and we need interpretations of the Pardoner's portrait and of his prologue and tale that explore the implications of his possible status as "mare" just as fully as criticism has already explored the implications of his possible status as "geldyng." It is neither likely nor desirable that such a reading will replace the view of the Pardoner as a eunuch; rather, it is to be hoped it will shed new light on familiar aspects of Chaucer's rich characterization.

As a contribution to this work, I wish to offer, in the first and longer part of this essay, a more detailed argument than has so far been attempted in favor of viewing the Pardoner as a possible homosexual.[2] In the second part, I consider the spiritual implications of the Pardoner's sexuality by redirecting attention to his bagful of pardons and relics. The initial references to these objects occupy a significant place in the middle section of the Pardoner's tripartite portrait in the General Prologue: he is not only a "geldyng or a mare" (ll. 669–91) but also both a "pardoner" peddling false relics (ll. 692–706) and a "noble ecclesiaste" (ll. 707–14). Through an interpretation of the Pardoner as homosexual, I hope to confirm what this structure suggests: that his pardons and relics constitute the essential link, the lifeline, between this sexually anomalous Christian and his church.

I.

For many of Chaucer's readers, the narrator's pronouncement is intimately linked with certain deservedly influential commentaries on the Pardoner's sexual status, and any reconsideration of the subject must acknowledge its debt to those studies and carefully discriminate its conclusions from theirs. In his ground-breaking review of medieval texts on medicine and physiognomy, Walter Clyde Curry opened discussion of the Pardoner's physical nature.[3] Although the point is seldom noticed, Curry interprets the narrator's pronouncement as offering a choice between impotence and effeminacy (p. 58). He treats the mention of these two sexual phenomena as serving to define a third possibility, underlying and unnamed, and then shows that the Pardoner's physical characteristics—long, fine hair; high voice; glaring eyes; and beardlessness—fit the descriptions of eunuchs offered by medieval doctors and physiognomists. All but one of Curry's sources, moreover, associate eunuchry with immorality, and some also insist that the congenital eunuch is more evil than the castrated eunuch. The sins attributed to eunuchs include dissoluteness, shamelessness, cunning, and viciousness. In what has proved the least convincing part of his argument, Curry contends that the other pilgrims, and Chaucer's audience, would have been able to go beyond the narrator's speculations to deduce that the Pardoner suffers from the (presumably rare) condition of congenital eunuchry.

Since in the view of the medieval experts the physical characteristics of all eunuchs are much the same, Curry's labeling of the Pardoner as a *congenital* eunuch is grounded not in unarguable physiognomical fact, as is sometimes believed, but in fallible literary interpretation. One argument appeals to the influence of source. Chaucer may have based his Pardoner, in part, on the characterization of a eunuch by the physiognomist Polemon (pp. 62–64), and Curry assumes that because Polemon's eunuch was a congenital eunuch, Chaucer's must be, too. A second argument rests on Curry's own estimate of the Pardoner's character; the depth of the Pardoner's depravity is seen as justifying his classification with the more malicious congenital eunuchs rather than with the comparatively benign castrated eunuchs (pp. 59–64). Moreover, by concentrating on the moral distinction between congenital eunuchs and castrated eunuchs, a prominent distinction in his sources, Curry distracts his readers from what he himself understands to be the different distinction in the General Prologue: that between "geldyng" and "mare." While he reveals the accuracy with which Chaucer uses the stereotype of the eunuch for some of the details of the Pardoner's portrait, Curry neither proves that the Pardoner is a congenital eunuch nor definitively exhausts the implications of the narrator's pronouncement.

The relationship of the Pardoner's eunuchry to his spiritual condition and to the larger themes of Chaucer's work was first addressed in a sophisticated way by Robert Miller.[4] Miller examines medieval biblical glosses that attempt to resolve a conflict in attitudes toward eunuchs in the Old Testament. Deuteronomy xxiii.1, reflecting a literal-minded racial and sexual perception of holiness, excludes eunuchs from the temple, while Isaiah lvi.3–5, taking a more spiritual approach, gives assurances that righteous eunuchs are among God's people. The medieval commentators found a solution to this conflict in a statement of Christ's discriminating among congenital eunuchs, involuntary castrates, and "eunuchs who have made themselves such for the Kingdom of heaven" (Matt. xix.12). Identifying the last group, the voluntary celibates in the service of God, as the eunuchs of Isaiah who will be accepted by God, the commentators go on to invent a second group of metaphorical eunuchs who will be rejected, as in Deuteronomy: those who, while capable of good works, deliberately remain spiritually sterile. Miller argues that the Pardoner's physical eunuchry is the sign of his deliberate spiritual sterility. His chosen role as *eunuchus non Dei* is seen as bitterly satiric, since he has a special responsibility as a churchman to be a *eunuchus Dei*, fruitful in good works.

If, however, Chaucer did use the Pardoner's physical condition as a sign in this way, he ran a considerable risk of undermining the very spiritual values he was attempting to communicate. Both Christ and the medieval commentators were reacting against the physical determinism of one strain of Jewish tradition. For them, involuntary eunuchry had no necessary moral significance at all; they were attempting to free the career of the soul from questions of genital competency.[5] Miller's Pardoner, in contrast, is a static figure. While Miller rightly emphasizes the free action by which the Pardoner would have become a *eunuchus non Dei*, he does not recognize in Chaucer's characterization a continuing human potential for change. Because the immutable physical fact of eunuchry is taken as the sign of the Pardoner's spiritual status, his soul cannot be allowed its own career independent of his sexual destiny. Despite this difficulty, Miller's study has done more than any other to establish the level of seriousness on which the problem of the Pardoner's sexuality should be addressed. Moreover, the biblical materials he has brought to our attention can now be seen as documenting one kind of consideration that medieval people gave to a question central to Chaucer's characterization of the Pardoner: What is the place of sexually different, or "deviant," persons in the scheme of salvation?

Wide acceptance of the conclusions of Curry and Miller has had the unintended side effect of dulling readers' responses to the Pardoner; this pilgrim, it seems, has been fully "explained." As Donald Howard puts it in *The Idea of the Canterbury Tales*, the theory of the Pardoner's congenital and "scriptural" eunuchry has become an excuse for not taking him seriously. In his dazzling treatment of the Pardoner as a grotesque, as a "feminoid" or "hermaphroditic" male, Howard succeeds in re-creating the strangeness of this pilgrim—his power to mystify, frighten, and fascinate. Partly from motives of anger and revenge, the Pardoner alienates himself from the community of human and divine values; in Howard's view, he becomes—like evil itself as defined in medieval philosophy, like the grotesques in manuscript illuminations, and like the very fragment of the *Canterbury Tales* in which his tale appears—something "on the periphery of the ordered world of created goodness," "marginal," "floating," "outside," "demonic" (pp. 338–41). Curiously, Howard accepts as fact the congenital and "scriptural" eunuchry that theorists have attributed to the Pardoner and claims that we know the character's sexual status while the narrator and the others do not (pp. 343–45). His discussion of the Pardoner nevertheless proceeds, rightly I think, as if we share the same general perspective as the pilgrims—that is, as if we too remain uncertain about the Pardoner's sexual status and thus experience the whole man as mysterious.

Howard fears that any interpretation of the Pardoner as homosexual would "explain" the Pardoner in the same deadening and unprofitable way as the belief in the character's eunuchry has and that the modern stereotype of the effeminate male homosexual would be anachronistically used to deny the Pardoner's mystery. While I agree that the danger of another reductive reading is real, a view of the Pardoner as homosexual would not necessarily have this effect; for the danger lies not in any particular sexual definition but in the manner of relating the Pardoner's sexuality to his spirituality. Nor is the stereotype of effeminate male homosexuality an anachronism; it is as authentically medieval as it is modern. Indeed, the medieval confusion of homosexuality with effeminacy and, as we shall see, with other sexual phenomena indicates both that Chaucer's contemporaries tried to explain homosexuality to themselves and that they failed to dispel the mystery it presented to them. It is true, however, that I cannot produce a Pardoner quite so enigmatic as Howard's, but this difference arises not from our disagreement about the Pardoner's possible homosexuality but from my unwillingness to accept, with Howard (p. 351), the Pardoner's definition of himself as a "ful vicious man." By turning our attention from the standard glosses on the Pardoner's sexuality to the literary characterization itself, Howard has brought the Pardoner alive again; but in his valuable explication of the Pardoner as a grotesque, he accepts too fully the Pardoner's own tortured and theatrical self-image. While giving detailed consideration to the possibility that the Pardoner is isolated from his heterosexual and homophobic peers by a condition of homosexuality, I emphasize the Pardoner's identity as a pilgrim in the fellowship of other pilgrims, motivated, even in his cupidity, by the love they all seek and experiencing an anguished self-division not unlike what others suffer.

The first step in a reconsideration of the Pardoner's sexuality must be the establishment of a gloss for "mare." "Geldyng" and "mare" are homely metaphors that must have had meanings both familiar and fairly precise for Chaucer's medieval audience; modern readers, however, face difficulties in recovering those meanings. Curry's influence is registered, but often inaccurately or incompletely, in modern editions of the *Canterbury Tales*. Among recent editors, only Donald Howard glosses both "geldyng" and "mare," and he interprets the first as "castrated eunuch" and the second as "congenital eunuch."[7] John Hurt Fisher preserves Curry's too narrow interpretation of "geldyng" as suggesting impotence, while Albert Baugh reflects what I think is the most common understanding of Curry's argument (and of the Pardoner's status): that "geldyng" means "eunuch" (without implying any differentiation of types) and that the Pardoner is a eunuch.[8] Neither Fisher nor Baugh, however, repeats Curry's interpretation of "mare" as a reference to effeminacy or offers any alternative gloss for that word. Finally, while both the *Middle English Dictionary* and the *Oxford English Dictionary* fully document the use of "geldyng" as a term for "eunuch," neither includes any evidence for a meaning of "mare" relevant to Chaucer's context.[9]

For many modern readers, the obvious possible translations for "mare" are "effeminate male" and "homosexual male." Until recently, though, there appeared to be no evidence that the word had been used in either of these senses. Then, in 1973, Jill Mann pointed to a Latin poem by the twelfth-century satirist Walter of Chatillôn in which homosexual men, also described as effeminate, are labeled "mares": "equa fit equus" "the horse becomes a mare" (*Medieval Estates Satire*, p. 146). While it is not certain that Chaucer knew Walter's works, they were relatively well known in England,[10] and the poem does add weight to the suggestion that "mare" may mean "effeminate male" or "homosexual male" or both. But even if there were no question about Chaucer's having read the poem, one supporting text would not constitute proof of his meaning.

We need not wait for the discovery of more supporting texts, however. The details of the Pardoner's portrait and the term "geldyng" create a context that suggests criteria for glossing "mare." "Mare" must be a term commonly used in Chaucer's day to designate a male person who, though not necessarily sterile or impotent, exhibits physical traits suggestive of femaleness, visible characteristics that were also associated with eunuchry in medieval times and that were thought to have broad effects on the psyche and on character. The gloss that most satisfactorily fulfills these criteria is "a homosexual." Chaucer did not know the word "homosexual," of course, since it did not enter the language until 1869,[11] but he might have referred to what we call homosexuality by making a biblical reference (to sodomites), a mythological reference (to Ganymede or Orpheus), a historical reference (to Julius Caesar, for example), or a philosophical reference (to sinners against nature).[12] As we shall see, the choice of "mare" has several important and related advantages: it avoids provoking an immediate response of condemnation, which other references might have invited; it focuses attention not on sexual acts but on a type of person in whose soma and psyche Chaucer apparently believed homosexuality to be deeply rooted;[13] and it suggests an attitude on the narrator's part in keeping with his character—a mixture of sympathy, amusement, and condescension.

Since several historical accounts are available, I shall not pause to document in detail the familiarity of Chaucer's audience with male homosexuality;[14] I should like to explore instead the situation reflected in my criteria for glossing "mare," the confusion of homosexuality with other sexual phenomena.

In using a word denoting femaleness, Chaucer reflects one ancient and widespread misunderstanding about male homosexuality, that it involves a man's becoming in some sense a woman. The concept of effeminacy provides one way of thinking about this supposed transformation, but care must be taken in interpreting references to effeminacy in the medieval setting. The *Middle English Dictionary* records only two uses of the word "effeminate," both in the sense "self-indulgent" or "unreasonable."[15] Satires on the fop, often described as long-haired and beardless, reflect a perception of feminization of behavior and appearance without any necessary suggestion of homosexuality (Mann, *Medieval Estates Satire*, pp. 147–48). In medieval Latin, however, *effeminatus* sometimes means "homosexual," as in the Vulgate Bible, and this sense had passed into English by the time of the King James Bible (Bailey, pp. 38–39, 48–53). There is some evidence, moreover, that the young aristocrat who aspired to fashion had to be careful to observe the boundaries that marked off effeminacy and homosexuality. At the end of a lengthy set of instructions on conduct, dress, and grooming in Guillaume de Lorris' *Roman de la rose*, for example, the God of Love tells the young lover:

> Cous tes manches, tes cheveus pigne,
> Mais ne te farde ne ne guigne:
> Ce n'apartient s'as dames non,
> Ou a ceus de mauvais renon,
> Qui amors par male aventure
> Ont trovees contre Nature.

> Sew your sleeves and comb your hair, but do not rouge or paint
> your face, for such a custom belongs only to ladies or to men of
> bad repute, who have had the misfortune to find a love contrary
> to Nature.[16] (II. 2:69–74)

Just as not all effeminate males were suspected of homosexuality, so not all homosexual males were perceived as effeminate. In his translation of Dante's *Inferno*, Mark Musa notes the contrast between the effeminate speech patterns of the sodomitical clerks in Canto xv and the more robust manner of the sodomitical soldiers in Canto xvi.[17] Since the substance of what constitutes effeminacy in males is culturally defined and subject to change, it is not necessary to find in the Middle Ages exact replicas of our current stereotype of effeminacy in homosexual males (including, for example, distinctive walk or hand movements); it is only necessary to show that certain types of feminized behavior and appearance in males were sometimes interpreted as evidence of homosexuality. Thus, even if the primary meaning of "mare" was "an effeminate male," a second meaning may have been "a possibly homosexual male."

Another ancient way of conceiving the male homosexual's supposed participation in the feminine was to think of him as a hermaphrodite. In Hellenic rites and legends, the hermaphrodite is a double god, a being with the overt equipment of both sexes (i.e., male genitals and female breasts), a symbol of unity, fruitfulness, and eternal life. In Hellenistic art, however, the hermaphrodite is an extremely feminized figure, though recognizably male, representative of one ideal of homosexual beauty.[18] Interest in this type of hermaphrodite revived during the twelfth-century resurgence of classical scholarship (Curtius, pp. 113–16). A late and perhaps unconscious reflection of this tradition, evidence of its thorough absorption into European thinking, appears in the treatment of the story of Sodom and Gomorrah in the Middle English *Purity*, a work commonly ascribed to the *Gawain* poet. The poet describes Lot's first glimpse of the angels as they pass through the crowded streets of Sodom toward his house; they are extraordinarily beautiful young men with beardless chins, rosy complexions, and luxurious hair like raw silk:

> As he stared into Þe strete Þer stout men played,
> He syȝe Þer swey in asent swete men tweyne;
> Bolde burnez were Þay boÞe, wyth berdles chynnez,
> Royl rollande fax, to raw sylk lyke,
> Of ble as Þe brere-flor where so Þe bare schew[e]d;
> Ful clene watz Þe countenaunce of her cler yȝen;
> Wlonk whit watz her wede and wel hit hem sem[e]d.
> (II. 787–93)

On one level the beauty of the angels is meant to suggest a spiritual excellence superior to all considerations and distinctions of human sexuality; but as A.C. Spearing remarks, it also explains something left unexplained in the biblical text: how the men of Sodom came to desire homosexual intercourse with the angels.[19] It seems likely that a hermaphroditic or feminoid male would have been suspected of sexual deviance.

An alternative to thinking of the male homosexual as a woman-man was to think of him as a nonman, for homosexuality was long

confused with eunuchry.[20] In Gautier de Leu's thirteenth-century
fabliau "La Veuve," for example, a widow who remarries finds the
vigorous sexual performance of her new husband on the wedding
night nonetheless disappointing:

> Nos avons çaiens un bruhier,
> un durfeüt, un hebohet.
> Ahi! con Damerdex me het
> qui fui des bons vallés aquius,
> et des cortois et des gentius,
> si pris cest caitif par nature.
>
> . . . .
>
> Et cis ribaus me tient plus vil
> que le fernier de son cortil,
> mais je sai bien, par Saint Eloi,
> qu'il n'est mie de bone loi,
> ains est de çaus del Mont Wimer:
> il n'a soing de dames amer.

> What have we here? An impotent,
> beardless ne'er-do-well! Ah me!
> The Lord must hate me bitterly,
> who turned away from fine young men,
> well born, courteous, and then
> wound up with this congenital bum!
>
> . . . .
>
> This scoundrel shows me less regard
> than he does the dungheap in the yard.
> However, by Saint Loy I know
> his moral code is just as low
> as that of those on Mount Wimer;
> for woman's love he doesn't care.[21]

The widow equates less than heroic sexual performance with impotence, impotence with beardless eunuchry, both of these with homosexuality, and all of these with heresy, for the reference to Mount
Wimer concerns a large group of *bougres* who were burned to death
for homosexuality and heresy in Champagne in 1239. The fabliau
makes fun of the widow and her insatiable appetite, but the intended

comedy of her speech must have depended partly on the pervasiveness of just such misunderstandings;[22] at the same time, the poet who made comedy out of the widow's confusion must himself have been in some degree superior to it. Like the French poet, Chaucer may be seen as making artistic use of what he perceived to be common misunderstandings of sexual phenomena. The Pardoner's possible eunuchry may contribute to the portrait of a homosexual since medieval people apparently strove to understand homosexuality by identifying it with now one, now another, sexual anomaly.

Seen against this background, Chaucer's portrait of the Pardoner in the General Prologue emerges as a pastiche of allusions to the three distinct sexual phenomena with which homosexuality was often confused—effeminacy, hermaphroditism, and eunuchry—and thus very probably to homosexuality itself. In the order of their appearance in the portrait the allusions are the description of the Pardoner's hair—its length and fineness suggesting effeminacy, eunuchry, and hermaphroditism and his grooming of it suggesting effeminacy; the Pardoner's concern with fashion, implying effeminacy; the references to goats and hares, suggesting hermaphroditism; the high voice, connoting effeminacy and eunuchry; the glaring eyes, associated with eunuchry; and the beardlessness, a symptom of effeminacy, eunuchry, hermaphroditism, and homosexuality. Furthermore, the glaring eyes and the references to goats, hares, and mares connote extreme lechery, which is at least as suggestive of sexual deviance as of sexual inadequacy.[23] What this catalog shows is that most of the allusions tend to be *multivalent*, and the reason is that the lines between these various sexual phenomena were fluid in medieval theory. It is impossible to say whether beardlessness, for example, was more likely to suggest eunuchry or homosexuality to a medieval person. Because of this fluidity, too, references to effeminacy, hermaphroditism, and eunuchry could serve as a code for homosexuality. Finally, while the categories "effeminate," "hermaphrodite," and "eunuch" can each account for some of the Pardoner's characteristics, only the category "homosexual" can account for all of them. For example, while the Pardoner's interest in fashion can be referred directly only to effeminacy (and not to eunuchry or hermaphroditism) and the narrator's allusion to goats only to hermaphroditism, both can be referred to homosexuality through what the medieval audience regarded as the mediating concepts of effeminacy and hermaphroditism.

Thus at a minimum it seems impossible to exclude the suggestion of homosexuality from the portrait. It is also impossible for the
reader not to be influenced by the opening frame for this physical
description: the presentation of the Pardoner's association with the
Summoner. The nature of this association has long been debated,[24]
but there is no doubt that the Pardoner is introduced to us traveling
with a male "friend" and "compeer" and that the two are singing,
in their contrasting voices, a love song, "Com hider, love, to me" (ll.
670–71). This tableau may be read in two ways. The Pardoner may
be seen as a frustrated heterosexual who associates himself with the
lecherous Summoner in order to deny his own impotence and to
acquire symbolically the Summoner's virility; or he may be seen as a
homosexual, ambivalent about disclosing his status, who nonetheless
becomes suspect through the public display of this ambiguous friendship. These are the two possibilities that the narrator makes explicit, I
believe, when he provides the closing frame for the physical description of the Pardoner: "I trowe he were a geldyng or a mare." Thus
these three parts of the Pardoner's portrait—the opening tableau, the
physical description, and the closing pronouncement—fit together in
a way that has not been fully appreciated. For the medieval audience,
with its confused and limited lexicon of sexual terms and concepts,
it was the physical description, I suspect, that was most ambiguous;
the opening frame first provided implicit guidance, and the closing
frame then explicit guidance, to its interpretation. Modern readers
may have a different experience, since the meaning of the Pardoner's
friendship with the Summoner has been clouded by controversy and
the meaning of the term "mare" has long been lost. In this situation,
the physical description, once it is set in the context of medieval sexual
theory, seems to me to provide the strongest evidence of the Pardoner's
possible homosexuality, which in turn helps us both to recognize a
possible implication of his association with the Summoner and to
gloss "mare."

Given, then, that Chaucer's text explicitly and implicitly raises
the issue of homosexuality, the narrator's treatment of the Pardoner
seems to unfold in this way. Faced with a somewhat bewildering set
of indications to interpret, the narrator rather shrewdly cuts through
the complexity to suggest that the Pardoner is either a nonman, that
is, a eunuch, or a woman-man, a homosexual. Indeed the phrase "I
trowe," which may denote either speculation or certainty,[25] serves to

dramatize the narrator in his role as interpreter, dealing confidently yet respectfully with resistant reality. There may even be an element of self-congratulation in his announced inability to decide exactly what the Pardoner's status is; the narrator may think that the double reference to eunuchry and homosexuality displays his sophistication. Actually, though, he is rather like the modern person who has not mastered the distinctions among homosexuals, bisexuals, transvestites, and transsexuals. One consequence of the narrator's characteristically limited perception is that we initially encounter the Pardoner as a kind of puzzle to be solved rather than as a pilgrim to be judged.

The animal imagery of the narrator's pronouncement also helps temporarily to isolate the Pardoner from moral judgment. The narrator perceives the Pardoner as someone conspicuously deficient in the animal sphere of perfection, lacking integrity of sexual identity, physical intactness, or procreative competency—the amoral perfections, elaborated in various cultural forms, that the narrator admires in the Monk and Harry Bailey. Though found wanting in one sphere, the Pardoner is perceived as supremely competent in another; thus the significance of the "but" as the narrator turns to the Pardoner's work in the world: "But of his craft, fro Berwyk into Ware, / Ne was ther swich another pardoner" (ll. 692–93). Sheer expertise, unrelated to its use or purpose, is one of the narrator's chief measures of value throughout the General Prologue (Mann, *Medieval Estates Satire*, p. 194), and this ideal, despite its moral limitations, has a special virtue in regard to the Pardoner since it embraces more than sexuality. For the narrator, the "pardoner" and the "noble ecclesiaste" are as important as the "geldyng" or the "mare." The narrator sets an example of not reducing the Pardoner to his sexuality, an example that at other levels of response Chaucer means us to emulate.

Nevertheless we cannot be so content with the narrator's tentative diagnosis of the Pardoner as the narrator himself is. As viewed by the medieval church, eunuchry and homosexuality had very different moral statuses; pace the doctors and physiognomists, eunuchry was not in itself regarded as sinful, while homosexual acts (the concept of a homosexual condition was not recognized by the moral theologians) were considered grave sins.[26] From this standpoint the narrator's self-satisfied conclusion that the Pardoner is one thing or the other is quite astonishing, for it reflects an essentially secular perspective. Since, however, we must view the Pardoner as a pilgrim—that is, not only as an animal being and an expert worker but also as a moral being with a spiritual destiny—we need to know more than the narrator is able to tell us. The narrator's comment on the Pardoner's sexual status preserves immutably for all time the narrator's own uncertainty about his fellow pilgrim. It does not fix to the same degree the mystery about the Pardoner himself, although the absence of any other explicit statement about his sexuality means that a choice between "geldyng" and "mare" or any extrapolation using both terms will always be an *interpretation*. Many critics, having chosen "geldyng," have traced the implications of their choice in readings of the Pardoner's prologue and tale; while admitting that the Pardoner may be a eunuch as well, I choose to emphasize his possible status as a "mare," or homosexual, and I should like to explore some of the consequences of my choice.

II.

It is rather widely agreed that the avarice the Pardoner boasts about is a screen sin, concealing some graver defect of body or soul or both.[27] Like his interpreters, the Pardoner betrays an interest in degrees of sinfulness, identifying one of the rioters in his tale as the "proudeste" (l. 716), another rioter (or perhaps the same one) as the "worste of hem" (l. 776), Harry Bailey as "moost envoluped in synne" (l. 942), and himself as "a ful vicious man" (l. 459). Also, as his constant preaching text, *"Radix malorum"* (l. 334), reveals, he is obsessively interested in underlying states of sinfulness, and other evidence suggests that he finds the root of all evil in the body. Although his semihysterical discussion of the so-called tavern sins seems not to rest on any positive values, it does have a unifying theme. All the sins are developed to some degree in a way that relates them to the human body.

Gluttony, of course, has a natural relation to the body, but the Pardoner's tracing of ingested food from "the tendre mouth" to the "shorte throte" (compared to a privy) to the "stynkyng cod, / Fulfilled of dong and of corrupcioun" and at last to the bowels with their "foul ... soun" (ll. 512–35) tends to turn all eating into an obscene act. He even treats the sin of Adam and Eve as an act of gluttony, ignoring its intellectual content. Similarly, cursing is treated not as a rejection of Christ's divinity and teachings but as an attack on Christ's body; all the examples the Pardoner provides refer to Christ's body and passion, and he later says of the rioters "Cristes blessed body [they] torente" (1. 709). Finally, gambling is most dramatically presented to us in an imagined scene in which the dice are referred to as "bones" (1. 656).[28] The treatment of these vices suggests an obsessive concern with the body as the source of sin, the instrument of sin, and the victim of sin. Significantly, avarice, the screen sin, is not presented as having an intimate connection with the body; instead it is decidedly intellectual, requiring of the Pardoner great cleverness in plying the tricks of his trade.

A key passage in the Pardoner's prologue hints more directly at what the concealed and deadly sinfulness in the body might be. The Pardoner describes one of his most ingenious tricks for persuading people to venerate his relics and offer alms:

> Goode men and wommen, o thyng warne I yow:
> If any wight be in this chirche now
> That hath doon synne horrible. that he
> Dar nat, for shame, of it yshryven be,
> Or any womman, be she yong or old,
> That hath ymaad hir housbonde cokewold,
> Swich folk shal have no power ne no grace
> To offren to my relikes in this place. (ll. 377–84)

The specificity about the woman's sin and the lack of specificity about the man's provoke interpretation. It seems likely that the unnamed sin shares a number of characteristics with infidelity: it is a sexual sin; it is peculiarly associated with one sex—with men, as culpable infidelity had long been associated with women; and it inspires a special opprobrium that arises from a cultural bias rather than from the principles of Christian ethics. Male homosexuality meets all these criteria.[29] Most important, the shame that attends the naming of the sin even in the confessional seems a clear allusion to homosexuality. Long before homosexuality was christened by Lord Alfred Douglas "the Love that dare not speak its name," it had been commonly referred to in some variation of the formula found in Chaucer's Parson's Tale: "thilke abhomynable synne, of which that no man unnethe oghte speke ne write" (x.909).[30]

It would be wrong to seem to deny, by qualification, the intense homophobia embodied in this notorious phrase, and yet it is important to recognize that there were shadings of opinion and feeling about homosexuality.[31] In the *Canterbury Tales* the Pardoner's behavior and the reactions of the other pilgrims reflect a setting in which a homosexual person, while possibly aware of the severe penalties sometimes inflicted on his kind, did not feel a proximate fear for his safety.[32] The Pardoner's flaunting of his friendship with the Summoner, though undoubtedly compulsive behavior, is probably not undertaken without some realistic assessment of the risks. As the pilgrims' apprehension about his ribaldry and Harry's false camaraderie suggest, what the Pardoner must confront in others is not their outright condemnation of him but their discomfiture, with its varying degrees of amusement, fear, sympathy, disgust, and ambiguous tolerance. In ministers of the church's sacraments, like Chaucer's Parson, the Pardoner would almost certainly encounter at least unthinking, if not vehement, reflections of that homophobia which the church had helped both to create and to perpetuate. In himself, the Pardoner has to contend with that self-hatred which internalizes the judgments of others. Ultimately the man who cannot confess the unnamed and unnameable sin is the Pardoner himself.

It may well be, moreover, that the Pardoner's inability to approach the confessional arises partly from his perception of the gulf between what the church was prepared to forgive and what he had to confess. As his portrait suggests, the Pardoner's homosexuality is a profound part of his being, an aspect that Chaucer could portray (and probably conceive of) only by projecting a biological cause.[33] The Pardoner himself seems to feel that he is in a state of alienation from Christ and the church, a state that is more than the sum of his sinful acts. *Mala*, or specific evil deeds, are not his concern; the *radix*, or root condition, is. But in the matter of homosexuality, as in matters of human sexuality generally, the church's moral theology tended to focus on acts, not on persons; and while it took account of a variety of actors, it defined them in terms of certain fixed statuses only: young or old, male or female, married or unmarried, clerical or lay. It understood homosexual acts only as the perverse behavior of basically heterosexual persons.[34] In other words, the church was prepared to deal with sinners like the scabby Summoner but not with the tortured Pardoner. The "inverted" Pardoner did not fit the church's definitions and could scarcely form a sincere purpose to amend a condition in himself he probably felt he had no power to change. Chaucer's study of homosexuality in the Pardoner seems to represent a deliberate intention to explore the inner reality of an outcast especially despised by his society and especially misunderstood by his church.

It is no accident that the man who cannot confess becomes a pardoner. Seizing on a theologically marginal church practice, the granting of indulgences, the Pardoner subverts the sacrament of penance he cannot use while simultaneously setting himself up as a substitute confessor. Officially, he had the power to offer almsgivers only remission of the punishment due sins already absolved by a priest. In practice, like many actual pardoners, he sold supposed absolution from sin.[35] While some of his customers may have been naïve Christians who could not appreciate the difference, others must have hoped to buy spiritual safety dishonestly, without reforming their lives. By exploiting the potential for self-deceit in those he imagines condemn him, the Pardoner attempts to convict his customers of being themselves "envoluped in synne." As he leads them away from the legitimate sacrament, it is as if he were saying, "If I cannot be truly forgiven, neither shall they be." At the same time, the Pardoner constantly enacts in reverse the scene of absolution he longs for. As he dispenses his own brand of absolution, often arousing in his audience true contrition (VI.430–31), it is as if he were saying, "If there is anyone the church will not forgive, I will forgive him," all the while hoping that the forgiveness he dispenses will magically flow back to cleanse himself.

This manipulation of the sacrament is one of the things the Pardoner does that tend to be obscured by what he says as he constructs a smoke screen of single-minded avarice. But his intimate association with confession betrays, beneath his practiced cynicism, the seriousness with which he regards the sacrament. Apparently he does not allow himself the easy out he offers others—the chance to buy forgiveness and satisfaction with money or specific good works. For himself the Pardoner requires true contrition, true purpose of amendment; he *does* believe that Christ's pardon is best.[36]

Interestingly, it was the subversion of the sacrament, more than the misappropriation of funds, that other churchmen principally complained of in actual pardoners. But Chaucer's association of his Pardoner with false relics may be a more imaginative touch, since it is not especially characteristic of the pardoners described in contemporary documents.[37] Perhaps nothing else about the Pardoner expresses so poignantly his anguish about his body as do the jars and bottles of old bones and bits of clothing he always carries with him. When

Harry Bailey charges that the Pardoner would try to pass off his "olde breech" "with [his] fundement depeint" as a relic and proposes to enshrine the Pardoner's testicles in a hog's turd "in stide of relikes or of seintuarie" (VI.948–55), the symbolic equivalence between the relics and the Pardoner himself becomes almost explicit. For many readers, Harry's crudity must suddenly and explosively bring to consciousness a truth they have already apprehended subliminally.[38]

Binding himself again to a marginal expression of the church's life, the veneration of relics, the Pardoner expresses both his fear, nearing conviction, that his own body, like the tavern in his tale, is the devil's temple (l. 470) and his faint but continuing hope that this same body may yet prove to be the holy temple of God. Because he uses false relics to make money and to entice others away from true contrition, the relics become, like his body, sources of sin to himself and to others. Moreover, by offering the relics for veneration, he dupes his customers into kissing what is symbolically the instrument of that sodomitical sin he and they have learned to despise. At the same time, the Pardoner seems always to be hoping that others will repose a genuine faith in his relics, a faith that will miraculously transform his relics and the body they represent into holy things. In all his traffickings with relics, the plea for money is partly a camouflage for the plea for the redemptive kiss. The relics he uses for this purpose *must* be false. His relics must be as unholy as he thinks his body is so that the hoped-for transformation can be "real." The Pardoner will never experience such a transformation, of course, since he will never be able to respect the faith of those he deceives and corrupts.

The notorious difficulty of accounting for the Pardoner's offering to the pilgrims relics he has already admitted to be false arises in part from overemphasizing the mercenary motive. But by taking the pilgrims into his confidence to a degree, the Pardoner has developed a more intimate relationship with this audience than he usually develops with his more gullible victims. In offering relics now, he is acting under an unusually strong compulsion to acquire that personal validation he is always seeking through them. Even on this occasion, though, the Pardoner's attempt to reach out to Harry Bailey and the community he represents is doomed by the inveterate ambivalence of the Pardoner's own attitudes.

The latent aggression in the Pardoner's statement that Harry "shalt kisse the relikes everychon" (l. 944) and the latent sexual implication in his command to Harry to "Unbokele anon thy purs" (l. 945) turn the scene into one of implied seduction or even rape; the Pardoner uses his homosexuality as a weapon. In addition, by characterizing Harry as "envoluped in synne" (l. 942) and offering to pardon Harry's sins, the Pardoner contemptuously portrays the heterosexual Christian as needing the absolution of the despised sodomite. But with the same gesture with which he assaults Harry's heterosexual sensitivities, the Pardoner asks for love; and with the same gesture with which he charges another with sin, he seeks forgiveness for himself. Understandably Harry reacts to the threats to himself in the Pardoner's behavior and does not hear the cry for acceptance. Example of natural manhood that he is, Harry retaliates by casting aspersions on the Pardoner's virility and by threatening castration (ll. 946–55). But as the reference to the true relic of Saint Helen's cross suggests, the ultimate issue is not perfection in the physical order but holiness in the spiritual order.[39] The Pardoner's defeat lies in the clear implication of Harry's obscenity that both the Pardoner's relics and his body are *not holy*.

The goal of the final scene, as of all the Pardoner's maneuvers, is a kiss. The scene does in fact end with a kiss, of course, though not one of the sort the Pardoner was seeking. The Knight engineers a reconciliation between Harry and the Pardoner that restores a degree of mutual tolerance while avoiding all the issues. We may be thankful, though, that the Pardoner does not receive the kiss that in rage and self-contempt he wished to extort from an abased Harry. It would truly have been an obscene kiss, not because of any homosexual element, but because of its sadomasochistic nature. Left unanswered, however, is the question whether the Pardoner will ever receive the kiss that in another sense he was seeking: not a kiss mirroring his own self-contempt or a kiss of ambivalent social tolerance but a kiss expressing genuine acceptance of his humanity—in Christian terms, a kiss confirming his part in the Father's creation and in the Son's redemption.

Through his manipulation of the sacrament of penance, the Pardoner covertly seeks forgiveness for what he takes to be his sinful condition; through his manipulation of relics, he covertly seeks affirmation that he is in some sense holy. The Pardoner lives his life through the church's rituals, sacraments, and sacramentals in a way that dramatizes both the pain of exclusion and the hope for ultimate inclusion. No other pilgrim is so saturated in the life of the institutional church as this accomplished singer of the liturgy, this eloquent preacher steeped in the lore of the pulpit, and this successful entrepreneur in absolutions and relics. Though believing himself the church's rejected son, the Pardoner has done everything he can to make himself a "noble ecclesiaste."

Given the position of the medieval church on homosexuality, this interpretation of the Pardoner might seem to offer new grounds for the still current belief that the Pardoner is, among Chaucer's pilgrims, uniquely evil. In my view it does no such thing. Ideally this interpretation should help us to penetrate the Pardoner's own obfuscatory characterization of himself as "a ful vicious man," a characterization that has already begun to receive the skeptical criticism it deserves. Making a useful distinction between behavior and state of mind, John Halverson shows that the Pardoner probably does less actual harm than the Friar and that his description of his own spiritual condition is preposterous, serving to mock those who accept it while disguising and protecting the Pardoner's true self. Halverson finds the Pardoner not evil, but deadly, "necrophiliac." While the relationship of the Pardoner to death is important and deserves the further study Halverson calls for (esp. pp. 191–92, 196–97, 199–201), I think it is already possible to say that the Pardoner's manipulation of relics and pardons betrays signs of spiritual life.

Interestingly, the subject of homosexuality offers Chaucer the opportunity to distinguish between behavior and state of mind in much the same way as Halverson does. Any physical acts in which the Pardoner expressed his homosexuality would be viewed by the medieval church as sinful, and Chaucer does not challenge this teaching. But he does challenge the belief that such sins are uniquely abhorrent, poisoning the whole character and extirpating all good and all potential for good. The Pardoner's elaborate way of relating to church and community through his relics and pardons reveals such hopeful signs as a latent belief in his own essential worthiness, a desire to be restored to God's grace, a desire to be socially useful, and a desire to give and receive love. The Pardoner's defenses, even against the best in himself, are so well entrenched, however, that the possibility of a transformation seems remote, though it cannot be denied. The Pardoner's preaching text, "*Radix malarum est Cupiditas*," is only one of the mottoes relevant to the judgment of this pilgrim; the other is the snatch of popular song on his lips when we first meet him, "Com

hider, love, to me." It is sometimes said that this song refers only to
carnal love, and to a love made distasteful by the characters of the
Summoner and the Pardoner. But just as Chaucer alludes here to that
charity which is the cardinal value of his pilgrimage, so the Pardoner,
however unconsciously, names this charity as the ultimate goal of his
own yearnings. Cupidity and love—each reader must decide what
relative weight to give to these two in judging the Pardoner, and the
weighting of the balances is not obvious.

The task of judging the Pardoner, like that of judging each of
the other pilgrims, makes the judges vulnerable, too, not least of
all Chaucer himself. A final question cannot be evaded. Why does
Chaucer treat the possibility of the Pardoner's homosexuality so allusively? Does his indirection betray some allegiance, or at least some
submission, to the phobic view that homosexuality is so abhorrent
it must not be spoken or written about? We must admit, on the one
hand, that here Chaucer may be showing a characteristic degree of
caution. On the other hand, Chaucer's very silences can be seen as an
allusion to the sin that should not be named.[40] Such an argument runs
the risk of being merely self-serving for the critic, of course; but if the
glossing of "mare" as "homosexual" is accepted, then the interpretation
of Chaucer's other allusions has a firm anchor in the literal meaning
of the text. Moreover, what I take to be this explicit suggestion of
possible homosexuality is never withdrawn or disproved. Thus readers
must engage in a work of interpretation that inescapably becomes
a moral exercise. Because the facts about the Pardoner's sexuality
are not given but must be established, readers cannot easily retreat
into one-dimensional judgments of this pilgrim; they are forced to
consider the whole character of the Pardoner in a way that should in
turn contribute to a nonreductive appreciation of his sexuality and its
spiritual implications.

Chaucer may have been inspired by a conviction like the one
with which the Parson closes his discussion of "thilke abhomynable
synne": "though that hooly writ speke of horrible synne, certes hooly
writ may not been defouled, namoore than the sonne that shyneth on
the mixne" (x.910). Chaucer may be seen as using his art, and especially its indirection and allusiveness, to challenge the sexual phobias
of his readers, requiring them mentally to juxtapose the Pardoner's
countenance with Christ's, even as the Pardoner himself has done by
wearing a vernicle on his cap (I.685). The vernicle, a representation

of Christ's face as it appeared on Veronica's veil, was commonly worn by Christians who had made pilgrimage to Rome.[41] There is nothing unusual about the Pardoner's wearing such an emblem (although another pilgrim to Rome, the Wife of Bath, is apparently not wearing one), but Chaucer's use of it is nonetheless thematically significant. The vernicle asserts the dignity of the Pardoner, whatever his sexual status, as part of Christ and reminds us that through his sexual sufferings the Pardoner participates in the crucifixion. But most important, the vernicle asserts the necessity of each reader's responding to the Pardoner in the context of Christian love, a necessity that cannot be evaded by appeals to the values of secular society or to the prescriptions of ecclesiastical leaders. The use of the vernicle is daring, the challenge to the reader risky; Chaucer is not always cautious.

It would be wrong to overstate the special relation of the vernicle to the Pardoner, however, and thus to isolate him once again in his supposed uniqueness. The vernicle might be mentally placed on the headdresses of all the pilgrims; there is not one of them who does not challenge the observer's capacity for insight and love. The Pardoner will not be rightly judged until we also subject to judgment our own fascination with him and until we perceive what he shares with the other pilgrims as clearly as we perceive what sets him apart. Chaucer, after all, suggests the balance at the very beginning; he gives us a "compaignye, / Of sondry folk" but "pilgrimes were they aile."

NOTES

1. *The Works of Geoffrey Chaucer*, ed. F. N. Robinson, 2nd ed. (Cambridge, Mass.: Houghton, 1957), p. 23. All subsequent references to the *Canterbury Tales* are to this edition.

2. Other arguments supporting the notion of the Pardoner's homosexuality, in the order of their earliest published form, are Muriel Bowden, *A Commentary on the General Prologue to the* Canterbury Tales (New York: Macmillan, 1948), pp. 274–76; Gordon Hall Gerould, *Chaucerian Essays* (Princeton: Princeton Univ. Press, 1952), pp. 58–60; Beryl Rowland, "Animal Imagery and the Pardoner's Abnormality," *Neophilologus*, 48 (1964), 56–60; Jill Mann, *Chaucer and Medieval Estates Satire: The Literature of Social Classes and the General Prologue to the* Canterbury Tales (Cambridge: Cambridge Univ. Press, 1973), pp. 145–52; and

John Gardner, *The Poetry of Chaucer* (Carbondale: Southern Illinois Univ. Press, 1977), pp. 301–03.

3. Curry, *Chaucer and the Mediaeval Sciences* (New York: Oxford Univ. Press, 1926), pp. 54–70.

4. Miller, "Chaucer's Pardoner, the Scriptural Eunuch, and the Pardoner's Tale," *Speculum*, 30 (1955), 180–99.

5. The medical and physiognomical texts Curry studied present a secular version of the physical determinism rejected by the biblical commentators. Thus if Chaucer knew both the scientific and the scriptural traditions of interpretation, he confronted not monolithic agreement but obvious conflict on the subject of eunuchry.

6. Howard, *The Idea of the Canterbury Tales* (Berkeley: Univ. of California Press, 1976), pp. 342–45.

7. Howard, ed., *Geoffrey Chaucer: The* Canterbury Tales, *a Selection* (New York: NAL, 1969), p. 88. These glosses seem to reflect both a closer adherence to Curry's views and an interpretation of the terms that differs from the one Howard adopts in *The Idea of the* Canterbury Tales (1976). In the latter work I cannot identify a gloss for "mare" that would elucidate what a medieval audience understood by the term. Howard says only that Chaucer's line suggests that the Pardoner "is sexually peculiar— that he lacks something: like a gelding the physical equipment, or like a mare the male gender-identity" (p. 343).

8. Fisher, ed., *The Complete Poetry and Prose of Geoffrey Chaucer* (New York: Holt, 1977), p. 22; Baugh, ed., *Chaucer's Major Poetry* (New York: Meredith, 1963), p. 253. Three other editors do not gloss either term: Robinson; E. T. Donaldson, ed., *Chaucer's Poetry: An Anthology* (New York: Ronald, 1958); and Robert A. Pratt, ed., *The Tales of Canterbury* (Boston: Houghton, 1974). In his Commentary, Donaldson adopts the view that the Pardoner is a eunuch (p. 900).

9. Applied to human beings, "mare" is usually a contemptuous term for a woman: "a slut." While both the *MED* and the *OED* cite *Canterbury Tales* I.691 s.v. "geldyng," neither treats Chaucer's use of "mare" in the entry for that word. Similarly, Thomas Ross, in *Chaucer's Bawdy* (New York: Dutton, 1972), has a page-long entry for "geldyng" (p. 94) but for "mare" offers only a cross-reference to an unhelpful entry for "horse" (pp. 145, 111).

10. Jill Mann, "Chaucer and the Medieval Latin Poets, Part B: The
    Satiric Tradition," in *Writers and Their Background: Geoffrey Chaucer*,
    ed. Derek Brewer (Athens: Ohio Univ. Press, 1975), p. 172.

11. The word was coined by a Hungarian doctor named Benkert;
    see Arno Karlen, *Sexuality and Homosexuality: A New View*
    (New York: Norton, 1971), p. 187. The gloss "a homosexual,"
    however—like "a eunuch," the common gloss for "geldyng"—
    does not accurately reflect the colloquial flavor of Chaucer's line.
    The best gloss for "mare" would probably be a slang term for the
    effeminate male homosexual.

12. Gen. xix. 1–11. The interpretation of the special sin of Sodom
    and Gomorrah as homosexuality was established in the first
    century A.D. by Palestinian Jews hostile to Hellenistic culture.
    On the rejection of this interpretation by modern biblical
    scholarship, see Derrick Sherwin Bailey, *Homosexuality and the
    Western Christian Tradition* (London: Longmans, Green and
    Co., 1955), pp. 1–28. On Ganymede, see Karlen, pp, 22–24.
    For translations of lyrics that contain allusions to Ganymede,
    see Ernst Curtius, *European Literature in the Latin Middle
    Ages*, trans. Willard R. Trask (New York: Harper, 1953), p. 116,
    and George F. Whicher, trans., *The Goliard Poets: Medieval
    Latin Songs and Satires* (New York: New Directions, 1949), pp.
    97–101. For Orpheus, see John Block Friedman, *Orpheus in the
    Middle Ages* (Cambridge: Harvard Univ. Press, 1970), pp. 8–10;
    Ovid's *Metamorphoses* x.83–84; and Jean de Meun's *Roman
    de la rose*, ll. 19651–54. For Caesar, see Dante's *Purgatorio*,
    Canto xxvi. For discussion, see Charles S. Singleton, trans., *The
    Divine Comedy* (Princeton: Princeton Univ. Press, 1973), II, Pt.
    II, 633–36.

    The sins against nature included not only sodomy between
    males but also homosexual contacts of all types by either sex;
    anal and oral intercourse, coitus interruptus, and departures
    from the "normal" position among heterosexuals; bestiality; and
    masturbation. See John Noonan, *Contraception: A History of Its
    Treatment by the Catholic Theologians and Canonists* (Cambridge:
    Harvard Univ. Press, 1965), p. 226.

13. Chaucer's conception seems identical with what is now
    sometimes called "true inversion," a conjunction of cross-sex
    identification (i.e., feminization in males and masculinization

in females) with homosexual choice of sex object. For criticism of the concept as a definition of homosexuality per se, see D.J. West. *Homosexuality* (Chicago: Aldine, 1967), pp. 59–62.

14. See Bailey, passim; Karlen, pp. 1–178, esp. pp. 66–103; and H. Montgomery Hyde, *The Love That Dared Not Speak Its Name* (Boston: Little, 1970), pp. 29–57.

15. Gower's *Confessio Amantis* VII.4304 and Lydgate's *Fall of Princes* III.1613. This usage reflects, of course, a tradition of antifeminism.

16. *Le Roman de la rose, par Guillaume de Lorris et Jean de Meun*, ed. Ernest Langlois (Paris: Librairie de Firmin-Didot, 1920), II, 111–12. The translation is Charles Dahlberg's in *The Romance of the Rose by Guillaume de Lorris and Jean de Meun* (Princeton: Princeton Univ. Press, 1971), pp. 60–61.

17. Musa, trans., *Dante's* Inferno (Bloomington: Indiana Univ. Press, 1971), pp. 127, 135.

18. Marie Delcourt, *Hermaphrodite: Myths and Rites of the Bisexual Figure in Classical Antiquity*, trans. Jennifer Nicholson (London: Studio Books, 1961). For modern scientific studies of hermaphroditism and homosexuality, see West, pp. 160–66, and John Money and Anke A. Ehrhardt, *Man and Woman, Boy and Girl: The Differentiation and Dimorphism of Gender Identity from Conception to Maturation* (Baltimore: Johns Hopkins Univ. Press, 1972).

19. *Purity*, ed. R. J. Menner (New Haven: Yale Univ. Press, 1920), p. 31; Spearing, *The Gawain-Poet: A Critical Study* (Cambridge: Cambridge Univ. Press, 1970), pp. 61–62.

20. Eunuchs had a recognized place in homosexual prostitution, and youths chosen as catamitic favorites were sometimes castrated. See Karlen, pp. 31, 229–33. Like effeminacy and hermaphroditism, eunuchry was sometimes thought of as creating a woman-man; see Curry, pp. 57–62, and Jean de Meun's *Roman de la rose*, ll. 20037–82. For modern scientific studies of eunuchry and homosexuality, see West, pp. 155–60.

21. Text and translation from Robert Harrison's *Gallic Salt: Eighteen Fabliaux Translated from the Old French* (Berkeley: Univ. of California Press, 1974), pp. 366–69. In a paper presented to the New Chaucer Society, 21 April 1979, in Washington, D.C., Charles Muscatine argued, on the basis of similarities between

the French work and the Wife of Bath's Prologue, that Chaucer knew "La Veuve" in some form, written or oral.

22. For example, the French words *bougres* 'Bulgars' (corrupted as modern English "buggers") and *herites* 'heretics' referred interchangeably to homosexuals and heretics after the church's suppression of the Albigensian heresy, which was thought to have originated in Bulgaria and to have encouraged homosexuality. See Bailey, pp. 135–44. It should be noted, too, that eunuchs, though sterile, are not necessarily impotent in the sense of being unable to perform the sex act. The church defined impotence broadly, however, to include all conditions that make it impossible to deposit "true semen" in the vagina. See T. Lincoln Bouscaren, Adam C. Ellis, and Francis N. Korth, eds. *Canon Law: A Text and Commentary*, 4th rev. ed. (Milwaukee: Bruce, 1966), pp. 534–37.

23. On the imagery of goats, hares, and mares, see Rowland, "Animal Imagery."

24. Summoners and pardoners sometimes worked together to defraud the faithful. See Charles R. Sleeth. "The Friendship of Chaucer's Summoner and Pardoner," *Modern Language Notes*, 56 (1941), 138, and Arnold Williams, "Some Documents on English Pardoners 1350–1400," in *Medieval Studies in Honor of Urban Tigner Holmes, Jr.*, ed. John Mahoney and John Esten Keller. University of North Carolina Studies in Romance Language and Literature, No. 56 (Chapel Hill: Univ. of North Carolina Press, 1965), pp. 197–207. In *Medieval Estates Satire*, Mann claims, citing two works by Walter of Chatillôn, that institutional corruption in the church was often described metaphorically as sodomitical and that here as elsewhere Chaucer turns the satirist's metaphor into the attribute of individuals (p. 147). When the case for the Pardoner's homosexuality has seemed to rest solely on his association with the Summoner or even more narrowly on the possible sexual pun in "stif burdoun" (I.673), it has rightly been judged weak. For arguments in support of an intended Chaucerian pun, see D. Biggins, "Chaucer's General Prologue A673," *Notes & Queries*, NS 6 (1959), 435–36, and B. H. D. Miller, "Chaucer, General Prologue A673: Further Evidence," *Notes & Queries*, NS 7 (1960), 404–06; for counterarguments, see Howard, *Idea*, pp. 344–45.

25. *OED*, s.v. "trow," v., 4: "to believe, think, be of the opinion, suppose, imagine; sometimes, to believe confidently, feel sure, be assured." For the second sense, *OED* cites *Piers Plowman*, A.I.133: "Þis I trouwe beo treuÞe!"

26. In seventh- and eighth-century penitentials, which remained in use for several centuries thereafter, homosexual acts were assigned penances of prayer and fasting comparable to those for adultery and murder. See John McNeill and Helena Gamer, eds., *Medieval Handbooks of Penance* (New York: Columbia Univ. Press, 1938). Thomas Aquinas ranked sodomy as a graver evil than heterosexual fornication, seduction, rape, or incest (*Summa Theologica*, 2.2.154.12). According to Noonan, Martin le Maistre, writing in the fifteenth century, was apparently the first Catholic moral theologian to suggest that homosexual inclinations might be due to sickness or biological causes (p. 357, n. 34).

27. G.G. Sedgewick, "The Progress of Chaucer's Pardoner. 1880–1940," *Modern Language Quarterly*, 1 (1940), 431–440. John Halverson, "Chaucer's Pardoner and the Progress of Criticism," *Chaucer Review*, 4 (1970), 184–202; and Alfred Kellogg, "An Augustinian Interpretation of Chaucer's Pardoner," *Speculum*, 26 (1951), 465–81.

28. This synecdoche, referring to the materials from which dice were sometimes made, may well have been established usage, although neither the *Middle English Dictionary* nor the *Oxford English Dictionary* cites an occurrence antedating the Pardoner's Tale.

29. In the three analogues to the Pardoner's trick cited by W. F. Bryan and Germaine Dempster, eds., *Sources and Analogues of Chaucer's* Canterbury Tales (1941; rpt. New York: Humanities Press, 1958), pp. 411–14, the sinners are women and the disqualifying sin is adultery. Apart from an introductory reference in one of the analogues to murders committed by both sexes, there is no mention of sins, named or unnamed, committed by men. Historically, female homosexuality has not provoked the same phobic reaction as male homosexuality. See Bailey, pp. 159–67, for sociopsychological attitudes underlying Christian teachings.

30. The Parson probably has in mind a variety of "sins against nature," since he says, "This cursednesse doon men and

wommen in diverse entente and in diverse manere" (X.910). The
Pardoner himself seems to echo the Parson's formula in these
lines: "Allas! a foul thyng is it, by my feith, / To seye this word,
and fouler is the dede" (VI.524–25). Ostensibly the subject is
excessive drinking, but the remark, coming in the middle of
an attack on the "wombe" "belly" or "uterus" (II. 521–36), may
suggest that for the Pardoner it is heterosexual intercourse that
is unmentionable and undoable. The Pardoner cites Paul as the
source of his remarks on the "worn be," and in Paul's epistle (1
Cor. vi.12–20) the subject is sexual sin, not gluttony.

31. Alain de Lille's twelfth-century philosophical work *De Planctu
Naturae* attacks homosexuality in the monasteries as the type
of all man's perversions of nature, and in the next century,
Jean de Meun has Genius, the priest of Nature, condemn
homosexuality and recommend castration as punishment (ll.
19636–86). The heroes of a handful of French fabliaux and
romances are charged with homosexuality, but always unjustly;
the reader never has to confront an actual homosexual hero.
(See Gerald Herman, "The 'Sin against Nature' and Its Echoes
in Medieval French Literature," *Annuale Mediaevale*, 17 [1976],
70–87.) In fourteenth-century Italy, however, Dante places some
sodomites in Hell, though not in the deepest circles (Cantos
xv and xvi), and others in Purgatory (Canto xxvi); and as Karl
Vossler observes, Dante confronts such sins "without profound
ethical abhorrence" (*Mediaeval Culture: An Introduction to
Dante and His Times*, trans. William Cranston Lawton [New
York: Ungar, 1929], II, 263). The sudden revelation of a
husband's homosexuality in Tale 6 of Day 5 of Boccaccio's
Decameron, perhaps the most prominent of many references to
homosexuality in the work, simply provides a climactic comic
fillip for the tale. Of special interest are indications that defenses
of homosexuality may have been current. Jean de Meun's Genius
refers to those who read Nature's rules backward and refuse to
understand their true sense (ll. 19636–64). Thomas Aquinas
considers and rejects several arguments to the effect that
homosexuality is not a grave evil, including the argument that
it causes no injury; Aquinas replies that God is injured (*Summa
Theologica*, 2.2.154.11–12).

32. Michael Goodich, "Sodomy in Medieval Secular Law," *Journal of Homosexuality*, 1 (1976), 295–302. In the thirteenth century some authorities on the Continent adopted statutes punishing homosexuality with confiscation of property, castration, or burning; but in England there was no civil law against homosexuality until 1553, and there is no record of anyone's being punished for such a crime before 1630.

33. Chaucer's problem has been shared by all who have tried to find a specific cause for homosexuality. Recently the view has begun to prevail that the capacities for heterosexuality and homosexuality are part of man's phylogenetic inheritance and that an individual's primary adaptation to either pattern is the product of a largely unconscious learning process. See Clellan S. Ford and Frank A. Beach, *Patterns of Sexual Behavior* (New York: Harper, 1951), passim; Wainwright Churchill, *Homosexual Behavior among Males: A Cross-Cultural and Cross-Species Investigation* (New York: Hawthorn, 1967), pp. 89–120; and Money and Ehrhardt, pp. 227–35. The American Psychiatric Association struck homosexuality from its list of mental illnesses in 1974.

34. This approach still reflects the official view of the Catholic church, although the church now also recognizes an "anomalous" condition of homosexuality for which the individual may not be wholly responsible. For the text of the 1975 papal statement, "Declaration on Certain Questions concerning Sexual Ethics," see *Human Sexuality: New Directions in American Catholic Thought, a Study Commissioned by the Catholic Theological Society of America*, ed. Anthony Kosnik et al. (New York: Paulist Press, 1977), pp. 299–313. For criticism of the statement, see John J. McNeill, S.J., *The Church and the Homosexual* (Kansas City: Sheed, Andrews and McMeel, 1976), esp. pp. 10–14. The church is moving toward the idea of a special homosexual condition at a time when the sciences are moving away from it.

35. Gerald R. Owst, *Preaching in Medieval England: An Introduction to Sermon Manuscripts of the Period, c. 1350–1450* (1926; rpt. New York: Russell and Russell, 1965), pp. 99–110, and Alfred L. Kellogg and Louis A. Haselmayer, "Chaucer's Satire of the Pardoner," *PMLA*, 66 (1951), 251–77.

36. I refer to the so-called crux of the Pardoner's Tale: "And Jhesu Crist, that is oure soules leche, / So graunte yow his pardoun to receyve, / For that is best; I wol yow nat deceyve" (ll. 916–18). Like other parts of the Pardoner's performance, including the sermon on the tavern sins and the trick of imputing sins to the unresponsive members of his audience, this benediction has several significances. It is a traditional formula that closes the Pardoner's storytelling in a conventional way; a setup that flatters the pilgrims and softens them up for the pitch for money that follows; a deliberately confusing statement meant to complete the Pardoner's revenge against the gentlefolk; a truthful assertion that the Pardoner, while a charlatan, is no heretic; and a poignant revelation that the Pardoner still hopes for a pardon more genuine than his own or that of the institutional church: Christ's pardon. See Sedgewick pp. 448–56, and Halverson, p. 198.

37. Owst, pp. 100–01, 349–51; and Kellogg and Haselmayer, pp. 215, 228.

38. In the famous Tale 10 of Day 6 of Boccaccio's *Decameron*, Friar Cipolla describes a fantastic pilgrimage he purportedly made to acquire relics. In his translation of *The Decameron* (Baltimore: Penguin, 1972), G. H. McWilliam states that the passage uses code language to describe homosexual experiences (p. 511).

39. For the possibility that these lines also contain an allusion to the famous relic of Thomas à Becket's hair breeches, see Daniel Knapp, 'The 'Relyk of a Seint': A Gloss on Chaucer's Pilgrimage," *ELH*, 39 (1972), 1–26. Perhaps Chaucer is suggesting that holiness may be found in unexpected places: in an old pair of breeches or in a homosexual pardoner.

40. Homosexuality was commonly discussed only allusively. In *De Planctu Naturae* Alain de Lille treats homosexuality through an elaborate allegory of grammatical terms, Dante does not name the sexual sin against nature that he treats in Cantos xv and xvi of the *Inferno*, and, as already noted, Boccaccio uses a code to refer to homosexuality in Tale 10 of Day 6 of his *Decameron*. In *Contraception*, Noonan traces the uses of silence and "cautious generality" in discussions of "sins against nature" in works of instruction for both priests and laity in the twelfth through the

sixteenth centuries (pp. 266–74). Confessors and preachers were often warned not to be specific lest they suggest new sins to persons innocent of them.

41. Jonathan Sumption, *Pilgrimage: All Image of Mediaeval Religion* (London: Faber and Faber, 1975), pp. 222, 249–50.

"IN THE PENAL COLONY"
(FRANZ KAFKA)

❧

"In the Interpretation Colony"
by Blake Hobby, University of
North Carolina at Asheville

Any reading that supposes, or in its procedure implies, that Kafka, already in possession of the truth, then merely encoded it in the process of writing, so that the business of doing literary criticism is *de*coding—any such reading must be wrong. Kafka's fiction is an act of seeking, it is a would-be discovery, invention, engendered of the truth. Seen thus its unfinishedness is itself expressive. Failure it may be, but in an endeavor very unlikely to succeed. And if the author, sentence by sentence seeking after truth, fails to arrive, how should the critic? (Preece, 19)

Our art is a way of being dazzled by truth: the light on the grotesquely grimacing retreating face is true, and nothing else. (Kafka, *The Blue Octavo Notebooks* 92)

We too must suffer all the suffering around us. We all have not *one* body, but we have *one* way of growing, and this leads us through all the anguish, where in this or in that form. Just as the child develops through all the stages of life right into old age and to death (and fundamentally to the earlier stage the later one seems out of reach, in relation both to desire and to fear), so also do we develop (no less deeply bound up with mankind than with ourselves) through all the sufferings of this world. There

is no room for justice in this context, but neither is there any
room for fear of suffering or for the interpretation of suffering
as merit. (Kafka, *The Blue Octavo Notebooks* 97)

Talking about the theme of sin and redemption in Franz Kafka's "In
the Penal Colony" (first published in 1919 as "In der Strafkolonie")
may not be novel, but it is significant. As early as 1941 Austin Warren
analyzed the story as an allegory for a sin-filled world in which God
had disappeared:

> The earth is a penal colony, and we are all under sentence of
> judgment for sin. There was once a very elaborate machine,
> of scholastic theology, for the pronouncement of sentence,
> and an elaborate ecclesiastical system for its administration.
> Now it is in process of disappearance: the Old Commander
> (God) has died, though there is a legend, which you can
> believe or not, that He will come again. Meanwhile the
> "machine" seems antiquated and inhuman to ladies, who are
> sentimental about criminals, and to the new governor, who is
> a humanitarian. (363)

Warren's assessment, given tongue-and-cheek, allegorizes the story,
turning the tale into a theological message about the death of God in
the modern world. What is allegory? Perhaps the best way to think
about allegory is the story behind the literal story, a symbolic way of
making meaning in which all the elements come together to signify
something. This way of interpreting seems natural. In the West, we
have inherited it from a long line of interpreters, from Augustine
to Dante to Aquinas to Cleanth Brooks and Robert Penn Warren,
whose method of "new criticism" articulated in *Understanding Fiction*
(1943) suggests that we read a work of literature as a stand-along
piece of artifice, looking for its organic unity. This way of approaching
understanding can be liberating, for we need not know anything about
the author, the historical milieu in which the work develops, or any
extratextual sources. Instead, what we need in order to confront a
text is the ability to read closely, thinking of literature as being self-
contained, looking for formal elements such as rhyme, meter, setting,
characterization, and plot and always keeping an eye out especially for
paradox, ambiguity, irony, and tension. Such reading yields the ability

to understand literature previously inaccessible. But such reading often eradicates a text's strangeness and irreducibility.

It is impossible to study Kafka without coming to terms with this sort of reading, one that attempts mastery by lining out a clear theme and often arriving at a moral conclusion. But what can we do if, as Julian Proece implies, such a totality and clear meaning eludes us? And what should we do if the author of the text—in this case the wily creator of expressionist and absurdist art we know as Franz Kafka—deliberately foils our attempts to arrive at a definitive interpretation and fashions a story about art, one whose meaning can never be fully arrived at? We confront such a dilemma with "In the Penal Colony." By looking at critical arguments that deal with sin and redemption, we see what can be agreed upon—namely that the text does deal with sin and redemption—and what can not be agreed upon—namely, what Kafka wishes us to take from his story.

Much of Kafka scholarship has focused on the parable as a form, one that enables Kafka either to encode a specific rhetorical intent or to capture the nature of paradox. This interest is often spurred by Kafka's diary entries and a short piece written late in life called "On Parables":

> Many complain that the words of the wise are always merely parables and of no use in daily life, which is the only life we have. When the sage says: "Go over," he does not mean that we should cross some actual place, which we could do anyhow if the labor were worth it; he means some fabulous yonder, something unknown to us, something that he cannot designate more precisely either, and therefore cannot help us here in the very least. All these parables really set out to say merely that the incomprehensible is incomprehensible, and we know that already. But the cares we have to struggle with every day: that is a different matter. (457)

In this passage Kafka describes parables as mysterious forms whose purpose lies in placing us before what we cannot understand and putting us in touch with the suffering endemic to the human condition. Heinz Politzer's influential study *Franz Kafka: Parable and Paradox* (1962) picks up upon Kafka's comments and casts his works in light of this predominantly religious literary form, taking the parables in the Bible as Kafka's muse:

> [Kafka's] parables are as multilayered as their Biblical models.
> But, unlike them, they are also multifaceted, ambiguous, and
> capable of so many interpretations that, in the final analysis,
> they defy any and all. Like literary Rorschach tests they reveal
> the characters of the interpreters rather than their own. (21)

Here Politzer delineates how Kafka's parables depart from their biblical
counterparts and tries to account for the range of interpretations already
encountered in Kafka scholarship at the middle of the twentieth century.

While Politzer posits a mystery at the heart of Kafka's works, as
a critic he finds it difficult to avoid decoding a specific message, one
that, in spite of its argument for open-endedness, limits the scope of
Kafka's narratives. We can see Politzer reining in such an interpretation as he describes the apparatus:

> This machine, whose composition and decomposition are
> described with equal perspicuity and love, is Kafka's prime
> symbol during these years. If his purpose was to concentrate
> in one universally valid image the process of dehumanization
> characteristic of the time of the First World War, then he found
> it here in this symbol of man's self-destructive ingenuity. If he
> sought to make externally manifest the hidden legal process
> of *The Trial*, then he found his symbol in this "peculiar piece
> of apparatus." If, finally, he attempted to catch a glimpse of
> transcendent existence behind the rationalized and organized
> reality of twentieth-century civilization, then his invention
> of a machine which combined the streamlined glamour of
> technology with the barbarous primitiveness of a divinely
> justified martial law was a real stroke of genius. (104)

Politzer provides a context for Kafka's works (World War I), but he
limits how we conceive of Kafka's tale. He challenges us to see the
apparatus as an example of post-World War I disillusionment, the sort
of disfigured reality present in Ernest Hemingway's *The Sun Also Rises*,
where the disillusioned drink, fish, and go to bullfights. *The Sun Also
Rises* bears the Gertrude Stein inscription as its epigraph: "You are all
a lost generation." By supplying this context, Politzer facilitates the
making of meaning, helping us connect a bizarre text with the history
of the early part of the 20th century. But, in doing so, he eradicates

the suprarational elements of the text, those that transcend any story of an era. For Kafka does not supply such a context. As an abstract expressionist writer concerned mostly with our interior world and the guilt we experience, Kafka does not write historical novels. It is virtually impossible to discuss Kafka's works without providing a specific context. When we supply a context, we interpret. When we interpret, we bring our perspective, by choosing which elements to emphasize and selecting what pieces to stitch together. As with so many other modernist writers, Kafka labors to create stories with seemingly endless possibilities for interpretation. Even if, as William Hubben tells us in 1962, "Kafka's main theme, then, is an ever-present sense of guilt, perhaps sin," we are still left trying to figure out the source of the guilt and the means and purpose of expiating sin (143). Such wondering may lead us, as it does for Martin Greenberg, to conclude that there is something imperfect about Kafka's art.

In *The Terror of Art: Kafka and Modern Literature* (1965), Greenberg, translator of Kafka's diaries, argues that "In the Penal Colony" is an aesthetic failure because Kafka grounds it in the historical and allows it to become an allegory of the modern world (Greenberg contends that Kafka's "dream narratives" such as *The Trial* and *The Castle* are more successful):

> *In the Penal Colony* takes place in historical time—the colony is a more or less recognizable possession of a European power of the late-nineteenth or early-twentieth century—rather than in the timeless subjective dimension into which the protagonists of Kafka's dream narratives awaken out of historical time. Its subject matter is the religious history of the world, which it recapitulates in terms of the old times and the new times of a penal colony. Like most of Kafka's stories, it is concerned with spiritual need, but it treats this subject in historical terms rather than through an individual who experiences the despair of spiritual darkness in the timelessness of his soul. It is an historical allegory. (108)

For Greenberg, "*In the Penal Colony* is not *about* the conflict between the moral and the religious; it falls victim to that conflict" (111), and "the failure of the story is the failure to be subjective—and through subjectivity to reach the truth" (112). Thus, he concludes the story is

too definitive and not open-ended enough, virtually the opposite position Politzer occupies in his book.

But as the cogs of the Kafka critical machine continue to turn,
those continuing to interpret the story do not shy away from religious
elements and the sin and redemption theme. In her 1979 analysis of
the story, Doreen Fowler contends that the Old and New orders in
the story represent the Hebraic and Christian traditions, with the new
order following "a harsher former order" and the officer appearing as
a Christ-like figure:

> Like God-the-Son who existed from time immemorial with
> God-the-Father and who aided in the creation of the world,
> the officer contributed to the institution of the penal colony
> from its inception: "I assisted at the very earliest experiments
> and had a share in all the work until its completion" (p. 193).
> Like Christ, son of God-the-Father, the officer pays filial-like
> devotion and allegiance to the old Commandant. The officer's
> youth further reinforces this resemblance to God-the-Son.
> Finally, the officer's willing sacrifice of himself in the place of
> the condemned man clearly suggests an analogy to Christ's
> suffering and death, which, according to Christian theology,
> were accomplished in order to redeem condemned humanity
> from the effects of original sin. (117)

According to Fowler, instead of celebrating Christ as a liberator from sin,
the story portrays Christ as the "last proponent of the old stern law":

> According to Kafka's construction of Biblical events, as
> suggested in "In the Penal Colony," Christ died for an opposite
> reason—in affirmation of man's guilt and the necessity of
> suffering for that guilt. The Christ-figure of Kafka's analogy,
> the officer, sacrifices himself in order to bear witness to the old
> order that identifies guilt with human existence and justice
> with punishment. *Thus, in Kafka's inversion of traditional
> Christian theology, Christ is not the originator of a new law of
> love and forgiveness. Rather, Kafka's Christ-figure is the last
> proponent of the old, stern law which decrees that atonement for
> human guilt is won only by suffering.* (116)

Alternately, Stanley Corngold in *Franz Kafka: The Necessity of Fiction* (1988) declares: " 'In the Penal Colony' casts doubt on the fact of anyone's guilt and hence on the efficacy of punishment for redemption. It does so radically for Kafka the author: it breaks up a paralyzing belief in the machinery of exculpation, and to this extent the story is redemptive" (235). As reading much Kafka criticism reveals, two critics dealing with the same thing can allegorize the story and arrive at two completely different interpretations.

While arguing that the historical period in "In the Penal Colony" is not expansive enough for the story's scope, Allen Thiher (1990) sees the story as an allegory of writing; a way of finding meaning, redemption, salvation, and justification for the law:

> What the immediate interpretive context should be is difficult to put succinctly, since this "punishment" is a parable that takes the history of Western culture as its largest referential framework; and this history is meaningful only as a history of the writing of that history. It is only by understanding history—and perforce the writing thereof—that we might gain access to the law and logos that we once believed were at the origin of our history. . . ."In the Penal Colony" spells out, as pun and literally, that the law and writing are two sides of the same thing—of that unnamable logos that we assume must exist. Writing is, in a quite literal sense, the means of finding access to the law, and hence of the redemption, justification, and salvation. (*Erlösung* is the received term for salvation Kafka uses, derisively, in the story itself.) In this exemplary story, then, the equation between writing and the law is savagely clear: writing is a way of finding the law as well as the form of the law itself. (51–52)

In the same year and with an equally astute reading of the tale, Arnold Weinstein (1990) sees the way that the machine functions as the role of art in a world where the connection with the divine word is lost:

> Kafka's writing machine is a made figure for the role of art and understanding in a world filled exclusively with signs and flesh. How can signs and flesh be connected, the thickness of matter by penetrated by the logos or spirit? The Word of the past, the

Word that spoke Truth and commanded Assent, is gone. But the writer remains.... The machine is indeed intolerable in its flagrant violation of the body, but it functions as a sublime symbol of Kafka's—and all artists'—aspirations: to read his work is to be penetrated by it: his words are inscribed in our flesh: our understanding of the story, of the Other, is to be both visceral and transcendent. The text is the machine: the metamorphosis is in us. (129)

Whether Kafka's text brings about the sort of change Weinstein claims, "In the Penal Colony" is a testimony to the power of art: the way a story can shake us, move us, and inspire us to return to it time and time again in search of meaning. In this sense, the story presents a moment of unveiling, where the suffering and horror at the core of existence affect us through the power of Kafka's art.

Franz Kafka's "In the Penal Colony" places readers before a religious spectacle, a ritualistic sacrifice. We read about the horrors of an apparatus that inscribes punishment on the flesh, reducing a human being to silence as it scripts atonement for sin. Were it possible to walk away comfortably knowing that Kafka crafted a meaningful allegory and believing we understood what Kafka was trying to say, we could begin talking about how the story instructs, informs, entertains, and brings us to a point of closure. Yet Kafka does not provide this clarity and leaves us, as Richard T. Gray (2002) argues, "without hope of interpretive mediation" ("Disjunctive Signs" 241). Such an inability to decipher engenders many varied interpretations. As Arnold Weinstein reminds us:

Like all of Kafka's best stories, "In the Penal Colony" is maddeningly rife with multiple contradictory interpretations. Some have made it announce Auschwitz and Dachau; others have seen in it a grim reminder of harsher Old Testament values, according to which our modern liberal world stands, either condemned or threatened; the brief tale has been read psychologically, psychoanalytically, anthropologically, historically, paradoxically, and parabolically. (120)

With Weinstein's thoughts in mind, we can see not only that Kafka intended us to struggle with the story, but also that our struggle with the story may be both the story's subject and the effect of its many elusive rhetorical devices. These critical voices reflect a half-century of thinking about the story, but, as we have seen, none of them has a definitive take, a way of authenticating an interpretation that arrives at a clear understanding of sin and redemption in the story.

Ultimately, we are left with a horrific meditation on interpretation. More than anything else, "In the Penal Colony" deals with the way we translate works of art into moral messages. In that sense, the tale is self-reflexive, commenting upon the very thing Kafka knows we will try to do with his story: reduce it to something meaningful in a clearly defined system, providing pithy phrases like the ones the apparatus cuts into the flesh. Kafka's grotesque work elevates art to the level of the spiritual, investing it with the power to overcome mechanized ways of understanding, and entrusting art to bear the burden of religion, whose ultimate truth is that we suffer, we die, and we are in need of redemption. Kafka's writing and the writing of the apparatus in the story simultaneously draw and repulse. But, unlike the traveler/explorer at the end of the story, we may never leave the colony, where thought at its best questions the past and at its worst dismisses everything as meaningless. Addressing fundamental questions about our existence and decrying our guilt, Kafka's is a religious art, one that praises our affliction and celebrates our failure to gain access to the law that might set us free. Rather than make a clear theological statement about religion, however, the story turns the very nature of art's ambiguity into a way of redeeming the world from signification, the West's wayward sin.

WORKS CITED OR CONSULTED

Brooks, Cleanth and Robert Penn Warren. *Understanding Fiction*. New York: Appleton-Century-Crofts, 1943.

Burns, Wayne. "'In the Penal Colony': Variations on a Theme by Octave Mirbeau." *Accent* 17 (1957): 45–51.

Corngold, Stanley. *Franz Kafka: The Necessity of Form*. Ithaca: Cornell UP, 1988.

Emrich, Wilhelm. *Franz Kafka: A Critical Study of His Writings*. Translated by Sheema Zeben Buehne. New York: Ungar, 1968.

Fowler, Doreen F. "'In the Penal Colony': Kafka's Unorthodox Theology." *College Literature* 6.2 (Spring 1979): 113–120.

Gray, Richard T. *Approaches to Teaching Kafka's Short Fiction*. New York: Modern Language Association of America, 1995.

————. "Disjunctive Signs: Semiotics, Aesthetics, and Failed Mediation in 'In der Strafkolonie." *A Companion to the Works of Franz Kafka.* James Rolleston, ed. Rochester N.Y.: Camden House, 2002.

Greenberg, Martin. *The Terror of Art: Kafka and Modern Literature.* New York: Basic Books, 1968.

Gross, Ruth V. *Critical Essays on Kafka.* Boston: G. K. Hall & Co, 1990.

Hawkins, Beth. *Reluctant Theologians: Franz Kafka, Paul Celan, Edmond Jabès.* New York: Fordham UP, 2003.

Heller, Erich. *Franz Kafka.* New York: The Viking Press, 1974.

Hubben, William. *Dostoevsky, Kierkegaard, Nietzsche, and Kafka: Four Prophets of Our Destiny.* New York: Collier Books, 1962.

Kafka, Franz. *Best Short Stories/Die schönsten Erzählungen.* Mineola N.Y.: Dover Publications, 1997.

————. *Franz Kafka, The Complete Stories.* New York: Schocken Books, 1971.

————. *Kafka's Selected Stories: New Translations, Backgrounds and Contexts, Criticism.* New York: W.W. Norton, 2007.

————. *The Blue Octavo Notebooks.* Cambridge, Mass: Exact Change, 1991.

————. *The Diaries: 1910–1923.* New York: Schocken Books, 1976.

Meyer, Michael. *Literature and Law.* Amsterdam: Rodopi, 2004.

Mirbeau, Octave. *The Torture Garden.* Olympia Press, 2008.

Pascal, Roy. *Kafka's Narrators: A Study of His Stories and Sketches.* Cambridge UK; New York: Cambridge UP, 1982.

Politzer, Heinrich. *Franz Kafka; Parable and Paradox.* Rev. and expanded ed. Ithaca, N.Y.: Cornell University Press, 1966.

Preece, Julian. *The Cambridge Companion to Kafka.* Cambridge UK; New York: Cambridge UP, 2002.

Rolleston, James. *A Companion to the Works of Franz Kafka.* Rochester N.Y.: Camden House, 2002.

Spann, Meno. *Franz Kafka.* Boston: Twayne Publishers, 1976.

Thiher, Allen. *Franz Kafka: A Study of the Short Fiction.* Boston: Twayne Publishers, 1990.

Thorlby, Anthony. *Kafka: A Study.* New Jersey: Rowman and Littlefield, 1972.

Warren, Austin. "Kosmos Kafka." *The Southern Review* 7.2 (Autumn 1941): 350–365.

Weinstein, Arnold. "Kafka's Writing Machine: Metamorphosis in the Penal Colony." Ruth V. Gross, ed. *Critical Essays on Kafka.* Boston: G. K. Hall & Co., 1990.

PILGRIM'S PROGRESS FROM THIS WORLD TO THAT WHICH IS TO COME (JOHN BUNYAN)

❧ ❧

"Forewords"
by H.R. Haweis, in *The Pilgrim's Progress* (1912)

INTRODUCTION

In this introduction to a 1912 edition of John Bunyan's Christian allegory *The Pilgrim's Progress*, H. R. Haweis maintains that the book "did for Protestantism what Dante did for Roman Catholicism—whilst exposing sometimes naïvely its weak points, it affirmed its doctrines, and popularized their application to current life." Haweis shows how Bunyan particularizes the Christian doctrine of sin and redemption to suit his audience.

☙

Next to the Bible, the "Pilgrim's Progress" is probably the book which has exercised more influence over the Religion of England than any other.

It did for Protestantism what Dante did for Roman Catholicism—whilst exposing sometimes naïvely its weak points, it affirmed its doctrines, and popularized their application to current life.

It supplied what Milton's "Paradise Lost" failed to give—some account of the ethics of the soul.

Haweis, H.R. "Forewords." *The Pilgrim's Progress.* By John Bunyan. Ed. R. Southey. New York: Harper and Brothers, 1912. 1–4.

From Milton we get our plan of salvation, but from Bunyan we get our conceptions of morality and our theory of spiritual development.

Perhaps few of those many who believe that the Bible is their sole spiritual guide realize the extent to which they see the Old Testament through Milton's eyes, and believe in the Gospel according to Bunyan.

There is yet another parallel. Bunyan supplied that imaginative touch and that glow of pictorial sentiment without which no religious message seems to win the masses.

He did with his "Pilgrim's Progress"—for a somewhat arid and stern Evangelicalism which repudiated the saintly legends and the material splendors of Rome—what Keble, with his "Christian Year," did for the dry bones of Anglicanism.

Keble made Anglicanism poetical. Bunyan made Evangelicalism romantic.

A greater than Bunyan or Keble adopted a similar method, when, as we read, "Without a parable He taught not the people." The extraordinary popularity of Bunyan's great book, one hundred thousand copies of which were circulated in his own lifetime, is not far to seek. He embodied his age—not its secular, but its religious side. No man could have been less influenced by the decapitation of Charles I, the accession of Cromwell, the restoration of that mundane merry monarch, Charles II. He lived through all these, in and out of prison, married and single, with his finger ever on the religious pulse of England; he was as little disturbed by wars and rumors of wars, political cabals and commercial bubbles, as were the great violin-makers of Brescia and Cremona by the political disturbances and bloody squabbles of the small Italian princelets of their day.

But in providing what the people really wanted, Bunyan was a master. They wanted the Bible; Bunyan gave it them. They felt its power; Bunyan showed them how to apply it. They kindled to its divine words, which they only half understood; Bunyan explained them. They needed, above all things, an infallible Book to replace the infallible Pope, whom they had knocked down. Bunyan not only told them that they might exchange the fallibility of men for the infallibility of God, but he provided for them such a battery of texts fitting every conceivable emergency and case of conscience that his New Bible Christian ceased to miss all those props of life and aids to devotion so skilfully devised for her children by the genius and varied mechanism of the Roman Church. And they got it all without the tyranny of Rome.

The impression a man of genius makes upon his age is in direct proportion to his intensity. The saints were vast accumulators of spiritual life. They were mighty reservoirs from which the people drank and went on their way rejoicing.

Emerson says the difference between great men and others is that there are more of them: they are many men rolled into one. They are macrocosms. That was true of Bunyan. Some men have some religious experience. Bunyan seems to have had all the spiritual experiences that could be had. There is no state, from blasphemy to ecstasy, which he had not sounded to its depths. Every event of his life, and every thought and sentiment came to him as so much teaching and discipline. What attracts us to him most is not the soundness of his judgment, nor his learning. The intellectual propositions which commended themselves to him seem to us often unreasonable, and his biblical learning, beyond a marvelous acquaintance with the letter of the Bible, is almost nil. He reminds us a little sometimes of the unlettered gospeler addressing his audience on the uselessness of all human learning and reasoning, when you might have the Word of God Himself to enlighten you.

"What, my brethren," he exclaimed, "is the use of it all? Did Paul know Greek?"

Had Bunyan known a little more Greek it would have done him no harm; and as to the comparative importance of Bible texts, why, it never occurred to him that a text was good for anything but edification, or that one text was not as good as another, if only it fitted an occasion. The Song of Solomon, or the Gospel of John, 'tis all one to good Bunyan. There is such a thing as idolatry of the Bible. It was the vice of his time, and to this day the Bible Christian suffers as Bunyan suffered (and the Church suffers too) from the defects of his qualities.

But his ingenuity is often marvellous, and one great source of his power is the often felicitous and sometimes fascinating use which he makes of texts.

"It was builded," he says of the Celestial City, "of Pearls and precious Stones, . . . so that by reason of the natural glory of the City, and the reflection of the Sun-beams upon it, Christian, with desire fell sick, *Hopeful* also had a fit or two of the same Disease. Wherefore here they lay by it a while, crying out because of their pangs, *If you see my Beloved, tell him that I am sick of love.*" This is as truly poetic as it is undoubtedly quaint.

Our "Pilgrim's Progress" is not only enlivened by conversations full of the deepest and surest spiritual instincts, so that it is a veritable manual of conscience cases, but it has what is so often wanting in persons of Bunyan's type of mind, the bull's-eye of wit, which is unexpectedly turned on to such persons as may be convicted of absurdity when they cannot be convinced of sin. The exposure of Mr. Talkative, who would chatter for any length of time about anything plausibly enough, but whose talk ended in smoke, or of Mr. By-ends, who was not to be condemned, according to himself, as a time server because his opinions always had the peculiarity of jumping with the times, or of Mr. Money-love, who found it possible to justify the morality of any action which brought him cash, are delightful cases in point.

His names alone are of quite monumental significance and suggestiveness. The jury in Vanity Fair, who tried Pilgrim and his friends, and consisted, amongst others, of Mr. Blind-man, Mr. No-good, Mr. Love-lust, Mr. Live-loose, and Mr. Hate-light, act and speak with delicious appropriateness.

"Away with such a fellow," "A sorry scrub," "My heart riseth against him," "Hanging is too good for him!" etc. Or consider the exquisite feeling which inspired Bunyan with such names as Greatheart, Hopeful, Faithful, Evangelist, or such as the Delectable Mountains, the Celestial City, and the King's Highway, and many more, which have become part of almost every Christian's imaginative outfit, as he follows in the footsteps of the great Pilgrim.

It is not necessary here to discuss Bunyan's theology. It was neither better nor worse than that of his age. The fires of hell, the forensic view of the Atonement, the material splendors of Heaven, his excessive reverence for the letter of the Book, belong rather to the form than to the essence of his doctrine, the center of which will always remain glowing with the love of God, bright with the discipline of the Soul, and radiating the enthusiasm of Humanity. These are the things unseen and eternal, which, when the Pilgrim awakes, he will surely find to have been, after all, no dream.

A PORTRAIT OF THE ARTIST AS A YOUNG MAN
(JAMES JOYCE)

"Sin and Redemption in James Joyce's
A Portrait of the Artist as a Young Man"
by Neil Murphy, Nanyang
Technological University, Singapore

Joyce's *A Portrait of the Artist as a Young Man* is constructed around a series of complex, resonant parallels between the metaphorical language of Christian mythology and Greek mythology. Joyce uses the imagery of Christianity to ultimately subvert its own substance, while initiating a transference of key Christian values to the artistic experience, or what Richard Ellmann called the "transvaluation of Christian images" (42). One of the focal points of the novel's structural and thematic tension is embedded in the allusive subtext of Stephen Dedalus's name: a conjoining of the first Christian martyr, St. Stephen, who was stoned to death, and the great mythic artificer, Daedelus, who survived an airy escape from Crete while his son, who flew too near the sun, died. A fusion of the Greek and Christian worlds, Stephen's doubly allusive name is indicative of the opposing forces within his character. Ultimately, of course, the Christian vocation that at one point appears central to Stephen's destiny gives way to that of the artist, to Daedelus. Throughout this shift, it is clear that the artistic life to which Stephen commits himself is a devotional mode of existence. So, while Stephen's desire to become an artist ultimately overwhelms the constraints of being a Jesuit priest, and even a Christian, the art he chooses is one that is infused with the language of

Christianity. So what appear to be irreconcilable aspects of his name are also conjoined, although in a definitively secular fashion. An extension of this is the way in which the traditional Christian concepts of sin and redemption are reconfigured through a series of transferences and reversals. Stephen's reinterpretation of Catholicism by way of his Daedalian aspirations becomes the source of his eventual artistic-spiritual redemption, while the vocational life of the Jesuits is depicted as a life of physical deprivation and denial of vitality. For Stephen, the religious life in effect becomes a sin against life.

The narrative design of *A Portrait of the Artist as a Young Man* is built on an amalgamation of religious and artistic themes, revealed in both the mythic significance of Daedelus's status as artisan and in Stephen's eventual reconstruction of himself as artist. The narrative aligns Stephen with Lucifer, both directly and indirectly. The reminders of the shining angel are everywhere; in the shape of wings, and wing beats, culminating eventually in the "wings of . . . exultant and terrible youth" (275) when Stephen prepares to take flight. The images used to describe Stephen during moments of sin—or preceding sin—are replete with significance. Stephen feels "cold lucid indifference . . . in his soul" when he begins the descent into sin and grows painfully aware that the "chaos in which his ardor extinguished itself was a cold indifferent knowledge of himself" (110). He is also consumed by "pride in his own sin" and a "loveless awe of God" (111). The hidden figurative kinship with the fallen angel extends throughout his period of sin, and reappears again in the metaphorical subtext to his flight from Ireland. We are also reminded in the sermons that Lucifer was a "son of the morning, a radiant and mighty angel" (126; from Isaiah 14:12) who had fallen, and of his traditional declaration of rebellion, "*non serviam: I will not serve*" (126; from Jeremiah 2:20), which later becomes a kind of artistic declaration of liberation for Stephen, one that coincides with his final rejection of Catholicism. The sermon also emphasizes that the sin of Eve (woman), influenced by the fallen angel Lucifer, is a sin of the flesh, just like Stephen's. Symbolically, such parallels push Stephen and the Shining One closer together in a silent brotherhood of resistance and wild abandonment. Like Lucifer's, Stephen's sin is a result of embracing life's opportunities, while rejecting the life of devotional service.

Throughout the novel, the characteristic rhetoric of religious quest becomes infused with that of the artistic. Even as a boy, the forbidding imagery of sin, punishment, and hell is everywhere in Stephen's consciousness, framing his particularized sense of being in the world; his daily existence is perpetually conditioned by a profound sense of sin and punishment. For example, Stephen comforts himself that he will not go to hell when he dies, because he has completed his prayers (16). He also wonders if it was a sin for Father Arnall to be in a "wax" or if it was permissible because the boys were idle (48). Stephen's early experience of punishment for a fake "sin," meted out by Father Dolan, results in Stephen developing a powerful sense of wrongdoing, punishment, and indignation. This is, of course, a perversion of the Christian pattern of sin followed by punishment with which Stephen is so familiar: His deep indignation is derived as much from the variation to the central narrative of his early experiences of Christian punishment, as it is from the implicit unfairness of Dolan's bloody-minded punishment. Furthermore, Stephen's agonized reaction is marked by a deep sense of humiliation: "[S]carlet with shame" he unraveled in his mind the intricacies of the unfair cruelty that had driven Dolan (53). Shame is the appropriate response to having transgressed, but Stephen's sense of shame is misplaced. The appropriate Catholic pattern has been muddied by the priest acting improperly. But Stephen's response mechanism takes some time to adjust to this fundamental rupture between his sense of the Catholic process and the living abuse of it. His sense of propriety is partially restored after his discussion with the rector, and his sense of obedience and humility is thereafter strongly emphasized: "He would be very quiet and obedient: he wished that he could do something kind for him [Dolan] to show him that he was not proud" (60–61). At this point, Stephen's need for the anchors of authority and moral certitude remain very strong, even though his victory is extremely shallow and his resistant urges have not yet found full expression.

When Stephen later confesses his sins of the flesh, a sense of shame again pervades: "His sins trickled from his lips, one by one, trickled in shameful drops from his soul festering and oozing like a sore, a squalid stream of vice. The last sins oozed forth, sluggish, filthy" (156). Throughout the novel, images of squalor and disgust repeatedly coincide with the language of sins. Stephen's cry of sexual desire is "but the echo of an obscene scrawl which he had read on the oozing wall of a urinal" (106), as he wanders along a "maze of narrow and dirty streets" (106). Disgust and sin are rhetorically linked; a dark, brooding

evil accompanies Stephen's sinful actions. When he sins with pros-
titutes, for example, he feels "some dark presence moving irresistibly
upon him from the darkness, a presence subtle and murmurous as a
flood filling him wholly with itself" (106). Traditional images of hell
are not far from his imagining consciousness: Stephen is painfully
aware of the "wasting fires of lust," the "dark presence," and the "wail
of despair from a hell of sufferers" (106). He positively oozes sin and
advances into another realm of existence, "another world ... awak-
ened from a slumber of centuries" (107). This other world suggests
another deep linkage between Stephen and the devil and offers crucial
foreshadowing of the sermon in the retreat. The sense of dislocation
from the fixed Catholic narratives of his former life is profound, even
though the language of those narratives remains the central defining
aspect of his new experiences.

The focal point for Stephen's salvation from his sins of the flesh is
the retreat, during which the process of redemption is characterized by
fear, a deep awareness, punishment, reverence, regret, and sorrow. More
significant in the context of the overall arc of Stephen's development,
however, is the recurring concentration on the oppositional claims
of flesh and spirit: Citing Matthew, "What does it profit a man to
gain the whole world if he suffer the loss of his immortal soul?" (118;
Matthew 16:26), the priest registers the claims of material reality over
those of the eternal spirit, repeatedly drawing attention to lower and
higher forms of existence, to the beast-like, and to the pure and the
holy, respectively. After the initial impact of the sermons, Stephen felt
that "[forms] passed this way and that through the dull light. And that
was life" (119). Material existence has become spectral, inconsequential;
when he later embraces art it coincides with a necessary *rapprochement*
with the stuff of material existence, "the wild heart of life" (185). But
for now the flesh becomes an emblem of sin and dullness.

Stephen twice seeks redemption. First via confession, repentance
and prayer, after the searing experiences of the retreat, and then via
the liberation of art, when he ultimately takes metaphorical flight. The
representation of Stephen's religious experiences is not always accompanied by the hellish imagery of sin and its consequences. A profound
sense of reverence also accompanies his childhood responses to the
trappings of Catholicism, as is clear from his respect for the sacristy,
that "strange and holy place" (41), and his enthusiastic embracing of
the spiritual path after his redemption from sin. Of course, Stephen's

response to his own secular existence, in certain meditative moments, is also depicted in a quasispiritual fashion. For example, his "silent watchful manner" (71) is embraced with almost religious zealousness, and he positively revels in "the joy of his loneliness" (71). These are recurring patterns of devotional response in Stephen, even when an experience is not strictly religious.

After the intense enthusiasm of Stephen's redemptive embracing of his religion begins to wane, a growing artistic awareness manifests itself, most obviously in Stephen's alertness to the sensual world and in his increasing fixation on language. The "swish of a soutane" attracts his attention, and "Les jupes" (167–168) generates a mini-reverie about an article of clothing worn by women. Gradually, his old critical eye reasserts itself and he begins to doubt some of the statements of his Jesuit teachers (169), and the "chill and order" of the religious vocation begin to repel him (174), expressed again in terms of the deprivation of body. Stephen now associates the priestly life with rising in the cold grimness of early morning and the fainting sickness of stomach. In an ironic repositioning, 'sins' *against* the flesh, or sins of self-deprivation, are now offered as negative images, as opposed to sins *of* the flesh. Stephen swiftly asserts his conviction that a life of religious vocation implicitly involves a denial of life, and he chooses another path to redeem his artistic soul:

> His destiny was to be elusive of social or religious orders. The wisdom of the priest's appeal did not touch him to the quick. He was destined to learn his own wisdom apart from others or to learn the wisdom of others himself wandering among the snares of the world. (175)

The fixed stasis of the Jesuit order, as he sees it, is represented as being in opposition to the needs of the artist, necessarily without fetters, free from authority. Stephen's salvation, when it comes, is affected through an aesthetic apprehension of reality:

> . . . a prophecy of the end he had been born to serve and had been following through the mists of childhood and boyhood, a symbol of the artist forging anew in his workshop out of the sluggish matter of the earth a new soaring impalpable imperishable being. (183)

The new vital bond between artistic being and materiality, between the imaginative mind and the body, is crucial here. The body, formerly the source of repugnant sin, now becomes a central component of Stephen's salvation and rebirth. And yet the flesh that was the source of his earlier anguish has also been transformed by his new visionary way of seeing. The first prostitute he slept with, "[a] young woman dressed in a long pink gown" (107), and the occasion of his sin, is also a prophetic echo of the girl on the strand who initiates his epiphany and signals his redemption. The contrast between the two events is tangible, particularly because the prosaic descriptions of the earlier encounter with the prostitute are barely memorable, unlike the highly charged Christian-influenced metaphors that accompany his epiphany:

> Her image had passed into his soul for ever and no word had broken the holy silence of his ecstasy. . . . To live, to err, to fall, to triumph, to recreate life out of life! A wild angel had appeared to him, the angel of mortal youth and beauty, an envoy from the fair courts of life, to throw open before him in an instant of ecstasy the gates of all the ways of error and glory. (186)

The deep religious tone of his response bespeaks a transference of devotional need from one sphere to another. She is an angel who enters his soul in communion with the holy silence of his artistic reverie, she is an emblem of life and the sensuality of living youth, she is his mortal angel, the replacement of pure spirit with the spirit of mortal aestheticism. In her Stephen has a perfect example of the flesh remade into art. As such she becomes an agent of his redemption.

Joyce's use of epiphanies does not mean the manifestation of Christ (as they traditionally might), but the epiphanies do serve an important figurative function in Joyce's efforts to create a secular art to rival the spiritual intensity of Christianity. The explanations of epiphany in Joyce's earlier unpublished novel *Stephen Hero*, a precursor to *A Portrait*, are fully immersed in the language of Christianity: "the revelation of the whatness of a thing . . . the soul of the commonest object . . . seems to us radiant" (217–218). The epiphany is the most complete example of Joyce's accommodation of Christian imagery; Joyce had experimented with simply writing out short epiphany episodes, of which 40 still exist, although most are much less extravagant than those readers encounter in his first novel (Joyce 1991, 161–200). In *A Portrait*, the "apparition" of the girl on the beach signals the initiation of Stephen's most sustained epiphany in the novel and fully utilizes the trope of the angel, while also conjuring the Virgin Mary, to elevate the essentially human aesthetic experience to the level of *claritas*. Later in the novel, Stephen, paraphrasing Aquinas, declares "the artistic discovery and representation of the divine purpose in anything or a force of generalization which would make the esthetic image a universal one, make it outshine its proper conditions" (231), but he then dismisses this and replaces it with a secular version that focuses on the "supreme quality [that] is felt by the artist when the esthetic image is first conceived in his imagination" (231). The transference of a Christian to a predominantly aesthetic religious experience is clear, as it is when he fully identifies with art, christening himself the "priest of eternal imagination, transmuting the daily bread of experience into the radiant body of everlasting life" (240).

Joyce's appropriation of his former religion's language to create metaphors that represent his vision of art is clear. But his decision to adopt the language of Christianity in order to erase the significance of the religious language itself is both provocative and ingenious. Joyce's commitment to Christian imagery reveals his awareness of the profound metaphorical sophistication of this body of images, from which he would draw inspiration throughout all of his work. A. Norman Jeffares has pointed out that Joyce owed much to the ordering cohesion offered by Catholicism, despite his essential rejection of the religion: "Stephen realizes that his true vocation is that of the artist, blending aesthetic experience with the logical ordering that he has learned from his Catholic upbringing" (Jeffares 222). And it is here that the central irony of his approximation of Christianity resides. Stephen sins and is redeemed by the traditional Christian procedure of confession, penitence, and forgiveness. But he then turns this process in on itself when the Christian vocation is presented as a grievous sin against the "fair courts of life," a sin of avoidance and sacrifice. Ultimately, the source of Stephen's redemption becomes the emblem of sin itself, which is subsequently redeemed by embracing reality. Stephen, like Christ, is resurrected from the dead and goes forth to pursue "the reality of experience" (275). Under the guise of the savior turned artist, he finds redemption.

WORKS CITED OR CONSULTED

Joyce, James. *A Portrait of the Artist as a Young Man*. London: Penguin, 1992.

———. *Stephen Hero*. Norfolk, Connecticut: New Directions, 1963.

———. "Epiphanies." Poems and Shorter Writings. Ed. Richard Ellman, A. Walton Litz, et al. London: Faber and Faber 1991: 161–200.

Ellmann, Richard. *James Joyce*. New York: Oxford University Press, 1983.

Jeffares, A. Norman. *Anglo-Irish Literature*. London: Macmillan, 1982.

THE PORTRAIT OF A LADY
(HENRY JAMES)

❦

"Isabel Archer as a Woman Clothed in the Sun"
by E.C. Curtsinger, in
The Muse of Henry James (1986)

INTRODUCTION

In his book on the novels of Henry James, Eugene Curtsinger reads *The Portrait of a Lady* as "an allegory of the Annunciation, itself perhaps the most dramatic moment in all of human history." By equating Isabel Archer with the Virgin Mary, Curtsinger explores the way Catholic theology and James's art intersect, each dependent upon the Great Muse (God), who invests his creation with a means of redemption from sin.

❦

The narrator of *The Portrait of a Lady* (1881) turns away from one of Henrietta Stackpole's comments, saying "this history . . . has too many other threads to unwind."[1] *The Portrait* is, indeed, a many-threaded novel, a rich weaving of bright and sombre strands into a gorgeous tapestry not to be undone by tugging at any several threads. I propose, however, to follow just one of the little fellows because, long and winding as he is, he passes near the hearts of Isabel Archer and Ralph Touchett, touches the tapestry's images of flower, bird, and star, and curls around

Curtsinger, E.C. "Isabel Archer as a Woman Clothed in the Sun." *The Muse of Henry James.* Mansfield, TX: Latitudes Press, 1986. 44–58.

the necks of Caspar Goodwood, Gilbert Osmond, Madame Merle, and little Pansy. Keep in mind that they are woven of many other threads, of course, and that my one small silver strand is merely a beginning.

I take up the thread at its far end where, in the closing moments of the novel, it is a filament of Isabel Archer's final scene with Caspar Goodwood. The scene, with Isabel on or beside a rustic bench as darkness gathers under the oaks at Gardencourt, is attended by lightning, comet, desert wind, and rushing water. That "the confusion, the noise of waters, all the rest of it, were in her own swimming head" does not diminish, for our little thread, the importance of James's pattern of cosmic imagery. The big sounds and colors are appropriate, obviously, to the worth of Isabel, the force of Caspar Goodwood, the great drama of the moment: she is seized by a new knowledge and she makes a climactic choice. Strangely enough, we seem not to have noticed, in a scant hundred years, the simple violent opposition of wind and water within the pattern of cosmic imagery. It's not Caspar's rushing torrent that carries Isabel away. It is the desert wind.

The water is all Caspar's.[2] He offers Isabel the world, which seems "to open out, all round her, to take the form of a mighty sea where she floated in fathomless waters. She had wanted help, and here was help; It had come in a rushing torrent." She might "sink and sink" in Caspar's arms, but she swims head and foot not to. His "white lightning" kiss only momentarily places her among those "wrecked and under water."

The comet, like the lightning, is Caspar's. He "had an idea, which she scented in all her being." When the idea "loomed large," Isabel "threw back her head a little; she stared at it as if it had been a comet in the sky." His idea, of course, is that he will give her his big wet world.

But who owns the desert wind? When Caspar asks her why she should go back to Rome and "that ghastly form," her marriage, Isabel's feelings are in pieces, one small and one large: "To get away from *you!*" she answered. But this expressed only a little of what she felt." Now comes the larger feeling, the new knowledge that "she had never been loved before," that all is different. Who loves Isabel Archer? Notice that her suddenly feeling loved takes her in response to Caspar's question about Rome, and that it identifies desert as the source of the newly-felt love:

> this expressed only a little of what she felt. The rest was that she
> had never been loved before. She had believed it, but this was

different; this was the hot wind of the desert, at the approach
of which the others dropped dead, like mere sweet airs of the
garden. It wrapped her about; it lifted her off her feet, while the
very taste of it, as of something potent, acrid and strange, forced
open her set teeth.

Caspar senses the desert wind as alien and opposed to him when it
forces open "her set teeth." Clearly, he identifies it with Rome and
her marriage. Watching her more closely than we, he says "It's too
monstrous of you to think of sinking back into that misery, of going
to open your mouth to that poisoned air."

The desert wind, the poisoned air, if they're not Caspar's, can
belong only to Gilbert Osmond. Naturally, we perish the thought that
this overwhelming desert love could be from Osmond. He is almost
universally regarded as a blackguard. He's the meanest man James ever
invented. He's the "sterile dilettante'" (292) who marries Isabel for her
money and wants to keep her lovelessly locked up in his fortress-like
Palazzo Roccanera.[3] But we do no harm by enjoying, for a moment,
this small thread in the huge tapestry.

Caspar says to Isabel, shortly before he comets, "your husband's the
deadliest of fiends." That the scene has Miltonic echoes—"The world's
all before us," as Caspar says—and is redolent of Eden has been noted
by other readers.[4] If we include Caspar's "deadliest of fiends" in the
pattern of cosmic imagery, and keep in mind James's characterization
of Isabel as virtuous woman and of Caspar as warrior, as armed man, [5]
we see that the prime archetype of the cosmic scene is, indeed, biblical.
It may come as a revelation:

> And a great sign appeared in heaven:
>
> A woman clothed with the sun, and the moon under
> her feet, and on her head a crown of twelve stars. And being
> with child, she cried travailing in birth, and was in pain to be
> delivered. . . . Woe to the earth, and to the sea, because the devil
> is come down unto you, having great wrath, knowing that he
> hath but a short time.
>
> And when the dragon saw that he was cast unto the earth,
> he persecuted the woman, who brought forth the man child.
>
> And there were given to the woman two wings of a great
> eagle, that she might fly into the desert unto her place, where

she is nourished for a time and times, and half a time, from the
face of the serpent.

And the serpent cast out of his mouth after the woman,
water as it were a river; that he might cause her to be carried
away by the river.

And the earth helped the woman, and the earth opened
her mouth and swallowed up the river, which the dragon cast
out of his mouth.

And the dragon was angry against the woman, and
went to make war with the rest of her seed, who keep the
commandments of God, and have the testimony of Jesus
Christ. (*Apocalypse 12*)[6]

Special woman, war-maker, watery assault, desert refuge. You don't
have to be a devotee of the Freudian hot-dog to catch the sexual
connotations of Isabel's open-mouthed receptions of the wind—not
of any violation by Caspar. But the phrasing, in James, is Saint John's
before it is Freud's: "the earth opened her mouth and swallowed up the
river." "'Open your mouth and I will fill it,' says the Lord" (*Psalms 81*).

Alas poor Caspar! The novel usually refers to him as "Caspar
Goodwood" or "Mr. Goodwood" except where he opposes Osmond.
Thomas Hardy's Boldwood may be a cousin to Caspar.[7] In our cosmic
scene, after his introduction as "Caspar Goodwood," his last name
stands alone, unrelieved by "Caspar" or "Mr.," six times in a row. Who
is this young comet Goodwood, Goodwood, Goodwood, Goodwood,
Goodwood, and Goodwood?: "And the third angel sounded the
trumpet, and a great star fell from heaven, burning as it were a torch,
and it fell upon the third part of the rivers and upon the fountain of
waters: And the name of the star is called Wormwood" (*Apocalypse
8*). The "Civil strife" Isabel pictures Caspar in may have been some
other war altogether than the American: "he might have ridden, on a
plunging steed, the whirlwind of a great war" (106).

How does Isabel fare as "A woman clothed in the sun, and the
moon under her feet"? The characters around her James refers to,
in the Preface, as the "heroine's satellites" (11). Many threads of the
novel may define Miss Archer as the huntress Diana,[8] but strung on
our silver thread she is Miss Sagittaria, the Archer. As the ninth sign
of the zodiac, she is between Capricorn and Scorpius. A moment of
the zodiac has the old goat, backed up by Aquarian waters, gazing at

her tail. She and the scorpion face each other. Her bow is bent, her arrow poised. Beyond the desert creature is Libra, ready for a pun: Caspar's lightning fades, and "when darkness returned she was free." This is fetched too far, of course, but we have to face the fact that real novelists are crazy people and don't think like the rest of us. Isabel's last name may not give her a sunny dress or a moon to stand on, but it places her in the heavens and readies her for cosmic scenes. As for Caspar, the zodiac, like the *Apocalypse*, puts a set of horns on him.

James's fondness of word-play is well known. His "Adina" is an anagram of *Diana*; in naming his characters, James "did not exclude even the most blatant of connotative possibilities."[9] If by our little thread Goodwood is Wormwood, his desert opponent is divine. But we don't have to relinquish our pretty pictures of Goodwood or our ugly pictures of Osmond merely because a thread in a great tapestry hints that one is satanic and the other sacred.[10] "Oh God!" says Madame Merle, in a moving moment, to Gilbert OsmonD (big *D* is mine) (435). "'God bless you!' said Gilbert Osmond" (264). We can ignore such pleasantries, of course, but what are we to do when we see that the dictionary defines the name *Osmond* as "Literally protection of God"?[11] As for *Gilbert*, it supplies the *G* without ringing other bells.

Since the novel is Isabel's, all the characters in it figure as the "heroine's satellites." Osmond tells Isabel she "can roam through space," and so she "ranged, she would have said, through space and surveyed much of mankind" (261, 270). Ralph notes her solar travel: "You seemed to me to be soaring far up in the blue—to be, sailing in the bright light, over the heads of men" (291). The zodiac may be seen as sunny Isabel's apocalyptic twelve-starred crown. Constellation, star, comet, planet: they circle the novel's sun or pass through her realm.

The Countess Gemini is by name a constellation and a sign of the zodiac. Serena Merle has "a sort of world-wide smile," "everything in her person was round and replete," and Ralph Touchett says that Serena "is the great round world itself!" (153, 230). What is the reason for her curious recurring smile, with "her handsome mouth drawn up to the left"? (153, 302–4). It is a reminder of Serena's "world-wide smile" and of Serena as world. "I was born before the French Revolution," she says. "I belong to the old, old world" (170). If Isabel admires and imitates Serena, "it was not so much because she desired herself to shine as because she wished to hold up the lamp for Madame Merle" (165). Osmond is once a moon: Isabel "had seen only half his nature then, as one saw the disk of the moon when it was partly masked by the shadow of the earth. She saw the full moon now—she saw the whole man" (357). Osmond's and Serena's astronomical positioning when they come together is almost comic: "on first meeting at any juncture," it is "as if they had approached each other obliquely and addressed each other by implication" (207). Lord Warburton is sometimes part of Isabel's sky: he "loomed up before her, largely and brightly," but Isabel "had a system and an orbit of her own" (95). Goodwood "had no system at all": "There was a disagreeable strong push, a kind of hardness of presence, in his way of rising before her" (95, 105). Mrs. Touchett, she of the wide travels and the "moral account book—with columns unerringly ruled and a sharp steel clasp," is a zodiacal Libra, balances precisely maintained, "as honest as a pair of compasses" (177, 190–91). Even Henrietta Stackpole has celestial moments, an "implacable glitter" (91). Ralph is moved by "the pure radiance of the young lady's imperturbable gaze" but resists "an inclination to frown as one frowns in the presence of larger luminaries" (110).

Characters, descriptions, scenes, dialogue, all are touched by the solar metaphor. Goodwood, entering Isabel's sky as an interloper, "seemed to see her whirled away into circles from which he was inexorably excluded" (142). There is a moment along "the Sacred Way" when Isabel is briefly unsatellited by her companions. As her imagination "hovered in slow circles," she becomes aware that "a shadow was thrown across the line of her vision." The free-wheeling Lord Warburton enters, rather like a planet coursing by. "I've nothing on earth to do," he says. "I've just come from the East. I'm only passing through" (245–46). Isabel is the surrounded sun when she is left alone in the gallery of the Capitol, "in the glorious room, among the shining antique marbles." She sits "in the centre of the circle of these presences, regarding them vaguely, resting her eyes on their beautiful blank faces; listening, as it were, to their eternal silence." Here, Warburton is identified with one of the classical presences, the Dying Gladiator, and we note that the old soldier will gradually fade from Isabel's universe (256–58). What a marvelous view when Saint Peter's is in orbit!: "It's very large and very bright," Isabel says (252). These and a thousand more images and phrases suggest that the sky of the *Portrait* is not static, its stars not intermittent symbols. The solar metaphor is a basic strategy of the novel and shines into its corners. James has in mind a bright, a vibrant theme of cosmic proportion and cosmic significance to bind it all together.

This is weighty stuff to hang by a thread. James brings it down to earth with birds and flowers. A bird is a star brought near: the Countess Gemini with her "look of shimmering plumage" is full of pecks and fluttery motion (218), Henrietta "shimmered, in fresh dove-coloured draperies" (80), a ralph is a raven, a merle is a blackbird. The bird imagery may find its source in the Apocalyptic eagle-wings of the sun-clothed woman. Ralph tells Isabel to spread her wings, Caspar "had never supposed she hadn't wings," and "she looked, as she sat there, like a winged creature held back" (192, 142, 323). Flowers are stars in the garden, characters relatively passive or ineffective, of small motion in the story: Lily, Pansy, Rosier who "had always smelt . . . of heliotrope" (365).

All these are satellites of the novel's lovely sun.

In our modern pose we like to run from certain kinds of literary analysis, as from a burning building, with cries of "allegory! allegory!" The trouble with allegory is that it disturbs our ontological faith that a rose is only a rose, and also that a reader momentarily freed from such flower metaphysics may tend to invent his own silly version regardless of what the writer writes. If the great James makes a novel whose flesh grows on a coherent allegorical heart and bone, then we have to be great readers. We leave the taboo to the ontologically devout. The fear that characters caught in allegory are vague automatons stripped of human values arises out of our failure to see that the deepest—the truest—motions of the human spirit are choreographed by the gods. We are never so human as when we dance in rituals allegorical and divine.

The allegorical thread I follow in the great weaving of the *Portrait* is simple, insistent, and clear. It binds together or illumines much that is scattered and puzzling in the literal action of the novel.

The Portrait of a Lady, by this one warm thread, is an allegory of the Annunciation, itself perhaps the most dramatic moment in all of human history: the angel Gabriel, sent from God, announces to the virgin Mary that "The Holy Spirit shall come upon thee, and the power of the most High shall overshadow thee. And therefore also the Holy which shall be born of thee shall be called the Son of God" (*Luke* 1). This time the Annunciation—so earnestly attempted in *Roderick Hudson*—magnificently succeeds. On a cosmic stage Isabel plays the part of Mary, Osmond is God, and Pansy, locked away from the world until Isabel is ready to receive her desert love, is Christ. The apparent absurdity of such a reading melts away as we follow the thread. The cosmic imagery of the novel would be, in fact, wasted without this mighty theme.

What I refer to as a Jamesian chasm between man and God is bridged—unexplainably, miraculously,—when the planet earth presents to the Almighty a woman worthiest to receive His seed. The child is bonded of earth and heaven but cannot begin human life until the woman knows, receives, the overshadowing Love. The *Portrait* is the story of the woman's journey to that event, of her gradually putting aside all worldly, all selfish things, of her motion toward saintly character and the great moment of belief and acceptance, of her formation, in a phrase, into the living portrait of the greatest lady. When Rosier sees Isabel "framed in the gilded doorway" (310), James, as Viola Winner points out, is "interpreting a great portrait."[12]

Readers have noted that Isabel is "half willing to be turned into a portrait," that she is "making a work of art of herself," that the stages of her journey fix her, finally, within the frame of an *objet d'art* hanging on the wall of Osmond's prison.[13] We have not noted, until now, that the painting she becomes is the Madonna. When Isabel first arrives at Gardencourt, Ralph exults at receiving "a Titian, by the post," "a Greek bas-relief," a "key of a beautiful edifice" (63). When Isabel receives the money, the inheritance is less cash than it is a mark of her character, divine gold in the lap of a worthy Danae: "She has looked as solemn, these three days, as a Cimabue Madonna!" says Mrs. Touchett (182). When Henrietta Stackpole spends a page on "her favourite work of art," a Correggio madonna—Caspar says he doesn't "remember pictures—especially that sort"—Isabel and Pansy a few pages later act out their version of the painting.

The Correggio gives us "the Virgin kneeling down before the sacred infant, who lies in a litter of straw, and clapping her hands to him while he delightedly laughs and crows" (382). James paints a canvas of "Pansy's virginal bower," an "immense chamber with a dark, heavily-timbered ceiling." He shrinks Pansy a bit, not quite to infant size, so that the chamber's "diminutive mistress, in the midst of it, appeared but a speck of humanity." He draws her on a pillow equivalent of straw, and addresses the two persons to each other: Pansy "kneeled down on a cushion in front of her, looking up and resting her clasped hands on her stepmother's knees." Isabel's perception of Pansy as "a childish martyr decked out for sacrifice" is at the heart of the Madonna's sorrow and joy. To insure that we see the painting, the artist names it for us: Pansy "exclaimed as if she were praying to the Madonna," and it is "the Madonna" who responds (390–92).

Isabel's whole experience of Pansy is a contemplation of becoming the mother of Christ. This she can do only after her final rejections of Caspar and the world he offers, and her recognition and acceptance of the powerful desert love. The famous "house of darkness, the house of dumbness, the house of suffocation" (360) so many readers picture her as returning to[14] is dark to Isabel only because she believes she is not loved by Osmond: "It was her deep distrust of her husband—this was what darkened the world. . . . she simply believed he hated her" (356). When she is taken by the desert wind, her flight is through the darkness and into the light (489). She runs out of our knowing and into the splendor, the divine sorrow and joy, the beautiful repose that we, like James, glimpse when we view the great portraits of the Madonna.

Christian theology and literary tradition—as in Milton, for example—have Christ existing before his human conception and birth into the world. James uses a Roman convent and Osmond's residences as figures for Pansy's place of pre-world life. The Florentine villa where we first see Pansy "seemed less to offer communication with the world than to defy the world to look in" (196). When Serena enters it, she brings in "something of the radiance of the outer world" (201). Her "*Je vous salue*" to the nuns is "a wordplay" on "Hail, Mary" and recognizes them as temporary mothers of the little Christa (202n). The "*couvent*" Pansy waits in "*n'est pas comme le monde*," a point emphasized by its French (199). The convent seems to Isabel—not realizing that she herself mysteriously is the key—like a "well-appointed prison, for it was not possible to pretend Pansy was free to leave it" (456). James, getting things ready for the birth of his little Christ, even places the convent, stashes the babe, in the quarter of Navona, the Piazza Romans know is crowded with displays of *creches* every Christmas season.[15]

Osmond's conversation with the nuns is a divine musing on the character and fate of Pansy as Christ. What he says of her is often echoed later by the narrator or other characters, the technique itself perhaps, shaping things to come out right. Pansy is "perfect. She has no faults," but "good as she is, she's made for the world. *Le monde y gagnera*" (199–200). She's "as pure as a pearl," and "would make a perfect little pearl of a peeress" (210, 349). She's twice "a little saint of heaven" (228, 458). She's a "convent flower," a "white flower" presented to Isabel's nose (220, 267). She's "princess," "shepherdess," "angel," "doll," all the best things that little girls are made of, the connoted specifications of James's pre-world Christ whose prime note is absolute obedience to the Father. The Swiss theologian Von Balthasar writes that "the way from the bosom of the eternal Father to the womb of the temporal Mother is a path of obedience, the most difficult and consequential of ways, but one which is trod on mission from the Father. 'See, I come to do Your will' (Heb 10:7)."[16] "I shall always obey him," Pansy says (270).

Her boy-friend Rosier at his simplest, which is by our allegorical thread, is an angel who will be attendant at whatever ceremony, birth or marriage, James might choose for Pansy's presentation to the world. Isabel met the boy with the rosy name when they were children visiting the lady with the light and shiny name, Mrs. Luce. Where else does one find an angel? Isabel "thought little Edward as pretty as an angel," with "features which she supposed to be angelic and which her new friend perfectly illustrated. . . . she had firmly believed for some time afterwards that the heavenly hosts conversed among themselves in a queer little dialect of French-English" (185). As angel, Rosier is a New Testament type, sweet rather than powerful. He "can't pronounce the names right in the Bible. They're very difficult, in the Old Testament particularly" (187). No wonder that when Rosier talks with Pansy she smiles "as if an angel had kissed her" (313). The romance, then, is not Pansy's disobedience of her father but only Pansy's wish to make her worldly debut and heaven's wish to get on with it. Osmond must oppose it, obviously, until Isabel is ready to accept the overshadowing Love. The angel Rosier might be surprised if Pansy suffered a sex change on entering the world, but James assigns sex to suit his art and only incidentally, I suppose, to please the angels.[17]

James likes to give his Isabel unnamed books to read or, more importantly, to hold unread. We see her reading "a history of German thought," "fretting the edge" of a volume of Ampere, or knowing the idea of "*wicked*" "only by the Bible and other literary works" (34, 261, 431). She poses often with a book not being read. When she tries "to lose herself in a volume she had brought from Gardencourt, she succeeded only to the extent of reading other words than those printed on the page." The interruption by Goodwood is followed by Isabel's again taking up "her book, but without going through the form of opening the volume" (135, 145). She spends "vague hours in turning over books in the library," or sits there "with a volume to which her attention was not fastened" (177, 178). "She pretended to read," "She was quite unable to read," and, on the afternoon of Warburton's and Goodwood's final visits, "her eyes often wandered from the book in her hand to the open window" (347, 482, 483).

The obvious comment that she is reading *The Portrait of a Lady*— that is, that the novel by another and perhaps more glittering thread than the one I follow is about the making of the novel or of a work of art, a painting—yields to the notice that Goodwood twice appears when she is near her Gardencourt, perhaps Edenic, book. His sudden appearance "seems to be both an illusion and a reality."[18] Is Goodwood of the book? Does he oppose the book? Why does he interrupt the book? Poor Caspar, with his satanic archetype riding him hard, wishes to save our second Eve from the picture-frame. We should note that The Book is a standard symbol in paintings of the Virgin Mary:

> In the hand of the Madonna, it may have one of two meanings: When open, or when she has her fingers between the leaves, ... then it is the Book of Wisdom, and is always supposed to be open at the seventh chapter. When the book is clasped or sealed, it is a mystical symbol of the Virgin herself.[19]

James's sketches of Isabel with book indicate her progress in Wisdom and holiness, and are rehearsals for the final painted oil. *The Sealed Book* has special meanings. It is "a symbol often placed in the hands of the Virgin in a mystical Annunciation.... The text of Isaiah (29: 11, 12) describes the vision of the book that was sealed, and could be read neither by the learned nor the unlearned."[20] I can't read *The Sealed Book* except in its hint that Isabel is on her way to being "the Virgin in a mystical Annunciation" which Caspar would like to prevent. If she could read it better, Goodwood wouldn't appear.

One becomes a virgin, I suppose, by medical science or by drinking—or sitting in?—the Castilian Spring at Delphi. Isabel's purity is noted—sometimes lamented—by many readers. She is "above all a young lady of principles," "less a fool than a saint." She is "morally incorruptible." Her "innermost self suggests a *virgo intacta*." Matthiessen writes that "Isabel, in spite of her marriage, has remained essentially virginal."[21] The first Mary is Virgin and Mother. The scarcely-mentioned boy-child Isabel bears to Osmond—the boy dies unseen by the reader—is a *pre-Christus*, a small but necessary touch by James if his virginal Isabel is to be, like Mary, a biological mother. *Pre-Christus* dies to make way for Christa.

By Christian tradition, Mary was of such purity that even in her mother's womb she did not bear the stain of original sin, had not, in other words, lost the Edenic inheritance squandered by Adam and Eve. It may be that Ralph's and James's gift to Isabel, the Gardencourt inheritance, is a figure for Mary's immaculate conception and Isabel's purity.[22] No wonder Serena is amazed. She runs to Osmond with her prize. Eons after Eden and the fall that separates the heavens from the earth, the world presents to the Almighty a woman who may be worthy and willing to bridge the gulf. "I'm frightened at the abyss into which I shall have cast her," Serena says (244). Her own wish for the Incarnation, for earth to present a madonna to God, is clear by her conniving, by her "*Je vous salue*," and by her vivid memory of two paintings coming together for a Biblical Visitation, a Perugino greeted by Saint Elizabeth's raised hands (211). Of course Osmond wouldn't have married Isabel without her money, as she laments. And of course she wishes to be loved for herself, not for her virtue and not for her use.

It takes the length of the book for Isabel to know that she is loved. Moments before her final meeting with Goodwood, Lord Warburton invites Isabel for a visit during Whitsuntide, "as you say you're not to be very long in England." James is telling us that Whitsuntide, the season of the Pentecost, the time of the descent of the Holy Spirit upon the apostles, is imminent. Since the Spirit has not yet taken Isabel, she doesn't yet know Love. Indeed, as James has her respond, emphasizing the season, "I'm afraid I hardly know about Whitsuntide" (484). That James places the Annunciation in Pentecost saves the Spirit a trip and enriches the powerful moment of His arrival. He comes not only to her, but also to us.

Saint Luke says "suddenly there came a sound from heaven, as of a mighty wind coming, and it filled the whole house where they were sitting" (*Acts 2*). Saint Henry James reports that "the hot wind of the desert"—with Goodwood doing his damnedest to prevent it—"wrapped her about; it lifted her off her feet, while the very taste of it, as of something potent, acrid and strange, forced open her set teeth." It fills her whole house. From this moment she is Loved. Surely, her fears of being used are melted away. A modern spiritual writer notes that "True silence is a suspension bridge that a soul in love with God builds to cross the dark, frightening gullies of its own mind, ... its own fears that impede its way to God."[23] Isabel's silent rush through the dark into the light is the very picture of the stilled spirit vibrant in the touch of God. As she goes beyond us and enters into the beauty, the joy, the suffering, and the mystery of saintly character, becomes the portrait of the Madonna, she is like that Mary who, as Von Balthasar says, "knows that she has not been used as a mere instrument. . . . She and God together are source."[24]

It may be that the Annunciatory thread in the tapestry of the *Portrait* makes possible, in Jamesian esthetics, the creating of worthwhile art. How's a fellow to write a great book if muses have retreated to Olympus forever, the gods no longer care, and Eden's celestial visitors, insulted, have gathered their best gifts out of the heart of man and world, gone back to heaven, raised the drawbridge, and slammed the door? James is no modern writer to spin out his guts on the page. The classical consciousness that man and his art are truly important only if both are touched by the gods is moved, almost inevitably, to seek refuge in the Christian myth. Writing the *Portrait* is a deeply imaginative exploration of myth, Isabel herself representing the creative reach of the writer:

> The working of this young lady's spirit was strange, and I can only give it to you as I see it, not hoping to make it seem altogether natural. Her imagination, as I say, now hung back: there was a last vague space it couldn't cross—a dusky, uncertain tract which looked ambiguous and even slightly treacherous, like a moorland seen in the winter twilight. But she was to cross it yet. (265)

When James discovers that Gabriel's angelic words take root in Mary Isabel's womb, the great abyss is beautifully bridged, the door is opened, and the sky's the limit for his art.

Difficulties remain, some of them in heaven. Gilbert Osmond—I refrain from abbreviating his name to G. Od.—is not purged of all his villainous qualities even though we recognize that most of them were Isabel's suspicions in the dark, before the illumination by the wind. We see in a new light "the beauty of his mind," his exquisite taste, his interest in "Correggios and crucifixes," his words, to Isabel, "transcendent and absolute, like the sign of the cross or the flag of one's country"

(358, 228, 446). But his snaky egotism, his envy of emperor and pope, his loving but iron rule of Pansy, his wish that Isabel "should adore me, if you will. Oh yes, I wanted that" (436)—these are not easily forgiven by the reader even after the illumination strikes. The characterization may be magnificent, but Osmond, like the God of the Old Testament, is not to be confined within our understanding.

Osmond is not the only version of divinity in the book. His sister and, perhaps, Lord Warburton seem to be leftovers from a classical sky, she all fluttery, chancy, accidental, amoral,[25] he rather like a sort of baptized Apollo. The Countess is wed to a brute of an unseen gambler. Though she takes her name from him, Gemini suggests she twins Osmond, competes with him, and it suggests, sooner or later, the twin stars of her constellation from whom Goodwood might have taken his first name. Caspar, like the Countess, is not a constructive force. As James carves out his conception of the universe, older remnants than the Christian are not yet pared away.

We presume that one doesn't become holy strictly by his own will and act. Osmond's subtle nagging of Isabel is James's version of the workings of divine grace as it forms the lady in saintly character. Isabel's final steps in perfection are marked by what she gives up, which is, stated simply, the world, the self, and the devil.

In a chapter of some considerable celestial positioning—Pansy above, Isabel descending, Madame Merle below—Isabel gives up the old world, "wished never to look at Madame Merle again" (457). Isabel's decision is tested when Goodwood tempts her. "The world's all before us," he says, but it turns to water, takes "the form of a mighty sea," and goes down the drain with Caspar. By giving up the world the Madonna saves it.

Isabel's wish for death is for the death of self, of ego, of the deep and inner voice that sings *me me me*, a wish for the final mysterious rendering of all oneself to God. "She envied Ralph his dying," and "She had moments indeed in her journey from Rome which were almost as good as being dead." She pictures herself in art after such a death: "She sat in her corner, so motionless, so passive, simply with the sense of being carried, so detached from hope and regret, that she recalled to herself one of those Etruscan figures couched upon the receptacle of their ashes" (465).

Ralph is many things in the novel, the gradually effaced hand of the writer, a "true Jamesian artist figure," the "other half" of Isabel, and even, when his ghost appears to Isabel in the final chapter, the spirit preface to the Spirit soon to descend.[26] By my little thread, Ralph is the sacrificed self of Isabel. When she "drops," Ralph says, "it hurts me as if I had fallen myself!" (291). When she hurts, Isabel's "ache for herself became somehow her ache for *him*" (363). When he dies—"'Oh my brother!' she cried with a movement of still greater prostration" (479)—her purification is almost complete. Thus Osmond's objections to Ralph fall into place as wishes for Isabel's perfection. Ralph's illness, all along, is her tenuous grasp of the world; to say it another way, his health is an inverse figure of her character.

Perhaps it's not so bad to be a painting, after all, with a vivid, important, forever sort of life going on in the frame. In Serena's glimpse of the Visitation, two paintings greet each other. Isabel's suddenly seeing Serena, late in the novel, is like "seeing a painted picture move" (456). The narrator reads Pansy's heart as she considers "her gentle stepmother" and "her magnificent father": "it may have stood almost as still as it would have done had she seen two of the saints in the great picture in the convent-chapel turn their painted heads and shake them at each other" (461). Let me suggest, without going into it, that James is dramatizing the difficult notion that sacred event, having happened once, is happening now and will always happen, rather in the fashion of primitive religious ritual whose dancers suddenly found themselves in company of the gods at the creation, or, in our time, as each Catholic mass is not in memory of but is the crucifixion. Art and religion come together here.

Strictly speaking, then, there is no allegory in the *Portrait*, for the *allegoria* is one with the novel's literal events. Thus James could see, in even such a small event as the taking of a tea, the history of man's involvement with the gods lived not again, but for the first and only time: "there are few hours in life more agreeable than the hour dedicated to the ceremony known as afternoon tea." The ritual happens during "a little eternity," "an eternity of pleasure." The old Adam on "the perfect lawn" of Gardencourt, Daniel Touchett, "the beneficent author of infinite woe," has his own large teacup, "of a different pattern from the rest of the set and painted in brilliant colours" (17, 358). That Pansy serves many a tea gives her something to do and suggests the little Christa's saving grace. One of Serena's precious cups, as Osmond wryly remarks, "has a wee bit of a tiny crack" (436). It may be, as Osmond suggests elsewhere, that "to-day the air has grown so dense that delicate things are literally not recognised" (420), but we sense that the crack in the cup is a mark of imperfection in earthly things, the great moat between man and the gods, and the Gemini split in heaven, some of which disappear later on, perhaps, when a golden bowl is shattered. What is the *Portrait* about? Why, the taking of a tea.

The sun-clothed woman of *Apocalypse* is variously identified with Israel, with the Church, with Mary.[27] Isabel dresses in black, in white with black ribbons, in mourning robes, in black velvet, in black brocade, but, as she says, her clothes "don't express me" (60, 92, 182, 309, 473, 175). Though she doesn't care to "glitter by arrangement," her "flame-like spirit" erupts with an occasional solar gleam because it can't hold back its light and because James wants us to catch, ahead of time, the brilliant beauty of her return to Rome: "a colour like a flame leaped into her face," she's "as bright as the morning," she has "a radiance, even a slight exaltation," and she walks "in no small shimmering splendour" (54, 213, 290, 206, 254, 276). There is, really, too much to say about her shining in the great tapestry of the *Portrait*. Wrapped in its golden thread, Isabel Archer is the woman clothed with the sun.

"We can surely account for nothing in the novelist's work," James says, "that hasn't passed through the crucible of his imagination."[28] The relationship of an artist to his art—however intimate and revealing—remains essentially mysterious. *Muse* may be only a pretty word for the imagination of the writer, but metaphor is dangerous. With the writing of the *Portrait*, the lady from Mount Parnassus is not merely baptized: she discovers that she is the virgin Mary.

NOTES

1. Henry James, *The Portrait of a Lady*, edited by Robert D. Bamberg (New York: W.M. Norton and Company, 1975), p. 418. The "thread" I follow is less visible in the 1881 *Portrait* than in the New York Edition of 1908, which Bamberg follows, giving also variations from the earlier edition. In this chapter, I use the Bamberg edition and cite it parenthetically in my text.

2. Arnold Kettle, in *An Introduction to the English Novel, Volume Two: Henry James to the Present* (New York: Harper and Row, 1960), notes that "Goodwood becomes identified with the torrent" (p. 31).

3. William T. Stafford, in *"The Portrait of a Lady*: The Second Hundred Years," *The Henry James Review*, 2 (1981), 91–100, says that he is "no longer irritated" with Osmond (100). Levy B. Levy, however, in *Versions of Melodrama: A Study of the Fiction and Drama of Henry James* (Berkeley: the University of California Press, 1957), leaves Osmond "suspended in an abstract void of evil" (p. 47). Cargill says that Osmond is "James's most completely evil character" (p. 87), and Walter F. Wright, in *The Madness of Art: A Study of Henry James* (Lincoln: the University of Nebraska Press, 1962), finds in Osmond a "will to destroy" (p. 88).

4. Richard Poirer, for example, in *The Comic Sense of Henry James: A Study of the Early Novels* (New York: Oxford University Press, 1960), comments on the "Miltonic echo" in Casper's plea (p. 245).

5. Dorothy Van Ghent, in *The English Novel: Form and Function* (New York: Holt, Rhinehart and Winston, 1953), points out that Caspar "appears always as an armor-man" (p. 225).

6. *The Holy Bible* (New York: John Murphy Company, n.d.). James, treating a somewhat Catholic theme, may or may not have used, as I do here, a Douay version.

7. Cargill discusses the Goodwood-Boldwood likenesses (p. 85).

8. Peter Buitenhuis, in *Twentieth Century Interpretations of "The Portrait of a Lady": A Collection of Critical Essays*, edited by Peter Buitenhuis (Englewood Cliffs: Prentice-Hall, Inc., 1968), notes that Isabel's "surname suggests the chaste Diana, goddess of the hunt" (p. 12).

9. Joyce Tayloe Horrell, "A 'Shade of a Special Sense': Henry James and the Art of Naming," *American Literature* 42 (1970), 203–30, 208, 203–04.

10. As Poirier says, "when we discover something covert it does not mean that we then give up or transform all that is obvious" (p. 245).

11. *Webster's New International Dictionary of the English Language*, edited by William Allan Neilson, Thomas A. Knott, and Paul W. Carhart, second edition unabridged (Springfield: G. and C. Merriam, 1959).

12. Viola Hopkins Winner, *Henry James and the Visual Arts* (Charlottesville: the University Press of Virginia, 1970), p. 73.

13. Tony Tanner, "The Fearful Self: Henry James's *The Portrait of a Lady*," in *Henry James: Modern Judgements*, edited by Tony Tanner (London: Macmillan, 1968), pp. 143–59. P. 147. Juliet McMaster, "The Portrait of Isabel Archer," *American Literature* 45 (1973), 50–66. 58.

14. Edward Wagenknecht, in *Eve and Henry James: Portraits of Women and Girls in his Fiction* (Norman: the University of Oklahoma Press, 1978), rejects Manfred Mackenzie's idea that Isabel's husband is "a 'villain' only in her imagination. This finds no support in the text," Wagenknecht says, "but Dorothea Krook also gives Osmond more charity than he deserves" (p. 45n).

15. Georgina Masson, *The Companion Guide to Rome*, revised edition (London: Wm. Collins Sons, 1972), p. 169.

16. Hans Urs Von Balthasar, *The Threefold Garland: The World's Salvation in Mary's Prayer*, translated by Erasmo Leiva-Merikakis (San Francisco: Ignatius Press, 1982), p. 30.

17. For a discussion of the inversion of sexual roles in James, see Ralf Norrman, *The Insecure World of Henry James's Fiction: Intensity and Ambiguity* (New York: St. Martin's Press, 1982), pp. 137–84.

18. Alden R. Turner, "The Haunted *Portrait of a Lady*," *Studies in the Novel* 12 (1980), 228–38. 237.

19. Cynthia Pearl Maus, *The World's Great Madonnas: An Anthology of Pictures, Poetry, Music, and Stories Centering in the Life of the Madonna and Her Son* (New York: Harper, 1947), p. 8.

20. *Ibid.*

21. Philip Rahv, *Image and Idea: Twenty Essays on Literary Themes* (Norfolk: New Directions, 1957), p. 65. Nina Baym, "Revision and Thematic Change in *The Portrait of a Lady*," *Modem Fiction Studies* 22 (1976), 183–200, 185. Michael Swan, *Henry James*, Bibliographical Series of Supplements to 'British Book News' on Writers and Their Work, general editor Bonamy Dobree (London: Longmans, Green, 1957), p. 15. Dennis L. O'Connor, "Intimacy and Spectatorship in *The Portrait of a Lady*," *The Henry James Review* 2 (1980), 25–35, 26. Matthiessen, p. 179.

22. Hugo H. Hoever, in *Saint Joseph Daily Missal*, edited by Hoever (New York: Catholic Book Publishing Company, 1961), says that the Feast of the Immaculate Conception was first

celebrated in England in the eleventh century and the doctrine defined as dogma in 1854 (p. 728). In other words, it was well known and considerably discussed in James's time.

23. Catherine de Hueck Doherty, *Poustinia: Christian Spirituality of the East for Western Man* (Notre Dame: Ave Maria Press, 1975), p. 20.

24. Von Balthasar, p. 44.

25. Ward writes that she is "neither good nor evil; she resides in the background of the story, aware of the sins of the past but incapable of redeeming the present" (p. 53).

26. Ora Segal, *The Lucid Reflector: The Observer in Henry James' Fiction* (New Haven: Yale University Press, 1969), p. 55; Tanner, p. 156; Maxwell Geismar, *Henry James and the Jacobites* (New York: Hill and Wang, 1965), p. 41.

27. J. Massyngberde Ford, *The Anchor Bible: Revelation* (New York: Doubleday, 1975), pp. 194–207.

28. *The Art of the Novel*, p. 230.

THE SCARLET LETTER
(NATHANIEL HAWTHORNE)

***

"The Complexities of 'Old Roger' Chillingworth: Sin and Redemption in Hawthorne's *The Scarlet Letter*"
by Robert C. Evans,
Auburn University at Montgomery

One of the many paradoxes in Nathaniel Hawthorne's *The Scarlet Letter* is that the character who at first seems the most sinned against eventually becomes the greatest sinner. Roger Prynne, the old, scholarly husband of Hester Prynne, enters the novel as the clear victim of his wife's adultery. She has undoubtedly betrayed him, as she herself readily admits: "'I have greatly wronged thee,' murmured Hester" (53). By the time the novel concludes, however, Roger Prynne—who has adopted the symbolic name "Roger Chillingworth"—has become the darkest and most malignant figure in the novel. Indeed, Hawthorne repeatedly refers to him as "old Roger"—a term often used as a nickname for Satan himself (Green 867). Part of *The Scarlet Letter*'s tragedy is the self-imposed degeneration of Roger Prynne, a man who corrupts himself because he can neither forgive nor forget the corruption of others. Hawthorne could easily have made Chillingworth a wholly malignant figure right from the start. Instead, however, the first appearances of Chillingworth are actually wreathed in ambiguities, ironies, and complexities, especially for anyone who is rereading the novel and knows what will happen later. Rather than depicting Chillingworth as a crude and uncomplicated villain, Hawthorne makes him a figure who seems simultaneously mysterious, sympathetic, and potentially dangerous. By paying close attention to the first appearances of Chillingworth, we can come to a greater appreciation of the subtlety of Hawthorne's art and a greater awareness of the nature and depth of Chillingworth's eventual sin. Only when we see how Chillingworth begins can we appreciate how far he falls.

The novel's first references to Chillingworth occur in a recollection by Hester as she stands, in Chapter II, in public humiliation on the scaffold. She remembers her husband as a "man well stricken in years" with "a pale, thin, scholar-like visage" (43). Ironically, the latter phrase might just as easily apply to Arthur Dimmesdale, her secret lover, especially after Chillingworth has spent years secretly tormenting the adulterous minister. Chillingworth, in effect, eventually helps to turn Dimmesdale into a physical copy of himself. This transformation is all the more ironic when we recall that both men are indeed highly learned and highly trained in the use of reason. Each man not only possesses a "scholar-like visage," but each has also spent years "por[ing] over many ponderous books" (43). Indeed, one of Chillingworth's greatest sins is that he eventually perverts the gift of reason—the gift that traditionally distinguishes man from the lower animals—by pursuing his ungodly vengeance. The fact that he is such a highly learned man eventually makes him all the more subtle, all the more cunning, and all the more dangerous. The fact that he is so intelligent also makes him all the more responsible for the sinful path he chooses to pursue and thus all the more spiritually self-destructive. By the end of the novel, Chillingworth has no one but himself to blame for the sins he has committed.

Chillingworth's physical appearance at first suggests that Hawthorne is planning to depict him as a rather crude villain. Hester remembers him as being "slightly deformed, with the left" (or "sinister") "shoulder a trifle higher than the right." He is called, in fact, a "misshapen scholar" (44). These details symbolically imply that his soul and character may be as "deformed" as his body. Indeed, when he first appears in Boston and is spotted by Hester from the scaffold, he is said to be "clad in a strange disarray of civilized and savage costume" (44). That phrasing, especially the word "savage," hints that Chillingworth's soul may already be tainted by heathenish sin. It is, however, the peculiar combination of the "civilized" *and* the "savage" that Hawthorne will stress again and again in his presentation of

Chillingworth. Indeed, part of what will make Chillingworth such a frightening figure is precisely that he will combine a "savage" hatred with "civilized" cunning. In the end, it will be Chillingworth's soul, far more than his costume, in "disarray," and in fact Chillingworth will emerge as far more "savage" than any of the "heathen" Indians with whom he has been living.

Chillingworth is "small in stature" (44), yet he deliberately diminishes himself even more, ethically and spiritually. He misuses the "remarkable intelligence" that is immediately apparent in his features, and by the conclusion of the novel, the "slight deformity" of his body will seem as nothing when compared to the enormous deformity of his soul (44). For a man who has been "chiefly accustomed to look inward," Chillingworth displays a remarkable lack of self-examination and self-perception. Hawthorne, however, refuses to initially present Chillingworth as a simple or total villain. He hints that Chillingworth may indeed have the potential for villainy, but he refuses at first to make the matter clear. Hawthorne does report that when Chillingworth first sees Hester, a "writhing horror twist[s] itself across his features like a snake gliding swiftly over them" (45). Such phrasing is almost too simple and obvious: Snakes have long been associated with evil, especially in Christian cultures, and Hawthorne is indulging in some especially unsubtle symbolism. Yet the phrasing suggests, at this point, Chillingworth's own shock and pain (his "horror") rather than any intended villainy. The narrator next reports that Chillingworth's "face darkened with some powerful emotion," but the precise nature of that emotion is left carefully unspecified, and so Chillingworth remains, for the moment, more a figure of mystery than of blatant evil. Likewise, when the narrator reports that Chillingworth "controlled" that emotion—whatever it was—"by an effort of his will" (45), that fact itself can be seen as indicating either admirable self-restraint or a desire to deceive. At this early point in the novel, then, neither we nor Hester can be quite sure what Chillingworth is thinking or what he intends.

Ambiguities and ironies continue to pervade the early description of Chillingworth. When an anonymous member of the crowd tells Chillingworth, "You must needs be a stranger in this region, friend" (45), the speaker cannot possibly know how accurate his words are. Having just come, with absolutely no preparation, upon the highly public scene of his wife being punished for adultery, Chillingworth must indeed feel like a "stranger," both in his own marriage and in Puritan Boston. Meanwhile, the fact that he is accompanied by a "savage companion" (45) will (once more) seem all the more ironic in light of his own later savage treatment of Dimmesdale, just as his reference to his time "among the heathen-folk" (45) is ominous and portentous in view of his own later heathenish behavior. Chillingworth tells his anonymous interlocutor that he has been "redeemed out of [his] captivity" among the Indians (45); but he will soon lead himself into a spiritual captivity far more serious than the physical imprisonment from which he has just been "redeemed." When the man with whom he is conversing tells Chillingworth that it must "gladden [Chillingworth's] heart" to have escaped his "troubles and sojourn in the wilderness" (45), he cannot know how painful every word of his statement is to Chillingworth. The word "troubles," for instance, must seem ironic to Chillingworth (whose real troubles have just begun), while the reference to an escape from the "wilderness" must seem ironic to any reader appraising what happens later in the book. Chillingworth, after all, is about to enter a moral "wilderness" of his own making that will be far worse than anything he has just escaped.

Further irony occurs when the anonymous citizen of Boston praises his town as a place "where iniquity is searched out and punished in the sight of rulers and people" (45), since the business of searching out and punishing iniquity (although not in plain sight) will be Chillingworth's self-appointed mission for the rest of the book. Equally paradoxical is the moment when the anonymous Bostonian is about to explicitly describe the nature of Hester's sin, and Chilling-worth, obviously pained, quickly cuts him off "with a bitter smile" (45). Yet just when Chillingworth might have reason to feel bitter, he wryly turns part of that bitterness against himself: "So learned a man as you speak of should have learned this too [the potential for adultery in a marriage between an old man and a young woman] in his books" (45). In other words, just when Chillingworth might be tempted to turn his full anger against Hester, he seems to accept (maturely, reasonably, and generously) a great measure of personal responsibility for what has happened. He is not yet a blackened villain; he is still a man who can appreciate his own role in having contributed to the circumstances.

Ironies in this initial appearance of Chillingworth in Boston continue to abound. At one point the anonymous citizen of Boston, referring to Hester's partner in adultery, speculates that "the guilty one stands looking at this sad spectacle, unknown of man, and forgetting that God sees him" (46). That description is applicable to Dimmesdale but will be even more applicable to Chillingworth by the end of the novel. Likewise, when Chillingworth responds by saying that "The learned man" (Hester's husband) "should come himself to look into the mystery" (46), he is being not only deliberately wry but also unintentionally ironic, because he will spend the rest of the book looking "into the mystery" of other people's sins in a way that will entangle him in even greater sins of his own. Finally, near the end of his conversation with the Bostonian, Chillingworth, speaking of Hester's partner in "iniquity," vows, "he will be known!—he will be known!—he will be known!" (46). He forgets, however, that Hester's partner already *is* known to God, the only judge who ultimately matters. Chillingworth's declaration is therefore less a sign of any disinterested concern for justice than an indication of his prideful (and sinful) yearning for personal revenge. By the end of the book, Chillingworth himself "will be known" by God for sins far more serious than those committed by Dimmesdale.

Chillingworth's next major appearance in the book also complicates our sense of his character in general and his sins in particular. When he visits Hester in prison in Chapter IV, he is himself a temporary resident there while the local magistrates confer with "the Indian sagamores respecting his ransom" (51). The prison in which Chillingworth finds himself, however, will be nothing compared to the prison of hatred in which he will soon confine himself. The latter will prove a kind of spiritual bondage from which he will never really be ransomed. Meanwhile, the fact that he presents himself to Hester as a physician is obviously ironic, since his role throughout the book is to exacerbate, rather than relieve, the sufferings of others, especially Dimmesdale. When Chillingworth promises Hester's jailer that he will help make her "more amenable to just authority" (51), his words are more ironic than he realizes, since he himself will soon proceed to violate the ultimate "just authority" of God's commands.

Throughout this prison visit, Hawthorne depicts Chillingworth in subtly ambiguous ways. Immediately after Chillingworth enters Hester's cell, his "first care" is given to Pearl, which makes him seem genuinely compassionate. The narrator immediately reports, however, that Pearl's "cries, as she lay writhing on the trundle-bed, made it of peremptory necessity to postpone all other business to the task of

soothing her" (51). Thus, while Chillingworth at first seems motivated
by mercy toward a suffering infant, his motives are revealed to be
significantly pragmatic. Similar ambivalence is evident when he speaks
to Hester "half coldly, half soothingly" or when he calls Pearl both
"misbegotten" (which suggests his bitterness) and "miserable" (which
suggests some pity). Likewise, when he tells Hester that he cannot
give her "a sinless conscience" (51–52), his words are both cutting and
compassionate. There are times in this episode when Chillingworth
seems satanic. For example, when he lays his "long forefinger on the
scarlet letter," the finger almost seems "to scorch Hester's breast, as
if it had been red-hot" (52). For the most part, however, he comes
across as surprisingly sympathetic, in every sense of that word. Indeed,
even Hester herself is willing to concede that his motives may not
be entirely malignant: She feels that he may be acting in accordance
with "humanity, or principle," although she also entertains the possibility that he may be acting from a kind of "refined cruelty" (53). The
important point is that Chillingworth's motives at first seem just as
mysterious (and therefore complex) to Hawthorne's readers as they
do to Hester. Chillingworth is not a cardboard villain. He is an intelligent, suffering human being and so is all the more responsible for the
suffering he ultimately causes. If Chillingworth were not as thoughtful
and capable of compassion as he is in this episode, he would not be as
guilty of genuine sin as he ultimately shows himself to be.

   When Chillingworth begins to talk seriously to Hester, he reveals
himself as both a "man of thought" and a man of some tenderness. He
accepts partial responsibility for Hester's sin, blaming it both on "my
folly, and thy weakness" (53). Yet his words here, like most of his words
throughout this scene, are double-edged. Any folly he exhibited in the
past is minor compared to the spiritual folly he will display later in
the book, and any past weakness that he attributes to Hester pales in
comparison with his weakness later in the novel. When Chillingworth
humbly describes himself as being, at the time he married Hester, "a
man already in decay" (53), his candor is admirable, but the spiritual decay he will bring upon himself as the narrative develops is far
greater than any physical decay. Similarly, the "physical deformity" that
Chillingworth readily admits is insignificant when compared with the
deformity of character he will exhibit later. Just as in the past he had
hoped to "veil" his physical defects, so in the future he will try to hide
and disguise his defects of spirit. And just as in the past he had tried

to "feed the hungry dream of knowledge" (53), so in the future he will be driven by an even more voracious desire for knowledge of an altogether different and darker kind. Chillingworth tells Hester that he literally has come "out of the vast and dismal forest," but what he doesn't then know is that he is about to enter a far more dangerous and dismal spiritual wilderness of his own making.

Practically everything Chillingworth says in this scene is ironic when read against the later plot of the novel. Chillingworth confesses that in the past he "lived in vain" (53), but his later life will be far more full of vanity than anything that came before. Similarly, he states that his world had once seemed "cheerless," but the only cheer he will experience in the future will be the perverse happiness of inflicting pain on others. He describes himself as having once been "lonely and chill" (53), but those days will be nothing compared with his spiritual isolation by the end of the text. He says that all he desired in the past was a "simple bliss" that he hoped "might yet be mine" (53). Such bliss might *still* be his if he were only capable of mercy. He destroys any chances of any kind of bliss when he chooses vengeance.

Chillingworth emerges in this scene as an exceptionally complex human being. On the one hand, he is capable of insightfully telling Hester, "We have wronged each other," and he is capable of promising her (in a sentence masterfully designed by Hawthorne), "Therefore, as a man who has not thought and philosophized in vain, I seek no vengeance and plot no evil. . . ." But this sentence does not end there; instead, it continues with two crucial words "against thee" (*SL* 53). Chillingworth's full capacity for evil and his full desire for revenge begin to become apparent. In some ways that desire is perfectly natural, but in other ways it is frightening and repugnant. Chilling-worth was presented as a character with whom we could sympathize to some degree, but now he emerges as a man whom we must reject and condemn.

When Chillingworth begins to smile "with a smile of dark and self-relying intelligence" (53), he begins to display, far more obviously than before, the egocentrism and intellectual pride that will make him the greatest sinner in the book. From this point on, in fact, the more he talks, the more his speech reveals ultimately damning ironies. He begins to employ religious language in highly self-indicting ways, as when he promises to be a man who "devotes himself earnestly and unreservedly to the solution of a mystery" (53). Similarly, he later promises that he will not "interfere with Heaven's own method of retribution" against Hester's secret partner and that he will not "to my own loss, betray him [the secret lover] to the gripe [the grip] of human law" (54). Yet interfering with heaven's methods is precisely what Chillingworth will do, to his own real spiritual loss. Thus, there is a special irony in Chillingworth's words when he vows that "Sooner or later, he must needs be mine! . . . Let him hide himself in outward honor, if he may! Not the less he shall be mine!" (54). It will be Chillingworth, at least as much as Dimmesdale, who will "hide himself in outward honor," and finally it will be Chillingworth, far more than Dimmesdale, who will be subject to a dark and vengeful power.

Chillingworth insists that Hester should not "betray" him, but it is finally Chillingworth who betrays himself. Chillingworth warns Hester not to "fail" him by revealing his secret, but it is Chillingworth who fails himself, spiritually, by maintaining that secret for so many years and using it to torment Dimmesdale. By the end of Chapter IV, Chillingworth—for the very first time—is described as "old Roger" Chillingworth (54)—a name with clear satanic overtones. By the end of that chapter, Hester links him with the legendary "Black Man" of the forest (another name associated with Satan), and she even wonders whether Chillingworth intends to seek "the ruin of [her] soul." In response, Chillingworth replies, with another cryptic smile, "Not thy soul. . . . No, not thine!" (55). Clearly he means to suggest that the soul he intends to ruin is that of her secret partner, but by this point it is clear that the soul most in danger is Chillingworth's. In this subtly composed chapter, Hawthorne carefully charts Chillingworth's own self-chosen spiritual degeneration. The man who seemed in some ways admirable and sympathetic at the beginning of the chapter has turned himself into a potentially satanic figure by the end. By the time Chapter IV concludes, Roger Prynne (the innocent victim) has turned himself into "old Roger" Chillingworth (the malignant sinner).

WORKS CITED OR CONSULTED

Green, Jonathon. *Cassell's Dictionary of Slang*. London: Cassell, 1998.
Gross, Theodore L. and Stanley Wertheim. *Hawthorne, Melville, and Stephen Crane; A Critical Bibliography*. New York: Free Press, 1971.
Hawthorne, Nathaniel. *The Scarlet Letter*. Person, 3–166.

Kopley, Richard. *The Threads of* The Scarlet Letter*: A Study of Hawthorne's Transformative Art*. Newark: University of Delaware Press, 2003.

Muirhead, Kimberly Free. *Nathaniel Hawthorne's The Scarlet Letter: A Critical Resource Guide and Comprehensive Annotated Bibliography of Literary Criticism, 1950–2000*. Lewiston, ME: Mellen, 2004.

Person, Leland, ed. *The Scarlet Letter and Other Writings*, by Nathaniel Hawthorne. New York: Norton, 2005.

Reynolds, Larry J., ed. *A Historical Guide to Nathaniel Hawthorne*. Oxford: Oxford University Press, 2001.

"SINNERS IN THE HANDS OF AN ANGRY GOD"
(JONATHAN EDWARDS)

"Jonathan Edwards"
by Leslie Stephen, in *Hours in a Library* (1909)

INTRODUCTION

First delivered on July 8, 1741, Jonathan Edwards's sermon "Sinners in the Hands of an Angry God" contains one of the most vivid descriptions of hell ever presented and is a strong apology for the Christian faith. In it, Edwards works to awaken his audience, to bring them to repent and atone for their sins. Writing at the turn of the 20th century, Leslie Stephen explores how Edwards "connects the expiring Calvinism of the old Puritan theocracy with what is called the transcendentalism embodied in the writings of Emerson and other leaders of young America."

JONATHAN EDWARDS[1]

Two of the ablest thinkers whom America has yet produced were born in New England at the beginning of the eighteenth century. The theorist who would trace all our characteristics to inheritance from

---

Stephen, Leslie. "Jonathan Edwards." *Hours in a Library, Vol. 1.* London: Smith, Elder, & Co., 1909.

some remote ancestor might see in Jonathan Edwards and Benjamin Franklin normal representatives of the two types from which the genuine Yankee is derived. Though blended in various proportions, and though one may exist almost to the exclusion of the other, an element of shrewd mother-wit and an element of transcendental enthusiasm are to be detected in all who boast a descent from the pilgrim fathers. Franklin, born in 1706, represents in its fullest development the more earthly side of this compound. A thoroughbred utilitarian, full of sagacity, and carrying into all regions of thought that strange ingenuity which makes an American the handiest of all human beings, Franklin is best embodied in his own Poor Richard. Honesty is the best policy: many a little makes a mickle: the second vice is lying, the first is running in debt; and

> "Get what you can, and what you get hold;
> 'Tis the stone that will turn all your lead into gold."

These and a string of similar maxims are the pith of Franklin's message to the world. Franklin, however, was not merely a man in whom the practical intelligence was developed in a very remarkable degree, but was fortunate in coming upon a crisis admirably suited to his abilities and in being generally in harmony with the spirit of his age. He succeeded, as we know, in snatching lightning from the heavens and the sceptre from tyrants; and had his reward in the shape of much contemporary homage from French philosophers, and lasting renown amongst his countrymen. Meanwhile, Jonathan Edwards, his senior by three years, had the fate common to men who are unfitted for the struggles of daily life, and whose philosophy does not harmonise with the dominant current of the time. A speculative recluse, with little faculty of literary expression, and given to utter opinions shocking to the popular mind, he excited little attention during his lifetime; except amongst the sharers of his own religious persuasions; and, when noticed after his death, the praise of his intellectual acuteness has generally been accompanied with an expression of abhorrence for his supposed moral obtuseness. Mr. Lecky, for example, whilst speaking of Edwards as "probably the ablest defender of Calvinism," mentions his treatise on Original Sin as "one of the most revolting books that have ever proceeded from the pen of man" (Rationalism, i. 404). That intense dislike, which is far from uncommon, for severe reasoning has even made a kind of reproach to Edwards of what is called his "inexorable logic." To condemn a man for being honestly in the wrong is generally admitted to be unreasonable; but people are even more unforgiving to the sin of being honestly in the right. The frankness with which Edwards avowed opinions, not by any means peculiar to himself, has left a certain stain upon his reputation. He has also suffered in general repute from a cause which should really increase our interest in his writings. Metaphysicians, whilst admiring his acuteness, have been disgusted by his adherence to an outworn theology; and theologians have cared little for a man who was primarily a philosophical specu- lator, and has used his philosophy to bring into painful relief the most terrible dogmas of the ancient creeds. Edwards, however, is interesting just because he is a connecting link between two widely different phases of thought. He connects the expiring Calvinism of the old Puritan theocracy with what is called the transcendentalism embodied in the writings of Emerson and other leaders of young America. He is remarkable, too, as illustrating, at the central point of the eighteenth century, those speculative tendencies which were most vitally opposed to the then dominant philosophy of Locke and Hume. And, finally, there is a still more permanent interest in the man himself, as exhibiting in high relief the weak and the strong points of the teaching of which Calvinism represents only one embodiment. His life, in striking contrast to that of his more cele- brated contemporary, ran its course far away from the main elements of European activity. With the exception of a brief stay at New York, he lived almost exclusively in the interior of what was then the thinly-settled colony of Massachusetts.[2] [...] Puritanism, though growing faint, was still powerful in New England; it was bred in his bones, and he was drilled from his earliest years into its sternest dogmas. Some curious fragments of his early life and letters indicate the nature of his spiritual development. Whilst still almost a boy, he writes down solemn resolutions, and practises himself in severe self- inspection. He resolves "never to do, be, or suffer anything in soul or body, more or less, but what tends to the glory of God;" to "live with all my might while I do live;" "never to speak anything that is ridicu- lous or matter of laughter on the Lord's Day" (a resolution which we might think rather superfluous, even though extended to other days); and, "frequently to renew the dedication of myself to God, which

was made at my baptism, which I solemnly renewed when I was
received into the communion of the Church, and which I have
solemnly ratified this 12th day of January 1723" (i. 18). He pledges
himself, in short, to a life of strict self-examination and absolute
devotion to what he takes for the will of God. Similar resolutions
have doubtless been made by countless young men brought up under
the same conditions, and diaries of equal value have been published
by the authors of innumerable saintly biographies. In Edwards'
mouth, however, they really had a meaning and bore corresponding
results. An interesting paper gives an account of those religious
"experiences" to which his sect attaches so tremendous an importance. From his childhood, he tells us, his mind had been full of
objections to the doctrine of God's sovereignty. It appeared to him
to be a "horrible doctrine" that God should choose whom He would,
and reject whom He pleased, "leaving them eternally to perish and
be tormented eternally in hell." The whole history of his intellectual
development is involved in the process by which he became gradually reconciled to this appalling dogma. In the second year of his
collegiate course, we are told, which would be about the fourteenth
of his age, he read Locke's Essay with inexpressible delight. The first
glimpse of metaphysical inquiry, it would seem, revealed to him the
natural bent of his mind, and opened to him the path of speculation
in which he ever afterwards delighted. Locke, though Edwards
always mentions him with deep respect, was indeed a thinker of a
very different school. The disciple owed to his master, not a body of
doctrine, but the impulse to intellectual activity. He succeeded in
working out for himself a satisfactory answer to the problem by
which he had been perplexed. His cavils ceased as his reason
strengthened. "God's absolute sovereignty and justice" seemed to
him to be as clear as anything he saw with his eyes; "at least," he adds,
"it is so at times." Nay, he even came to rejoice in the doctrine and
regard it as "infinitely pleasant, bright, and sweet" (i. 33). The Puritan
assumptions were so ingrained in his nature that the agony of mind
which they caused never led him to question their truth, though it
animated him to discover a means of reconciling them to reason; and
the reconciliation is the whole burden of his ablest works. The effect
upon his mind is described in terms which savour of a less stern
school of faith. God's glory was revealed to him throughout the
whole creation and often threw him into ecstasies of devotion (i. 33).

"God's excellency, His wisdom, His purity, and love seemed to appear in everything: in the sun, moon, and stars; in the clouds and blue sky; in the grass, flowers, and trees; in the water and all nature, which used greatly to fix my mind. I often used to sit and view the moon for continuance, and in the day spent much time in viewing the clouds and sky, to behold the sweet glory of God in these things; in the meantime singing forth, with a low voice, my contemplations of the Creator and Redeemer." Thunder, he adds, had once been terrible to him; "now scarce anything in all the works of nature" was so sweet (i. 36). It seemed as if the "majestic and awful voice of God's thunder" was in fact the voice of its Creator. Thunder and lightning, we know, suggested characteristically different contemplations to Franklin. Edwards' utterances are as remarkable for their amiability as for their non-scientific character. We see in him the gentle mystic rather than the stern divine who consigned helpless infants to eternal torture without a question of the goodness of their Creator. This vein of meditation, however, continued to be familiar to him. He spent most of his time reflecting on Divine things, and often walking in solitary places and woods to enjoy uninterrupted soliloquies and converse with God. [...] Evidently he possessed one of those rare temperaments to which the severest intellectual exercise is a source of the keenest enjoyment; and though he must often have strayed into the comparatively dreary labyrinths of metaphysical puzzles, his speculations had always an immediate reference to what he calls "Divine things." Once, he tells us, as he rode into the woods, in 1737, and alighted according to custom "to walk in Divine contemplation and prayer," he had so extraordinary a view of the glory of the Son of God, and His wonderful grace, that he remained for about an hour "in a flood of tears and weeping aloud." This intensity of spiritual vision was frequently combined with a harrowing sense of his own corruption. "My wickedness," he says, "as I am in myself, has long appeared to me perfectly ineffable; like an infinite deluge or mountains over my head." Often, for many years, he has had in his mind and his mouth the words "Infinite upon infinite!" His heart looks to him like "an abyss infinitely deeper than hell;" and yet, he adds, it seems to him that "his conviction of sin is exceedingly small." Whilst weeping and crying for his sins, he seemed to know that "his repentance was nothing to his sin" (i. 41). Extravagant expressions of this kind are naturally rather shocking to the outsider; and, to those who are incapable of sympathising, they may even appear to be indications of hypocrisy. Nobody was more alive than Edwards himself to the danger of using such phrases mechanically. When you call yourself the worst of men, he says, be careful that you do not think highly of yourself just because you think so meanly. And if you reply, "No, I have not a high opinion of my humility; it seems to me I am as proud as the devil;" ask again, "whether on this very account that you think yourself as proud as the devil, you do not think yourself to be very humble" (iv. 282). That is a characteristic bit of subtilising, and it indicates the danger of all this excessive introspection. Edwards would not have accepted the moral that the best plan is to think about yourself as little as possible; for from his point of view this constant cross-examination of all your feelings, this dissection of emotion down to its finest and most intricate convolutions, was of the very essence of religion. No one, however, can read his account of his own feelings, even when he runs into the accustomed phraseology, without perceiving the ring of genuine feeling. He is morbid, it may be, but he is not insincere; and even his strained hyperboles are scarcely unintelligible when considered as the expression of the sentiment produced by the effort of a human being to live constantly in presence of the absolute and the infinite.

[...]

The pastor, it may easily be supposed, was not popular with the rising generation. He had, as he confesses with his usual candour, "a constitution in many respects peculiarly unhappy, attended with flaccid solids; vapid, sizy, and scarce fluids; and a low tide of spirits; often occasioning a kind of childish weakness and contemptibleness of speech, presence and demeanour; with a disagreeable dulness and stiffness, much unfitting me for conversation, but more especially for the government of a college," which he was requested to undertake (i. 86). He was, says his admiring biographer, "thorough in the government of his children," who consequently "reverenced, esteemed, and loved him." He adopted the plan, less popular now than then, and even more decayed in America than in England, of "thoroughly subduing" his children as soon as they showed any tendency to self-will. He was a "great enemy" to all "vain amusements;" and even after his children had grown up, he enforced their abstinence from such "pernicious practice," and never allowed them to be out after nine at night. Any gentleman, we are happy to add, was given proper opportunities for courting his daughters after consulting their parents, but on condition of conforming strictly to the family regulations (i. 52, 53). This Puritan discipline appears to have succeeded with Edwards' own family; but a gentleman with flaccid solids, vapid fluids, and a fervent belief in hell-fire is seldom appreciated by the youth even of a Puritan village.

[...]

This simplicity is significant of Edwards' unique position. The doctrine of Calvinism, by whatever name it may be called, is a mental tonic of tremendous potency. Whether in its theological dress, as attributing all events to the absolute decrees of the Almighty, or in its metaphysical dress, as declaring that some abstract necessity governs the world, or in the shape more familiar to modern thinkers, in which it proclaims the universality of what has been called the reign of law, it conquers or revolts the imagination. It forces us to conceive of all phenomena as so many links

> "In the eternal chain
> Which none can break, nor slip, nor overreach;"

and can, therefore, be accepted only by men who possess the rare power of combining their beliefs into a logical whole. Most people contrive to shirk the consequences, either by some of those evasions which, as Edwards showed, amount to asserting the objective existence of chance, or more commonly by forbidding their reason to follow the chain of inferences through more than a few links. The axiom that the cause of a cause is also the cause of the thing caused, though verbally admitted, is beyond the reach of most intellects. People are willing to admit that A is irrevocably joined to B, B to C, and so on to the end of the alphabet, but they refuse to realise the connection between A and Z. The annoyance excited by Mr. Buckle's enunciation of some very familiar propositions, is a measure of the reluctance of the popular imagination to accept a logical conclusion. When the dogma is associated with a belief in eternal damnation, the consequences are indeed terrible; and therefore it was natural that Calvinism should have become an almost extinct creed, and the dogma have been left to the freethinkers who had not that awful vision before their eyes. Hobbes, Collins, and Hume, the three writers with whom the opinion was chiefly associated in English literature, were also the three men who were regarded as most emphatically the devil's advocates. In the latter part of the eighteenth century, it was indeed adopted by Hartley, by his disciple Priestley, and by Abraham Tucker, all of whom were Christians after a fashion. But they reconciled themselves to the belief by peculiar forms of optimism. […] But Edwards, though an optimist in a very different sense, was alone amongst contemporary writers of any speculative power in asserting at once the doctrine that all events are the result of the Divine will, and the doctrine of eternal damnation. His mind, acute as it was, yet worked entirely in the groove provided for it. The revolting consequences to which he was led by not running away from his premises, never for an instant suggested to him that the premises might conceivably be false. He accepts a belief in hellfire, interpreted after the popular fashion, without a murmur, and deduces from it all those consequences which most theologians have evaded or covered with a judicious veil.

Edwards was luckily not an eloquent man, for his sermons would in that case have been amongst the most terrible of human compositions. But if ever he warms into something like eloquence, it is when he is endeavouring to force upon the imaginations of his hearers the horrors of their position. […] Read that sermon (vol. vii., sermon xv.), and endeavour to picture the scene of its original delivery. Imagine the congregation of rigid Calvinists, prepared by previous scenes of frenzy and convulsion, and longing for the fierce excitement which was the only break in the monotony of their laborious lives. And then imagine Edwards ascending the pulpit, with his flaccid solids and vapid fluids, and the pale drawn face, in which we can trace an equal resemblance to the stern Puritan forefathers and to the keen sallow New Englander of modern times. He gives out as his text, "Sinners shall slide in due time," and the title of his sermon is, "Sinners in the Hands of an Angry God." For a full hour he dwells with unusual vehemence on the wrath of the Creator and the sufferings of the creature. His sentences, generally languid and complex, condense themselves into short, almost gasping asseverations. God is angry with the wicked; as angry with the living wicked as "with many of those miserable creatures that He is now tormenting in hell." The devil is waiting; the fire is ready; the furnace is hot; the "glittering sword is whet and held over them, and the pit hath opened her mouth to receive them." The unconverted are walking on a rotten covering, where there are innumerable weak places, and those places not distinguishable. The flames are "gathering and lashing about" the sinner, and all that preserves him for a moment is "the mere arbitrary will and uncovenanted unobliged forbearance of an incensed God." But does not God love sinners? Hardly in a comforting sense. "The God that holds you over the pit of hell, much as one holds a spider or some other loathsome insect over the fire, abhors you, and is dreadfully provoked; He looks upon you as worthy of nothing else but to be cast into the fire; ... you are ten thousand times as abominable in His eyes as the most hateful and venomous serpent is in ours." The comparison of man to a loathsome viper is one of the metaphors to which Edwards most habitually recurs (*e.g.* vii. 167, 179, 182, 198, 344, 496). No relief is possible; Edwards will have no attempt to explain away the eternity of which he speaks; there will be no end to the "exquisite horrible misery" of the damned. You, when damned, "will know certainly that you must wear out long ages, millions of millions of ages, in wrestling and conflicting with this Almighty merciless vengeance: and then when you have so done, when so many ages have actually been spent by you in this manner, you will know that all is but a point to what remains." Nor might his hearers fancy that, as respectable New England Puritans, they had no personal interest in the question. It would be awful, he says, if we could point to one definite person in this congregation as certain to endure such torments. "But, alas! instead of one, how many is it likely will remember this discourse in hell? It would be a wonder if some that are now present should not be in hell in a very short time, before this year is out. And it would be no wonder if some persons that now sit here in some seats of this meeting-house in health, and quiet and secure, should be there before tomorrow morning."

With which blessing he dismissed the congregation to their dinners, with such appetites as might be left to them. The strained excitement which marks this pleasing production could not be maintained; but Edwards never shrank in cold blood from the most appalling consequences of his theories. He tells us, with superlative coolness, that the "bulk of mankind do throng" to hell (vii. 226). He sentences infants to hell as remorselessly as the *durus pater infantum*, Augustine. The imagination, he admits, may be relieved by the hypothesis that infants suffer only in this world, instead of being doomed to eternal misery. "But it does not at all relieve one's reason;" and that is the only faculty which he will obey (vi. 461). Historically the doctrine is supported by the remark that God did not save the children in Sodom, and that He actually commanded the slaughter of the Midianitish infants. "Happy shall he be," it is written of Edom, "that taketh and dasheth thy little ones against the stones" (vi. 255). Philosophically he remarks that "a young viper has a malignant nature, though incapable of doing a malignant action" (vi. 471), and quotes with approval the statement of a Jewish Rabbi, that a child is wicked as soon as born, "for at the same time that he sucks the breasts he follows his lust" (vi. 482), which is perhaps the superlative expression of the theory that all natural instincts are corrupt. Finally, he enforces the only doctrine which can equal this in horror, namely, that the saints rejoice in the damnation of the wicked. In a sermon called "Wicked Men useful in their Destruction Only" (vol. viii., sermon xxi.), he declares that "the view of the doleful condition of the damned will make them (the saints in heaven) more prize their own blessedness." They will realise the wonderful grace of God, who has made so great a difference between them and others of the same species, "who are no worse by nature than they, and have deserved no worse of God than they." "When they shall look upon the damned," he exclaims, "and see their misery, how will heaven ring with the praises of God's justice towards the wicked, and His grace towards the saints! And with how much greater enlargement of heart will they praise Jesus Christ their Redeemer, that ever He was pleased to set His love upon them, His dying love!"

Was the man who could utter such blasphemous sentiments—for so they undoubtedly appear to us—a being of ordinary flesh and blood? One would rather have supposed his solids to be of bronze, and his fluids of vitriol, than have attributed to them the character which he describes. That he should have been a gentle, meditative creature, around whose knees had clung eleven "young vipers" of his own begetting, is certainly an astonishing reflection. And yet, to do Edwards justice, we must remember two things. In the first place, the responsibility for such ghastly beliefs cannot be repudiated by any one who believes in the torments of hell. Catholics and Protestants must share the opprobrium due to the assertion of this tremendous doctrine. Nor does Arminianism really provide more than a merely verbal escape from the difficulty. The "semi-Pelagian" Jeremy Taylor, for example, draws a picture of hell quite as fearful and as material as Edwards', and, if animated by a less fanatical spirit, adorned by an incomparably more vivid fancy. He specially improves upon Edwards' description by introducing the sense of smell. The tyrant who fastened the dead to the living invented an exquisite torment; "but what is this in respect of hell, when each body of the damned is more loathsome and unsavoury than a million of dead dogs, and all those pressed and crowded together in so strait a compass? Bonaventure goes so far as to say that if one only of the damned were brought into this world, it were sufficient to infect the whole earth. Neither shall the devils send forth a better smell; for, although they are spirits, yet those fiery bodies unto which they are fastened and confined shall be of a more pestilential flavour." It is vain to attempt an extenuation of the horror, by relieving the Almighty from the responsibility of this fearful prison-house. The dogma of free-will is a transparent mockery. It simply enables the believer to retain the hideous side of his creed by abandoning the rational side. To pass over the objection that by admitting the existence of chance it really destroys all intelligible measures of merit and of justice, the really awful dogma remains. You still believe that God has made man too weak to stand alone, that He has placed him amidst temptations where his fall, if not rigidly certain in a given case, is still inevitable for the mass, and then torments him eternally for his wickedness. Whether a man is slain outright, or merely placed without help to wander at random through innumerable pit-falls, makes no real difference in the character of the action. Theologians profess horror at the doctrine of infantile damnation, though they cannot always make up their minds to disavow it explicitly, but they will find it easier to condemn the doctrine than effectually to repudiate all responsibility. To the statement that it follows logically from the dogma of original sin, they reply that logic is out of place in such questions. But, if this be granted, do they not maintain doctrines as hideous, when calmly examined? It is blasphemous, we are told, to say with Edwards, that God holds the "little vipers," whom we call "helpless innocents," suspended over the pit of hell, and drops millions of them into ruthless torments. Certainly it is blasphemous. But is an infant really more helpless than the poor savage of Australia or St. Giles, surrounded from his birth with cruel and brutal natures, and never catching one glimpse of celestial light? Nay, when the question is between God and man, does not the difference between the infant and the philosopher or the statesman vanish into nothing? All, whatever figment of free-will may be set up, are equally helpless in face of the surrounding influences which mould their characters and their fate. Young children, the heterodox declare, are innocent. But the theologian replies with unanswerable truth, that God looks at the heart and not at the actions, and that science and theology are at one in declaring that in the child are the germs of the adult man. If human nature is corrupt and therefore hateful to God, Edwards is quite right in declaring that the bursting bud must be as hateful as the full-grown tree. To beings of a loftier order, to say nothing of a Being of infinite power and wisdom, the petty race of man would appear as helpless as insects appear to us, and the distinction between the children or the ignorant, and the wise and full-grown, an irrelevant refinement.

It is of course true that the patient reception of this and similar doctrines would indicate at the present day a callous heart or a perverted intellect. Though, in the sphere of abstract speculation, we cannot draw any satisfactory line between the man and the infant, there is a wide gap to the practical imagination. A man ought to be shocked when confronted with this fearfully concrete corollary to his theories. But the blame should be given where it is due. The Calvinist is not to blame for the theory of universal law which he shares with the philosopher, but for the theory of damnation which he shares with the Arminian. The hideous dogma is the existence of the prison-house, not the belief that its inmates are sent there by God's inscrutable decree, instead of being drafted into it by lot. And here we come to the second fact which must be remembered in Edwards' favour. The living truths in his theory are chained to dead fancies, and the fancies have an odour as repulsive as Taylor's "million of dead dogs." But on the truths is founded a religious and moral system which, however erroneous it may appear to some thinkers, is conspicuous for its vigour and loftiness. Edwards often shows himself a worthy successor of the great men who led the moral revolt of the Reformation. Amongst some very questionable metaphysics and much outworn—sometimes repulsive—superstition, he grasps the central truths on which all really noble morality must be based. The mode in which they presented themselves to his mind may be easily traced. Calvinism, logically developed, leads to Pantheism. The absolute sovereignty of God, the doctrine to which Edwards constantly returns, must be extended over all nature as well as over the fate of the individual human soul. The peculiarity of Edwards' mind was, that the doctrine had thus expanded along particular lines of thought, without equally affecting others. He is a kind of Spinoza-Mather; he combines, that is, the logical keenness of the great metaphysician with the puerile superstitions of the New England divine; he sees God in all nature, and yet believes in the degrading supernaturalism of the Salem witches. The object of his faith, in short, is the "infinite Jehovah" (vi. 170), the God to whose all-pervading power none can set a limit, and who is yet the tutelary deity of a petty clan; and there is something almost bewildering in the facility with which he passes from one conception to the other without the smallest consciousness of any discontinuity.

[. . .]

God is to the universe—to use Edwards' own metaphor—what the sun is to our planet; and the metaphor would have been more adequate if he had been acquainted with modern science. The sun's action is the primary cause of all the infinitely complex play of forces which manifest themselves in the fall of a raindrop or in the operations of a human brain. But as some bodies may seem to resist the action of the sun's rays, so may some created beings set themselves in opposition to the Divine Will. To a thorough-going Pantheist, indeed, such an opposition must appear to be impossible if we look deep enough, and sin, in this sense, be merely an illusion, caused by our incapacity of taking in the whole design of the Almighty. Edwards, however, though dimly aware of the difficulty, is not so consistent in his Pantheism as to be much troubled with it. He admits that, by some mysterious process, corruption has intruded itself into the Divine universe. The all-pervading harmony is marred by a discord due, in his phraseology, to the fall of man. Over the ultimate cause of this discord lies a veil which can never be withdrawn to mortal intelligence. Assuming its existence, however, virtue consists, if one may so speak, in that quality which fits a man to be a conducting medium, and vice in that which makes him a non-conducting medium to the solar forces. This proposition is confounded in Edwards' mind, as in that of most metaphysicians, with the very different proposition that virtue consists in recognising the Divine origin of those forces. It is characteristic, in fact, of his metaphysical school, to identify the logical with the causal connection, and to assume that the definition of a thing necessarily constitutes its essence. "Virtue," says Edwards, "is the union of heart to being in general, or to God, the Being of beings" (ii. 421), and thus consists in the intellectual apprehension of Deity, and in the emotion founded upon and necessarily involving the apprehension. The doctrine that whatever is done so as to promote the glory of God is virtuous, is with him identified with the doctrine that whatever is done consciously in order to promote the glory of God is virtuous. The major premiss of the syllogism which proves an action to be virtuous must be actually present to the mind of the agent. This, in utilitarian phraseology, is to confound between the criterion and the motive. If it is, as Edwards says, the test of a virtuous action that it should tend to "the highest good of being in general," it does not follow that an action is only virtuous when done with a conscious reference to that end. But Edwards overlooks or denies the distinction, and assumes, for example, as an evident corollary, that a love of children or friends is only virtuous in so far as it is founded on a desire for the general good, which, in his sense, is a desire for the glory of God (ii. 428). He judges actions, that is, not by their tendency, but by their nature; and their nature is equivalent to their logic.

His metaphysical theory coincides precisely with his theological view, and is generally expressed in theological language. The love of "Being in general" is the love of God. The intellectual intuition is the reflection of the inward light, and the recognition of a mathematical truth is but a different phase of the process which elsewhere produces conversion. Intuition is a kind of revelation, and revelation is a special intuition.

[...]

So far, Edwards is unassailable from his own point of view. Our theory of religion may differ from his; but at least he fully realises how profound is the meaning of the word, and aims at conquering all human faculties, not at controlling a few external manifestations. But his further applications of the theory lead him into more doubtful speculations. That Being, a union with whom constitutes true holiness, is not only to be the ideal of perfect goodness, but He must be the God of the Calvinists, who fulfils the stipulations of a strange legal bargain, and the God of the Jews, who sentences whole nations to massacre for the crimes of their ancestors. Edwards has hitherto been really protesting against that lower conception of God which is latent in at least the popular versions of Catholic or Arminian theology, and to which Calvinism opposes a loftier view. God, on this theory, is not really almighty, for the doctrine of free-will places human actions and their results beyond His control. He is scarcely omniscient, for, like human rulers, He judges by actions, not by the intrinsic nature of the soul, and therefore distributes His rewards and punishments on a system comparable to that of mere earthly jurisprudence. He is at most the infallible judge of actions, not the universal ordainer of events and distributor of life and happiness. Edwards' profound conviction of the absolute sovereignty of God leads him to reject all such feeble conceptions. But he has now to tell us where the Divine influence has actually displayed itself; and his view becomes strangely narrowed. Instead of confessing that all good gifts come from God, he infers that those which do not come from his own God must be radically vicious. Already, as we have seen, in virtue of his leading principle, he has denied to all natural affections the right to be truly virtuous. Unless they involve a conscious reference to God, they are but delusive resemblances of the reality. He admits that the natural man can in various ways produce very fair imitations of true virtue. By help of association of ideas, for example, or by the force of sympathy, it is possible that benevolence may become pleasing and malevolence displeasing, even when our own interest is not involved (ii. 436). Nay, there is a kind of moral sense natural to man, which consists in a certain perception of the harmony between sin and punishment, and which therefore does not properly spring from self-love. This moral sense may even go so far as to recognise the propriety of yielding all to the God from whom we receive everything (ii. 443), and the justice of the punishment of sinners. And yet this natural conscience does not imply the existence of a "truly virtuous taste or determination of the mind to relish and delight in the essential beauty of true virtue, arising from a virtuous benevolence of the heart" (ii. 445). God has bestowed such instincts upon men for their preservation here; but they will disappear in the next world, where no such need for them exists. He is driven, indeed, to make some vague concessions (against which his enlightened commentators protest), to the effect that "these things [the natural affections] have something of the general nature of virtue, which is love" (ii. 456); but no such uncertain affinity can make them worthy to be reckoned with that union with God which is the effect of the Divine intervention alone.

Edwards is thus in the singular position of a Pantheist who yet regards all nature as alienated from God; and in the treatise on Original Sin he brings out the more revolting consequences of that view by help of the theological dogma of corruption. He there maintains in its fullest sense the terrible thesis, that all men are naturally in a state of which the inevitable issue is their "utter eternal perdition, as being finally accursed of God and the subjects of His remediless wrath through sin" (vi. 137). The evidence of this appalling statement is made up, with a simplicity which would be amusing if employed in a less fearful cause, of various texts from Scripture, quoted, of course, after the most profoundly unhistorical fashion; of inferences from the universality of death, regarded as the penalty incurred by Adam; of general reflections upon the heathen world and the idolatry of the Jews; and of the sentences pronounced by Jehovah against the Canaanites. In one of his sermons, of portentous length and ferocity (vol. vii., sermon iii.), he expands the doctrine that natural men—which includes all men who have not gone through the mysterious process of conversion are God's enemies. Their heart, he says, "is like a viper, hissing and spitting poison at God;" and God requites their ill-will with undying enmity and never-ceasing torments. Their unconsciousness of that enmity, and even their belief that they are rightly affected towards God, is no proof that the enmity does not exist. The consequences may be conceived. "God who made you has given you a capacity to bear torment; and He has that capacity in His hands; and He can enlarge it and make you capable of more misery, as much as He will. If God hates anyone and sets Himself against him as His enemy, what cannot He do with him? How dreadful it must be to fall into the hands of such an enemy!" (vii. 201). How dreadful, we add, is the conception of the universe which implies that God is such an enemy of the bulk of His creatures; and how strangely it combines with the mild Pantheism which traces and adores the hand of God in all natural objects! The doctrine, it is to be observed, which is expanded through many pages of the book on Original Sin, is not merely that men are legally guilty, as being devoid of "true virtue," though possessed of a certain factitious moral sense, but that they are actually for the most part detestably wicked. One illustration of his method may be sufficient. The vileness of man is proved by the remark (not peculiar to Edwards), that men who used to live 1,000 years now live only 70; whilst throughout Christendom their life does not average more than 40 or 50 years; so that "sensuality and debauchery" have shortened our days to a twentieth part of our former allowance.

Thus the Divine power, which is in one sense the sole moving force of the universe, is limited, so far as its operation upon men's hearts is concerned, to that small minority who have gone through the process of conversion as recognised by Edwards' sect. All others, heathens, infants, and the great mass of professed Christians, are sentenced to irretrievable perdition. The simplicity with which he condemns all

other forms, even of his own religion, is almost touching. He incidentally remarks, for example, that external exercises may not show true
virtue, because they have frequently proceeded from false religion.
Members of the Romish Church and many ancient "hermits and
anchorites" have been most energetic in such exercises, and Edwards
once lived next to a Jew who appeared to him "the devoutest person
that he ever saw in his life" (iv. 90); but, as he quietly assumes, all such
appearances must of course be delusive.

Once more, then, we are brought back to the question, How could
any man hold such doctrines without going mad? or, as experience has
reconciled us to that phenomenon, How could a man with so many
elevated conceptions of the truth reconcile these ghastly conclusions
to the nobler part of his creed? Edwards' own explanations of the
difficulty—such as they are—do not help us very far. The argument
by which he habitually defends the justice of the Almighty sounds
very much like a poor quibble in his mouth, though it is not peculiar
to him. Our obligation towards God, he says, must be in proportion
to His merits; therefore it is infinite. Now there is no merit in paying
a debt which we owe; and hence the fullest discharge of our duty
deserves no reward. On the other hand, there is demerit in refusing to
pay a debt, and therefore any shortcoming deserves an infinite penalty
(vi. 155). Without examining whether our duty is proportional to
the perfection of its object, and is irrespective of our capacities, there
is one vital objection to this doctrine, which Edwards had adopted
from less coherent reasoners. His theory, as I have said, so far from
destroying virtue, gives it the fullest possible meaning. There can be no
more profound distinction than between the affections which harmonise with the Divine will and those which are discordant, though it
might puzzle a more consistent Pantheist to account for the existence
of the latter. That, however, is a primary doctrine with Edwards. But
if virtue remains, it is certain that his theory seems to be destructive
both of merit and demerit as between man and God. If we are but
clay in the hands of the potter, there is no intelligible meaning in our
deserving from Him either good or evil. We are as He has made us.
Edwards explains, indeed, that the sense of desert implies a certain
natural congruity between evil-doing and punishment (ii. 430). But
the question recurs, how in such a case the congruity arises? It is one
of the illusions which should disappear when we rise to the sphere of
the absolute and infinite. The metaphor about a debt and its payment,

though common in vulgar Calvinism, is quite below Edwards' usual
level of thought. And, if we try to restate the argument in a more
congenial form, its force disappears. The love of God, even though
imperfect, should surely imply some conformity to His nature; and
even an imperfect love should hardly be confounded, one might fancy,
with an absolute enmity to the Creator. Though the argument, which
is several times repeated, appears to have satisfied Edwards, it would
have been more in harmony with his principles to declare that, as
between man and his God, there could be no question of justice. The
absolute sovereignty of the Creator is the only, and to him it should be
the conclusive, answer to such complaints. But, whatever may be the
fate of this apology, the one irremovable difficulty remains behind. If
God be the one universal cause of all things, is He not the cause of evil
as well as good? Do you not make God, in short, the author of sin?

With this final difficulty, which, indeed, besets all such theories,
Edwards struggles long and with less than his usual vigour. He tries to
show, and perhaps successfully, that the difficulty concerns his opponents as much as himself. They can, at least, escape only by creating
a new kind of necessity, under the name of contingency; for God is,
on this theory, like a mariner who has constantly to shape his course
to meet unforeseen and uncontrollable gusts of wind (v. 298); and to
make the best of it. He insists upon the difference, not very congenial
to his scheme, between ordering and permitting evil. The sun, he says
(v. 293), causes light, but is only the occasion of darkness. If, however,
the sun voluntarily retired from the world, it could scarcely evade
the responsibility of its absence. And finally, he makes the ordinary
distinction, and that which is perhaps the best answer to be made to
an unanswerable difficulty. Christ's crucifixion, he says, was so far bad
as it was brought about by malignant murderers: but as considered by
God, with a view to all its glorious consequences, it was not evil, but
good (v. 297). And thus any action may have two aspects; and that
which appears to us, whose view is necessarily limited, as simply evil,
may, when considered by an infinite intelligence, as part of the general
order of things, be absolutely good. God does not will sin as sin, but
as a necessary part of a generally perfect system.

Here, however, in front of that ultimate mystery which occurs
in all speculation, I must take leave of this singular thinker. In a
frequently quoted passage, Mackintosh speaks of his "power of
subtle argument, perhaps unmatched, certainly unsurpassed amongst

men." The eulogy seems to be rather overstrained, unless we measure subtlety of thought rather by the complexity and elaboration of its embodiment than by the keenness of the thought itself. But that Edwards possessed extraordinary acuteness is as clear as it is singular that so acute a man should have suffered his intellectual activity to be restrained within such narrow fetters. Placed in a different medium, under the same circumstances, for example, as Hume or Kant, he might have developed a system of metaphysics comparable in its effect upon the history of thought to the doctrines of either of those thinkers. He was, one might fancy, formed by nature to be a German professor, and accidentally dropped into the American forests. Far away from the main currents of speculation, ignorant of the conclusions reached by his most cultivated contemporaries, and deriving his intellectual sustenance chiefly from an obsolete theology, with some vague knowledge of the English followers of Locke, his mind never expanded itself freely. Yet, even after making allowance for his secluded life, we are astonished at the powerful grasp which Calvinism, in its expiring age, had laid upon so penetrating an intellect. The framework of dogma was so powerful, that the explosive force of Edwards' speculations, instead of destroying his early principles by its recoil, expended its whole energy along the line in which orthodox opinion was not injured. Most bold speculators, indeed, suffer from a kind of colour blindness, which conceals from them a whole order of ideas, sufficiently familiar to very inferior minds. Edwards' utter unconsciousness of the aspect which his doctrines would present to anyone who should have passed beyond the charmed circle of orthodox sentiment is, however, more surprising than the similar defect in any thinker of nearly equal acuteness. In the middle of the eighteenth century, he is still in bondage to the dogmas of the Pilgrim Fathers; he is as indifferent to the audacious revolt of the deists and Hume as if the old theological dynasty were still in full vigour; and the fact, whatever else it may prove, proves something for the enduring vitality of the ideas which had found an imperfect expression in Calvinism. Clearing away the crust of ancient superstition, we may still find in Edwards' writings a system of morality as ennobling, and a theory of the universe as elevated, as can be discovered in any theology. That the crust was thick and hard, and often revolting in its composition, is, indeed, undeniable; but the genuine metal is there, no less unmistakably than the refuse.

NOTES

1. *The Works of President Edwards*, Worcester (Mass.), 1808.
2. The population of Massachusetts is stated at 164,000 inhabitants in 1742, and 240,000 in 1761.—See Holmes's Annals.

THE WASTE LAND
(T.S. ELIOT)

"'Hints and Guesses' in *The Waste Land*"
by Michael Gillum,
University of North Carolina at Asheville

Although the concept of salvation might be applied in secular as well as religious contexts, a sin, properly speaking, is an offense against God or God's law. We might question whether there can be sin in *The Waste Land*, since God seems to be absent from the poem's world. Raised by a pious Unitarian mother, Eliot separated himself from the church as a young man but, according to his biographer Lyndall Gordon, never stopped feeling drawn toward religious experience. In midlife, five years after *The Waste Land*, Eliot would formally convert to Anglican Christianity. However, in the period leading up to that poem, Eliot was a nonbeliever. Later he told Stephen Spender that, at that time, he was "seriously considering becoming a Buddhist" (quoted in Sultan 175). In Eliot's 1920 volume, poems such as "A Cooking Egg," "The Hippopotamus," and "Mr. Eliot's Sunday Morning Service" treat aspects of Christianity satirically. However, "Gerontion" and stanzas 3 and 4 of the "Sunday Morning Service" reveal a sense of loss over the absence of living faith. That feeling is certainly evident in *The Waste Land*. Not only the desperate sense of loss but also fleeting glimpses of the transcendent in that poem foreshadow Eliot's future conversion.

The empty world of the poem—the urban wasteland and the desert—is haunted by its absent God. In Part 1, the fortuneteller Madame Sosostris says, "I do not find / The Hanged Man" (54–55).[1] In his note to line 46, Eliot says he associates this card of the Tarot deck "with the hooded figure in the passage of the disciples to Emmaus in Part V." In this roundabout way, Eliot indicates that the Hanged Man who did not turn up in the card reading represents Christ. Of course we would not expect Madame Sosostris, a dabbler in pagan mysteries, to "find" that card. She represents an aspect of the debased modern culture from which the poem is trying to escape. So is Christ elsewhere present in the wasteland? Not clearly so. Part 5, "What the Thunder Said," begins with a somewhat veiled description of the Passion of Christ:

> After the torchlight red on sweaty faces
> After the frosty silence in the garden
> After the agony in stony places
>
> . . . .
> He who was living is now dead
> We who were living are now dying
> With a little patience [.] (322–330)

Apparently Jesus "is now dead," crucified but not risen again. His life and death do not redeem the shriveled death-in-life condition of the wasteland people, "dying / With a little patience."

Later in Part 5, the questing speaker sees "the hooded figure in the passage of the disciples to Emmaus," where, according to Luke 24:13–31, two of his followers eventually recognized the resurrected Christ. But in the poem's version, there is no recognition:

> Who is that third who walks always beside you?
> . . . .
> Gliding wrapt in a brown mantle, hooded
> I do not know whether a man or a woman
> —But who is that on the other side of you? (360–366)

Eliot's note makes this blurry presentation even blurrier by referring us to "an account of one of the Antarctic expeditions" (360) where the extra person seen by the explorers was merely a hallucination. Therefore, either Christ appears to the quester of Eliot's "What the Thunder Said" but is not recognized, or he is a hallucination not really present at all. Beyond that, the spectral figure seems more menacing than reassuring. Nevertheless, these passages and footnotes about the

Hanged Man and the "hooded figure" direct our attention to God's absence from the wasteland. Since the death of God is literally the point of departure for the quest in Part 5, the quest itself must be a search either to recover faith or to discover some substitute for it, some other saving truth. But before getting to that, we must consider what it is that the wasteland needs to be saved *from*.

The poem includes a cryptic pattern involving women being assaulted and injured by men—cryptic in that it unfolds mainly through literary allusions and Eliot's notes. In Part 2, "A Game of Chess," the nervous upper-class woman ("Belladonna" in the Tarot passage) sits beneath a tapestry or painting of Philomela, who was raped and mutilated by King Tereus (97–103). Philomela, transformed into a nightingale, sings for a second time in Part 3 (203–206). Also, Eliot's note to line 138 refers to Middleton's *Women Beware Women*, where a game of chess masks a rape or forcible seduction that is happening at the same time. This connection is so obscure that no reader could have made it without Eliot's prompting, and there is little apparent similarity between the old play and this section of Eliot's poem. As far as we know, Belladonna is not raped, yet Eliot associates her with rape victims. These allusions to rape do not clearly parallel the other sexual acts in the poem, which appear to be consensual, though exploitative and degrading. The poem also contains hints of women being murdered:

> White bodies naked on the low damp ground
> And bones cast in a little low dry garret,
> Rattled by the rat's foot only, year to year. (193–195)

Here the initial speaker of "The Fire Sermon" juxtaposes a sex act on the riverbank with bones cast into an attic. Whose bones? There is an implication of murder successfully concealed. Eliot's note to line 293 refers to Dante's la Pia, who was murdered on her husband's orders (Southam 179).

Another abused woman is Ophelia, who goes mad and commits suicide by drowning after being spurned and insulted by Hamlet. In Shakespeare's play, she speaks her last farewell in the words quoted by Eliot in line 172, at the end of the pub scene. Hugh Kenner, one of Eliot's critics, sees dim echoes of this drowned-woman motif in the Hyacinth Girl with wet hair (38) and again in the opening of Part 3, where "fingers of leaf / Clutch and sink into the wet bank" (173–174). Kenner connects the motif to Eliot's 1939 play *The Family Reunion*, where Harry confesses to drowning his wife, and to *Sweeney Agonistes*, where Sweeney says, "Any man might do a girl in." Kenner also interprets the corpse that Stetson planted in his garden (71) not as a male vegetation god out of *The Golden Bough* but as a murdered wife or lover (Kenner 161–165). Additionally, Cleopatra, who committed suicide after bringing ruin to Antony, and Dido, who committed suicide after being cruelly abandoned by Aeneas, enter the poem through allusions and notes. Eliot's note to the word *laquearia* (92) evokes Dido through a connection that, again, no reader would make without the note. Eliot's notes are determined to draw attention to female victimization even when it is invisible in the versified part of the text.

The poem's covert theme of fantasized violence against women may well derive from Eliot's feelings about his failing first marriage to Vivien Haigh-Wood,[2] a mutual disaster that contributed to her mental illness and blighted Eliot's life for decades. The angry, desperate exchange between the nervous woman and her husband in part 2, lines 111–138, is commonly understood to reflect the Eliots' marital relationship. These dark feelings, only murkily expressed in the poem, arouse a powerful sense of guilt that surfaces especially in the accusation of Stetson (69–73). It is as though the tangled "textual unconscious" of *The Waste Land* resents women as a source of temptation and a cause of suffering, yet at the same time feels guilt at having harmed women and sympathizes with their suffering at the hands of men. At the level of Eliot's personal psychology, this submerged private material may be what constitutes "sin" and a need for redemption in *The Waste Land*. However, the poem also has broader and more visible concerns about patterns of failure in modern culture.

The Waste Land carried an unusual amount of sexual content for its time. In Part 1, we find the ambiguous romantic encounter in the hyacinth garden (35–41), framed by quotations that remind us of the grand but illicit passion of Tristan and Isolde in Wagner's opera. Part 2 alludes to the myth of Philomela's rape and exposes sexual tensions in the marital relation of Lil and Albert. Part 3 presents a series of debased sexual relationships beginning with the "nymphs" (London typists and shopgirls) seduced and abandoned by "the loitering heirs of City directors" (180). Sweeney, a character who appears in other poems by Eliot as a sensual brute, will visit Mrs. Porter, who, according to the bawdy soldiers' song that Eliot quotes, is the keeper of a brothel (Southam 168). Mr. Eugenides proposes a homosexual tryst with the narrator; then the "typist home at teatime" (222) endures the clumsy advances of her pimply boyfriend; and finally the Thames daughters confess their loss of virginity under squalid circumstances.

Despite all this activity, the title of Part 3, "The Fire Sermon," seems somewhat misleading or even ironic. As Southam explains, "The Fire Sermon was preached by the Buddha against the fires of lust, anger, envy and the other passions that consume men" (165). However, in Eliot's "Fire Sermon," no fires of passion are evident. Mr. Eugenides's proposition to a near-stranger is as calculated as the business transaction they have just concluded. The typist is indifferent to her "lover" and to their sexual encounter: "[S]he is bored and tired" (236). The Thames daughters are similarly passive and mechanical: "By Richmond I raised my knees / Supine on the floor of a narrow canoe" (294–295). Thus, the poem does not treat the sexual behavior of the wasteland's people as flaming sins of passion but as symptoms of a pervading emotional and spiritual deadness.

As Brooks and others have emphasized, this condition of living death is what the wasteland needs to be saved from (88). It is diagnosed in the title of Part 1, "The Burial of the Dead," as well as in the opening lines, where the speaker resents the evocative scent of lilacs reawakening memory and desire and misses the anesthetic blanket of "forgetful snow." He would rather stay dead. Marie (12–17) is bored and lonely, alive only in her memories of the past. In the last paragraph of Part 1, the zombie bank clerks plod across London Bridge, linked with spiritual death through Eliot's allusions to the *Inferno*. After line 12 or so, it is eternal winter in the urban wasteland: "the brown fog of a winter dawn" (61), "the sudden frost" (73), "the brown land" (175), "a cold blast" (185), "on a winter evening" (190), "the brown fog of a winter noon" (208), "the frosty silence in the gardens" (323). The colors of the wasteland are brown, black, violet, and red; the only thing green or blue is the adulterated firelight in Belladonna's artificial environment (95).

The prophetic voice in Part 1 asks whether there are any signs of vigorous life in the wasteland, where winter feeds "a little life with dried tubers" (6–7):

> What are the roots that clutch, what branches grow
> Out of this stony rubbish? Son of man,

> You cannot say or guess, for you know only
> A heap of broken images [....] (19–22)

If there are signs of life, we—and the voice seems to challenge readers personally—cannot recognize these signs because we know only a chaotic "heap" of fragments. Our relation to culture is disordered. The contemporary European culture represents the accumulation of its past: religion, poetry, national myths, and so on. But by now the accumulation is so vast that it no longer forms clear patterns. Westerners hold in common no central symbols and ideas adequate to support community and confer meaning upon individual lives but see in the cultural residue only the "withered stumps of time" (104). This metaphor of culture as rubbish and broken images is central to the very method of *The Waste Land*, with its quotations of poetry its allusions to philosophy, religion, and myth and its snatches of ancient and foreign languages (six of them, plus archaic English, and even the rooster in line 392 speaks French or Italian). Rather than ending his four major sections with reassuringly conclusive statements, Eliot places puzzling fragmentary quotations at these key spots: a line of Baudelaire's French ends Part 1, Ophelia's farewell Part 2, the Buddha and St. Augustine Part 3, and finally an explosion of fragments in five languages wind up the poem. To be simply bewildered by all this would be an appropriate first response, because the reader's sense of disorder and confusion is part of the poem's meaning. While research into the contexts will suggest particular meanings for these quotations, they function more generally as "a heap of broken images," suggesting a loss of intelligible meaning.

In the midst of the poem's concluding volley of quotations, the speaker says, "These fragments I have shored against my ruins" (431). This line points to a possible way out of the wasteland: Perhaps a cultivated individual might select pieces of junk and treasure from the cultural attic and reorganize them into a life-sustaining pattern of values. However, "shoring" is a defensive action against siege, and it sounds as if the walls, like London Bridge, are coming down regardless. The line that follows is "Why then I'll fit you. Hieronymo's mad againe" (432). In the original context, the dramatic entertainment by which the half-crazy Hieronymo "fits" his company in *The Spanish Tragedy* is actually a stratagem for murdering his enemies, hardly a step toward redemption through high culture. The poem's conclusion suggests that any salvation from the personal and cultural wasteland must be sought somewhere beyond culture and history. Dante and Shakespeare are not strong enough medicine.

In "Dry Salvages" (1941), one of the *Four Quartets*, Eliot speaks of "hints and guesses" that can lead us toward "the point of intersection of the timeless / With time," suggested by images such as "a shaft of sunlight, / The wild thyme unseen, or the winter lightning [...]" ("Dry Salvages" Part 5). In *Four Quartets*, Eliot, at that time writing as a committed Christian, speaks repeatedly of moments when a partial experience of the transcendent breaks into our defective temporal reality. Even in *The Waste Land* there are hints and guesses, momentary flashes of experience that suggest something higher and better. If the modern city is "Unreal," where is the Real? A line struck from a draft of the poem quotes an answer from Plato: "Not here, O Glaucon, but in another world" (*Facsimile* 31). But in present experience there may be intimations. For example, the Hyacinth Girl's lover remembers looking "into the heart of light, the silence" (41). Although critics don't agree as to whether he recalls an experience of ecstasy or one of failure and despair, he uses the language of religious mysticism. "Looking into the heart of light" might be a positive experience, even if it is lost beyond recapture.

Several hints of transcendence involve music from "above," in both a physical and metaphoric sense. Belladonna's picture displays

> The change of Philomel, by the barbarous king
> So rudely forced; yet there the nightingale
> Filled all the desert with inviolable voice
> And still she cried, and still the world pursues,
> 'Jug Jug' to dirty ears. (99–103)

The rape victim Philomela, retaining her moral purity, sings her pain "with inviolable voice," filling the desert with a perfect music that cannot properly be heard by our "dirty ears." The nightingale's song is a traditional metaphor for poetic art, but here it is something beyond art, a music that transcends our fallen condition. The nightingale sings again amid the sexual corruption of "The Fire Sermon" (203–206), immediately after the quotation in French from Verlaine's sonnet "Parsifal" (202). The latter, in its original context, also describes pure music descending from a higher place, as a boys choir sings in the dome of the chapel where Parsifal venerates the Holy Grail. Later in Part 3,

"This music crept by me upon the waters" (257) quotes Shakespeare's *The Tempest*. In that context, Ferdinand heard a transcendent music originating in Ariel's magic, and the song had the power to settle both the fury of nature and the fury of his own passion. Likewise, in Eliot's following lines (258–265), the speaker feels calm and cheerful in a mood missing since the interlude in the Hofgarten (8–11). In Part 5, the quester in the desert thinks of birdsong and the "sound of water over a rock / Where the hermit-thrush sings in the pine trees / Drip drop drip drop drop drop drop" (356–358). Although the falling water and the music from above are absent from the actual scene, the speaker must remember them from some previous experience.

Some of the "hints" are explicitly Christian. London's Lower Thames Street strangely juxtaposes a fish market, a pub, and a wonderful, small Anglican church:

> And a clatter and a chatter from within
> Where fishmen lounge at noon: where the walls
> Of Magnus Martyr hold
> Inexplicable splendour of Ionian white and gold. (262–265)

"Inexplicable" in the context of the wasteland, the beauty of this baroque church's interior hints of something beyond. As we have seen, "What the Thunder Said" includes an encounter with a "hooded figure" who may or may not be the resurrected Christ. Eliot's notes overlay Part 5's ordeal in the desert with the Christian legend of the Grail quest. But this quester comes to an "empty chapel, only the wind's home" (389). Apparently the quester finds nothing there, only "dry bones." Nor does he continue to the King's palace and recover the Grail. With this truncation, the poem denies any Christian affirmation. Yet some breakthrough has occurred:

> Only a cock stood on the rooftree
> Co co rico co co rico
> In a flash of lightning. Then a damp gust
> Bringing rain [.] (392–395)

Again we should notice the "from-aboveness" of the cock's cry, the lightning flash, and the subsequent voice of the thunder-god. The passage implies some sense of contact with the transcendent.

So is the voice of the thunder the vehicle of salvation in *The Waste Land*? According to the Hindu fable that Eliot borrows, the thunder god says "DA," a meaningless root syllable functioning as a riddle. Then three different audiences make three different guesses at the god's intended meaning, respectively *datta, dayadhvam,* and *damyata,* which Eliot translates as "give, sympathize, control" (402). Then in the myth, but not in Eliot's poem, the god says that each is correct, or rather all three together constitute a program for saving oneself. Eliot's speaker in this section further interprets "give, sympathize, control" in terms of his own life experiences, considering in what ways he may have fulfilled the commands. This passage makes the point that, even if humans could receive divine revelation, they would still have to interpret it.

However, the interpretations of Eliot's speaker are so oddly off the point that he might have misconstrued the god's commands. By "give," the god probably meant to practice charitable actions and give alms, yet the speaker responds by thinking of a romantic or perhaps sexual experience, the giving of one's heart or body: "blood shaking my heart / The awful daring of a moment's surrender" (403–404). Next, the speaker answers the command to "sympathize" (or "be compassionate") by thinking first of his own emotional isolation before acknowledging the equal isolation of others: "I have heard the key / Turn in the door once and once only" (412–413). Finally, in the Hindu fable, the remaining command meant to "control yourself" (Southam 192). However, the speaker dodges the point of self-control by thinking about a past occasion when he might have controlled another's heart (might have begun a love affair?) but failed to do so: "your heart would have responded / Gaily, beating obedient / To controlling hands" (421–423).

Critics have offered many other interpretations of these three puzzling responses to "give, sympathize, control," but if we take the statements on their own terms rather than forcing them into compliance with the god's actual commands, the speaker offers the best account that he can of meeting the requirements. But he must understand how far he has fallen short. By shifting the god's ethical commands onto these grounds of personal intimacy, the answers reinforce the poem's theme of failed romantic or sexual love. They powerfully evoke the emotions of sexual passion, personal loss, loneliness, and regret for lost opportunity. However, they are too self-centered and needy, and too focused on the erotic aspect of life, to be adequate responses to the divine words. Since Eliot had studied the classic Hindu texts for two years at Harvard, he must have been aware of these discrepancies. If the voice of the thunder offers a program for salvation, no human presence in the poem is capable of following it through. The divine challenge has led only to the admission of failure. However, the text will repeat the commands as the next-to-last line of the poem, suggesting that they may yet offer promise as a path that has not yet been tried.

Despite the apparent failure, something happens in "What the Thunder Said." Compared to the static or circular quality of the first four sections, in the fifth there is movement toward a goal. Moreover, the wasteland culture appears to be breaking up. Earlier there were crowds of people tamely crossing London Bridge or "walking around in a ring" (56). By contrast, in Part 5 there is mob violence, "torch-light red on sweaty faces" (322) and "hooded hordes swarming / Over endless plains" (369–370). The delirious speaker wonders

> What is the city over the mountains
> Cracks and reforms and bursts in the violet air
> Falling towers
> Jerusalem Athens Alexandria
> Vienna London
> Unreal [,] (372–377)

Frank Lentricchia compares this apocalyptic vision of contemporary history to Yeats's "The Second Coming" and says Eliot "defines his modernity in *The Waste Land* as that intuition of being on the verge of upheaval—the breakup, the smashing, and the sinking of a whole era" (277). The speaker's personality may be cracking up as well ("Hieronymo's mad againe"), while the poem itself collapses into a heap of fragments at the end. Although frightening, this breakup could be a positive clearing away of whatever inhibits life in the wasteland. Still, the poem offers no clear positive vision. In the end, there is no redemption in *The Waste Land*, only the piercing awareness that something is lacking. The speaker sits upon the bank, fishing (424–425). Fishing at least is a hopeful activity.

NOTES

1. Quotations of Eliot's verse are from *Collected Poems 1909–1962*; I cite *The Waste Land* by line number.
2. For Eliot's first marriage, see Ackroyd 61–68, 81–84.

WORKS CITED OR CONSULTED

Ackroyd, Peter. *T. S. Eliot: A Life*. New York: Simon and Schuster, 1984.

Brooks, Cleanth. "*The Waste Land*: Critique of the Myth." 1939. *Critical Essays on T. S. Eliot's The Waste Land*. Ed. Lois A. Cuddy and David H. Hirsch. Boston: G. K. Hall, 1991. 87–112.

Eliot, T. S. *Collected Poems 1909–1962*. New York: Harcourt Brace Jovanovich, 1993.

———. The Waste Land: *A Facsimile and Transcript of the Original Drafts*. Ed. Valerie Eliot. New York: Harcourt Brace Jovanovich, 1971.

Gordon, Lyndall. *T. S. Eliot: An Imperfect Life*. New York: W. W. Norton, 1999.

Kenner, Hugh. *The Invisible Poet: T. S. Eliot*. New York: McDowell Oblensky, 1959.

Lentricchia, Frank. *Modernist Quartet*. Cambridge UK: Cambridge U.P., 1994.

Southam, B. C. *A Guide to the Selected Poems of T. S. Eliot*. 6th ed. New York: Harcourt Brace, 1994.

Sultan, Stanley. *Eliot, Joyce and Company*. New York: Oxford UP, 1987.

THE PLAYS OF TENNESSEE WILLIAMS

"The Anti-Hero"
by Esther Merle Jackson, in
The Broken World of Tennessee Williams (1956)

INTRODUCTION

Esther Merle Jackson focuses on the anti-hero as an image of the modern person in Williams's plays, claiming that such protagonists in Williams's works reveal "the nature of suffering as it appears in the life of the twentieth century." Placing his plays in a broad context that includes the works of the ancient playwrights, Shakespeare, and Williams's contemporaries, Jackson shows how Williams's "catalogue of transgressors in search of salvation" reflects our search for meaning in the modern world.

ᑟᕁᑐ

Caught in the form of limitation
Between un-being and being.

One of the most controversial aspects of the drama of Tennessee Williams is his use of an anti-heroic protagonist as an image of man. Williams appears to reject the Aristotelian concept of the protagonist

Jackson, Esther Merle. "The Anti-Hero." *The Broken World of Tennessee Williams.* Madison, WI: U of Wisconsin P, 1956. 68–87.

294 The Plays of Tennessee Williams

and to substitute for it an anti-hero, the personification of a humanity neither good, knowledgeable, nor courageous. In Blanche, Alma, Brick, Kilroy, Val, Chance, and Shannon, we see this anti-heroic image of man. Even those figures who command some sympathy, characters such as Tom in *The Glass Menagerie* and Catharine—the victim of *Suddenly Last Summer*—may be described in the language of T. S. Eliot as "non-beings"—"Caught in the form of limitation / Between un-being and being." Williams claims that such is the image of modern man—poised as he is between the contrary imperatives of his world. As he examines humanity through the patched glass of his synthetic myth, the playwright perceives a creature transfixed in a moment of stasis, halted at the point of transition in the process of becoming.[1]

In the "East Coker" movement of *Four Quartets*, T. S. Eliot describes the moral universe out of which the anti-hero has emerged:

> ... There is, it seems to us,
> At best, only a limited value
> In the knowledge derived from experience.
> The knowledge imposes a pattern, and falsifies,
> For the pattern is new in every moment
> And every moment is a new and shocking
> Valuation of all we have been. We are only undeceived
> Of that which, deceiving, could no longer harm.
> In the middle, not only in the middle of the way
> But all the way, in a dark wood, in a bramble,
> On the edge of a grimpen, where is no secure foothold,
> And menaced by monsters, fancy lights,
> Risking enchantment. Do not let me hear
> Of the wisdom of old men, but rather of their folly,
> Their fear of fear and frenzy, their fear of possession,
> Of belonging to another, or to others, or to God.
> The only wisdom we can hope to acquire
> Is the wisdom of humility: humility is endless.[2]

Williams throughout his work—fictional, poetic, and dramatic—portrays the humanity mirrored in Eliot's lines. He attempts to show us man "On the edge of a grimpen, where is no secure foothold, / And menaced by monsters, fancy lights, / Risking enchantment." The reasons for these adjustments in the image of man are clear. The definition of the hero given in the *Poetics* of Aristotle does not adapt itself to the contemporary perception of reality. For Aristotle, like Plato, conceived virtues to be relatively static concepts.[3] His hero is the personification of "good," a man possessing a significant distribution of those qualities which the philosopher believed to characterize the highest levels of human life. Aristotle thought moral stability, like intelligence, to be the concomitant of aristocratic birth. His definition of character thus reflects the political, social, ethical, and religious biases of his own age: "There remains, then, the character between these two extremes; that of a man who is not eminently good and just, yet whose misfortune is brought about not by vice or depravity, but by some error or frailty."[4]

Although contemporary dramatists accept certain aspects of the ethics of Aristotle, they do not feel that his definition of the hero is in every sense an accurate description of a virtuous man in the twentieth century. Arthur Miller, for example, points out that many aspects of Aristotle's system of ethics are today obsolete. The image of man in the twentieth century, writes Miller, must be rooted in an open system of values appropriate to a democratic society.[5] Tennessee Williams writes that the most pressing moral problem of man in the twentieth century is to avoid extinction: "to beat the game of being against non-being."[6] The crux of the argument which has led to the modification of the Aristotelian hero lies in changes in the perception of experience, in the accumulation of new knowledges about and new hopes for the human species.

One of the most dramatic of the changes which have affected the idea of the hero is that embodied in the science of psychology, for classic ideals of "goodness," "nobility," and "courage" have, under psychological scrutiny, assumed a significantly different aspect. Equally affecting, perhaps, has been the political history of modern Europe: a record of suffering, wars, and conflicts which have exacted a tremendous physical, spiritual, and psychological toll. Because of a new sense of historical crisis, the hero, a man of action, has grown less appealing as an image of present moral and ethical aspirations than the anti-hero, a man of reflection and contemplation. But perhaps an even more profound change in perspective is represented in the growing influence of the Judaeo-Christian ethic on the moral aspirations of the common man. Despite the apparent record of history, the principles of Christianity have become, in the past century, a more meaningful part of a common standard for human action. The substitution of the "inner-oriented" ethic of the Christian protagonist for the "outer-directed" heroism of the Greek hero is one of the significant contemporary adjustments in Western drama. It is this change which has materially altered the idea of tragic action and which has produced a new concept of dramatic character.[7]

In a discussion of contemporary form, René-Marill Albérès describes the contemporary anti-hero as a "theological protagonist." He is an image of man seeking to know the universe, to define its purpose, and to discover his ultimate meaning in its pattern. Albérès describes the contemporary motive in these words: "The contemporary theatre, like the novel, becomes a research and a quest. It makes itself idealistic, its characters force themselves toward that which they can never find."[8] For Albérès the anti-heroic quest is a journey toward moral commitment. Williams seems to confirm this judgment in his play *The Night of the Iguana*; he gives in this work the account of a heretic, the story of the world-weary priest Shannon who searches the earth for the face of God. Shannon follows the moral progression described by St. John of the Cross as the "dark night of the soul." He proceeds in contrary motion, in flight from the presence of God; but, like St. John, he finds that the "way down" leads up. Shannon declares that his search has brought him finally to that presence which he has sought:

> Yes, I see him, I hear him, I know him. And if he doesn't know that I know him, let him strike me dead with a bolt of his lightning. (Act II, p. 78)

Williams' construction of his anti-heroic protagonist, his "negative saint," is based on a radical perception of new dangers for mankind, as well as on the recognition of new modes of courage. What are these dangers? In *A Streetcar Named Desire* the playwright cautions the spectator against societal regression, against the capitulation of humanity to the laws of the jungle. In later plays—*Cat on a Hot Tin Roof, Camino Real, Suddenly Last Summer, Sweet Bird of Youth*, and *The Night of the Iguana*—he warns against the moral and spiritual disintegration of mankind. To interpret present dimensions of the human dilemma, Williams creates a protagonist who is conceived in anti-traditional terms. Brick, Kilroy, Catharine, Chance, and Shannon are not "mankind" in the sense of classic, neoclassic, romantic, or realistic definitions. They are images of a humanity diminished by time and history. They are each characterized by an inner division, by a fragmentation so complete that it has reduced them to partialities. They are "un-beings," caught in the destructive life process. They are fragments of debris, thrown up by "time the destroyer."[9] In the short story *One Arm*, Williams describes this anti-heroic man: "He never said to himself, I'm lost. But the speechless self knew it and in submission to its unthinking control the youth had begun as soon as he left the hospital to look about for destruction."[10]

The portrait of the anti-hero is not confined to the work of this playwright. Its fusion of pessimism and mysticism was the trademark of both the poetic realists and the early expressionists. The image of an anti-heroic man may be seen in the plays of Strindberg, Tolstoy, Ibsen, and Chekhov, as well as in the writings of expressionist artists such as Oskar Kokoschka. Moreover, this same contour is apparent in the work of existential dramatists such as Jean-Paul Sartre and Albert Camus. Some of the most telling portraits of the anti-hero have appeared in the work of the orthodox Christian dramatists Paul Claudel and T. S. Eliot. Claudel's *Partage de Midi*, like Eliot's *Murder in the Cathedral*, interprets an anti-heroic image with eloquence. Eliot gives the human condition anti-heroic description in these lines:

> Man's life is a cheat and a disappointment;
> All things are unreal,
> Unreal or disappointing:
> The Catherine wheel, the pantomime cat,
> The prizes given at the children's party,
> The prize awarded for the English Essay,
> The scholar's degree, the statesman's decoration.
> All things become less real, man passes
> From unreality to unreality.
> This man is obstinate, blind, intent
> On self-destruction,
> Passing from deception to deception,
> From grandeur to grandeur to final illusion,
> Lost in the wonder of his own greatness
> The enemy of society, enemy of himself.[11]

Clearly, this view of character is not entirely the creation of the twentieth century. Rather, it represents the intensification of perspectives which have been present throughout the history of Western letters. Albert Camus observes that much of existentialist dogma parallels the fundamental teachings of Jesus Christ. Certainly there are clear correspondences between existential teleologies and New Testament pronouncements on man's guilt, his search for truth, and his need for faith. Expressionism, existential theory, and "radical" Christian theology are agreed that man may find salvation only in love—in sympathy for his fellow man. Williams finds, then, considerable support for his vision of humanity from Christian theology and existential philosophy, as well as from the modern arts. His anti-hero is the symbol of a widely recognized condition: a "sickness unto death." Like the classic protagonist, the anti-hero searches for a mode of healing. But unlike the earlier protagonist he does not expect to find it. That which forbids his immediate salvation is himself. For the anti-hero is possessed of a profound fault, not merely of a single flaw, but of a comprehensive condition of evil, an inner impurity far greater than the Greek *hamartia*. Albérès describes this inner condition as "original sin."

* * *

The playwright gives shape to his anti-hero through the manipulation of a mythic glass; that is, Williams reveals his flawed image of man by showing his relationship to archetypal patterns. Throughout his work, Williams superimposes parallel visions—shadow images—of modern man. His anti-hero is a man of many identities; his Tom a "Hamlet," his Catharine a "Cassandra," his Brick an "Orestes," his Big Daddy an "Agamemnon." In *Orpheus Descending* his use of this technique of multiple vision is vivid. The Orphic figure Val descends into the underworld of Williams' mythical Mississippi town and there is brought to destruction by reveling maenads—Vee, Carol, and Lady—who envy his strange and magical music. Perhaps less obvious is Williams' use of a simultaneous treatment of character in *A Streetcar Named Desire*. Blanche—the poetic figure—descends into the underworld described as "The Elysian Fields." The symbology is set forth in the protagonist's opening speech (Scene I, p. ii): "They told me to take a street-car named Desire, and then transfer to one called Cemeteries and ride six blocks and get off at—Elysian Fields!"

In the critical scene preceding Blanche's destruction, Williams gives Orphic voice to the night:

> [... *The night is filled with inhuman voices like cries in a jungle.*
> [*The shadows and lurid reflections move sinuously as flames along the wall spaces.*
> [*Through the back wall of the rooms, which have become transparent, can be seen the sidewalk.* ...] (Scene X, p. 148)

There is in this work a second source of character interpretation which, like the Orphic myth, has its major presentation in Greek mythology. Williams has found one of the antecedents for his anti-hero in the figure of the Euripidean Orestes. The Oresteian protagonist, like the contemporary image, is an anti-hero. He is a symbol of man in flight from the consequences of his own transgression, in search of his identity in the universe. Modern European dramatists, for reasons associated with their own intellectual history, have been more inclined to develop studies of the Aeschylean pre-tragic protagonist Prometheus. Throughout the work of Sartre, Anouilh, and Camus we see the outline of Prometheus in revolt against cosmic law. H. D. F. Kitto describes "Promethean heroism":

> We may now inquire what is the relation of Aristotle's theory to Aeschylus. The answer is roughly, None whatever. Aristotle's tragic hero, who must be neither good nor bad, but average (or a little better) and "like" us, is the Sophoclean hero who in himself prefigures the human tragedy, all of it. ... The Aeschylean hero, who is not intended to sum up and typify in his own breast the tragic strength and weakness of man, need not be a blend and therefore cannot be "like" us; he must be only the sinner with so much characterization as to make him intelligible.[12]

The Americans, on the contrary, have been attracted to the late tragic apprehension of Euripides, especially by his images of Orpheus, Electra, Medea, and Orestes. While O'Neill reflects a certain interest in "Promethean man" in plays such as *Mourning Becomes Electra* and *Lazarus Laughed*, Williams, Miller, Inge, and, more recently, Albee conceive a protagonist closely akin to the anti-heroic image of Euripides.

The differences between these two apprehensions are significant. Promethean anti-heroism is revolutionary in nature. The pre-tragic protagonist of Aeschylus is, like Milton's Satan, a rebel: he is a creature in revolt against a powerful and inscrutable divinity. Albérès describes this Promethean anti-heroism:

> A man raises himself among other men. He sets himself up, by the requirement that he chooses to follow in a total solitude, social and metaphysical. . . . They [the heroes] wish to be alone, and it is in this sense that they refuse, from the beginning, the solutions of other men, the guaranteed, proven solutions. . . . Solitude defines the conditions of the hero, and his heroism is that he has not been born to accept the help of proven formulae. Prometheus is alone because he is the only one to dare, and his solitude expresses only the audacity of his enterprise.[13]

The Oresteian hero, treated in Aeschylus' trilogy, comes into sharper focus in the work of Euripides. For Euripides' Orestes—undoubtedly a fragment of a longer study—is the product of a particularly modern sensibility. Orestes is not a tragic hero in the Sophoclean tradition. He is, rather, an image of man concerned with his own power, responsibility, and complicity, in the evil of the universe. Unlike the Sophoclean hero, the Euripidean anti-hero is himself the microcosm of universal evil as well as the image of universal good.

In an eloquent essay on Greek tragedy, Edith Hamilton attributes the continuing appeal of the Euripidean anti-hero for writers to the timeless nature of this playwright's perception. She describes Euripides as the "first modern mind." Miss Hamilton suggests that Euripides, writing at a point of crisis in Athenian history, was compelled to formulate answers to many of the problems which now confront the contemporaries: a decline in religious faith, the acceleration of knowledge, political crises, and shifting moral values. She describes the peculiarly modern consciousness of the Greek dramatist:

> He feels, as no other writer has felt, the pitifulness of human life, as of children suffering helplessly what they do not know and can never understand. . . . Out of the pages written more

than twenty-three hundred years ago sound the two notes which we feel are the dominants in our world today, sympathy with suffering and the conviction of the worth of everyone alive. . . .

There is an order of mind which is perpetually modern. All of those possessed of it are akin, no matter how great the lapse of time that separates them. . . .

Always those in the vanguard of their time find in Euripides an expression of their own spirit. He is the great exponent of the forever recurring modern mind.[14]

Miss Hamilton describes Euripidean anti-heroism in terms which might well apply to the contemporary protagonist of Tennessee Williams:

Above all, they [the modern minds] care for human life and human things and can never stand aloof from them. They suffer for mankind, and what preoccupies them is the problem of pain. They are peculiarly sensitized to "the giant agony of the world." What they see as needless misery around them and what they envisage as needless misery to come is intolerable to them. The world to them is made up of individuals, each with a terrible power to suffer. . . . [15]

She traces the roots of the anti-heroic perception:

They behold, first and foremost, that most sorrowful thing on earth, injustice, and they are driven to it by a passion of revolt. Convention, so often a mask for injustice, they will have none of; in their pursuit of justice at any cost they tear away veils that hide hateful things: they call into question all pleasant and comfortable things. They are not of those who take "all life as their province"; what is good in the age they live in they do not regard; their eyes are fixed upon what is wrong. . . . [16]

The Oresteian anti-hero is not, then, the virtuous man of Aristotelian description; he is, on the contrary, the symbol of a guilty humanity, the distillation of a fatal weakness in man. He cries out:

O! human nature, what a grievous curse thou art in this world!
and what salvation, too, to those who have a goodly heritage
therein![17]

Moreover, Orestes is a transgressor whose sins are supported, rather
than diminished, by intelligence. For his fault is his lack of human
compassion. While the gods have indeed preordained the punishment
of Clytemnestra for the murder of Agamemnon, Orestes makes a free
choice to act as her executioner. The brutal manner of his crime—a
murder devoid of pity, calculated in vengeance, and executed without
a trace of compassion—strikes horror even in the heartless gods.
Orestes thus demonstrates a capacity for evil which is anti-human in
its very aspect. Jean-Paul Sartre, in his modernization of the Euripidean legend, describes Orestes as a man who defies the gods in order
to assume full responsibility in the universe:

> Foreign to myself—I know it. Outside nature, against nature,
> without excuse, beyond remedy, except what remedy I find within
> myself. But I shall not return under your law; I am doomed to
> have no other law but mine. Nor shall I come back to Nature,
> the Nature you found good; in it are a thousand beaten paths all
> leading up to you—but I must blaze my trail. For I, Zeus, am a
> man, and every man must find out his own way. . . . [18]

It is, then, primarily in consequence of his own choice that Orestes
suffers. How does he suffer? The sophisticated dramatist Euripides,
living at the beginning of the decline of the Greek Empire, saw in the
sense of guilt a more ruinous form of pain than any devised by the gods
or by man's enemies. In the opening scene of his *Orestes*, he portrays
a man whose body is wracked by this corrosive inner disease: guilt.
Orestes demonstrates all the symptoms of spiritual disintegration that
afflict the modern anti-hero: the malaise, the fevered hallucinations, and
the attacks of rage.[19] For his consciousness of transgression, Orestes pays
the penalty of fragmentation, disorientation, and despair.

Orestes, clearly a more highly developed protagonist than the more
primitive Agamemnon, suffers not for the existence of sin in the universe
but for his consciousness of his own error. In Aeschylus' treatment of the
subject, Orestes' madness has been prophesied by the Furies:

Woe on you, younger gods! the ancient right
Ye have o'erriden, rent it from my hands.
I am dishonored of you, thrust to scorn!
　　But heavily my wrath
Shall on this land fling forth the drops that blast and burn,
Venom of vengeance, that shall work such scathe
As I have suffered; where that dew shall fall,
　　Shall leafless blight arise,
Wasting Earth's offspring—Justice, hear my call!—
And thorough [through] all the land in deadly wise
Shall scatter venom, to exude again
　　In pestilence on men.[20]

In Euripides' *Electra*, the curse of the Furies is conveyed to Orestes by the Dioscuri:

> [B]ut haste thee to Athens, seeking to escape these hounds of hell, for they are on thy track in fearful wise, swart monsters, with snakes for hands, who reap a harvest of man's agony.[21]

The Euripidean myth, like the drama of Williams, is concerned not merely with defining the nature of sin; it seeks to find a human answer to suffering. Aeschylus, consistent with his theological orientation, summons man before the gods, where accused humanity is given a suspended sentence, a conditional acquittal. Euripides, on the other hand, places the responsibility for evil fully on man and challenges him to find a solution for the ills of his world.

* * *

The image of the anti-heroic Orestes seems always to have been present in the transgression-conscious American literature.[22] It is a clear motif in works such as *The Scarlet Letter*, *Billy Budd*, and *Moby Dick* as well as in William Faulkner's Euripidean studies of the mythical South. The Oresteian myth is a more subtly defined element of interpretation in the work of other Americans: in that of Walt Whitman, Robert Frost, T. S. Eliot, Emily Dickinson, and Edna St. Vincent Millay. In the works of all of these writers there appears the contour of the guilty protagonist, *man in exile*, in flight from his own transgression. D. H. Lawrence has commented that the study of guilt—the residue of the Puritan heritage—is one of the most persistent themes in American literature.[23] But the theme of metaphysical guilt is also an important element of modern European literature. The anti-hero of Tennessee Williams belongs to the lineage of Shakespeare, Goethe, Dostoevski, Gide, Kafka, and Thomas Mann, as well as to that of Hawthorne, Melville, and Faulkner. Like these writers, Williams explores one of the most persistent themes in modern letters: the significance of human transgression.

In order to examine this metaphysical problem, Williams sets in motion an anti-heroic cycle of human experience. Like Dante's poet, his anti-hero traverses the downward way in his "dark night of the soul."[24] Blanche, in *A Streetcar Named Desire*, describes her descent in the spiritual cycle:

> There are thousands of papers, stretching back over hundreds of years, affecting Belle Reve as, piece by piece, our improvident grandfathers and father and uncles and brothers exchanged the land for their epic fornications—to put it plainly! . . . The four-letter word deprived us of our plantation, till finally all that was left—and Stella can verify that!—was the house itself and about twenty acres of ground, including a graveyard, to which now all but Stella and I have retreated. (Scene II, p. 45)

Blanche, in her downward progress toward salvation, comes to the realization of her own responsibility for suffering. She becomes aware that she suffers more for her own transgressions than for the actions of her guilty ancestors. Like Orestes, she has made a guilty choice: a choice which has involved her in the suffering of others. She suggests that she is the effective cause of her husband's death. In her moment of partial "enlightenment" she describes the critical moment when she withdrew "sympathy" from a morally helpless being:

> He'd stuck the revolver into his mouth, and fired—so that the back of his head had been—blown away!
>
> It was because—on the dance-floor—unable to stop myself—I'd suddenly said—"I saw! I know! You disgust me . . ." And then the searchlight which had been turned on the world was turned off again and never for one moment since has

there been any light that's stronger than this—kitchen—candle.
(Scene VI, pp. 109–10)

Blanche records her descent into the hell of suffering. She describes her agony:

> I, I, *I* took the blows in my face and my body! All of those
> deaths! The long parade to the graveyard! ... And funerals are
> pretty compared to deaths. ... You didn't dream, but I saw! *Saw,*
> *Saw!* And now you sit there telling me with your eyes that I
> let the place go! How in hell do you think all that sickness and
> dying was paid for? Death is expensive, Miss Stella! ... (Scene
> I, pp. 25–26)

The play begins at a point late in the development of the anti-heroic cycle. In his record of this movement, Williams exposes Blanche's progressive fragmentation, her progress toward the last circle of hell. In *A Streetcar Named Desire*, Williams concludes his development at the ultimate point of descent; that is to say, this play closes without a clear resolution.

If his earlier works trace the protagonist's descent into the private hell of consciousness, it is only in later plays that Williams begins the description of the long and torturous ascent of the anti-hero to a limited enlightenment. We see some hint of resolution in *Summer and Smoke* in the redemption of Dr. John by the young and lovely Nellie. Similarly, in *Cat on a Hot Tin Roof*—a vivid transposition of the Oresteian myth—there is some suggestion of hope in the renewed bonds of sympathy between the dying father and son, as well as in the possibility of a new life which may cancel out old sins. A second movement—the ascent to light—is more clearly marked in *Camino Real*, a play in which Williams offers, as savior of mankind, the American soldier of fortune Kilroy, a protagonist who redeems the world with a simple display of sympathy. A more complete cycle of understanding is suggested in *The Night of the Iguana*, where the world-weary Shannon finds God through the friendship of Hannah, a woman who offers him sympathy.

A review of the whole body of Williams' work would seem to indicate that the playwright has not as yet completely resolved the problem of reconciliation in his cycle of anti-heroic development. He has succeeded in stating the case against man, in describing his anti-heroic condition. Moreover, he has formulated the general outlines of a kind of virtue appropriate to this condition. His greatest achievement, perhaps, is his definition of present conditions of heroism. For in his drama the anti-hero engages himself to suffer the agony of conscience, to confront hidden truth, and to accept the heavy burden of metaphysical guilt. Blanche, Alma, Brick, Kilroy, Chance, Val, Catharine, and Shannon may be described in these terms:

> That which distinguishes the character from those who surround him is that a problem poses itself for him, a problem which others ignore or dare not confront; it is that he is more and more tormented. None of these persons who have attracted our great writers is remarkable in the sense of those who have preceded them. They are men like others, but they ask themselves certain questions while others allow themselves to live.[25]

* * *

If the willingness to engage inner conflict is the nature of heroism in the theatre of Williams, his organization of character is designed to reveal such action by exploring, in relation to the protagonist, the full range of possibilities affecting his moral choice. The anti-hero, in this sense, is not a man; he is a schematic presentation of extended moral possibilities. In each of his characters Williams presents a composite image, a montage of the roles which together comprise the anti-heroic character. Alma, in *Summer and Smoke*, speaks of this view of character:

> I've thought many times of something you told me last summer, that I have a *doppleganger*. I looked that up and I found that it means another person inside of me, another self, and I don't know whether to thank you or not for making me conscious of it!—I haven't been well. . . . For a while I thought I was dying, that that was the change that was coming. (Scene XI, p. 115)

In his presentation of character, Williams follows the method of exposition which in modern theatre is associated with the theories of Luigi Pirandello. For Pirandello defined dramatic character as an agglomeration of roles:

> For the drama lies all in this—in the conscience that I have, that each one of us has. We believe this conscience to be a single thing, but it is many-sided. There is one for this person, and another for that. Diverse consciences. So we have this illusion of being one person for all, of having a personality that is unique in all our acts. But it isn't true. We perceive this when, tragically perhaps, in something we do, we are as it were, suspended, caught up in the air on a kind of hook. Then we perceive that all of us was not in that act, and that it would be an atrocious injustice to judge us by that action alone . . . [26]

In this theory, Pirandello attempted to provide for modern drama a concept of character consistent with the relative perspective of twentieth-century thought: to create an image of man in all of his complexity, in the full reality of his inner disharmony. It is important to observe that Pirandello's theory corresponds not only to the relative vision of artists such as Picasso, but also to that of the great creative thinkers such as Jung.[27] Like Jungian psychology, Pirandello's theory defines character as a loosely unified grouping of identities. Pirandellian Man, like Jungian Man, is a configuration of masks. He is an image of man in search of a reconciling symbol, in need of a self above selves.

This pattern of organization, despite its intellectual validity, presents serious theatrical problems. How can such a concept of character be realized in the sensible form of the drama? European playwrights such as Brecht have solved this problem by introducing into the drama large quantities of discursive material. They explain the conflicted nature of the protagonist's character through the use of monologues, films, notes, and other "teaching devices." Americans such as O'Neill and Miller have also on occasion used such techniques. Although Williams makes some use of the interior monologue, he has been inclined to figure inner conflict in more theatrical terms. He follows the example of Shakespeare in revealing character through schematic arrangement. Like Hamlet, Blanche DuBois reveals her inner nature by playing out her conflicted roles: schoolteacher, Southern belle, poet, sister, savior, and prostitute. Similarly, Alma, Brick, Quixote, Chance,

Val, Shannon, and others play out a range of characters, as they don first one mask and then another.

Although it was interpreted by Pirandello, this idea of character development should be credited to Shakespeare. Indeed, it may be described as the "Hamlet organization": for the anti-heroic Hamlet is perhaps the most effective theatrical example of this multiple concept of human personality. Hamlet is organized from simultaneous visions in much the manner of the modern anti-hero. Shakespeare rationalized his use of montage by attributing to his protagonist the consciousness of an actor. Mark Van Doren describes Hamlet's character as a "spectacle forever suspended":

> Hamlet is an actor. Like any character in whom Shakespeare was greatly interested, he plays a role. He plays indeed many roles, being supreme in tragedy as Falstaff was supreme in comedy. . . . Like Falstaff he shows the man he is by being many men. . . . He acts with the King and Queen, with Ophelia, with Polonius, with the court at large; taking on and putting off each role as occasion dictates, and at the climax of the tragedy wearing all of them simultaneously.[28]

Shakespeare, then, revealed the nature of Hamlet's character by exposing the possibilities of *action* and *being* contingent upon a moment of choice. In the course of his time upon the stage, Hamlet plays many roles; he is alternately prince and jester, lover and knave, courtier and politician, poet and ribald jester.

A study of the work of Williams would seem to show that he takes this "existential" Hamlet as his point of departure in his organization of anti-heroic character. For he seeks to affirm in character the present; his protagonists have little real past and no hope for a future. They are locked within a moment of choice. The form of Williams is thus a record of a critical instant in individual destiny. The stage for action is consciousness: it is a consciousness filled with spectres who are in effect extensions of the self. This principle is perhaps most clearly demonstrated in *The Night of the Iguana*, one of his latest plays. Here, as in other works, Williams creates a mythical way station in his progression of understanding. To this "point" he brings a number of characters, each personifying a particular virtue or vice in the consciousness of the protagonist. The aged poet is at one extreme of the continuum. A man who has lost the will to live, he is countered by a young and eager girl. The energetic German family is posed against the casual Mexicans; the corrupt agent Latta against the anti-heroic Shannon; the saintly Hannah against the "insatiable widow" Maxine. *The Night of the Iguana* is a kind of modern *Everyman*, a moment when the protagonist watches his own vices and virtues parade across the great stage of his consciousness.

A more subtle use of the Hamlet device may be seen in an earlier work, *The Glass Menagerie*. For Williams creates in this drama a conscious self: the observing and reflecting "Tom" who projects the flow of experience from his own recall. Within his stream of consciousness there exists another "Tom," the acting self. As the play progresses, it becomes evident that each of the other members of Tom's family represents a position in his pattern of understanding. *The Glass Menagerie*, like O'Neill's *The Great God Brown*, is an exploration of life possibilities, a review of the roles conceived by an anti-heroic man. In *The Glass Menagerie* Williams conceives three of these masks: that of Amanda, the self of natural life; of Laura, the self of poetry and illusion; and of the father, the self of action. Tom explains his choice of a life role in these words,

> I didn't go to the moon, I went much further—for time is the longest distance between two places.....
> I left Saint Louis. I descended the steps of this fire-escape for a last time and followed, from then on, in my father's footsteps.... (Scene VIII, p. 123)

In *The Glass Menagerie*, as in the other major works of Tennessee Williams, the protagonist pursues his "odyssey," his journey toward selfhood. Within the "lyric instant," the moment of escape from the corrosive life process, the protagonist conducts his search for a principle through which he may bring meaning to experience. He does this by exploring the alternatives mirrored within this image of his own consciousness. Williams thus examines a comprehensive theme of twentieth-century arts, the search for identity: the journey toward meaning. It is because of his perception of a moral crisis that Williams has abandoned more flattering images of man. Apparently shocked and frightened by the growing threat of human annihilation, he suggests that the theatre cannot afford to exalt man, to praise and to commend his nature. He insists that the proper function of the modern drama is to expose man's hidden nature, to search out his motives, to discover his limits, and, ultimately, to help him to find a mode of salvation. There is little doubt that in his anti-hero Williams states the case against modern man effectively. However, he has been able to evolve only a limited resolution for his cycle of suffering. He concludes that the only hope for man is compassion. It is love that redeems the damned city of Camino Real and sets the "water to flowing again in the mountains."

The anti-heroic protagonist of Williams is designed to reveal the nature of suffering as it appears in the life of the twentieth century. He is intended as the object of pity and terror in the modern world. A question is often asked about this aspect of Williams' work: Of what meaning is the fate of his emotional, spiritual, and moral cripples? The answer given by Williams reflects the gradual usurpation of the pagan idea of tragedy by the Christian concept of human worth. For the Christian ethic holds every man a sinner, redeemable only through love. Similarly, it insists, as does Williams, that all men are anti-heroic; that these figures, no more than others, are guilty of the human condition. In this context, Williams' catalogue of transgressors in search of salvation is a true symbolism—his anti-hero, the very present image of man.

NOTES

Note: The quotation following the chapter title is from a poem by T. S. Eliot, "Burnt Norton," which appears in *Four Quartets* (London: Faber and Faber, 1949), p. 20; copyright 1943, by Harcourt, Brace & World, Inc., and reprinted with their permission.

1. Williams, like Eliot and others among twentieth-century artists, accepts a dynamic theory of reality. Like post-Hegelians such as Bergson, Williams regards art as the image of process, and form as a "still" picture drawn out of the moving spectacle. See Henri Bergson, *An Introduction to Metaphysics*, trans. T. E. Hulme (New York: The Liberal Arts Press, 1949), pp. 25–27.

2. "East Coker" in *Four Quartets* (London: Faber and Faber, 1949), pp. 26–27; copyright 1943, by Harcourt, Brace & World, Inc., and reprinted with their permission.

3. See also Aristotle *Ethics*, trans. D. P. Chase (London, 1911).

4. Butcher, *Aristotle's Theory of Poetry* . . . (New York, 1951), p 45.

5. Arthur Miller, Introduction to the *Collected Plays* (New York, 1957), pp. 8–12.

6. Introduction to *The Rose Tattoo*, p. ix.

7. Such a change in perspective appears in late Greek drama, especially in plays such as *Oedipus at Colonus*, a work which shows many correspondences to "Christian drama." In the main, however, the movement toward an "inner direction" must be attributed to the passage of Christian perspectives into the medieval drama.

8. René-Marill Albérès, *La Révolte des écrivains d'aujourd'hui* (Paris, 1949), p. 141. (The translation is my own.)

9. This is Eliot's phrase. It appears in "The Dry Salvages," the third of *The Four Quartets* (London: Faber and Faber, 1949): "Time the destroyer is time the preserver," p. 40, line 115; copyright 1943, by Harcourt, Brace & World, Inc., and reprinted with their permission.

10. In the collection *One Arm and Other Stories*, pp. 9–10.

11. T. S. Eliot, *Murder in the Cathedral* (New York: Harcourt, Brace and Company, 1935), Act I, pp. 41–42; copyright 1935, by Harcourt, Brace & World, Inc., and reprinted with their permission.

12. H. D. F. Kitto, *Greek Tragedy: A Literary Study* (rev. ed.; New York, 1954), p. 116.

13. Albérès, pp. 125–26.

14. Edith Hamilton, *The Greek Way to Western Civilization* (New York, 1948), pp. 197–98.

15. *Ibid.*, p. 199.

16. *Loc. cit.*

17. Euripides *Orestes*, trans. E. P. Coleridge, in *The Complete Greek Drama*, eds. Whitney J. Oates and Eugene O'Neill, Jr. (New York, 1938), II, 114.

18. Jean-Paul Sartre, *The Flies* in *No Exit and Three Other Plays*, trans. Stuart Gilbert (New York, 1955), p. 122.

19. The indebtedness of Freud to Euripides is clearly illustrated in this work.

20. Aeschylus *Eumenides*, in *The Complete Greek Drama*, I, 298–99.

21. Euripides *Electra*, in *The Complete Greek Drama*, II, 105.

22. See Doris Falk, *Eugene O'Neill and The Tragic Tension* (New Brunswick, New Jersey, 1958).

23. See D. H. Lawrence, *Studies in Classic American Literature* (New York, 1923).

24. The Bochum critics thought Dante to be among Williams' strongest influences, especially in *Camino Real*.

25. Albérès, p. 125.

26. Luigi Pirandello, *Six Characters in Search of an Author* in *Naked Masks: Five Plays*, ed. Eric Bentley, trans. E. Storer (New York, 1952), pp. 231–32.

27. This Jungian language also seems to be employed by Pirandello. The relationship between Jung and Pirandello has not, to my knowledge, been fully explored.

28. Mark Van Doren, ed., Introduction to *Four Great Tragedies* (New York, 1955), p. 208.

Acknowledgments

Augustine. "Enchiridion to Laurentius on Faith, Hope, and Charity." *Seventeen Short Treatises of S. Augustine, Bishop of Hippo.* Oxford: J.H. Parker, 1847. 85–159.

Curtsinger, E.C. "Isabel Archer as a Woman Clothed in the Sun." *The Muse of Henry James.* Mansfield, TX: Latitudes Press, 1986. 44–58. © E.C. Curtsinger. Reprinted by permission.

Gindin, James. "Gods and Fathers in F. Scott Fitzgerald's Novels." *Modern Language Quarterly* (March 1969): 64–85. © The Modern Language Association of American. Reprinted by permission.

Haweis, H.R. "Forewords." *The Pilgrim's Progress.* By John Bunyan. Ed. R. Southey. New York: Harper and Brothers, 1912. 1–4.

Jackson, Esther Merle. "The Anti-Hero." *The Broken World of Tennessee Williams.* Madison, WI: U of Wisconsin P, 1965. 68–87. © Esther Merle Jackson. Reprinted by permission.

Kennard, Jean E. "William Golding: Island." *Number and Nightmare: Forms of Fantasy in Contemporary Fiction.* Hamden, CT: Archon Books, 1975. 176–202. © Jean E. Kennard. Reprinted by permission.

Knight, G. Wilson. "Coleridge's Divine Comedy." *The Starlit Dome: Studies in the Poetry of Vision.* London: Oxford UP, 1941; Barnes and Noble reprint, 1960. 83–178.

Maida, Patricia D. "Light and Enlightenment in Flannery O'Connor's Fiction." *Studies in Short Fiction* 13 (Winter 1976): 31–36. © *Studies in Short Fiction.* Reprinted by permission.

McAlpine, Monica E. "The Pardoner's Homosexuality and How It Matters." *PMLA* 95.1 (January 1980): 8–22. © The Modern Language Association of America. Reprinted by permission.

Santayana, George. "Dante." *Three Philosophical Poets: Lucretius, Dante, and Goethe.* Cambridge, MA: Harvard UP, 1910. 73–135.

Stephen, Leslie. "Jonathan Edwards." *Hours in a Library, Vol. 1*. London: Smith,
    Elder, & Co., 1909.
Wells, B.W. "Goethe's *Faust*." *Sewanee Review* Vol. 2 (August 1894): 385–412

Index